by Mari Sandoz

OLD JULES — 1935
SLOGUM HOUSE — 1937
CAPITAL CITY — 1939
CRAZY HORSE — 1942
THE TOM-WALKER — 1947
CHEYENNE AUTUMN — 1953
THE BUFFALO HUNTERS — 1954
WINTER THUNDER — 1954
MISS MORISSA — 1955
THE HORSECATCHER — 1957
THE CATTLEMEN — 1958
HOSTILES AND FRIENDLIES — 1959
SON OF THE GAMBLIN' MAN — 1960

OLD JULES

Old Jules

BY

Mari Sandoz

WITH ILLUSTRATIONS

HASTINGS HOUSE

PUBLISHERS   NEW YORK 22

Copyright, 1935,
By Mari Sandoz

———

All rights reserved

Published October, 1935

Twentieth Anniversary Edition 1955
Reprinted 1960

ONE can go into a wild country and make it tame, but, like a coat and cap and mittens that he can never take off, he must always carry the look of the land as it was. He can drive the plough through the nigger-wool, make fields and roads go every way, build him a fine house and wear the stiff collar, and yet he will always look like the grass where the buffalo have eaten and smell of the new ground his feet have walked on.

— BIG ANDREW

FOREWORD

LINCOLN, NEBRASKA
March 23, 1935

TO THE JUDGES
Atlantic Non-Fiction Contest
8 Arlington Street
Boston, Massachusetts

GENTLEMEN: —

Old Jules is the biography of my father, Jules Ami Sandoz: I have also tried in a larger sense to make it the biography of a community, the upper Niobrara country in western
Nebraska.

The book grew out of a childhood and adolescence spent
among the story-tellers of the frontier, for the frontier,
whether by Turner's famous definition or by any other, is a
land of story-tellers, and in this respect remains frontier in
nature until the last original settler is gone.

It grew, then, out of the long hours in the smoky old
kitchen on the Running Water, the silent hours of listening
behind the stove or in the wood box, when it was assumed
that of course I was asleep in bed. So I — the Marie of the
story — heard all the accounts of the hunts, the well accident, the fights with the cattlemen and the sheepmen; was
given hints here and there of the tragic scarcity of women,
when a man had to "marry anything that got off the train,"
as Old Jules often said; knew the drouths, the storms,
and the wind and isolation. At school we heard other versions, partly through the natural cruelty of childhood, partly
because a feud was on and we were actually outsiders in the
school.

But the most impressive stories were those told me by

Old Jules himself, perhaps on the top of Indian Hill, over-looking the spot where a man was hung under his leadership, and the scene of six years of lawing that drove his second wife into the insane asylum.   Perhaps he limped through the orchard as he talked, with me close behind, my hands full of ducks or grouse or quail.   Perhaps I followed among flowering cherry trees, carrying the plats to the orchard. Perhaps I drove the team on long trips while he smoked and talked of his own dreams and his joys and his disappoint-ments.   And always was I too frightened of him to voice either approval or surprise.

Although there was apparently no affection between us, my father somehow talked more sincerely to me, particularly when we went hunting, than was his custom.   During these stories he never looked at me — almost as though he were talking to himself, without feeling any compunction to "throw in another grizzly."   Perhaps it was because of my cringing cowardice from ridicule (I 'm well over that now). He could be certain that I would not laugh.

Sometimes it seems that a quirk of fate has tied me to this father I feared so much, even into my maturity.   The three crucial moments in his life after I could take part in our family life involved me as an unwilling participant: the snakebite, the near-killing of the Strasburgers and my near-ending with the same gun, and the final moment when he died.

Out of these events came the need to write this book, augmented by the one line my father wrote me in 1925, when I received honorable mention in the Harper Inter-collegiate Short Story Contest, guarded by the name of Marie Macumber.   He discovered my activities, sent me one line in his emphatic up-and-down strokes: "You know I consider writers and artists the maggots of society."   The book became a duty the last day of his life, when he asked that I write of his struggles as a locator, a builder of com-munities, a bringer of fruit to the Panhandle.

Before I wrote one word of *Old Jules* I took notes on all references to the Panhandle in all the important papers of the state from 1880 to 1929, and more complete notes on every Panhandle or near-Panhandle paper from its establishment to the end. The gleanings fill three heavy notebooks. . . . Then of course I read all the frontier literature and history obtainable, with a study of frontier economics and politics. . . . In the archives of the Nebraska State Historical Society I went through the entire Ricker Collection, containing interviews with all the old-timers the late Judge Ricker of Chadron could find in twenty years of diligent search. I exposed my mother to months of inquisitional inquiry and interviewed everyone available. Most valuable, however, were the 4000 letters and documents in the files — no, boxes — of Old Jules himself, a little mouldy from the leaky flat roof of our Kinkaid home, but generally intact. His habit of revising has saved many of his violent letters for me, in his own characteristically forceful push-and-pull penmanship.

As I read, the stories of my childhood came back to me with new significance. And as I arranged and rearranged the bits of information in what seemed the closest verisimilitude to life as those people lived it in the Running Water country, the duty became a privilege. Not one character, included or regretfully put aside, would I have one whit different: not my mother, who had the courage and the tenacity to live with this man so many years, or the Surbers, to whom many of us owe what joy we derive from music and from art; not Nell Sears; Jim the convict; the Peters'; Andy Brown, the yellah boy; the family that are the Schwartzes and that constituted the bit of glamour of our community; Tissot; Freese; Dr. Walter Reed, or Old Jules himself. These people have endured, and as I review them from the vantage point of twice knowledge my eyes mist. A gallant race, and I salute them.

I can promise affidavits from the Nebraska State Histori-

cal Society on any event of moment, as, for instance, the
Niobrara Feud, the cattleman murder of the brother of Old
Jules, and so forth, from newspapers of the period. As to
my historical and personal integrity as well as my portrait
of the time and the community, I refer you to Dr. A. E.
Sheldon, Superintendent of the Society, State Capitol, Lincoln, with whom I have worked at various times for years —
in the capacity of associate editor of the *Nebraska History
Magazine* and director of much of the research for the last
two years. Dr. Sheldon homesteaded northwest of Valentine in 1886, published a newspaper at Chadron in the nineties, and knew Old Jules well. I refer you also to Frank
L. Williams, Managing Editor, *Nebraska State Journal,*
Lincoln. Mr. Williams spent his cub-reporter days in western Nebraska in the eighties and knew the Old Jules of the
orchard days.

Thank you,

MARI SANDOZ

CONTENTS

ILLUSTRATIONS

OLD JULES

THE PEOPLE

OLD JULES . . . . Jules Ami Sandoz

    HIS SWEETHEART . . . . . . Rosalie

    HIS WIVES:
      No. 1 . . . . Estelle
      No. 2 . . . . Henriette
      No. 3 . . . . Emelia
      No. 4 . . . . Mary

His parents, children, brothers, sister, uncles, cousins, and so forth

THE DOCTOR . . . . Dr. Walter Reed

THE MAN WITH THE WINCHESTER . Gentleman Jim

THE TWO FRIENDS . . . . . . Johnny Jones and Elmer Sturgeon

THE TWO JESTERS . . . . Paul Nicolet and Jules Tissot

THE ROADHOUSE KEEPERS . . . . Jacob Schwartz, his sons and daughters

THE TWO KILLERS . . . . . . Dave Tate and Ralph Nieman

THE CATTLEMEN . . . . Richards and Comstock, Modisett

THE REGION: The upper Niobrara country — the hard-land table, the river, and the hills

I

SPRING

THE border towns of Rock and Cherry counties were shaking off the dullness of winter. Galloping hoofs, the boom of the forty-four, and the measured beat of the spike maul awakened the narrow single streets running between the tents and shacks. Sky pilots plodded from town to town, preaching a scorching and violent hell. But west of there the monotonous yellow sandhills unobtrusively soaked up the soggy patches of April snow. Fringes of yellow-green crept down the south slopes or ran brilliant emerald over the long, blackened strips left by the late prairie fires that burned unchallenged until the wind drove the flames upon their own ashes, or the snow fell.

All winter the wind had torn at the fire-bared knolls, shifting but not changing the unalterable sameness of the hills that spread in rolling swells westward to the hard-land country of the upper Niobrara River, where deer and antelope grazed almost undisturbed except by an occasional hunting party.

But now the grass was started. Out of the East crawled the black path of the railroad. Colonies of homeseekers in covered wagons pushed westward. From the plains of Texas a hundred thousand head of cattle came, their feet set upon the long trails to the free range lands. In the deep canyons of the Niobrara, wolves and rustlers skulked, waiting, while the three or four ranchers already in the hills armed themselves for the conflict.

And out of the East came a lone man in an open wagon, driving hard.

Jules, hunched down on the wagon seat, a rifle between his knees, followed up the north fringe of the river bluffs from the little town of Verdigre near the Missouri. For three weeks he had whipped his tired team onward, always with impatience, as though to-morrow would be too late. But there was really no hurry. His Swiss-made map showed the sandhills a wilderness with many small lakes and streams, remote, uninhabited — wild fruit, game, and free land far from law and convention. There a man could build a home, hunt and trap in peace, live as he liked.

Little about this dark-bearded young man in ragged, camp-stained clothing suggested the dapper student who swaggered the streets of Zurich three years before, whose shave was as necessary as breakfast. An old cap, greasy and scorched from service in pan lifting, sat low upon eyes as strange and changing as the Jura that towered over his homeland. They were gray, and glowed at a lusty story well told, withdrew in remote contemplation of the world and the universe, or flashed with the swift anger and violence of summer lightning.

At twenty-two, after four years of medical school, Jules instigated another of his periodic scenes. A larger allowance was the pretext. Three thousand francs was not enough for the son of a gentleman in the university. Would they have him clean his own shoes?

This time he aroused more than his mother's short-lipped anger that always ended in tearful yielding to this eldest and most beloved son. His father's anger broke through a military restraint. So the fine Jules would play the millionaire? Did he forget that there were yet five brothers and the young Elvina to be fed and clothed and educated? Perhaps it would be well if he learned to clean his own shoes.

The son stood up to the father. Were the summer months he had spent as railway mail clerk, a life fit only for the slow wits of a stable hand, as nothing? Yes, his allowance had been increased, but he knew why.

To separate him from the little Rosalie who worked beside him in the mail service, and who was not considered good enough for one of a family celebrating the four hundredth year of its foundation. They would have finer daughters-in-law. Very well. Let their favorites, Paul and Henri and Nana, bring them. He, Jules, would go to America. And he would take the Rosalie with him.

But, as his father predicted, the little Rosalie would not go. So he left his home on the blue waters of Lake Neuchâtel alone, crossed the sea, and came as far west as his money permitted, to northeastern Nebraska. There he filed on a homestead and became a landed man, with twenty dollars, a stamp collection begun as a boy, a Swiss army rifle, and a spade. Letters in French and full of this wonderful country crossed the sea to Rosalie. She answered affectionately, but she still could not bring herself to follow her Jules to an American frontier farm, pointing out instead their total unfitness for peasant life.

So — after three years of disappointment — Jules married the first woman that would have him.

When the young wife, Estelle, refused to build the morning fires, to run through the frosty grass to catch up his team, Jules closed her mouth with the flat of his long, muscular hand, dumped their supply of flour and sugar to the old sow and pigs, and loaded his belongings upon the wagon to leave her and Knox County behind him forever.

Because, in 1884, Valentine was the land office for the great expanse of free land to the west and south, Jules stopped there. The town was also the end of the railroad and the station of supply and diversion for the track crews pushing the black rails westward, for the military posts of Fort Niobrara and Fort Robinson, for the range country, and for the mining camps of the Black Hills. Sioux came in every day from their great reservations to the north, warriors who as late as '77 and '81 had fought with Crazy Horse and Sitting Bull; law was remote, and the broken hills or the Sioux blanket offered safe retreat for horse thief, road agent, and killer.

Because the town was probably full of thieves, Jules camped in the sparse timber of the river valley. After a supper of antelope steak he kicked the coals from his fire and climbed the hill towards the double row of lighted windows.

The flat plain of Valentine was dotted with the dark bulks of covered wagons, hungry oxen, picketed horses — settler caravans and freighters camped for the night in their push westward. Jules stopped to talk to a knot of silent men squatting around a fire — Germans, they told him at last, going to the north table, two days out. They stared curiously at the dark, bearded young man, tall in the gleam of the fire, fine long hands and delicate wrists dangling from shrunken coat sleeves. *Ja*, they had heard of the sandhills. They sucked loudly at their pipes when he said he would go there.

Seeing, Jules left them and went down the one street of Valentine. He dodged behind the horse-lined hitch-racks as a dozen galloping cowboys came into town, yelling, shooting red streaks through the darkening sky, stirring up a dust that shimmered golden in the squares of light that spilled from the tents and shacks. In the doorway of the largest saloon and gambling house between O'Neill and the Black Hills the homeseeker hesitated.

Despite the blaze of tin lamp reflectors along the walls, the interior was murky, heavy with the stench of stale alcohol and winter-long unbathed humanity. Restless layers of smoke crept over the heads of the crowd. Hats pushed back, their hands on their hips, the frontiersmen listened to a short, stocky man sitting on the wet bar, their narrow eyes moving covertly over their neighbors. Jules edged closer with the other newcomers to listen to the strange American words.

It seemed that the stocky man brought news. The vigilantes down the Niobrara were riding again. That meant, he reminded his listeners, a cottonwood, a bridge, or a telegraph pole and a chunk of rope for somebody. The vigilantes had come as far west as Valentine before, taken men away and left them dangling for the buzzards. They took Kid Wade from the sheriff at Bassett only a month ago. Hung him to a telegraph pole and sold the rope at fifty cents an inch. They said he was a horse thief. That dodge always worked.

Now the vigilantes were riding again and all opposition would be taken care of in the usual way.

Jules looked curiously into the frightened faces of the land seekers about him and started away to buy a glass of beer. It was all just another joke on the greenhorns and soon the laughing would begin.

At the bar a half-drunken youth, several years younger than Jules, was talking big. "Let the viges come. We'll make 'em eat lead," he drawled, and spit into the sawdust at his feet.

"Shut that running off the mouth, Slip," a whisper warned, somewhere near Jules. The youth called Slip poured himself another glass of whiskey, running it over. He gulped the liquid and spit again.

"I ain't afraid of any goddamn viges," he told them all, his hand on his heavy cartridge belt.

A shot set the glasses and bottles to ringing and started a wave of relieved talk and natural laughter as Slip turned and set his glass back upon the bar. A mushroom of powder smoke rose from the crowd and crept lazily toward the dark rafters.

Jules laughed too now, not as the others, but with keen enjoyment. This was as the shooting through the darkness outside, a show, the Wild West of which he had read, with a great smell of powder and brag. It was fine. Then he stopped, a little sick. The youth was bending low over the bar and from his mouth ran a string of frothy blood. Slowly he went down, his fingers sliding from the boards.

The sun-blackened men about him melted back, their hands frankly on their guns now. A hunchback and a negro pushed between them, carrying the sagging figure out. The swinging doors came to rest behind them and still no boot creaked.

At a shoulder signal from the bartender two men finally pushed forward, pounding empty glasses on the wet wood. Gradually the front line crumbled; glasses clinked, while one after another the newcomers escaped into the night. A blond-bearded Polander climbed upon a barrel and pulled away at a red accordion. Two girls came out of the boxes at the back and slipped companionably into the double line at the bar. Gradually the crowd thickened again. Everything was as usual.

Bewildered and angry at this, his first death, Jules let himself down into the handiest chair. Across the pine table from him sat a man twisting a finger into his walrus moustache, engrossed in his own thoughts and a mug of beer.

"But will the officials not try to apprehend the murderer, lock him up?" the newcomer finally demanded, in the stilted English of the foreigner.

A heavy eyelid went up slowly and came down. " 'T ain't healthy, times like this, to be too interested in the remains nor anybody what mighta been involved." The man stopped, fished in his sagging pocket, and brought up some newspaper clippings.[1] Shaking out the tobacco, he handed them across the table. Cautiously Jules took them and read of the surprising activities of the vigilantes, while the man talked on.

[1] From the St. Paul *Phonograph*, February 15 and 29, 1884.

Transgressors Dealt With by Vigilantes.

SIOUX CITY, February 5.—Reports have reached here from the upper Elkhorn country, in Nebraska, that Kid Wade, dea er of the Nebraska outlaws and horse thieves, has been hung by vigilantes, who have headquarters at a place called "The Pen," at the mouth of the Long Pine. They have arrested a large number of men in various parts of northern Nebraska and taken them away to this place, where they are tried and disposed of in a manner unknown. But as they are never seen again, it is supposed that they are shot, hanged or conducted out of the country. The terrible earnestness of the vigilantes and the mystery of their ways cause men to shudder when their doings are mentioned. It is positively certain that they have lynched eleven men, and it is equally sure that others have met the same fate, but how many, or by what means, only the grim executioners can tell. "Kid" Wade was captured at Lemars three weeks ago. He seemed to realize the fate that awaited him, but manifested no more concern than if going about his ordinary business.

4LONG PINE, February 7.—Kid Wade was found this morning hanging to a whistle-post ten miles east of Long Pine. Coroner Shofford, of Long Pine, held an inquest to-day and found that he came to his death by hanging by parties unknown. The vigilantes left this place yesterday morning with Wade. The sheriff of Holt county took him from them, but on the way to Holt county ten or fifteen masked men took Wade from the sheriff.

Vigilantes' Law in Cherry County.

SIOUX CITY, February 16.—Sheriff Carter, of Cherry county, Nebraska, has been notified by the vigilance committee to leave the county immediately. The vigilantes claim that he is in collusion with the Nebraska horse thieves beyond a doubt. Sheriff Carter announces a fixed determination to stay, denies the charges made against

him, and has sworn in a posse of thirty men
for his protection. The sheriff and his men
are all armed to the teeth, awaiting hostili-
ties. The leader of the vigilantes has post-
ed up a notice that no man living can escape their vengeance, least of all Sheriff
Carter. Further developments are anxiously awaited.

"Kids like that Slip there what steals maybe a hame string
and shoots off their mouth got no business in this man's
country, Frenchy.   Of course, most of it 's just likkered-up
track hands and cowboys and soldiers or reservation bucks.
But there 's horse stealing, rustling, and skin games going
constant.   Then — " dropping his voice — "of course
there 's our viges."

"It is so?" Jules tapped the clippings.

"Yeh, claiming the courts is run by crooks, no protection
for their stock or lives."   The man turned his head over a
thick shoulder and looked about.   "I guess 't ain't no secret,
but the county judge and the sheriff is supposed to own
every sliver in this goddamn dump.   The viges has ordered
the sheriff to leave the county.   He swears in a posse of
thirty men with Winchesters and awaits developments."

Could this be so?

Wondering what his father would say, the recent citizen
of the orderly, uneventful little Swiss republic leaned upon
his folded arms and considered these people more closely.

In that packed room only one man stood out.   He was
alone at a corner table, with a rifle standing in the crook of
his arm, the barrel against his young beard, his dark hair
turning up in silky drakes' tails under the large belly-tan
hat.   His legs were exceedingly long, so long that his fine
soft boots extended out upon the floor beyond the small
table.   But no one bumped against them and no one sat
with him.   Undisturbed, aloof, he sipped a small glass of
whiskey.

"Yeh." The old freighter made the most of his fresh audience. "Like the paper says, the other morning they's a notice tacked up on this shack, mind you, saying that the viges gets what hair they's after. So far nothing's happened, as I knows, unless — " He jerked a stubby thumb towards the doors.

"But do the people here believe that the vigilantes are always right?"

The man choked, sputtering beer through his moustaches.

"Right? Who's stopping to ask about right if they has the crack shots on their side?"

So that was how it went here. Jules ordered two beers.

The country west the old-timer dismissed with a grand sweep of the replenished mug. "No-count, unless you got money enough to start a cow outfit and guns enough to fight the rustlers off. Starve to death farming. Never rains, cold as blazes in winter. They brought a feller up from the lake country south of here last week. Both hands froze, fingers rotting off, crazy as a shitepoke."

Jules, who never listened to what he would not hear, rose abruptly and took a turn through the crowd, wishing he had brought one of his guns with him instead of hiding both the rifle and his secondhand ten-bore in the buckbrush along the river.

He pushed away a girl who put her arm about his shoulders. There was no telling — probably diseased. He took no chances.

The man with the rifle was still there, turning the tiny glass between his lean brown fingers, watching the light in the amber liquid. "One-man outfit," the freighter had called him, "not running with no pack here."

Jules was not quite certain what these phrases meant, but there was something about the man. Not even the women, wandering about with large-mouthed laughter in search of pay dirt, went near him. In the glare of the tin reflectors the blued barrel of his Winchester gleamed, a repeater, a beautiful weapon, as true steel is beautiful.

To avoid the milling, dusty street Jules cut around the corner of the saloon and stumbled over something — a man, stiff and cold. Probably the youth who defied the vigilantes, chilling for shipment home.

The homeseeker pressed his back against the board wall for a moment. Inside, the Polander was still sweating over a fast polka. Boots stomped, while far away a revolver echoed twice, followed by a faint "Yi-hoo!" Jules touched the dark bulk with his foot. Sometimes the sparrow, like the eagle, dies far from his nest.

But only a most important man, a general or a senator, would be shipped across the sea. He scratched his beard. Surely digging would be easier in the sandhills than in the stony graveyards of Neuchâtel, and if there was none to wield the spade the wolves would clean the bones well.

Shivering a little, he slipped away into the pitchy darkness.

Back at his wagon, Jules pulled his Vetterli from its hiding place in the buckbrush. He raised it to his shoulders several times. The gun came up well, but it was only a single shot. Heavily he crept into his bed roll.

The next day he tried to trade the old Swiss rifle for a secondhand Winchester, but such guns were in great demand on the border and there were other needs for the forty dollars remaining from the relinquishment of his Knox County claim. There would be much to buy, — farm tools, seed, food, ammunition, shoes, drugs, — all the things of life in a new land.

The old storekeeper puttered about among his stacks of gaudy Indian goods, the thick woolens he kept for the freighters and the leathers for the ranch hands. Finally he took Jules into a back room and showed him the bales of furs caught up the Niobrara by Indian and white trappers

— beaver, mink, an occasional otter, endless muskrats, not worth more than eight or ten cents, skunk, coyotes, gray wolves, and badgers from the bluffs and hills. But beaver and otter — those were the furs.

So Jules added a dozen steel traps to his supplies, and a book on trapping and first aid for the frontiersman. He obtained plats and information at the land office, listened with interest to the story of a hard-land region west of the sandhills, and made arrangements to have all mail held until he returned.

"That may be a long time, feller. Lots of things kin happen out where you 're going," the postmaster commented dryly.

"I am a crack shot," Jules told him stiffly.

"Oh, are you!" The man looked the camp-stained homeseeker up and down. "There 's other things catchin' where you 're going besides lead colic."

But he made a note of the mail instructions and stuck the paper on the last of the long row of spikes jammed full of similar slips. Jules wrote letters to his friends in Knox County, young professional men: a doctor, a lawyer, an architect, all who had come across the sea in answer to his earlier letters. They had been disappointed in America, but now he would lead them to a better land. And last he wrote a letter to Rosalie, dropped a blob of red wax upon the flap and pressed it down with his grandfather's seal — a man with a seedling tree standing on newly ploughed ground, facing the rising sun. Then once more Jules set his face westward.

Every day the country grew more monotonous. The gash cut by the Niobrara sank deep between sandstone and magnesia-white bluffs; the grass was longer, yellower, less washed by the winter snows. Because the bluffs crowded close to the stream the homeseeker kept out of the valley, only descending into it for water and wood. The washed ruts of the army trail leading west to Fort Robinson did not interest him. There would be less game along the trail and less freedom on land within sight of troops.

The days brought pale, wind-streaked skies, yellow coyotes slinking into gullies, and endless small game: rabbits, grouse, quail. Wedges of wild geese honked their way north, and along the river the swift wings of ducks whistled over the brush and the clear, sand-bottomed stream. He saw many antelope and deer, and one morning a large, dun animal with high shoulders and broad pronged antlers grazed peacefully against the higher reaches of the sparsely timbered hillside. An elk. The young hunter's Vetterli came up, then dropped, stock down, to the ground. Arms crossed over the muzzle, Jules watched the beautiful animal, so nearly the color of the grassy slope that it vanished unless silhouetted against the dark green of the pines. At last he slipped away.

Towards noon a yellowish haze crept up the horizon. The wind rose in panting gusts, settled into a steady push, almost as tangible as a wall. The flying sand cut the man's face. Despite the sharp-lashed whip, the horses turned their tails into the wind. Finally Jules gave up, unhitched, and slept away the day behind a sandstone cliff over the river. The next morning was still and clear, and the rested horses set off on a trot that soon slowed to a walk in the loose sand, hock deep, blown from bare stretches over the grass. But the wind-uprooted trees, the denuded knolls, brought only a grunt from the homeseeker. He refused to see any significance in them. Instead he considered the coming Presidential election. Cleveland, the governor of New York, was an aggressive young Democrat. If nominated he would carry the election, build up world trade, bring good times for the poor man. Without tariff there would be no international conflicts, no wars. That reminded him of Estelle in Knox County. Lazy, good for nothing, did n't want to raise children. So long as there were wars it was woman's duty to make soldiers.

Last year's sunflowers stood taller, their stalks thicker, sturdier. Jules climbed off his wagon. His study of government bulletins, his knowledge of botany in the Old Country, convinced him that where sunflowers grow corn will grow also. And except for the few cowboys at the Hunter ranch the country was open, free. The grass was almost untouched; cow chips rare.

About two o'clock on the afternoon of the twentieth of April, the day before Jules's twenty-fifth birthday, which he had completely forgotten, the hills gave way and before him was the silver ribbon of the Niobrara, the wooded slopes barely tinged with palest green, topped by yellowish sandstone bluffs. Farther on was a plain, flatter than the palm of a man's hand, and reaching into the dim blue hazes each way. Far off to the left was a flat butte, box-like. To the extreme right were low hills, similar to those left behind.

But the land straight ahead, the Flats, as the Hunter cook called it, was absolutely bare, without a house, even a tree — a faint yellow-green that broke here and there into shifting aspects of small, shimmering lakes, rudimentary mirages. There, close enough to the river for game and wood, on the hard land that must be black and fertile, where corn and fruit trees would surely grow well, Jules saw his home and around him a community of his countrymen and other homeseekers, refugees from oppression and poverty, intermingled in peace and contentment. There would grow up a place of orderliness, with sturdy women and strong children to swing the hay fork and the hoe.

Leaning upon his Vetterli, his cap pushed far back from his eyes, he surveyed the Running Water, his new homeland.

II

MIRAGE

The Niobrara, its sand bottom still soft from the flood waters of March, was smaller here than in Knox County. But the current ran swift and strong and its load of abrasive yellow sand had cut deep through sandstone and volcanic ash and lime rock, baring bones of mastodon and beds of petrified snails.

But the homeseeker had no time for these things to-day. Jules pounded his thin-necked team through the stream and up a snake-head gully to the horizon-wide hard-land table. Where the occasional sunflower along the soldier trail reached to his shoulder, he sank his spade two blades deep through the tough nigger-wool sod. The soil was black, smooth, smelling of spring. Here the settler dropped the harness from his team. When his fire of diamond willow crackled, he skinned a grouse, and fried it all. If a man would plan well, he must eat.

His long hands about his ragged knees, he looked into the red fire. Soon Rosalie would be beside him, Rosalie and neighbors, lights all over the Flats, friendly in the dark that was unrelieved to-night.

At last he lay down to sleep.

The next morning Jules took his traps to the river, and while a blue kingfisher poised over the stream and fell like a plummet, he set several number ones where the dainty tracks of a mink embroidered the mud. Two larger traps he hid cunningly where a gnawed young cottonwood lay half

in the water.   He caught two muskrats, a mink, and two
beaver feet, chewed off at the steel jaws of the trap.   It was
too bad to leave an animal crippled to suffer.

Before the kerosene that had slopped against the grub
box was evaporated and the coffee was tolerable again, Sol
Pitcher, a surveyor from Verdigre, drove out of the dusk to
the campfire.

The two talked over their supper.   The cook at Hunter's
had said: "You 'll find Frenchy scratching the dirt on the
Flats until July comes to cook his liver and lights."

"Trying to discourage settlers," Jules grumbled, over a
leg of cottontail.

"Yeh," Sol admitted as he wiped the gravy from his catfish moustaches.   He liked the country, was disappointed
that the impractical Jules had put off finding the government corners [1] of his land while he planted young ash and
cottonwood and box-elder seedlings from the river.   A
wave of population was due.   There would be money in
locating.

For two days they plodded their ponies over the table
westward from Box Butte to a wide prairie-dog town, thousands of little crater-like holes, with the derisive dogs bobbing out of sight with a flirt of the stubby tails, to scold and
bark as soon as the men were past.   Jules shot one to ex-
amine it — a gnawer, with teeth like a little beaver.   He
spattered the head of a rattlesnake on one of the mounds.
Then he saved his ammunition.

They found several fine, whitened buffalo heads and a
few depressions that lined up with the compass, but no num-
bered stakes as the government bulletins promised.   Hoping

[1] The government surveys in this region were completed in 1881.   The
section corners were marked with four holes, one in each of the cornering
sections, the soil thrown together in a central mound, and a stake bearing the section numbers driven into this mound.   The Homestead Act,
effective January 1863, allowed each *bona fide* settler 160 acres of land.
The entry was by legal description and the entryman swore that he had
seen the premise before filing.   "Squatting" had lost all legal status.

that the weather had brought them down, they dug in the holes. Finally Jules threw the spade from him.

"Damn the luck!   Prairie fire burn me the stakes or somebody maliciously destroy them!"

"Yeh, guess you 're right, Jule," the calmer Sol agreed, picking up the spade. The next day Sol headed north towards the railroad survey, where locating would be more profitable around the new town sites.   Three soddies would make a town, with lots to sell.

After his friend was gone, Mirage Flats was suddenly empty, bare as a burnt-out world.   When a small puffball of dust came down the army trail from Fort Robinson, far to the west, Jules leaned with folded arms across the muzzle of his gun beside the deep ruts, and watched them trot by: three light wagons, officers, educated men with a mounted escort.   They barely acknowledged his greeting.   Only one more granger scalp if the Sioux broke out.

Back at his wagon Jules set the rifle against the wheel and poured out a cup of cold coffee from the blackened syrup pail, looking after the troopers until the clot of dust dipped down towards the Niobrara.

Suddenly he flung the dark liquid and the cup from him, and piled his plough, his axe, and his spade into the wagon. In the morning he would go back, not to Estelle and Knox County, — to Neuchâtel and to Zurich, to his friends Surber and Karrer, — to Rosalie.

But that night, while, with the point of his pocket knife, he probed frying balls of baking-powder biscuit in antelope-steak gravy, tired hoofbeats pounded over the prairie.   A covered wagon broke from the darkness, the lathered flanks of the horses heaving.   A man leaped down, deep shadows of night on his naked cheeks.

Jules reached for his rifle and stepped back into the darkness.

"Don't shoot! My God, man, don't shoot!" the frightened youth begged.   "My wife 's dying — and I can't find a woman to help her."

Suspiciously Jules came forward, scratching his beard. "In thaire?" he asked, thumbing towards the wagon.

Together they climbed upon the doubletrees, Jules carrying his lantern and his gun. Inside, between boxes and bundles, lay a young woman, little more than a child, her eyes unmoving caverns in the light.

Jules pushed his cap back and clambered out. He set the pan off and began eating rapidly with his knife, mouthing the hot food, his rifle still in the crook of his arm. Behind him in the shadows hovered the stranger. Once more he searched the dark of the Flats, shielding his eyes from the campfire and lantern glare. There was nothing, only those in the circle of the light.

"You can't sit there — eating — and let her die!"

Without answering Jules speared another chunk of steak and put it into his mouth. Slowly the man plodded to his team and gathered up the lines.

"Heah? — Oh, hell! — Put on a bucket of water to boil," Jules ordered.

At a hoarse cry from the wagon he gulped a cup of black coffee and carried the lantern into his tent, his back a black, moving shadow. From a small bottle with a red skull and crossbones he measured the equivalent of a grain of wheat of white powder into a tin cup.

"What you giving her?" the husband whispered.

"Morphine. Kill some of the pain. Now make me room and get me some clean rags."

While the boxes and bundles came out of the wagon Jules thumbed through his doctor book, washed his hands carefully, pared his fingernails close, and pulled his blunt scissors from the boiling water with a stick. Then he carried out the instructions of the book as unfeelingly, as coldly, as though the woman were one of the animals he had so often seen his veterinary father care for, the father who still hoped that this eldest of six sons would be a doctor.

The woman was spent by long hours of labor and he needed all the ingenuity and recollection his Swiss heritage could bring to his strong, narrow hands and the pitifully scant equipment he had. But she had endurance, youth, and courage, and Jules was without knowledge of pain. The horizontal rays of the early sun found the camp asleep — one more potential tiller of the soil on Mirage Flats.

And this morning the discouragement of yesterday was gone. With the help of the young father, Jud Haskins, Jules unloaded once more and started a dugout, a place for his belongings, something to mark his claim. Almost every day pin dots of black broke from the obscurity of the blue-veiled horizon. Only the impression that his place was safely entered protected it from claim jumpers.

Two weeks showed that it was not good with the Haskins baby. Although the young mother ate much fresh game and every day a bit from their lean store of potatoes and flour, the little Jules cried all night, his mouth like a starving birdling's. The settler swore and thumbed the doctor book.

Then one evening he found a note pinned to his clean blankets. The Haskins' hoped to find a doctor and cow's milk at Fort Robinson. The fresh bread hanging from the ridgepole of the tent was for him, and the big jar of grape butter. And God bless him.

With a curse Jules crumpled the note and threw it into the fire. He sat a long time with his hands hanging between his muddy knees. When the clean coffeepot boiled over, he stirred.

"Every man need a good woman," he told the Flats.

Jules was n't long alone. Homeseekers were drawn to the little tent and the mounds of new dirt. Sometimes they brought news from Valentine: shootings, vigilantes, settlers, and the progress of the railroad west. In return they got locating help and advice and settled over the Flats. Or they moved on to the railroad survey. And when that happened Jules felt a personal defeat.

Early in May a man, his wife, and a daughter of eighteen shivered through a three-day drizzle at Jules's camp. They laughed at the settler's pan-fried bread and his coffee pounded with a hammer in the corner of a flour sack. But they listened eagerly enough when he talked of preëmptions and timber claims and read the Homestead Act to them from the bulletin that was only a mess of little black jiggers on white paper to them.

The third evening Jules brought some of his drying hides, with the animal smell still upon them, into the land seeker's wagon, insisting that the girl stroke the glossy back of a mink, dusky purple-brown in the light.

"Soft like *samat*," he bragged, and brushed the fur quickly to her pale cheek.

"Oh," she shuddered. "The awful thing! Take it away!"

"Dirty foreigner!" the mother called after Jules. But he did n't care. He threw himself on his bed, his hands under his head, his knees up in the darkness, and laughed until he choked. Fine ladies, these, with no family, no education, nothing.

The next morning the world glistened with the blue-white of a new snow under the hot sun. Instead of the covered wagon of the homeseekers there was only a blackish bare spot with two dark tracks leading away to the south, across the level country, headed back to Kansas.

The girl, then, was gone. He had dreamed last night, as a young lover dreams, of Rosalie, the dark curls of her neck soft under his fingers. Thinking of her, he kicked the snow into the wheel tracks. Perhaps this was Sunday and they should be walking in the leafing woods, he and Rosalie, the mosses green and springy underfoot.

But he was hungry. Never forehanded, the storm caught him without firewood. His team, too, was gone. His horse, Jim, tired of cropping nigger-wool roots, pulled up

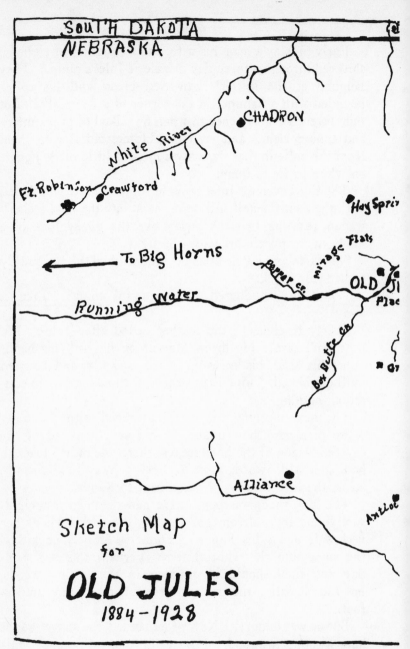

SOUTH DAKOTA
NEBRASKA

CHADRON

White River

Ft. Robinson   Crawford

Hay Sprin

Mirage Flats

← To Big Horns

Pepper Cr.

OLD JU

Plac

Running Water

Box Butte Cr.

Gr

Alliance

Antioc

Sketch Map
for →

OLD JULES
1884-1928

AUTHOR'S WORKING MAP

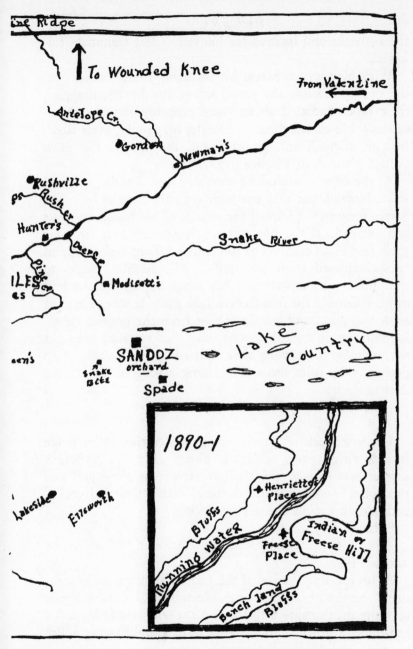

ine Ridge

To Wounded Knee

from Valentine

Antelope Cr.

Gordon

Newman's

Rushville

Rusher

Hunter's

Pierce

ILES

Modisett's

Lake Country

SANDOZ
orchard

Snake
Butte

Spade

1890-1

Lakeside

Ellsworth

Henrietta's
Place

Bluffs

Running Water

Freese
Place

Indian or
Freese Hill

Bench land
Bluffs

OF OLD JULES COUNTRY, *with Inset of* FREESE TROUBLES

the ash stake and foraged for himself. The teammate followed.

With his shotgun across his forearm, Jules started over
the prairie towards the river, where the horses, dragging
their ropes Indian fashion, were probably sunning themselves. He cursed them — Estelle, his family, even Rosalie; his stomach still growled and the sun on the snow
burned his eyes to a lightish gray.

At the edge of a bluff he stumbled over a stake, a corner
stake, blurred, but with the numbers still discernible. The
horses forgotten, he freed the needle of his pocket compass
and stepped off the line towards his camp, each step one
yard, north and east. The sun climbed, faint curls of steam
twisted upward from the bluffs. Mirage Flats began to
shimmer as sun on water. Only when he had the numbers
of his claim did the homeseeker look up. It was noon; the
snow was gone, and bobolinks rose from the prairie, spiral-
ing into the air until they were only specks against the light
sky, raining melody as they coasted to the earth. Cap
pushed back, Jules listened and sang a song of his student
days in Zurich.

Once more everything was good.

His first week on the Running Water the settler made
friends with a party of Oglala Sioux. He was dipping a
keg of water from the shallow stream as they galloped
through a break in the buffalo-berry brush, their half-naked
bodies dark against the silvery thicket.

"Hou!" they called.

The white man straightened up, answered "Hou!" as he
watched them.

At his greeting the last of the Indians stopped. "Frenchman," he shouted, white teeth gleaming. He wore a pair
of white man's pants with the seat cut out, moccasins, and a
red-tipped feather in his hair — a lean, straight young figure
on a bay and white calico pony.

The entire string whirled their ponies into a circle about the settler, rested their rifles across their horses, and nodded their approval of this supposed Frenchman. Through the young Indian, White Eye, they indicated that their camp was across the river.

That evening Jules rode into the Sioux broken circle of tipis set among the hackberry and box elders at the foot of Indian Hill. White Eye led him to a large fire where most of the men squatted about in blankets, smoking.

They greeted the white man with raised palms, offered him the fragrant pipe ornamented with a lock of long yellow hair, and asked where he came from. An old man, wrinkled as last year's potato, nodded. He had been to the Missouri. It was far; many sleep. They made their friend welcome on the Running Water.

The Oglalas told Jules many things about the country, the winters, the summers, the hunting. They spoke slowly, sadly, of the buffalo days, — when the great herds spread northward, — as Jules's father spoke of the age of Pericles. Now the buffalo was no more. One, two, on the Snake, in the sandhills, and then it is done.

As they talked children raced through the camp with bows and horseweed lances, dogs barking. Women in red or blue calico and bordered blankets falling to the beaded moccasins cooked over smaller fires. Some turned thick corn-meal cake from one frying pan into another. Some stirred dark messes in huge government kettles.

Until the Oglalas returned to their reservation, Pine Ridge, in June, Jules went often to the camping ground, used no man knew how long. Twice he picked eagles out of the sky for them. In return for the wing fans the old men liked and the fine breath feathers for their headdresses, they gave Jules a covered army kettle, laughing deep in their blankets when he asked, "Where come from?" They offered the white man half of the camp property for his German buckshot mould. He parted with it reluctantly for a light saddle which he needed most urgently and they apparently hardly at all.

From the Indians Jules learned to guide Old Jim with his knees, leaving both hands free for the rifle. They taught him weather and game sign, sharpening his ears and his eyes as a fine stone whets a blade of steel. They took him to Deer Creek, one sleep away, at the edge of the deep hills, on a hunt.

Their ponies loped untiringly over the low swells, through chophills, and out into tiny, bunch-grassed valleys between soapweed-studded sand buttes that seemed to move aside as the hunters approached.

They climbed their horses up Deer Hill, so called because buckbrush grew almost to the bald towering top. Resting at the edge of the blowout, a deep crater sifting yellow sand down the slope in high winds, they looked off to the lesser hills shouldering each other away into the horizon in every direction. To the east, the Oglalas said, was the land of the Gone-Before-Ones, with many hundred elk in the winter, antelope the year round, deer in every brush patch, clear lakes for the washing of the hides, and sand cherries, plums, and chokecherries for the women. But it was not good to go there before the death song.

"Why not?" Jules demanded.

No one knew. Strange things happened to those who went. If they came back, the tongue was twisted and none could understand.

Jules looked with interest at the rounded hill contours blurring to the far horizon. There, away to the east, where a tiny bit of lake gleamed blue-white between high, well-grassed ridges, one might find quiet and peace and rest when age slowed the blood and the children were grown.

But it would be bad in a blizzard. He remembered the story the freighter told of the man with hands and feet rotting, "crazy as a shitepoke," which seemed to be a queer bird that rose heavily from the rushes along the Niobrara and made the peculiar pumping noise in the evening. Thunder-pumper, Sol Pitcher called him.

At Deer Creek, a winding little stream with slough grass almost meeting over the clear thread of water, they camped. Towards evening the women came in, some horseback, bobbing like rolled feather ticks on the loping ponies, the others in two government wagons. The next day the hunters killed fifteen antelope and three buck deer, two of the deer and four antelopes falling before the Vetterli.

"Straight Eye," the Indians called Jules as they squatted about the fire of fast-disappearing buffalo chips.

The women stripped the meat and threw it on the drying racks they fetched with them. Laughing, a tall girl offered to cure some for the watching white man. She was light brown, her eyes soft, her body not too compacted by reservation diet for this Jules.

"Tell her I am married," he said.

A quick laugh followed White Eye's interpretation, and a long silence. Uneasily Jules picked up his Vetterli and went to the picketed horses. At a grunt from the older men White Eye brought him back. It was only the kindness due a guest in the tipi of an Oglala. In marriage she would have a chief, bring her father many horses.

Jules was glad to be taken back. It was nearing night. Old Jim was tired and Jules himself stiff with saddle-wolf. To show his self-sufficiency, he salted a piece of tender meat to preserve it. By the next morning the sand under the sack was browned with the precious juices that are strength. The women saw and, among themselves, made the sad, kindly noises of a friendly flock of chickens.

On the way back the Indians stopped on a particularly rough spot where the chophills lay like dun waves of a storm-tossed sea, caught and held forever in naked, wind-pocked knobs. Green yuccas crowded towards the higher hills like dark sheep running before a storm, and in the hol-

lows were tight, tub-sized nests of bull-tongue cactus, the
sections broader than a big man's hand.

"Running Water, which way?" White Eye asked.

Jules squinted for the sun, but there was none, only a
high, opaque sky blanketing.   He reached for his compass,
but the leader held up his hand, palm out, and made peculiar
digging motions.   Then Jules laughed with them.   Every
hollow, every blowout scooped by the wind pointed away in
the same direction, the southeast.

"*Sacré!*   Never git lost in this country!"

Between hunts and helping settlers find corners and lines,
Jules worked at his dugout, two thirds in the ground, roofed
with sod over straight ash poles.   He tried breaking his own
ground, but found that it was not easy to manage a team and
hold the plough in nigger-wool sod.   It jerked and bucked;
the handles pounded his legs, blistered his hands, and there
was no smooth band of black behind him, only torn, twisted
strings of sod that would not turn or flatten.

"Takes a strong back," he consoled himself, "and a thick
head."

After that Jules began to charge a locating fee, one day
of breaking.   On the new ground he planted corn or beans
with the spade, striking the blade into the ground once at
every step, dropping the seed and closing the groove with
his foot as he walked.   Cut, drop, step — up and down the
field.

Not all the homeseekers who came stayed.   Some ignominiously returned to their relatives, others pushed on to the
greener fields beyond the horizon: more wood, and water,
less isolation and work.   One evening as Jules was skinning a broad-stripe skunk beside his tent two covered wagons
came up the soldier trail.   They sought a turn-off north.

"No road, no travel that way," the locator told them
shortly, busy cutting around the scent bag of the animal.
"Better land here and plenty game along the river."

"Mebby, but they's talk of the railroad coming through, an' the womenfolks wants to live clost to town." The driver of the first wagon spit a brown splotch into the curling grass and swung a long whip over his team. The dry wheels squeaked forward. Two women looked through the round hole in the back of the second wagon, holding their noses. In disdain Jules flung the carcass after them.

The influx of settlers meant talk on politics and science and the news. Outsiders brought reports of a panic in New York, the failure of the Marine Bank, the nomination of Jay Gould's Blaine on the Republican ticket, and Cleveland, the exponent of civil service to Jules, on the Democratic.

The country was evidently going to the dogs again. Corruption in high places; railroads taking all the little fellow could scratch together. But nevertheless the settlers watched with impatience the slow westward creep of steel from Valentine.

Gradually the homeseekers formed the habit of dropping in at the dugout. They hunched themselves on boxes of provisions and ammunition, whittled, pared their nails with their knives, looked at Jules's books, — science, medicine, geography, or history, — thumbed the mail-order catalogue, or just talked. Now and then Jules moved the lantern from its place on the Nebraska statutes to settle some point.

On special occasions he opened the big brown stamp album, kept in the box on the ridgepole with his drugs and poisons. With hands carefully washed in water that must be carried from the Niobrara, he examined any loose stamps under magnifying glass, held them to the light to catch the watermarking, and fixed them into place. Some day he would fill the gaps, most of them.

Every time he followed a departing guest into the night for a neighborly last word, the dozens of lights blinking out on Mirage Flats reminded him that the country was settling fast. Soon there would be land fights.

Before he drove the hundred fifty miles to Valentine, Jules spent a whole day writing letters, driving his pen in a strong, harsh slant across the page. His brothers and his uncles in Switzerland must know of this land that fit the shoulder like a well-cut coat. Here there were sunsets rivaling anything he had seen in Italy, and land that needed no manure carried to it on bent back. To Rosalie he wrote another letter. Surely she would come now, and quickly. He did not tell her of Estelle, but wrote of the fine thunderheads here, rising into the sky with more magnificence to him than the Jura of his childhood; and of the mushrooms in the woods, food for a king.

At Valentine Jules filed immediately, even before he had a glass of beer, for the homeseeker trails into the frontier land-office town were deep and worn. There were two letters, one from his sister Elvina. Papa stilled hoped for a doctor in the family. Rosalie wrote as ever, but nowhere did she promise to come.

Jules traded for supplies his spring catch of hides and a couple of eagles he shot on the way down. The eagles sold well; the hides the trader threw into a pile on the greasy counter.

"Springy, catched too late, not worth much. See that green spot?" The trader pointed to a dark stain in the skin on the flesh side. "That means a thin hide. Catch them in cold weather, when the skin's prime. An' you better scrape the fat off the badgers next time; dry better, look better. Musta been a good winter up the river, them animals comin' out so greasy. A good year for skunk and badger oil; fry it out; bring you a little money too."

That evening Jules turned in at the saloon where he had seen the youth killed. It was jammed, with more gambling, more and louder women.

"How, Frenchy! God, but you 're getting to be a dirty cuss. Ain't they no water out west?" asked the old freighter

at the identical table, still twisting his fingers into his moustache ends, as though he had n't moved.

"Water is for crops — and cows," Jules said. Every
drop he used was carried a mile and a half. He ordered
the beers and got the news in return. A couple of killings
in town, nothing special, just settlers fighting over entries.
Looked like Sheriff Carter was going to leave the country,
maybe feet first. Several of the vigilantes from down the
Niobrara were out on bail, charged with doing considerable
horse stealing on the side. Every day strings of wagons
went west and every day the drags came back. Twenty
thousand head of young stock trailed through in one week.

"Is that so?" Jules scratched his beard and forgot his
drink. "Looks like the cattlemen intend to hog the country."

"Yeh, it 's their meat — " the freighter said, twisting the
uncurling moustaches hopefully.

"Like hell — it 's the country of the poor man with a
gun," Jules roared. His rifle across his arm, he stalked
away through the crowd, stopping here and there before men
who might be looking for land, telling them of the Mirage
Flats. Three young men from Iowa promised to come as
soon as their outfits pulled in on the unreliable freight.

The man with the Winchester was nowhere in Valentine.

At the post office Jules wrote another half-dozen letters
to his countrymen at Verdigre, a general letter to the Swiss-
American publications in the East, and one to a paper reaching the middle-class in Neuchâtel, urging all who wanted
land to come, and come quickly. The letter to Rosalie he
opened again and added a postscript: "If you do not come
now it will be too late." And as he sealed the envelope
with the man carrying the young tree he meant all of it.

When he ordered his mail held until called for, even if
that were six months, the postmaster offered to send it out
with that of the new colony under Reverend Scamahorn, west
along the survey somewhere. The parson would soon have

a post office at Gordon.   Until then he got his mail at the Newman ranch.

"I don't risk my life going to Newman's or any other ranch," Jules said flatly.   Nor did he intend to go to Gordon for it.   He wrote to Washington, asking that a post office be established on the southeast quarter of section three, township twenty-nine, range forty-five, west.   That done, he set out for Mirage Flats and home.   In his eagerness he forgot to have his kerosene can filled.   And he drove his team even harder than before.

III

JEST AND DEPARTURE

By the first of July Mirage Flats was settling up, a covered
wagon here, a dugout and the square, patient faces of oxen
there. Strips of nigger-wool sod lay straight and flat as
bands of metal or greened into rows of two-speared, heat-
curled corn. By now no plough would penetrate the brick-
hard soil. Dry-land whirlwinds picked up bits of grass and
weeds, tossed them high into the air, dropped them capri-
ciously back upon the prairie, and zigzagged on. Heat
dances and illusionary lakes rippled away the noon hours on
the whitish horizon. Already some of the settlers turned
their bronzing faces from these signs of aridity and, with a
deepening of the sun scowl between their eyes, lifted the
lids of their water barrels, wondering how long before the
rising yellow sand bars of the Niobrara would choke the
little channel a man now could almost jump across.

But the hardier, the more ambitious, were not content
with drinking water from the tepid little stream. They
turned their faces toward Valentine, to file before some claim
jumper did it for them, to bring back provisions if the money
lasted. Anyway to bring back well supplies, rope, wind-
lasses, buckets.

The well Jules started early in the spring he gave up as
more than a one-man job. What he needed was a strong
wife. Several Sundays he rode his Jim horse up to Rush
Creek, near the railroad survey. Although Matilda Lehrer
never had much to say, her laugh was like beading cider at
the bunghole. But to Jules her fragrant hot bread and her

sure hand on the hammer and the spade meant more just now. Then somebody told her that the romantic foreigner was married.

"I don't see what difference that make," he argued. "If she want me I get a divorce."

But Matilda's mother, with cheeks hanging like a gray dish towel from the peg that was her nose, folded her hands over her stomach. Jules got on his horse and spurred out of her sight.

July was brittle with sun. Through the noon hours grouse squatted behind the ragged sunflowers along the soldier trail, mouths open, wings out, tame as chickens under a Slav's table.

The drouth sucked up the water holes south of the river and the Hunter ranch stock came in droves to the Niobrara. Any night the wild steers might drift up on Mirage and eat out the settlers. Shotguns boomed along the river. Jules filled several shells with salt and laughed as the cattleman's stock retreated.

One afternoon, when he had worked a furious half hour chopping the sod about his whips of trees and cleaning out the tough weeds, two homeseekers stopped for their last filing instructions. Glad of the respite, Jules squatted on the shady side of the wagon with them and filed his gleaming hoe.

A cowboy, headed west for the upper Hunter ranch, reined off towards the loafing settlers. His wild-eyed dun side-jumped at Jules's pile of bleaching buffalo skulls and broke away in a run. The rider jerked the horse to his haunches, bloody froth flying from the spade bit. Back before the settlers, he shifted his heavy Colt, tossed a leg around the saddle horn, and rolled a cigarette. He had been up to the tent town of Gordon, about thirty miles away. It was going strong as a sheepman's socks. Everything wide open; draw played in the dust of the street.

So?

Yeh, even had a resident sky pilot who organized a church along in May, with seventy-five people scattered around his tent, sitting on the woodpile, wagon tongues, empty whiskey kegs, and the ground making a noise fit to stampede a herd of longhorns clear down on the Cimarron. But the collection was a mite disappointing, and after the praying the new congregation milled into the nearest saloon to wet their gullets and celebrate the organization of the first Methodist Church west of Valentine, much to the consternation of the rustling, straight-shooting parson.

"Rustling — shooting?" Jules inquired. "Preachers steal cattle too?"

The horseman grabbed for his cigarette and laughed.

"Naw, you got the wind wrong. The parson ain't a rustler, he's a *rustler* — works hard scratching souls together for Kingdom Come. He wouldn't chaw slow elk, starving. But he's bit off a tough chunk — saving souls up there. They's liquor enough running in the street of Gordon to lay anything excepting Nebraska dust."

It might be worth going up.

"Yeh, but better not tie your Sunday-school money in your shirt tail."

"What you mean?"

The horsebacker slapped his worn chaps. "You'll lose it when they steals your shirt, you greenhorn." Suddenly the man leaned forward, his arms crossed on the saddle horn, his light, sun-squinted eyes cold upon them. "But you grangers 'll never have no money. It don't never rain in this damned country and you'll stop lead or stretch rope if you keeps shootin' cattle."

The two newcomers dropped back. Jules stood his ground, and pushed his cap away from eyes hard as the file in his hands. Deliberately he spit upon the ground at the man's stirrup.

"You don't run me off! I see the cattle business in hell first."

The ranch hand caressed the worn butt of his Colt absently. "Fighting words, hoe man," he said. "But it'll be a different tune — and you better roll up this snag of fence you got strung around here or it won't be healthy for you."

With that he pinched the fire from his cigarette butt, flipped it into the breaking, and sank his spurs. The clean-limbed half mustang dropped into a short, easy lope, stringing a trail of dust across the Flats.

Jules had no heart for more weed chopping.

After supper several neighbors came across the curled, dead grass to sit on the piles of dirt. They talked and looked at a newcomer's pamphlet on railroad land sales. "The New Canaan," one called the Panhandle.

Big Andrew, who could lay twice as much sod in a day as any other on the Flats, lifted his buffalo shoulders a little and pulled his pipestem from his red beard. "Canaan — Promised Land they call it?" He looked off over Jules's corn, dark, rattling a little in the wind of dusk. "Yah, a panhandle, to the Promised Land."

"I ain't seen much milk and honey," a truck gardener from Missouri complained.

Jules stirred from his preoccupation. "It will come," he said.

They laughed comfortably, as men who had known each other for a long time instead of weeks and days.

Off to the west lightning winked almost continuously, but no one said anything about rain. "You can see the flash three hundred miles," Jules had told them earlier in the summer.

"Three hundred miles? Who in hell you stringing now?" they scoffed.

"Stringing — fooling? I don't fool when I talk business."

So they smoked in silence now, or picked their teeth with grass. Before night settled they walked out to Jules's sod corn, dark figures plodding through the late dusk. The corn was still good, would make thirty bushels to the acre, maybe, with a little rain. Chewing the drying leaves, they talked of the coming railroad, with markets for their produce. Then there would be law, with probably a new county cut off from Sioux as Cherry had been, with county officials.

"It will be important to get good ones, in sympathy with the settlers," Jules pointed out, and told about the cowboy that afternoon.

"Hell, no cattleman 'll bother us much on the Flats. Grass here 's too short for nothing but sheep or horses."

Jules did not answer. They could not see that the Flats were almost settled. They knew nothing of the world's hunger for land. He left them and brought out his smoky lantern and his rifle and ran a soft-brushed ramrod through the barrel. Blinking a little in the light, the others talked — of drinking at Valentine and Gordon, about women; particularly about women, and for once Jules had no smutty story to offer. Nor did he bring out dripping tin cups of new currant wine from the keg working in the corner of the dugout. Big Andrew cupped the fire in his pipe with his palm and noticed that Jules's shirt was torn clear down the back, and that when he stooped white skin showed — white skin over delicate bones. There was something defenseless about the human back, particularly Jules's.

The settlers scattered early to-night, the newcomers taking Andrew to their wagon to ask about the locator. Funny cuss; cleaned his gun twice this afternoon.

The big fellow moved heavily on the wagon tongue. "Yah, maybe he see what we don't. He is like the tree that grow on the bluff of the river — the pine. He get the wind and the storm that do not touch us who are the cottonwood and the willow near the water. But his root is strong and he see the cloud from far off — and the sun before she shine on us."

"Talking about water — I don't see 's any of you 're getting much."

Jules did n't leave his corn while the Hunter cattle grazed the Niobrara Valley. Once when three steers wandered up through a gully he took half the powder out of two shotgun shells and peppered their tough hides with buckshot.

When his corn was curled and gray, and the potato and bean plants seemed harsh sticks with dry leaves, the rain came. It fell for three hours, so hard that the Flats was a sheet of water. Jules pushed out to throw up a ridge of sod about the mouth of his dugout. Even so he had to rescue his bed, his catalogues, and his guns from the floor.

The rain brought a buzz to the Flats. The settlers, young with the land, talked big as the surviving sod corn and the potatoes pushed their bursting bosoms up under the shadows of the new vines. But the first week in September brought fog, a flurry of snow, and a clear, bright morning that spread ice over the water barrels and whitened the unmatured corn. It killed the beans and the big melons that Jules and the coyotes watched so jealously.

The next morning wagons rumbled away over the Flats towards Pine Ridge for lumber. Unless another hard soaker came soon there would be no sod cutting for building.

Here and there hunched tiny stacks of hay, not enough for the cattle, nothing at all for the horses. Jules had only his team, accustomed to desultory care, and some of the settlers who did not have even the three dollars locating fee he now charged hauled dry brush from the Niobrara for him to a pile behind his dugout. This he chopped when needed, in three-foot lengths, and pushed through the fire-box door of his cookstove as it burned, disregarding the smoke.

"Well, I 'll be damned! You are the laziest yet," a neighbor remarked.

"Me lazy? I got the best sod corn and beans in the country and a couple hundred trees growing. In addition I located over a hundred settlers that will stay."

"Yeh, I guess that 's right enough," the man admitted, not convinced.

During the late summer Jules's letters brought three young French Swiss from Ohio. Paul Nicolet was the light one, with a small, pointed head and a delicate upper lip. Jules Tissot, nicknamed "The Black," was narrow-eyed, and yellowish skin grew far up between his bony fingers. Jules Aubert, the writer and spokesman of the three, was like his letters, judicious, cautious, articulate without brilliance — an open handwriting in blue ink on good blue-gray paper. He found work at once at a new ranch on Minnetonka, Pine Creek, as the white man called it, at fifteen dollars a month.

The three accepted Jules's dugout, still without wood floor or door, as their headquarters. Within a week they were calling themselves "the Company." Because three by the same name were too many, and perhaps because of his aversion to practical jokes, the current frontier humor, their host became Old Jules. Soon he was Old Jules to all the Flats.

Nicolet and Tissot helped with the well. In return the locator would take the newcomers to Valentine to file on land he had managed to keep covered for their coming. A holiday, a little wine, a little music, perhaps a little women — who can say? And as they planned they ate young prairie chicken flavored with wild garlic and roasted to the point of disintegration in the army kettle. And with it they drank deep red wine of the black currants from along the river.

Then they talked of the Old Country and of course of women, Tissot the loudest. He was the sort who jerked a peasant girl's head back by her thick braids and pressed his kisses upon her.

"Conquering a woman who hates you — a-ah, that is worth the effort!" and the red of his dark lips showed wet.

"I like mine tame."

Aubert agreed with Jules. But The Black was a devil of a fellow.

Jules told of his pranks in the mountain village where he had been sent to learn German among fat cheeses and buxom blonde maidens. He laughed until he choked at the recollection, swearing he had his fill of thick calves forever. A little nostalgically they talked of the vineyards, like green robes embroidered in purple, spreading down the mountainside, of the wine-pressing time, the sparkle of the juice, and the dances. They sang a little, sentimentally in bad German, or lustily in French about the "Little Pot under the Bed," and the "Boatman's Daughter." Then there was the "Marseillaise." For Jules there was always the rousing "Marseillaise."

During the day he filled buckets in the well that Nicolet and Tissot drew up from the narrow hole. Sometimes they waved a coat over the opening to frighten the excitable Jules, or made the full buckets dance over his head and laughed at his fiery cursing until they had to lean weakly against each other from laughing. But usually they were busy enough pulling the rope or nailing curbing together to follow the digger. Needless expense, this curbing, some thought, with lumber scarce, but after a cave-in near Gordon upon the digger it was concluded that Old Jules's way was probably better.

One exceptionally warm evening they dried their soil-caked clothing in the evening sun. The Black Tissot teased a toad drowsy with fall. At last he dropped it into the well, listening for the plop as it hit far below. "You are a fool!" Jules told him angrily. But good humor returned easily to-night. To-day his spade had struck water. To-morrow they would clean out the well, the next day off to Valentine. There would be mail, a letter from Rosalie. Surely she would come before the first blizzard, before winter blocked the roads.

Somewhere a belated prairie-dog owl called a friendly "Who, who!" An arrow hawk fell noisily upon the fall's last mosquito. Lights winked faintly out upon the Flats.

Jules's lantern had burned dry the night before, and when the chill rose up out of the river valley they went to bed.

Eighteen days later a wagon escorted by troopers swung to a halt before the log hospital at Fort Robinson, and Old Jules, his eyes sunken into a fever-burned mask, was carried away. By the time he regained consciousness, Dr. Walter Reed, the post surgeon, had examined this granger. The man was covered with dark bruises, but everything was overshadowed by the crushed left ankle, swollen to the size of a water bucket, black and green with infection, the leg to the loin swelled to a shininess and lividly streaked. Eighteen days — perhaps it was too late even for amputation.

But when the emaciated man was prepared for the operation he sat up, his gaunt cheeks flushed a violent red under his beard, his bloodshot eyes glittering.

"You cut my foot off, doctor, and I shoot you so dead you stink before you hit the ground."

The attendants pinned the man back, but they could not stop the tongue or the eyes. The doctor, tall, slight, not much past thirty, stood over this patient, so different from the regular run of stolid grangers that were brought to him sick and dying. He saw a strong, straight nose, wide-winged, a fine forehead, narrow hands, eyes that commanded even through the veil of fever. Long the doctor looked down into those eyes that never wavered, although the patient's clawed hands gripped the narrow edge of the table to retain consciousness. He was not begging but commanding that his leg, rotting though it was, and dying, be left to him, defying anyone to take it from him.

The thin line of the doctor's moustache twitched. "My orders are amputate. But your wish to die in one piece shall not be ignored." He gave a salute, one that was only half mockery. "And it would be just like your particular brand of damn fool to pull through."

The doctor was right. Jules did pull through, but not without a great deal of agony to himself and to this doctor who could never learn proper impersonality toward his patients. The first few nights it took two men to hold Jules when he tried to fling himself out of bed upon Nicolet and Tissot, when he cursed his father and his mother for driving him away to America. Then there were times when he talked to Rosalie, the Rosalie who might be waiting at Valentine, and once of the man with the Winchester in the saloon. These two came with the sleep of the doctor's morphine.

His leg in a sling, with tubes in the crushed ankle dripping bloody pus, the infection slowly drained away; the swelling went down. By then the doctor and the attendants, and through them the entire fort, had the story of Old Jules.

It seemed that when the final pail of mud had been dumped on the mottled brown and yellow piles of clay, the two helpers pulling Jules from the well could not resist a little joke. They jerked the rope several times, laughing until they had to wrap it about a corner plank while Jules, dizzy in the twisting bucket, looked down at the water far below him and knew that under it was rock. They pulled again, and jerked, pulled and jerked — once too often. Near the top the frayed rope broke and the well-digger plunged sixty-five feet to the bottom, his foot doubled under him.

Two weeks later soldiers headed for Fort Robinson found a man lying along the trail. It required three stout troopers to take the rifle from him and then he collapsed in a rush of French, German, and English curses. They gave him water and got two settlers, Scribner and Sturgeon, to haul him to the fort.

During the first two months at the hospital Jules went over the accident a hundred times. The two frightened helpers had pulled him out and, bowing before the blast of his anger, tried to bathe and bandage him, Tissot pale and a little defiant, Nicolet with tears in his light, boyish eyes. When Jules calmed he took a dose of morphine and considered. He was in no condition for a hard trip a hundred and fifty miles down the Niobrara with no hospital to receive him. And even now the land came first. The filings of the three must be made immediately. To Aubert, who came that evening, he gave his last twenty-five dollars for winter supplies, took another dose of morphine, and went to bed. They would pound the horses on the tails; be back in a week if possible.

But the ankle did not get better and the pain grated like a rasp through the mist of morphine and wine. Hunger and the need for water drove him out the third day. He crawled to the well, dragging the swollen foot after him like a wounded animal. Then he waited at the edge of the garden for an hour for a rabbit to come within shooting distance. Because he had no kerosene there was no light. Everyone thought he was gone to Valentine. No one stopped.

The seventh day Jules shot a chicken hawk that lit on a fence post. Carefully, with his gun steadied on a box, he shot, but it was a long time before he could get back to the dugout and set the gaunt, blue corpse of the bird on to cook. He drank the dark, wild broth and gnawed the meat that was never tender enough to eat.

The eighth day and the ninth the young Swiss did not return. Jules's morphine was gone, and the wine, with its dulling alcohol. Delirium and unconsciousness swept over him like wind-driven fog. At last he dragged the heavy, swollen leg to the soldier trail and lay down to die.

After a few weeks Dr. Reed saw that the patient would probably recover. He cut off the morphine and substituted whiskey and a pipe. When Jules set his bed afire at night, his tobacco and matches were taken away at ten o'clock, but without his pipe he let no one sleep and so he was told to burn himself up.

The doctor brought in some of the Frenchmen about the fort, particularly Baptiste Garnier, half-breed interpreter, the man General Crook termed the best hunter in the West. This Little Bat had the terse, figurative tongue of his Siouan mother. Two years before, when Dr. Reed came to the fort, the tough element, still hanging about from the Black Hills gold rush and the agency days just past, sized up the slight build of the new post physician: the delicate forehead, the sensitive mouth under the narrow moustache. They laughed with peculiar unpleasantness. But not Little Bat. "He is like a new rifle, this doctor, light as nothing in the hand but shoots far and true." The comparison tickled Jules's fancy when he heard it. Yes, a fine, new rifle. And when Little Bat heard about the beaver feet Jules caught, he laughed. "Drown them — with sack of sand," he advised.

When the fever first left him, Jules, at the strong insistence of Dr. Reed, wrote to his father. The two young men found a great deal to discuss: science, politics, Switzerland; and always Jules's career as a doctor. To the young Swiss, cut off from all contact with the educated for three years, these hours with the post surgeon were fine and precious. But in Jules, as in every man, there lurks something ready to destroy the finest in him as the frosts of earth destroy her flowers. In spite of himself he became derisive.

"You don't learn nothing in the American universities. Damn poor doctoring you fellows do!" he jeered.

Dr. Reed bit his moustache, felt the patient's steady wrist, and went sadly away.

Instead of the customary Christmas letter, Jules wrote Rosalie a short, cold note, speaking of himself as a cripple who could be of little value to her now even as an acquaintance. He sealed it with three blobs of red wax pressed down with his grandfather's seal from the box of papers the thoughtful Sturgeon had brought along. For a moment he looked at the bit of brass, with its intaglio of the man and sprouting tree against a rising sun. Then he put it away and turned his face to the wall.

Now he wrote no more, saw no one except the breeds and the enlisted men who taught him American card games, profanity, and smut. They had no patience with pinochle, the only game he knew, learned secretly in his father's stable in Neuchâtel, so he learned seven-up and pitch and black-jack.

Late at night, sometimes, he wondered what had happened to the three young Swiss who left him alone on the prairie. They should have been back days before the soldiers came. Probably let the horses run away; perhaps were caught in a prairie fire or killed by road agents. More probably they went back to Ohio or the Old Country. They owed him more than that, that Nicolet and Tissot.

So the days dragged their misery-soiled trail over him. During the nights his leg ached in the sling and the wind whistled about the adobe and log shacks of the fort.

In November Jules got a letter in the smooth, pleasant hand of Jules Aubert, on his blue Swiss correspondence pa-per, saying: —

DEAR FRIEND:

We arrived at your house the day after your departure for Fort R., and the following Sunday Mr. Scribner, who conducted you, came to tell us that one of us ought to go to see you during the course of a week and bring you an extra shirt and a pair of trousers. I planned to go at the beginning of last week but crops which we gathered and threshed by hand hindered me. . . .

We made hay for your ponies and charge ourself to lodge them and feed them during the winter in order that we may serve you by this little while we haul the lumber for our houses. Tissot is going to the post to-morrow and I send you a shirt which was in your trunk. As for the trousers, I have n't found any, but I think you won't need them for the moment.

Winter is approaching and we have to build a stable for four horses and a house for ourselves. . . .

We were n't able to bring back any merchandise from Valentine for the reason that we had twelve bushels of wheat and oats . . . and one of the horses got sick, perhaps the colic, going down. . . . In consequence I hold at your disposal the $25 which you entrusted to me for merchandise. Please tell me if I should send this to you. In that case I should like to have a receipt for the $25 I paid you for the forge in order that if anyone comes to reclaim it I will be able to let him see the receipt. Moreover I have sold 13 pounds of beans at 8 cents a pound and four bushels of potatoes at 25 cents each, making $2.04. I am sending a receipt for the bill from Mons. Sparks Brothers, for the $20 that I sent to them for you.

As soon as we shall have finished our house we shall go live there and put all your property in your house and close the entrance in such a way that no one can get in. . . .

We learn with pain that you have been obliged to go to a doctor and that perhaps it will be necessary to amputate a foot. We hope that all will go well and that you will recover rapidly and that soon we will have the pleasure of seeing you here in good health. We beg you to receive our affectionate salutations.

In the name of the Company,

JULES AUBERT

P.S. We were able to take our claims as we understood them and thank you for the good service you have done us.

"Wants a receipt for his money. Thinks I won't come back and they can get all I got!"

In February he received another letter from the three. It was full of news. Certain paragraphs he read and reread:

Everyone left the country at the beginning of the winter and we are the only ones left for at least five miles around. Even Big Andrew has gone, no one knows where. We are still staying in your house, seeing that the snow had hindered us from hauling the lumber necessary to build. It has diminished a little these last days and yesterday I made two trips to the river. Last night it began to snow again and here we are, halted for some days.

It has been impossible to come to visit you. A man named Clark was obliged to leave his wagon en route to Valentine in December and it was not until recently that I was able to go hunt him up.

Nor has everything happened for the best here. Nicolet had six wagons of hay burned by a prairie fire. The last of November while going to see a timber claim for his brother coming from Ohio, his black horse fell in the middle of the river and despite all our care to dry him, he perished during the night. Mr. Bourne, who lives five miles northwest, lost two horses and one mule and 55 head of cattle and he does n't know where half of them perished. . . . Nor have you been exempt from misfortune. I found your black pony stretched out behind the stable. In spite of all my efforts I could not hold him on his feet. The next day we went to the stable again but in vain. He died, so of the four horses we have only two. . . .

I sold the remainder of your store for seven dollars, which I hold at your disposal.

I reclaimed your revolver and your rifle from Scribner. He brought them to me immediately. He left his claim the third of December, as did Bourne, Sturgeon and others. We have been to the Hunters' ranch to look for work. We will cut posts for fences for the next month. Perhaps we could work there all summer, only I have not the $200 to prove up my preëmption and in consequence must live on it this summer.

Perhaps there will be some way of coming to an understanding about cultivating your place, if you make reasonable conditions. Perhaps I might also buy your pony if you are disposed to sell it.

Receive, dear Friend, our best wishes for your speedy recovery and for the New Year, which has just begun, also the sincere greetings of your altogether devoted,

JULES AUBERT

"Devoted, hell! Eat up my grub, kill my pony, now want my other one and my farm land!"

There were other letters; two of them were from Matthews, an Iowan Jules located on the Flats. The first letter was full of accounts of foot injuries. One acquaintance had had his leg amputated, a little at a time, up to his hip. But he was making a living selling shoe strings in Chicago. "Nerve up and you will come out all right. I wish I was with you to take care of you."

The second letter rambled on in a friendly manner and ended in a dun for twenty dollars due on his stove. They were all buzzards, these friends, like buzzards sitting on a fence waiting for a sick cow to die.

"*Soldat!*" Jules called, motioning to a private he knew who was walking past the frosting window. The man came in and they played seven-up, using Mat's letter for a score pad.

While Jules dealt, the private bit off a chew. "God, but it is cold out. I been on the border for almost three years now and I ain't never seen such a chilly spell. Man just came in from that knot of tents and shacks on Chadron Creek. Grub got scarce, so about a week ago a young feller takes his gun and busts out to bring in a buck. The wind commences to move the snow around. He did n't come back, and it being thirty-two below that night he ain't been seen since. The man that just come over on snowshoes took two days to make what 's just a little jaunt in the summer time. They wants the troops to turn out and find the lost hunter and Uncle Sam 's always willing to oblige."

"You think they find him?" Jules asked as he picked up the cards.

The man hit the spittoon with true military marksmanship. "Oh, yeh, they 'll find him — when the snow goes off in the spring, by watching the buzzards."

Late that night another blizzard howled between the high buttes and down about the fort. Jules lay awake and thought of many things — of Rosalie and the children they might have, of the herd of a thousand elk reported wintering in the sandhills, south of the river.

He thought, too, of the other stories the soldiers told, ghost stories. Of an Indian with a buffalo robe, a knife hidden in his hand, stalking before the guardhouse, his head down, his one feather pointing into the sky: the ghost of Crazy Horse, the greatest Sioux war chief of them all. Little Bat told Jules the story: how Crazy Horse was tricked into the guardhouse and bayoneted through the kidney. It was said that ever since, for eight years, he walks.

"What he want?" Jules asked.

Nobody could guess. Some said he had to walk so every dark of the moon until the last Indian he led against Custer was dead. Others said he was looking for the man who killed him.

"Old woman stories," Jules scoffed, but somehow Crazy Horse reminded him of the man in the saloon at Valentine, the one with the beautiful Winchester. Lone men, both of them, self-reliant. It would be good to be so.

One of the warmer days in February a grinning private brought in a young woman. Jules turned as far as the sling would permit. The woman stared a moment, clasping the baby in her arms close to her.

"Oh!" she cried. Then Jules recognized her. It was Nina Haskins and her little Jules. She kissed the man's clean cheek. "Oh, I 'm so sorry about your foot. I just had to come before I left for home."

"Your man, he 's leaving the country?"

"No." She shook her head. "Jed 's buried up on the north table. He — he got caught in a blizzard."

"Oh, hell!"

"So I 'm going to Sidney to take the train — " She blinked rapidly and then smiled. "But don't you think you might say you are proud of your namesake?" The eight-month-old boy reached out his arms and laughed at the thin, white man, so different from the wind-burned, bearded one that spanked him into life. The next moment the woman was gone towards the door, burying her face in the child's wraps.

One afternoon Dr. Reed came to Jules's cot with a small envelope bearing a Swiss stamp.

Jules took the letter slowly. It was addressed to the doctor two months before in his father's handwriting and asked humbly for word of his injured son and special kindness for him.

"My reply is on the back," the doctor told Jules, and went away. Almost afraid to see what this man had to say of him, he read: —

I beg that you will pardon my delay in answering your favor of Dec. 27th '84. I am happy to inform you that your son, Mr. Jules Sandoz, still remains under my care in the Post Hospital of this Fort, and that, although not fully recovered, he is doing very well. His injury was a very severe one — being a compound, comminuted fracture of the left ankle-joint, with dislocation. He was admitted to Hospital on the 18th day after receipt of injury, & had truly a horrible joint. I at once placed him under ether, removed the astragalus entire & a part of the os calcis and intl malleolus. Drainage tube was then carried through joint & wound dressed antiseptically & placed in plaster of paris splint.

I may say that had I been permitted to fully exercise my judgement, I should have amputated at the ankle-joint, but your son would not consent. The wound is nearly healed, & I anticipate that he will yet have a useful foot.

You may rest assured that he shall have my best attention.

Jules folded the letter slowly and slipped it into the envelope, already addressed. It was taken away and still Dr. Reed did not return. Perhaps he had been called out.

Most of the grangers left the country before the first snow, Jules had been told, but now and then a half-frozen traveler was brought to the post or a desperate, half-wild man came plodding through the snow. Perhaps forty miles out there was sickness, a woman insane, or a baby coming. Patiently the doctor bundled himself against the cold, mounted a sturdy post horse, and, with his aide, set out into the teeth of the blizzard, or across the white night at nearly forty below zero.

"This country will develop — in time," he told Jules once. "But not until the ground is soaked in misery and in blood."

"Yah, I guess that 's so," agreed Jules, without looking up from the scraping of the bowl of his pipe. He admitted it reluctantly, for not many months ago the land had been almost without flaw in his eyes.

IV

THE RETURN

THE annual January and February thaws only crusted the snow. Travel was almost impossible. Even the tough feet of the few cattle that survived the winter left reddish stains where they struggled through the drifts in search of bare spots on wind-blown knolls. The snow-cleared paths about the fort were iron underfoot.

Then, one night, about two o'clock, the ice in the creeks and rivers of the Panhandle popped like pistol shots. The air was a warm breath to face. Little Bat heard and, recognizing the sound, rushed into the night in his underwear. He sniffed, listened to the faint, high wind song, and ran hilarious through the barracks.

"It is the chinook! In a week the geese they fly!"

By morning the wind had eaten into the hard snow banks. During the next week the gullies roared with gray water that cut deep washouts, filled the buffalo wallows, and turned the tiny creeks into boiling cascades. The Niobrara cracked. Huge masses of ice piled and jammed in the bends and the river spread to the willows of the second bottoms. The deluge of snow water from the west swept the channel clean and left blocks of dirty ice piled high on the banks.

In the draws dead range cattle bloated until they looked like kettledrums or exposed gaping holes under the ribs where coyotes and gray wolves had eaten and slept and eaten again during the winter, without the need to face the blizzards that swept down from Dakota.

The grass started around many a dugout and shack in the

Panhandle that spring, without a foot save the cottontails'
to press it down.   A little later many door and window holes
glared vacant as skulls.   Sometimes even the roofs were
stolen by those who had immediate need for them.   Other
places were objects of watchful waiting until the length of
desertion rendered the claim contestable.   Perhaps the waiting settler waived the preliminaries and moved in immediately.   Then, if the homesteader returned, a fight with fists,
possibly with guns, ended in one remaining while the other
left or was hauled away.   The law was remote; the nearest
sheriff almost at the Wyoming border, west of Fort Robinson, a good three days' ride away.   A man made his own
rights here or had none.

The saloon settlements at Gordon, at Rush Creek, and at
Chadron awoke, threw off the paralysis of winter-blocked
roads and depopulation.   The people laughed, drank, gambled, fought, and loved, for women were coming in, their
own, with whom they quarreled, and those of the roadhouses, over whom they fought.   But chiefly they built, for
this summer the railroad would surely come.

Once more Jules, crippled Old Jules for all time now,
set his face towards the hard-land fringe west of the sandhills.   The blue military overcoat, with its short cape, em-
phasized the slouch of his shoulders.   The pallor of his
fine-textured skin accentuated his nose, straight-ridged and
wide-gabled, over the close-clipped dark beard.   The brows
seemed heavier too, as though to protect the remote, hurt
gray eyes that still burned with defiance.

The wagon moved slowly eastward, past the dark morning face of Crow Butte, where the Sioux Indians were out-
witted by their former brothers, the Crows, and where the
people of Dull Knife staved off ultimate tragedy at the
hands of the white man a few days longer.   At the brow of
the ridge Jules looked back to Fort Robinson, a tiny smudge
of log and dobe buildings along the foot of the far bluffs.
He had spent months there, long, painful months, and all

he had for it was a stiff ankle, still oozing a little gritty pus, and two crutches leaning against the wagon seat where his rifle should be. He cursed the foot, his fellow settlers, Scribner and Sturgeon, who hauled him to the fort, and more particularly Dr. Reed.

If they had waited another day, just one more day. Now he was only a hopeless cripple with empty pockets, sick, discouraged, even naked if it were not for the army clothing, two complete outfits, Dr. Reed ordered issued to him. The settlers on Mirage Flats, whom he 'd helped all he could, failed him; deserted with the first bad snow. Only the cattlemen stayed. With them in possession of the country there was no place for him, no place for his homeseekers. He would borrow money of Nippel or others of his friends at Verdigre, go back to Neuchâtel, complete his doctor's training, marry Rosalie, an intelligent doctor's wife. . . .

The wagon lurched over the water-gutted Indian trail.

"Oh, my foot!" he roared. The driver paid no attention, not even changing the flat whistle through his teeth.

A long time Jules looked at the offending foot, the crutches. He had been the best walker in his class — always the leader in their week-end hikes to remote villages. To go back now, a miserable cripple, among them all. He could not do that. Even an animal hid from his kind when injured.

He did not see the brilliant web of prairie sun, the tinge of green spreading over the rolling buffalo-grassed hills, the antelope bounding away from the trail, to stop curiously on a knoll when there was no pursuit. For Old Jules there was nothing but his clumpy foot discovered by every jar of the springless wagon.

Suddenly a little valley opened before them, with a long, thin strip of sod stretching away over the prairie; a bug-like speck that was a team with a ploughman creeping along the edge. Jules saw that and sat up. The man was a fool, ploughing sod so early. It would all grow back to grass.

Late May or early June, that was the time for breaking, when the grass was well started. Turn it under then and it died and rotted. *He* would have more ground broken this spring. The strip along the trees.

Pushing his trooper hat away from his eyes, Jules watched the first flock of geese against the southeastern horizon, flying high with the south wind. He dug his cob pipe from his pocket, stuck the stem between his bearded lips, and fought the wind for a light. He puffed with satisfaction. Little Bat had predicted well. Next week the geese would be thick on the Running Water.

The day Jules came back to the Flats there was no mirage, only the mud of slow rain on gumbo. He watched his home rise out of the prairie, first the well, with its windlass like a gallows' head, then the mound that was his dugout — nothing more. The wire about the young trees was scattered over the grass; the posts gone into the gray pile of ashes before the door, the huge stack of brush behind the dugout with them. The stovepipe over the roof was blown away, and much of the roof. Inside the dugout it was dark, mouldy, and bare. The stock of goods that he hoped to sell for a few dollars, his blankets, his reloading tools, his ammunition, his rifle, even his box of books and his letters, were gone. Only three law books and a stack of catalogues and government pamphlets too worthless to carry away remained, muck-covered and moulding from the snow water that left a ring three feet up the wall. Strangely slow and dull for a man of his temperament, as though weighed down by the yoke of years, the returned settler let himself down to an upturned keg and dropped his hands between his thin knees. A long time he stared at the rusty stove and the rain drips spattering on the lids. Gradually he became conscious of a glassy, blinking eye looking at him from a round mound under the stove. A toad, so early. "By golly, the lazy bugger, steal me my house!" Jules laughed aloud,

slapping a blue-clothed thigh.   He stirred out to gather up
a few handfuls of grass.   This he dried over the flame of the
wrapping paper from his bundles.   The keg he chopped into
firewood, and in the red light of the cookstove he thought
about his plum and apple trees, all except half a dozen green
to the tips.   Once more he planned.

The next morning a wagon rumbled over the army-trail
ruts, and Jules Aubert, standing erect, feet braced, a squint-
eyed, browned man of the plains by now, drove up.   He
brought Jules's books and his letters and other odds and
ends.   Most important, he brought the twenty-five dollars
and the shotgun.   But the wood, the groceries, and the ammunition were used up; one of his ponies was dead and the
rifle stolen.

The smoke rising from Jules's redeemed stovepipe and
the boom of his ten-bore along the Running Water brought
neighbors to inquire after his health and to eat pot roast
of wild goose in the flickering skunk-oil light.   After supper
they filled their pipes at Jules's tobacco box and noticed
that his skin was thin and white as a plucked quail's and
that gray was creeping along his temples.

Jules cleaned his cob pipe and talked of the winter with
the flair for exaggeration he learned from the old-timers
about Fort Robinson.   "When telling stories," one said to
him, "Jim Beckwourth allus sized up his crowd.   If they
was too ignorant to know fightin' a grizzly bare-handed
makes a good story, he 'd just throw in another grizzly."

When the faces of the men floated in the smoke that
seemed as reluctant as they to go from the dugout, the talk
turned to crops and planting and trees, and from that to
politics, the coming railroad, the new county that was sure
to be organized soon.   Big Andrew, back for the summer
at least, moved his weight from one elbow to the other.
Ja, this year the boom would come.   Matthews and his
friend Lamoureau smoked on, nodding assent.   It was already started when they left Iowa.

Among the first to come to visit was Nicolet, his skin burned red, his small blue eyes moving quickly away from the crippled foot. The last, almost, was Tissot, arrogant, saying in a voice too low for the usually preoccupied Jules to hear: "Now he have the excuse not to work!"

For an hour the talk was cautious, like steps on rotten ice. Then someone noticed that Old Jules was afire. They pounded the smouldering from his coat and rescued his pipe that he slipped burning into his pocket.

It was a good joke, and so Tissot stayed to supper of fresh catfish Jules had seined from Pine Creek. He even left his gun to be repaired, without charge.

On his way back from Valentine, Sturgeon unloaded two boxes of groceries and ammunition and a sack of mail at Jules's dugout. The settler ran expertly through the letters, sorting out his own. One he opened with clumsy fingers. It was from Rosalie, still affectionate, kind. Oh, it was too bad, this accident to her Jules. But she loved her injured man even more than the whole one! He might not be able to go into the railway mail service beside her as she had hoped. But his father would be proud to see this brave eldest a doctor, and doctors with slight limps are so *distingué*, did n't her Jules think so too? But America — she could not bring herself to come to America. Had it not given him only bad luck?

Jules crushed the letter between his palms and threw it into the wood box, gathered up his gun and crutch, and went out to the dog town west of the tree patch for a rabbit for breakfast. But during the night he crept from his bed and found the ball the letter made. By the light of his skunk-oil lamp he read it again.

The spring of 1885 a new wave of settlers broke and spread over the hard-land table of the upper Niobrara. Almost every quarter section was scarred by spade and plough. Earth-walled homes went up or down, soddies or dugouts, or a combination of both. Their occupants came from offices where they made neat rows of figures until their backs were round and their chests sunken; from steel mills, horny-handed, with bad eyes; from Eastern farms lost to loan sharks; from everywhere. They came to escape injustice or justice; to find freedom from paternal restraint; to make money. They came.

This year there were more women, not many, but more, and some of these single. Whatever their status in Indiana, or Iowa or York state, where competition was keener, here they were all sought after as heiresses or, more to the point, good cooks.

Convinced once more that Rosalie never intended to come to America, Jules sent back her photograph and commanded her never to write to him again. Then he washed his face and hands and plastered his hair down inexpertly with water. He even considered changing his shirt, only to find he already had both of them on. Not having a looking-glass, he couldn't tell much about the results, but, hoping for the best, he pounded Old Jim about the Flats.

The first rebuff sent him limping angrily to his horse. Hooking his crutch over the horn and resting his weight on his left knee, in the stirrup strap, the bad foot back out of the way of accident, he loped homeward.

He located new settlers; in return they backset his old land and broke out more. But he must have ammunition, food.

At Dr. Reed's suggestion Jules wrote to his father for a hundred dollars before he left Fort Robinson. Now, in answer, came the third son, Paul. Jules met him at Rushville with elder-brotherly gruffness, accentuated by his suspicion that he came to return the wanderer to paternal domination. Then, too, his crippled foot and his greasy army pants put him on the defensive before this agile, well-groomed young man whom he remembered as a long-necked boy of sixteen. Paul was shorter than Jules, slighter, but with the same quick, nervous manner. His forehead was less imposing, his eyes a little less commanding, and a kindly, humorous twist lurked in his lips. Secure in his position as third child, he developed few inhibitions. He greeted Jules with affectionate enthusiasm, lamented the accident to the foot, brought news of the Old Country.

The father and mother were well. William (next to Jules in age) was n't getting on with his wife. He drank, was violent and brutal one day, in highest good humor the next, and never attended to business. It could n't go on like that much longer. . . . Elvina, the only sister, would teach French in Toronto. Emile played the flute and had a good time. Henri? Henri would study surgery. He would be the doctor of the family.

So?

Jules pounded the ashes from his pipe, apparently not noticing the implication that his career as a doctor had been given up at home.

"And Nana?"

"Nana is still Nana, very amusing, very little. He does not grow."

So they talked as they drank the slim bottle of white wine their mother sent to Jules with the father's hundred dollars. And the world became a good place once more, even for a man with a bad ankle.

Paul stayed. He did n't file on land immediately because the good places on Mirage Flats were covered. Perhaps someone would overstay his six months' leave, or get discouraged. If not — well, one filed where one could, he told Jules, shrugging his shoulders. He was not without the gift of reconcilement.

In the meantime Paul tried to clean up the dugout and Jules, but farther than keeping his running ankle scrupulously clean, the impatient elder brother could not be moved. He wore his shirts until they fell off, bathed when the river was tepid, washed his hands before and after dressing his foot, and his face practically never. Soap, he protested, burned fine skins like his.

Jules bought another pony and took Paul into the hills on hunts. His manipulation of his Jim horse with his good knee, his remarkable skill with the borrowed rifle, amazed and pleased Paul. Jules showed his brother some tricks in antelope hunting, such as jigging his hat up and down on his rifle over the edge of a knoll to entice the curious creatures into close range. But for himself he liked best the shots that tested his marksmanship — where he must estimate distances, and drop, and wind. "There are two sights to your gun. Do not shoot until you have seen them both — and then, *March'la!*" But Paul was not a good marksman.

Nor could he follow the impassioned visions of his older brother. There was, however, a point of similarity. Neither had the self-control and calm necessary to manage horses well. When Paul climbed on Old Jim, already weighed down with guns, a frying pan, coffeepot, tin cups and other camping accoutrements, as a hundred times before, the horse gave one awkward buck and threw his rider over the woodpile.

Jules limped up anxiously, but when he saw Paul brush himself off with a rueful face, the older man laughed. A horse, even as a lady, may have his untouchable spots, and Old Jim's left flank was one of them.

"How do you know so much about horses — and ladies?" Paul asked, wiping a drop of blood from his skinned nose.

"Heah? — Oh, I find out."

The first time Paul went to the river on a hunt alone, he shot something red in the brush. Instead of venison he had a dead calf belonging to the Hunter ranch. He could not understand laxity in law enforcement, and against all the advice and scoffing Jules could manage, Paul rode away towards the Platte River. If he found any good land Jules was to follow, leave behind him the unpleasant reminders of his injury.

After a couple weeks a letter from Paul came north by a settler he sent to Jules. The good land along the river bottom was all taken up. "I have seen the Platte, which my companion, an American freighter, calls 'a mile wide and an inch deep,' laughing inordinately. This American humor I cannot understand. Why is it funny to call a stream a mile wide that is not a fourth of that — and an inch deep that will make a horse swim in the channel?"

Jules had never seriously considered leaving the Niobrara, the Running Water, and the community growing up about him. Early in June he spurred Old Jim about the Flats and along the river, circulating a petition for a post office. Once more he wrote letters.

Most of the settlers were busy. Crops looked good, despite the drouth, and those who had been there the year before were not so restless when one week of shimmering heat dance followed another. The recently arrived Iowans plodded through their corn, from shipped-in seed, tall but curling, and knew it could not live another day.

The thing that worried Jules and the others who farmed the year before was the short growing season. Corn that was to be hard must be matured by the tenth of September at the latest. Not an ear of last year's crop was solid.

"I intend to pick the best for seed every fall," Elmer Sturgeon told them. "I 'll find some ripe enough to grow. Develop an early strain that way."

Jules scratched the tender spot under his chin. "Too slow."

Others suggested crossing with squaw corn and calico, although it might cut stalk and yield.

"There is probably an early corn; I 'll write to Washington." Jules was already digging through his pockets for a pencil.

Big Andrew caressed his pipe with his horny, splay fingers, puffing calmly. "All these things will come."

Before the Fourth of July wagons were fitted out for camping. Bows and tarps that had been set up on the ground to cover excess goods or to house an old hen and her chickens, with sod along the bottom to keep the skunks out, were repaired and mounted on wagons. Horsebackers, teams of gaunt ponies or plodding plough critters, moved like giant apparitions over the mirage lakes towards Rushville, the new town west of Gordon, and already booming itself for the county seat of a county yet to be formed.

A few weeks before, the handful of tents and shacks was moved up from Rush Creek to the railroad tracks which somehow always miss any town located along a survey. One of the first buildings to take to wheels was the saloon, pulled by fourteen horses; the single board shack swaying drunkenly over the rough road, an American flag flying from the false front. Beside the driver rode a woman in a wine-colored silk dress. The men hailed her boisterously.

"Hi, there, Jen!"

"Not taking no chances with the liquid refreshments, are you, Jen!"

She thumbed her nose at them, quite elegantly, with a dainty lace handkerchief, so as not to offend Matilda Lehrer and her mother watching under their slat bonnets.

Now the board saloon was ready at Rushville, with a bare pine bar and pitch frying out in amber drops from the sunny wall. Beside it huddled three or four tent competitors, the bars of planks laid across barrels, two-by-fours spiked in place for footrails, a few shovels of sawdust sprinkled over the gray earth.

By ten o'clock the celebration crowd milled through the dusty street — sunburned, peeling newcomers, noisy or bewildered or overcautious, in raw contrast to the rich brown skin and easy bearing of those with some length of residence in the dry, windy Panhandle.   The few women, mostly in calico and gray sunbonnets, worked about the camp wagons scattered around three sides of the town.   Across the tracks was the big attraction, the broken-circle camp of the Sioux under Young Man Afraid of His Horse.

Where the tents and pine shacks stopped and the burnt prairie began, beyond the race track, stood the pine-bough-circle shelter for the big Sioux dance.   In the centre, around the tall pole, the *wakan* or holy tree, wove the Indian dancers, their breech-clouted brown bodies painted in greasy yellows, vermilions, black and white.   They executed a peculiar toe-and-heel back slip-step, leaping, springing, all to the beat of flat palms on a wet skin drum.   About them a circle of women bounded on stationary feet, chanting a monotonous "He-yah, he-yah."   It was all energetic enough, but lifeless; the essence, the religious significance gone; the dance debased for a white man's holiday.

After the long, intricate ceremonies the tired braves fell back, the women squatted upon the ground, and a grotesque Omaha dancer sprang forward, stopped, crouched, his white-ringed eyes glaring under a buffalo headpiece.   His bare, painted breast was piled with strings of beads, shells, and elk teeth.   Over his fine metallic legs hung long strips of dyed fur and bells caught in red anklets, and on his buttocks flopped a rosette of eagle feathers with a long animal tail reaching below his calves.   Suddenly he flew into a wild furious dance, leaping and contorting himself, the long tail switching as he went through his eccentric movements, always with the back slip-step, to the drumming of the older men and their chant of strange songs.   Thump-tum, thump-tum.   Their hands made a hollow, green sound.

Old Jules pushed his way through the crowd.   "By golly, look at that fellow sweat!" he commented appreciatively to a group of Indian women sitting inside their blankets.   They showed pleasant white teeth at his tone of approval and motioned him to sit.

Before he could decide, a painted Indian in fringe and scalp-trimmed buckskin arose and lifted his hand in greeting.   It was White Eye.

"Ah, walking stick bad medicine, Straight Eye.   We look for you on Running Water for the fall hunt."

"I been to Fort Robinson."

The Indians gathering about him nodded.   A quiet, austere chief signaled to White Eye.   When he returned he brought a message: "I have heard good things of you, Straight Eye, and my heart is glad that you are back.   Come to my tipi after the dance and I give you long rifle.   Indian get from white man.   Think you are dead.   Keep.   Now you come; give it back."

Jules shook his head.   He knew who had his gun.   He had seen one of his neighbors slip it into the bed as he appeared unexpectedly at the door.   But Jules followed White Eye to the tipi after the dance, the tipi of Young Man Afraid of His Horse.   Jules had heard from the Frenchmen at Robinson of this last great hereditary chief of the Oglalas — fine stories of his unassuming demeanor, his faithfulness to his people.

Inside, on buffalo robes, sat a dozen of the head men, dressed in eagle-feather headdresses and beaded buckskin. Across from the opening was the older man, with no beads now, no paint, no feathers, and yet he was easily the finest there, this Young Man Afraid.

A long time the Swiss stared, but the chief gave no sign to this deepest discourtesy to a Sioux.   Finally Jules sat and smoked, but inattentively.   The thing that had drawn him to the man with the Winchester at Valentine he found once more, here, and in an uneducated Indian.

The other white man in the circle, Dr. McGillicuddy, agent at Pine Ridge, talked to him of his own days at the Fort.   Finally a Vetterli was handed to Jules.   It did not have his brazing where his trigger guard had been broken.

There was a "Hou!" of approval as he refused the gun. It was good, and when the cherries are black and drying on the stem they would visit the straight-tongued *Washicu*, the white man who does not lie.

In the middle of the afternoon a train, an engine and a few cars, puffed into sight. The crowd lined out along the new steel and ties, thrilled at the tremble of the earth, the chatter of the cars to each other, as if none had ever seen the like before.

Then they returned to the saloons. Jules, hobbling about with one crutch and a borrowed rifle, was not drinking. He had only one round silver dollar and his shotgun between him and starvation. Big Andrew from the Flats, half drunk but always generous, bought him a drink and a lunch. Cheered by the liquor and the food, Jules talked, and the violent tongue with the sunken cheeks, the deep-set eyes expressing extravagant dreams for this land, arrested attention even in this holiday crowd.

"You aimin' to raise corn here?" a cowboy setting up a ranch by the brand and rope method said pityingly. "Why, man, you 're crazy. Look at the heat, drying up the prairie so it 'll burn like powder by the first of August. Don't be a damn fool! Ain't the country done you enough dirt?"

The allusion to his foot was too much. Jules pushed his way out through the crowd. But he came back.

"If the country 's so damn bad, why you staying?" he demanded of his tormentor.

"Wall, I ain't stayin' to stir dirt hard as dobe bricks, nor to encourage poor little sunflowers to commit suicide by tryin' to grow on it. I been through this country with cows from Texas for six years, hand runnin', and I ain't seen more than a drop of rain in July yet."

Jules squinted up at the sky. "According to the government books I got, those sheep clouds mean rain or snow in twenty-four hours."

That fetched a roar of laughs and back-slappings. Even the Flatters could n't believe that.

"I cain't do nothing about the snaow," shouted a hilarious cow-puncher with silver-studded gauntlets. He raised his glass of whiskey and dashed the liquid against the back of the weather prophet's neck. "But there 's yer rain!"

Jules pivoted on his good foot, the sharp eyes seeking the culprit, his hand sliding along the rifle to the trigger guard. But a dozen silent men held empty whiskey glasses. Defeated, he hobbled away.

By evening the dust thickened until the light of the oil lamps from the doorways shivered as in a fog. On a platform couples danced polkas and square dances, others waiting their turn, the men clinging to their partners while still others elbowed six deep around any woman who demanded a moment's rest. Boots, spurs, guns, stale whiskey, loud banter, a fight or two, and over it all the noise of an accordion and a fiddle played by men on teetering chairs placed on empty barrels.

A playful cowboy tearing past snipped out the three lanterns with three deft shots. The fiddle squawked, the accordion expired with a wheeze. The sudden dark was thick, cut now and then by violet flashes of heat lightning ignored by the old-timers as only harbingers of more drouth. When they got the lanterns going again, the accordionist was missing. His instrument was there, but he never returned for it.

Scarcely had the dancing begun again to the screech of the fiddle when a roaring wind swept down upon the little border town. The guy ropes of the tents sang, the canvas flopping. The crowds scattered towards the wagons and other shelter. The next second the storm broke; the sky was streaked in a shifting, twisting pattern of red lightning; thunderbolts crowding upon each other shook the ground. Then the rain came. In a wave it swept before the wind. Wagons teetered and rolled. In a newcomer's shack a woman screamed. With the next gust half of the tents went down. During the lull that followed, while men ran forth to grab sliding guy ropes and catch loose horses, the third wave came, and then there were no further lulls. All night the water drove down in solid walls upon the new town of Rushville.

The next morning the sun came up calm and clean over the devastated border holiday. The lower portion of the camping ground was a pond in which wagon beds and empty kegs and cases floated idly. Buildings, half completed, were flattened and mud-covered. The roads were gutted, while in the gullies wagons, lumber, endless trash and barrels, were piled and covered with muck. Men and women, with soil-caked feet, searched among the piles for their belongings. But there were few real laments, and those were lost under the general hilarity that it could actually rain here in July. This morning everyone was young and strong again, with land and hope. Nothing was impossible to-day.

Jules, leaning on his hoe, squinted into the west. Sun going low and no supper. The weeds of his ten acres of trees were high, the sunflowers blooming, the smaller trees being choked. And his corn, his beans, his potatoes. He had no money to hire help. So he chopped furiously for a half hour, despite his bad ankle. Then his mind began to work and he stopped to plan. Some day the country would all be settled, the cattlemen gone. Then he would have a fine big orchard, with rows half a mile long, and vineyards such as his father never saw. But what he needed was a good wife; they all needed good wives.

Pounding the ashes from his pipe, he exchanged the hoe for his crutch and went to the house to meet the usual evening callers, sure to ride up or perhaps walk across the phosphorescent evening Flats for their mail or for gossip. There was always news. A few weeks before, Jules had received a yellow form letter, telling him a post office had been established at his dugout. He went to Rushville im-

mediately to get his supplies, including the regular forms
and fifteen dollars' worth of stamps, and a six-foot board.
With black grease from the wagon axle and a corn cob he
painted the words POST OFFICE in eight-inch letters.   This
he nailed over his door, a foot and a half above the ground
of Mirage Flats.   Then he hobbled away, to the army trail,
to admire it.   Business-like.

Late in August Jules rode across the country looking for
an earlier corn, for trapping grounds and potential wives
for his community.   He stopped at Chadron, already a busy
town of a hundred and fifty shacks and tents.

Here Jules saw three hundred thousand dollars' worth
of bullion come in from the Black Hills on a stagecoach
with four express guards, guns strapped low, Winchesters
across their knees.   Three hundred thousand dollars out
of a hillside — and he without the price of a bed.   But he
could always camp with some settler out on the table.   So
he talked the afternoon away in Angel's saloon, and heard
of the bad-man bartender imported to discourage promiscu-
ous shooting.   The cowboys from the Three Crow ranch
scared him out.   One of them knocked the gun out of his
hand, grabbed his long red beard, and emptied his Colt
through it.   The bad man took the next train back to
Omaha.

But the country would not always be so, and remembering Jim Beckwourth's advice, Jules's trees became thousands,
his corn grew to six feet and would yield sixty bushels to
the acre.   Everyone on the Flats would be in the millionaire class in no time, and the day was coming when there
would be no tariff, and the farmer would receive a fair price
for his produce.   The fresh audience flattered him, but he
knew he must find a camp before dark.   As he hobbled out
toward the hitch-racks a high-seated buggy with a spirited
team swung a wild curve out of a side road into the street
and was upon him.   With a long, frightened vault upon
his crutch, Jules cleared himself, but the rim of the wheel

caught the wooden prop and flung it from him, throwing him into the dust as the team plunged away.

The settler roared curses after the driver, spitting out the stem of his pipe and reaching for the bowl in the dust.

The team pulling hard on the bit, the man swung back to see if the cripple was injured. Jules gave the wild horses one look and fled to the hitch-racks. The buggy vanished in a cloud of dust.

"The owner of the Three Crow ranch," somebody told Jules. "Bartlett Richards."

So? Jules looked after him again. He had seen that outfit deep in the sandhills not a month earlier.

There was always news at Jules's dugout, companionship, good talk. Often, too, there was a glass of wine, pieplant at first, currant later in the summer. He got all the government reports on dry farming, took several papers that brought world news. But the settlers were more interested in local items: 1,283,121.86 acres of land handled through the Valentine land office in 1884, filings and proofs; home-seekers on every trail.

"And only one of my family here to get any of it," Jules lamented. "This land is going to be valuable some day."

In fact it was valuable now. The papers reported that the 7U ranch of 22,000 head of cattle, 1100 acres of hay land, complete with cow ponies, ranch buildings, and haying tools, sold for $500,000 to the Ogallala Land and Cattle Company down near the Platte, making that ranch one of the largest and strongest in the Panhandle of Nebraska. Sheedy, the owner, was a sick man. He sold out cheap.

"Cheap? Five hundred thousand dollars ain't cheap for this land if you was to get it all," Ned Manson, a settler with ranching ambitions and the remains of a quart of whiskey, said with a twist of his loose face.

Jules lifted his greasy cap and scratched his tousled hair. "Almost all government land. Not worth much if Cleveland's proclamation means anything."

"What 's that?" Manson asked, wiping his lips after another drink from his bottle.

"No-thing," Jules said, with artificial detachment, "except that the President ordered all the fences down around government land on the Brighton ranch."

"Yeh? But that 's down around Custer County, ain't it — two-three hundred miles south and east of here. Better land. This country 'll never be worth anything except for cow bait. Ain't you read about the stock train, a whole train filled with range cattle for the market, leaving Chadron last week? This is a cow country."

"The time is coming when the big outfits will all be gone — when the little fellows get a show — and coming soon."

Although that was just what Ned Manson would have wanted when sober, now he was already a big cowman. Jules's certainty irked him.

"I say the ranchers will have the country soon!" And to emphasize his words he banged on the table littered with maps and government reports. Jules was up, his face gray in the dim light.

"*Na*, be still," Big Andrew reasoned. "They are not coming to-night."

But the locator already had his gun down from the pegs over his bed. Andrew and Nicolet and Aubert were silent in the shadows. Manson got to his feet a little unsteadily. Jules was just going to clean his gun, like he was always doing.

Slowly the barrel came up, stopping at the man's heart.

"Already working against me! Git off the place!"

Swiftly the man stumbled out into the night. Jules hung up his rifle and slumped to his box, saying nothing.

Only Big Andrew dared protest.

"You do like a drunk man yourself," he said, as he tied a string around his mail.

"I have had no drink this week."

"I know."

Left alone, Jules sat with his head on his hands, a dark, lonely figure beside the little light flickering over a saucer of oil.

V

A CHECKERED SUIT

By the first of August Mirage Flats was hard as metal under the hoofs of Old Jim and the trails smoked far behind him. The Niobrara fell until its backbone bleached in long sand bars soon furred over with seedling willow and cottonwood. The corn and potatoes stopped growing. Dead, the newcomers wailed. Waiting for the August rains, Jules predicted, but without his usual emphasis. His mind was on other, bigger things.

After Jules wrote a dozen letters to Lincoln asking for local government in which the settler had a part, a delegation from the towns and ranches called on the governor. The east end of Sioux County was cut off and officials appointed until the first of January for the new county of Sheridan. Bennett Irwin, foreman of the Newman ranch, near Gordon, but in Cherry County, was one of the new commissioners. The judge and the county attorney were from the cow town itself. Johnny Riggs, brother-in-law of Irwin and foreman of the Hunter ranch, was appointed sheriff. Not a settler among them.

"I could see it coming," Jules lamented. "The country and the court's in the hands of the cattleman already."

"Wait until election — we have the votes," the religious little Iowan, Johnny Burrows, comforted, firm in his conviction of a God in His heaven.

"Yeh, but haf you heard who is the new depooty sheriff? It is the Doctore Middleton!" Honest Hans, the little German a couple of miles north, was happy to impart the scandalous news.

"The old rustler and hoss thief?" Jug Byers demanded
skeptically.

Jules nodded. "It means Hunter and Newman cattle
will be protected and the rest of the country be damned."

It looked that way. Still, Jules pounded his Jim horse
over the Flats once more to get out the vote for the special
election.

The county-seat fight would be a three-way split: Gordon,
the largest town, whose backing was the Newman ranch,
really in Cherry County; Rushville, the Hunter ranch town,
and Hay Springs, the settler trading point. Rushville defeated Hay Springs 919 to 839. The dazed Flatters fig-
ured late into the night on the margins of the paper announcing the outcome. Where did all those Rushville votes come
from?

To the amazement of many settlers, several hundred of
the votes were cast in their own precincts, bought up by the
cattleman town. Angry knots of men gathered about the
saloons and talked of checkered suits and rope. But the
charges were so frankly admitted that the mob, without a
leader, melted in defeat.

On the Niobrara the young Swiss hunched over his bad
ankle. To him this selling out of the settler to the cattleman was one more proof of the American's indifference
to corrupt officials and the prostitution of his rights as a citizen. First there was the unmarked shooting of the youth
in Valentine. Now this thing had happened here on the
hard-land fringe of the Running Water, where he had elected
to settle, to live the rest of his life, where he had hoped for,
worked for, fine things.

When his neighbors were gone he saddled up and rode
through the darkness towards Deer Creek. All the way the
hills, usually so friendly, squatted far away in the night and
gave him no welcome.

At sunup he stopped his tired horse at a spring and roasted
a young grouse over the fire. Fed, and warmed by the fire,

he was still dark and cold as cast iron within.   He had chosen
to come to America, America the land of the free, to find
that corruption followed upon the heels of the settlers as
wolves once trailed the buffalo herds.   One year of settlement and it had come.   Must he keep moving always
ahead, always alone?   He would pack up for the wilds of
Canada.

That evening as Old Jim climbed wearily out of the Niobrara Valley homeward, long shadows of men afoot and
on field-gaunted horses moved across the Flats.   It warmed
Jules to see them.   For the first time that day he found satisfaction in his life.

Young Hans took his game from him, held his crutch,
unsaddled the horse, and then joined the others in the cool
dugout.   Once more they talked of the election, and this
time Jules joined in.

"Tammany politics," he termed it as he drew the entrails
from a young duck and threw it on the table with several
others that Johnny Burrows had neatly picked.

"Sell votes, get money for tobac, no?" Hans suggested as
he stacked an armful of wood behind the stove.

The walking sky pilot who had dropped in for supper
laid down the potato he was peeling and dragged out his
worn pocket Bible.

"Tobacco money, hell," Jules scoffed — "and by golly,
you preacher, if you want any grub you better skin them
spuds."

Before the fierce gray eyes and the bloody hunting knife
Jules waved absently under his nose, the sky pilot peeled
potatoes until he had a huge finger-smudged mound on the
table, sneaking frightened, watery looks at this rough man
with whom he had elected to spend the night.   He made no
more attempts to turn the conversation from county elec-
tions to religion, even drank the after-supper cup of currant
wine Jules poured out to him and placed the empty cup back

in line for refilling, while the others pulled long, sanctimonious faces and nudged their neighbors.

Then there were stories, ribald ones. Hans, too, told one to-night, incongruous on his soft, girlish lips. And Jules finished with one that choked him with laughter. Even Johnny Burrows forgot and grinned a little sourly. And as they scattered over the moon-bleached Flats for their homes, they talked of the look on the sky pilot's face as the last one of them was leaving.

"He thinks maybe he find the devil sure this time," Hans told Johnny.

"Jules should not act and talk so. It gives people a wrong opinion of us," the Iowan said patiently.

In the dugout Jules was ordering a dozen old army rifles.

The next week the quiet, conservative Elmer Sturgeon stooped through the doorway of Old Jules's dugout. The election secret was out. Sheriff Riggs had brought in 226 votes from the Hunter ranch alone. The county commissioners were rejecting 184 of these. Hay Springs claimed the county seat and Rushville was going to court.

Jules nodded, thumbing the statutes on his ragged knee. "I know, but according to the law the canvassing board got no right to go behind the returns. If the election is set aside they can vote again. But Hay Springs won't get it. The cattleman outfits will never let the county seat out of their hands."

"You may be right, Jules," the conservative Johnny Burrows conceded, as he speared a new wick for the lamp with wire and dipped it into the lead kettle of warm oil.

"Ja, I think it is so," Hans agreed, pulling his pant leg down over his underwear from which he had just cut the wick.

Jules sucked the clogging stem of his homemade chokecherry pipe. "That way the Rushville gang can run the country and nobody's safe if they git it in for him." He stopped to fill his pipe from a cheap pound sack, puffed a minute. "But if they impose on us too bad," he spit into the fire and watched the red coals running around the bottom of the lid, "you can drive a man to take the law in his own hands."

The group looked at each other in the flickering light, straightening back in their seats. Old Jules was business-like.

As it proved, the county commissioners were denied the right to go behind the returns.

During the summer young Hans often came riding through the twilight, his hat under his arm, a red, kerosene-soaked handkerchief tied about his head to keep the buffalo gnats away: a gay, whistling cavalier on a plough-gaunted horse. Sometimes he stopped to pick a handful of prickly prairie roses growing along the sandy slope of a gully, pink-striped with scarlet, great splotches of pale light in the dusk, and heavy with fragrance. On those evenings he talked of his Anna, waiting for him in the Old Country.

One evening Charley Sears, the youngest of a family fresh from Kentucky, brought his fiddle to Jules's dugout. They all sprawled on the edge of the roof while the young Irish-man played a few tunes. When he laid the instrument down Hans took it up, plucked the strings, twisted at the keys, and tried the bow, but it was alien to his horny hands now. At last he gave it up. Jules played a practice piece, very badly, with exaggerated count, his knees crossed, his bad foot jerking in time as he squinted through the dusk at his fingers.

"Ach, how I should like to hear my Anna sing Schumann to-night — " Hans's voice died away without finishing, his work-blistered hands scraping across his two-day beard.

"Wagner — he is the man for this strong land," Big Andrew said.

"I took my *Schatz* Rosalie to hear Wagner, many, many

times — and now she won't come to America," Jules told them.

"She will come," Hans said optimistically, "as my Anna will come. If it rains — ach, if I have luck, she will come soon, my Anna."

"It is not good to live alone," Andrew said slowly, doubtfully, for he was afraid of women, afraid they would laugh at his thick, powerful shoulders, his hands hard as Jules's anvil.

That night they separated early. Jules sat alone outside until late, not smoking. In the darkness he forgot his rags and dirt, his stiff ankle, the crutch beside him. He was back four years, young again, whole again, and with Rosalie.

Much of the settler talk was about women. In the saloons, at the post offices, on the road, they discussed them — those of the various roadhouses, even the nest of negroes not far from Rushville, and then, with little change of epithet, they switched to talk of the young women of the community who showed no roadhouse tendencies whatever.

Sheepishly a newcomer unfolded a paper from his pocket. It was a double sheet, entirely given to matrimonial prospects, with alluring descriptions and photographs of women dressed in garments of varying vintage. But these men were not experts in such matters. The one in the centre of the page, of a girl of about twenty, with a dozen ostrich tips from her hat drooping over a bare shoulder, intrigued them.

"She would look different in a sunbonnet," John Burrows said severely, disapprovingly.

"Or when she gits round like a barrel," another added.

By fall Jules's ankle was healing so well that he seldom used his crutch about the place any more, hobbling along instead on the clubby foot in a large overshoe stuffed with excelsior. He managed to cut six acres of corn, taking it slowly. He made several trips into the hills, once with

Young Man Afraid of His Horse, twice with Matthews and Lamoureau; each time bringing back all the game their horses could carry: deer, antelope, and the meat of a young elk. Part of it they distributed among the neighbors and the rest they traded for sugar and coffee at Rushville.

Generally they camped somewhere on Deer Creek, but once Jules led them deep into the forbidden land of the Indians, to the little blue lake he saw from Deer Hill. The broken chops reared into high ridges, the north slopes smudged with wild plum and chokecherry patches, and between lay broad, deep valleys, the grass reaching to the stirrup and sweet with mint. Game was plentiful and tame in the buckbrush and on the hillsides, now and then range cattle, wilder than antelope, dashed away through the cuts and passes between the hills.

The third day they stopped their horses on the crest of a ridge and looked down into the narrow canyon of Snake River. The swift, clear stream cut its bed deep through sandstone and magnesia-white bluffs that pushed in, disputing the water's flow at every bend. Autumn brush spilled down the steep slopes, with here and there a slim ash or box elder pointing high through the plum thickets and matted wild grape.

Mat and Lamoureau led the horses down the steep descent while Jules hobbled and slid the best he could. Suddenly he stopped and called. The others came to him and sat down at his side. Over them, and as far as they could see in the dim leaf haze, the thicket was roofed with a solid clustering of wild grapes, blue with bloom. The thorny brush that supported the vines was almost bare, but the ground underneath was purple-red with overripe plums, sweetish, decaying food for the swarms of wasps humming drowsily as they worked.

"Fruit enough for a whole village," Jules said grandly. "Plum jell, grape wine."

"You're right," Mat agreed.

Two days later they started back. At the crest of the hill Jules held his Jim horse in and looked down upon Snake River. Once more he felt something of his first sight of Mirage Flats — a man alone looking upon a good place to live.

With the fall work almost done, Jules's dugout attracted more and more settlers, for news or to escape the need of living with themselves for an hour or so. Sometimes they talked about him a little, calling him a funny cuss, each in his own way. It was almost as if his mind slanted, like cloth cut on the bias, and yet sometimes Elmer Sturgeon or Big Andrew wondered if it was not better so, more adaptable to its own strains and stresses, and surely more interesting.

Jules and his visitors laughed easily, uproariously, particularly if the wine was well fermented and not yet vinegar. But on one point they were serious enough. In this country a man needed a wife, somebody to look after him, do the chores. Some went farther — a helper in the field, at least until she provided children old enough to take her place.

The Ainsworth *Journal* was running a matrimonial column, begun as a joke, but soon clothing itself in seriousness. The apparently guying surface was discounted by men who needed a cook. The circulation climbed. Other papers imitated. Openly the letters were studied, those by men for style, those by women with a deeper purpose.

"Ach, there she is, my future bride," laughed the blond and sunburned Hans. "Listen!"

DES MOINES, *September* 18, 1885

EDITORS:

I see by your paper that there are several young men in your city willing to get married. I would like to meet Mr. Sam Jones and take my chances.

Yours with a view to matrimony,

MOLLIE SMITH

"Maybe Mollie would have me — No?" he asked, turning his back and pointing to the holes in the seat of his pants where considerable sun-tanned Hans showed through.

Jules looked up from his paper. "Here we got no women and in Utah they got too many. The government is trying to make them turn all over one back into circulation. I could use four myself — one to cook my breakfast, one to chop weeds, one to carry home the game I shoot, and one to sleep with."

When the old settler, as they already considered him, was in an expansive mood his neighbors tossed alien ideas before him and watched him pounce upon them like a wolf, rip them, tear them, and turn away unsatisfied, yet not entirely so, for Jules liked the exhilaration of this fierceness in himself.

But if he suspected that they were playing with him he grew morose, hunched into himself in the dim light of the kettle of oil or, rising in wrath over them all, drove them from the place. Then for several days he was alone, unless a traveler stopped or someone came for strychnine or gun repairs or in urgent need of balsam copaiba.

By the time his neighbors came back he was glad to have an audience, talked big, praising himself and his Mirage Flats until his confidence returned.

Election day brought winter, six to eight inches of snow, the wind whipping it into long, frozen scarves behind every Russian thistle, soapweed, or cow-chip pile. Bachelors living alone pored over copies of matrimonial papers or wrote more letters back East, hoping that some girl of their acquaintance might be wiliing to come West.

But as soon as the storms let up, the men could get away from the isolation. They could go to the warm, friendly saloons to talk, to drink if they had a few cents in their pockets, or a little game or a few furs to trade. But not their women. They had only the wind and the cold and the problems of clothing, shelter, food, and fuel. Sometimes their voices shrilled, sometimes they died to dark silence.

Early in January George Klein pushed his team through the snow to Pine Ridge for wood. When he came home he found his house dark, the fire out, and his wife and three children dead — gopher poison and an old case knife worn to a point. The woman had been plodding and silent for a long time, but her husband had hoped for better crops, better times, when he could buy shoes for the children, curtains for the window, maybe a new dress for his wife and little luxuries like sugar now and then.

"If she could a had even a geranium — but in that cold shell of a shack — " a neighbor woman said sorrowfully as she helped make white lawn dresses for the three children, something nice for their funeral.

"There 'll be more killing themselves before long unless they get back to God's country," was the prediction. And it was true. One of two young Swedes who got lost in the sandhills came out completely crazy. His brother hung himself from a manger.

In the meantime the snow piled so deep that no wheel turned on the railroad for days and remote shacks saw no visitor for weeks. During the long evenings the more discerning settlers began to see what Jules tried to point out from the start, a tightening of the cattleman lines about the short-grass Flats, to feel something the mustang must feel in his first corral.

For several years the Newman and Hunter ranches hired line riders to turn the stock back from the hills. Even so an occasional swift blizzard drifted whole herds into them. The enterprising Irwin, still foreman at Newman's, sent twelve good cow hands equipped with grub and bed wagons into the hills. They found much stock in fine condition, although it was April and the winter had been long and hard.

The outfit worked the hills for five weeks, gathering and holding eight thousand head of branded stock belonging anywhere from Broken Bow, towards the centre of the state, to Chadron. In addition, they found a thousand mavericks, some five years old, which, according to custom, were branded with the iron of the outfit finding them. It was a profitable venture and aroused ranching ambitions in even the camp cook.

Now the last sandhill taboo was broken and the cattlemen, crowded out by settlers east of the sandhill country, along the Platte, and on the table about Chadron, moved into this, their last stronghold. Cattle were taken into the broad meadows of the lake region to fatten and to winter on the steep south hill slopes where the long grass was never entirely snow-covered. Great round-ups, bringing representatives from Dakota and the Platte, became a feature of the sandhill cattle year.

Big herds of longhorns still trailed in, bawling, wilder than deer, from the South, but their place was gradually being taken by trainloads of smooth young she stuff, with Hereford bulls to improve the strain. The wild steer was passing, and valuable cattle meant valuable grass. More outside money, foreign money as the settlers called it, came in. The men running the ranches were only tools for large Eastern or English concerns. They strung barbed wire over the hills, enclosing the government land and protecting it with gun-carrying forces of cow hands. Not that they needed to use the guns against anything more threatening than a wolf or a maddened cow. Not yet. But they'd soon be getting too big for their britches.

And every year brought more settlers, more land-hungry people. By this time they were reduced to contesting or locating in the range south of the river, claimed by the cattlemen. Many listened to the stories of wind that made blowouts of any land ploughed there, and of gun-packing cow-boys, and preferred buying relinquishments or contesting on the table. In the spring of '86 there were several deserted claims on the Mirage Flats and along the river, and Jules helped newcomers to these. But the contesting privilege was open to abuse. Every town had half a dozen actual and would-be lawyers. Some of them lived honestly on the many inevitable conflicts that arise in frontier communities. Then there were the contest sharks, contesting fifty or a hundred claims at a time, claims upon which the entryman was living. If he fought he was sure to win, but at the expense of lawyer fees. For a sum the contest would be dropped. Settlers known to have a little ready money were compelled to buy themselves out several times a year.

Old Jules dipped his pen hard into his drying ink and wrote violent letters with impressive strings of signatures to Washington. He was told the abuse was not uncommon and that a civil damage suit was the only recourse.

When Jules was asked, "Had any contesting down your way?" he caressed the smooth lock of the rifle across his arm.

"There probably never will be."

"But what can be done with such crooks?"

"Nothing, I guess, only run them out of the country."

Perhaps making an example of one or two . . .

On a dark, late spring day a crowd of men gathered in a saloon near the end of main street in Rushville, still the county seat. They did n't say much, just passed a few quiet words. They did not even mention the name of C. C. Akin, contesting attorney. But there were lines about the mouths of these men and their eyes were hard as worn ploughshares.

Quietly a long, lean, little-known settler went up the street to the frame hotel while a few of the others slipped around to the back. At his signal from a window, the rest moved towards the front door and went in their boots heavy on the bare boards of the lobby.

After a while they came out and down the middle of the street, dragging Akin with them.   Men, boys, even a woman or two, ran up from every direction until the crowd overflowed the street, but no officers came.   The lawyer was taken into a store near the depot.   The crowd waited outside, silent, patient, while from the windows across the street looked curious and sometimes smirking faces.

Suddenly something like a half-plucked animal shot from the door.   It was Akin, stripped naked, covered with tar and feathers, body, head, and face, running for the open prairie; the mob yelling at his heels spurted the dust behind him.   Twice he fell in his fright, and like a desperate animal he was running again before he was up, running until he was far out on the plain, only a dark speck with nobody near.

The men straggled back to town and scattered.   Some went into the saloons to get a drink; others with no taste for drinking now climbed on their horses and cut across the open country home.

"That 'll end the son of a bitch around these diggings!" remarked an old prospector who had followed gold from Sutter's Fort to the Black Hills.   "The settlers' interests must be protected," Chamberlain, a banker dealing in land mortgages, said piously.   Ash Parks, from Mirage, who had bought off four contests, spit into the dust at the banker's feet and walked away.

Jules came home from Rushville late that night with nothing to say.   Parks and Jug Byers were as close-mouthed. In a few days the sheriff gathered up twenty-two of the tar-and-feather party.   Six of the men were fined five dollars each and given a day in jail.   There being no jail, the prisoners were "carefully watched," as the *Standard* said. Put the time in playing poker in the back of the saloon with the county judge, some of the church people charged.

"Not much money changing hands in bogus contests any more," Jules chuckled, as he looked over the legal notices, his first comment on the affair.

"Mob rule is against the tradition of our great country," Johnny Burrows complained, but mildly.

"Tradition, hell!" Jules shouted at him over the paper. "What you know about tradition here — country raw, still full of buffalo bones, an insult to the nose of a honest man with the stink of the Indians you butchered to steal their land. Tradition? Tradition of lead and blood!"

"For the land sakes, Jule, don't get so excited. You were glad enough to come and take up a piece of the country."

"You damn right — and the Indians made me welcome."

"Why they not give you squaw to make the dog soup?" Hans teased.

"My wife got no need to cook dog. I can supply plenty game."

That was true, they agreed. Later they followed Jules out into the bright night to see the streak of the bullet from his borrowed rifle cross the face of the full moon. And then they went back to the dugout and talked long of guns and powder, and watched Jules mould shiny lead bullets, not so accurate as the steel-jacketed ones, but cheaper and true enough at close range. Hans sniffed the hot lead and amused himself dipping the bottoms of the bullets in melted beeswax and setting them up in rows like soldiers to cool.

For a few months there was peace from contest sharks.

Summer came about like all the other summers. One day it was winter and the next the mercury climbed to ninety. Several bachelors who left the country in the fall brought back brides. Jed Brown met his girl in Rushville and married her. Hans was still reading letters from his Anna, carrying them around until they broke at the creases. "Married men," Jules argued, "stay home more, make better farmers."

There was a great deal of ploughed ground on the hard-land table now, and other crops besides corn — wheat, rye, oats, and potatoes — were doing well. Everyone was young

and the sky was high above them, the horizons far, and the
tragedies of the winter were forgotten.

Chadron, not to be outdone by Rushville this year, was
putting on a big Fourth of July celebration. Jim Dahlman,
the mayor, a Texas trail driver and an early ranch hand at
Newman's, invited Red Cloud of Pine Ridge and two hundred and fifty of his Indians to lend a frontier tang.

Three days before the celebration, Red Cloud arrived in a
long sausage of dust raised by fifteen hundred Sioux and
Cheyennes, bringing their families, their ponies and dogs,
and their weapons. In the silent tipis they pitched against
the sky were warriors who helped scalp the men of Custer;
Sioux who were with Sitting Bull four years before; Cheyennes who had been with Dull Knife and saw their women
and children butchered only eight years before within sight
of their campfires to-night. And down below them lay a
foolish little white man's town, full to the sideboards with
whiskey. If any leaked into the camp of Red Cloud, or if
an over-enthusiastic celebrant's bullet found a red skin . . .

To those who came complaining of the number, old Red
Cloud talked through an interpreter, putting always a third
person between them and himself.

"My young men like to make the feast — and the battle,"
he said. So, of course, they were feasted, even though there
was some difficulty in rounding up enough steers for so many
hungry Indians. Nor were they trail-gaunted longhorns,
or grotesque lump-jaws, such as the beef contractors sold
the government for them. These were fine, smooth stock.
Even so, the predominance of feather, beads, and paint was
not particularly exhilarating to anyone except Jules, who
camped with his friend White Eye.

The big event of the celebration was a hundred-mile race
about an oblong track. It was much advertised and the
discrepancy between the early posters and the later ones as
to purse was overlooked. The real money would change

hands in open bets. Every town along the Northwestern had several race horses backed to the limit by the local sports.

Early in the morning ten entries, including several blooded horses, started. Two dozen men quick on the draw were deputized to discourage sudden onslaught upon stake-holders or the death of any horses from lead colic, as happened down towards Sidney the week before.

The crowd, well ornamented with painted and feathered Indians, packed close about the track, yelling as the dust thickened until the horses were only thundering blurs. Before the race was half over one horse came to a dead stop, his sides dripping blood in roweled arcs. Another somersaulted and lay still. A fine, slender-legged racer staggered to her knees, groaned, and died.

"Clear the track!" the official shouted each time. Ten men were hired to drag the down animals away.

Finally only three were left — rangy mustang stock. Old Baldy, a cow pony belonging to the mayor and worth about fifty dollars, won, just able to walk in.

It was a big race and a dry one, and the crowd pushed into town for a real throat-wetting, only to be met by the news that the Humane Society had sworn out warrants for all connected with the event. Resourcefulness is a prerequisite for frontier survival. The officials induced twenty young Sioux in full paint and regalia to run a foot race through the one street of Chadron. The warrants were never served.

And the morning of the sixth, Red Cloud and his warriors struck camp and trailed back to Pine Ridge. Then there was nothing except burning crops and the browning prairie to talk about, so Jules went home too.

Money is scarce in a new agricultural community. Every man works for himself and trades help with his neighbors during harvest and threshing. Jules farmed by exchange. He sold ammunition, usually at cost, reloaded shells, re-

paired guns, and cut gunstocks from blocks of walnut, working with strange care, like a sculptor. He located and surveyed, and now and then there were a few pigs or calves or
colts to castrate — all on time. Those who owed him and
would pay ploughed his field, seeded, cultivated, and harvested his crop. There was seldom enough to pay his ammunition and grocery bills in town. During the winter he
trapped, hunted along the Running Water, went deep into
the hills for coyotes and gray wolves. He shot and sold
antelope, shipped barrels of frozen ducks and grouse, perhaps geese, and bought and shipped furs with his own catch.
Never a good trader, too often he paid more than he could
get. The little income from the post office he spent for
stamps to bring more settlers to the country. Duns did not
worry him, for he believed in the future.

Occasionally Jules went to a neighbor's for a square meal,
bringing fresh game, or carrots, perhaps, and tomatoes.
He wore his clothes until they dropped off. But the time
finally came when he must raise two hundred dollars for
his preëmption [1] somehow. So his stamp collection went,
at a tenth of its value.

Because the Flats was stocking up, Jules finally wrote to
his father for money to fence his place. Probably because
he had not repaid what he borrowed when Paul came, the
father replied in impatience. Land was not fenced in Switzerland. If it must be in America, why not with wood, or,
failing that, why not dig a ditch around it?

Dig a ditch around three hundred twenty acres!

Nothing more was done, and when Lamoureau's cattle ate
up his garden and much of his crop, Jules went to court.
Unfortunately Lamoureau was the mail carrier and it ended
by Jules driving him from the place with a gun. It cost

---

[1] Under the Preëmption Act, as much as 160 acres might be entered, to
be paid for in a given length of time at $1.25 an acre, residence to be main-
tained until payment.

him the precious post office — which was taken over by Lamoureau's wife.

The day she came for it Jules went on a long hunt. He could not face the empty pigeonholes in the corner where his neighbors' letters, catalogues, and papers had been. So this was how the government repaid a man for building up the country: took his post office away because someone working against him would swear to lies. But the shrewd old settler was fooling no one. He knew he had no right to drive anyone from a public place.

Jules came back calmer, but determined. He wrote more letters. Plenty of good free land left for everyone. Openings for a blacksmith, a storekeeper, and a lawyer in the town of Sandoz which he had planted in the wilderness. That it was fifteen miles from the railroad was unimportant to him.

The winter of 1886–1887 cleaned out many Dakota ranchers, including the stock of the four-eyed young New Yorker, Theodore Roosevelt, but it was n't bad in the Panhandle. Sod corn had yielded twenty bushels to the acre, some of it solid enough to keep. With grain for the horses, the ribbons of sod would roll from the breaker bars next spring.

Everyone was young and optimistic, and sociable. The communities split into the dancers and those with Methodist feet, as Elmer Sturgeon called them. The former attended everything, even the dances at the edge of the sandhills. They sprinkled sand over the slick ice of the Niobrara crossing. If a horse went through the channel they pulled him out and drove him warm. Often Jules went too, just to lean against the wall or sit on the end of a bench made of native planks across boxes and kegs, talking politics and crops with the less pushing or popular, watching Nell Sears jig until her red face flamed and her brother John joined in, while Charley played the fiddle. And when they finally dropped into somebody's hastily vacated place or on someone's lap, the floor was cleared for a set.

> Gents bow out and ladies bow under,
> Hug 'em up tight and swing like thunder,

until the girls' skirts flew and their feet left the floor, amid shrieks. Someone sang, "Susanna, don't you cry for me." Perhaps Elmer Sturgeon could be coaxed to add his "Love is such a funny, funny thing," to the evening, standing straight and stylish in his highly glazed paper collar and full suit while most of the others wore rough work shirts with only a sprinkling of half-washed linen collars, badly ironed. If they had coats, all but Elmer shed them early, for the room must be kept warm for the babies sleeping in two rows across a homemade bedstead or on the floor under the plank bench where the women sat.

Perhaps there was a debate: Resolved, that Grant was a great butcher instead of a great general; or, Resolved, that the Irish should be free. Once they tried to get up a debate on the farmer-railroad controversy, but no one would produce arguments for the rail plutocrats. In any case the final telling argument was a quotation from either the dictionary or the Bible. Once there was a test of authority, the Bible versus the dictionary, and the end was a devil's lane between two erstwhile good neighbors.

Sometimes there was a dialogue at the literaries, painstakingly prepared and put on without scenery with Joe Parker's homemade plank sled for a stage, so small that a couple of good stalking steps landed the actor in the lap of a close spectator.

Here the young men came, lonely, often badly fed, for a little good cooking and to woo the few girls, sometimes winning them, sometimes not. It seemed Johnny Burrows, dependable as his ox team, was to be successful.

"By golly, he's a rustler," Jules remarked the spring before, when he saw the broad field of breaking the lean little man had turned up with the slow plough critters. Soft-spoken, religious, he was exceptional. But he was one of those opinionated folk who are never forgiven, and when he forgot himself so far as to correct the grammar of his Lucy at a spelldown, she rose to her fullest height, an inch greater than his, gathered up her swirling skirts, and looked down upon her escort.

"I 'll have you know, Mr. Burrows, that I talk like I please!" With that she pushed her way towards the door and departed on the arm of a gay, stiff-collared youth who knew little and cared less about grammar and who would never raise an ear of corn in his life.

"Let her go to hell," Jules advised. "You can't hold them when they want to run."

But Johnny only worked a little harder, got a little thinner, spoke a little softer, particularly after Lucy married the gay man.

If a blizzard came up the crowd piled into the hay-packed wagons and covered their heads with horse blankets and robes. Nor did the wooing seem to suffer — not until the team stuck in a snowdrift or the driver got lost. But many were like Jules, compelled to face the storm long miles alone, the snow caking their eyelashes and beards as they pounded the saddle horses homeward to cold, dark holes in the ground.

Sometimes young Hans went with Jules, but he was not so gay now, for his Anna wrote less frequently. Then for a month he rode over to Jules's every mail evening, where he and Big Andrew and the others still got their mail just as they had while he had the post office.

There was no letter from Anna. Hans had hoped to have her with him long before this, but it went slow. Not only must he have the passage money, but there must be a house for her. His Anna could not live in a dark hole in the ground; not his Anna who sang Schumann.

"If you had two hundred dollars to pay on your preëmption you could borrow some."

"Ach, if I had two hundred dollars to pay I would be like a kaiser," Hans laughed, but not quite as he did two years before.

At last a letter came. Hans read it at Jules's light and then stumbled to a box in the corner, covering his face with his hands. Jules was reading a paper and paid no attention. Finally the youth got up and went out.

Half an hour later Elmer Sturgeon brought him back. The young German looked dazed; the pupils of his blue eyes large black holes.

"Found him stumbling over the army trail, falling down in every rut. He 's not drunk. Must be sick."

"You don't say." Jules looked at his eyes, felt his pulse. "Something pain you?"

Dully Hans shook his head. Together they put him to bed and Jules burnt a little sugar in a pan, poured in a big cup of wine and added a pinch of ginger, and made Hans drink it steaming hot. After a little he sat up, dropping his hands loosely over his knees.

"My Anna — she is not coming, never. She is married."

"Oh, hell!" Jules slumped forward in his chair. That was the way with women. Finally he got up and brought Hans another cup of wine. But the young German would n't take it and, carrying his cap, he left, Elmer following him out.

Unannounced, another brother, Emile, came across the sea to the Running Water. When Jules looked up and saw before him the gay music maker of the family in his own doorway, it was suddenly as if everything in America had never been. They talked all night, these two, of Neuchâtel, of home. It was still the same, everything always the same. But here in America — three years before only the prairie and the army trail; now homes everywhere. There was still free land on Pine Creek, with plenty game and fish. It was good to grow with the land.

Early in the fall Jules had received one of the beautiful, drawn-character letters from Charles Nippel, his architect friend in Verdigre. He was going into politics. Of course Jules knew that Estelle had a divorce. Jules had n't heard, nor had he heard about the son, Percy, she claimed was his.

"Women who won't obey their husbands are worthless — no telling where they pick up their babies," he told Big Andrew.

That evening he cut a new wick from his undershirt and refilled his lead kettle with skunk oil, sent his visitors away, and wrote to Rosalie. When the crumpled paper lay about the wood box he read aloud what he had written, the shadow of his gestures exaggerated on the wall. Yes, it was good, and he sealed it with the man holding the tree.

The reply came very soon, telling Jules that his dear friend was so pleased to hear from her old love in America again. She was, oh, so sorry he had such bad luck. First his foot and now they, the best companions and friends, must have a misunderstanding. It made her very unhappy. Would he forgive her and be the nice friend he once was?

Jules saddled up Old Jim and went to Chadron to have a photograph taken. His wool shirt was a bit too wide in the collar and he did n't have a tie, but there was no denying that his gray-brown eyes carried a light that made every photograph a thing of life.

Forehanded, for once, he ordered a dozen.

Then he settled down to wait with what patience he could muster. The months dragged by and Rosalie did not come, did not even write. At last he cursed her, Estelle, all women, and spent a lurid night in Chadron with the worst one he could find. And then, because his need of a wife had become great, he asked her to marry him. She laughed in his face.

"Your feet stink!"

When he was sure that he had not infected himself, he wrote a letter to Elvina of his need for a helpmate. Paul, too, had written the sister of Jules's problem. "He will not look after himself. He cures all his neighbors for nothing. He has brought a dozen children into the world when the money and time were short. In that he takes after our fathers. He has never lost a mother or a child, a good record here, where so many die. But he will not, as I say, look after himself. He lives like a pig. He has a good farm and the genius to make things grow and thrive as none else. He should have a good wife, one who will help him and manage him."

Elvina looked about among her acquaintances. There was her friend Henriette, a classmate from Switzerland, now teaching French and manners in a private home in Boston. She was well educated, cultured, with a mind of her own and tired of childish tyrannies and the crudities of a newly rich family. It would be an undertaking for a city woman if Paul spoke justly, but it was worth trying. She wrote to Henriette, sending most affectionate greetings and casually mentioning letters "from her beloved brother Jules who is postmaster in Nebraska, etc., etc., but is so lonesome away from people of his own kind." And to Jules she spoke of her dear friend, even enclosing a sheet of Henriette's fine script.

In April 1887, Henriette came to Rushville and married Jules.

VI

HENRIETTE

Hunched down on the board that served as a seat, his gun
across the wagon bed before him, Jules returned from Rushville in jubilant spirits. He swung his whip and sang lusty
songs in French and German. The greasy cap, the faded
blue army coat, and the old blanket over his knees completely covered his new ten-dollar suit. But despite that
he looked different. His beard was gone, baring a cleft
in his short chin; his moustache was trimmed, his hair cut.
His skin, fine-textured and smooth, was clean, almost white
compared to that of the burnt men who hung curiously about
the depot to-day.

Beside Jules sat his new bride. Henriette seemed small,
shivering in her coat of good cloth and struggling with the
wind to keep her feathered hat pinned to her dark hair.

Now and then she stole a look at this brother of her friend
Elvina, her husband now, and always her strangely dark gray
eyes slid quickly away, over the wide Flats, dull with mid-
April, yet with the promise of sudden spring already in the
air. She considered the habitations: sod houses, frame
shacks weathering to soft prairie tones, the low earth humps
of dugouts. Most of the places showed signs of activity,
strips of stubble falling under the black furrows of the
plough, newly strung wire fences shimmering. And, as in
Rushville, everyone seemed to know her husband, to greet
him with boisterous friendliness, inquiring for news, asking
his opinion on trees, crops, politics, and the weather, while
they eyed his new wife. Each time Jules squinted at the
dark wall rising higher in the northwest.

"Rain to-night — probably snow. Git, git!" He whipped the team on, and the big trunk that was Henriette's and the little box of groceries that belonged to both, but for which the woman had paid, jumped as the team crossed the old army trail.

"Well, I be hung for a horse thief! You oughter see the woman Old Jules has wrangled himself," Jed Brown remarked to Big Andrew, to whom he had hurried with the news. "Got a few hundred dollars of her own, Jules was telling me, and he shore needs that. Good enough looker too, and dressed in silks like a fancy woman, but she ain't that kind. She's refined."

"No! — Well, Jules, he write a good letter and is not bad to look on when he is clean like to-day, before he go to the train. If I do not have to come home to look after my mare and foal, I stay. He look fine, like judge, maybe, or senator. And he know how to talk with big words and make you believe," Big Andrew admitted.

Yes, everyone knew how he could talk, and everyone, particularly the women, wondered how this venture could end.

Jules did not take Henriette to his dugout immediately. After considering a photograph of this woman with lace at her wrists, he decided it should not be so, at first. The dugout was full of muddy traps gathered in from the river, a few green hides, and all the accumulated filth since Paul went to the Platte. Later Henriette would clean it. For the present he made arrangements to use the Rutter shack, near the river, and all above ground.

It was dark when Jules and his bride arrived, and because he had forgotten to buy kerosene he ate crackers and cheese and drank part of a bottle of wine by the light of the cookstove. He scarcely noticed that Henriette did not eat or that she was as a stick of wood, her hands fastened on the lace handkerchief in her lap. When it was time for bed she roused herself and slowly, with uncertain movements, she spread new linens from her trunk over the blankets she suspected were dirty if she could see them clearly. Once she stopped and looked about as one just awakening. It could not be true — this. This moulting crow could not be the eagle she had seen in the letters from Elvina's brother.

Train-weary, her body aching from the jolting lumber wagon, she crept into bed.

Towards morning it began to rain. The roof leaked, a little at first, then more. Soon everywhere. Henriette sat on the wet straw tick all the next day with a purple umbrella over her head, crying noiselessly while Jules raged that there was no fuel. Plainly the white hands of his wife would be incapable of wielding a successful axe against the toughness of wet wood. So he plunged out, dragged in a fallen ash tree, and chopped it into appropriate lengths on the floor. At last he got the fire going and while one stoveful burned he dried another in the rusty oven, his socks steaming behind the stove. He made half a gallon of coffee and dug out the remainder of the crackers and cheese. As he pushed a cup towards Henriette he warned her that he was not the man to wait on a woman. She shook her head. She was not hungry.

Fed and warmed, Jules filled his pipe and listened to the rain as the dusk gathered. He watched the fire-tinted drops run along the rafters and bound off the umbrella.

Suddenly Henriette laughed aloud. "It is like Chopin — 'The Raindrop,' " and she hummed a bit of it.

Jules liked that. Their piano teacher at home had played it sometimes when he stayed to chocolate after lessons. They all practised a little, but only Emile and Nana had the ear. Reminiscently he hummed tunes of the homeland, sang a song Rosalie taught him in the spring: —

Ach, bleib' bei mir, und geh' nicht fort.
Dein Herz ist ja mein —

a lonely sadness creeping into his voice. But a new leak
hit his cap, streamed down his neck, and cut the song short.

"*Sacré!* — and they try to tell me this is a dry country!"
he exploded in English, laughing as at a huge joke. He
hung his wet cap on the stove hook to dry and crawled into
bed beside Henriette, rubbing his stubbly cheek against her
arm.

The fourth morning the sun came out. The light snow
that followed the rain was gone by noon, and the river bottom was suddenly green with spring. Little remained of
the whole incident except the water stains on Henriette's
silk dress, nothing at all to mar the hope of Jules.

He did not know that the first time he left the house his
wife brought out Elvina's letter praising her brother in
extravagant terms, tore the double sheet across once, and
dropped it into the hot bed of ash-wood coals. So ended
a long friendship.

The end of the week Jules took his wife to Valentine to file
on a homestead across the river from Indian Hill. They
were barely back when the winter's severest snowstorm hit
the Panhandle. The shack on the river shook in the wind
until the snow piled to the roof. But by this time Henriette was prepared for even a blizzard in May. The morning
after the storm she went out into the glowing whiteness.

"Oh, Jules," she called. "Come quickly."

He threw down his newspaper and, grabbing his rifle,
limped out. "What is it?" he demanded, looking about.
"What is it?"

"The snow — is it not beautiful?"

"Oh, hell, bother me when I 'm reading."

But Henriette ignored his grumbling. She put her arm
through his and together they followed the wind-swept
ridge to the top of the bluff overlooking two miles of blue
river, a blue ribbon dropped carelessly in snow. The leafy

trees and brush along both sides bent under the load of whiteness, and over it all the brilliant sky pressed down and filled every gully, every crack and crevice in the snow, with delicate harebell blue.

To Jules the appeal of beauty was strong but momentary. In a moment the rabbit tracks leading off across the country stole his attention. He showed the long succession of Y's to his wife, explaining the rabbit's absurd way of placing his hind feet ahead of his fore ones and the jack rabbit's trick of doubling back and side-jumping into the snow to watch his trail.

"I must write my pupils in Boston of the clever creature."

Jules's face, well beard-smudged by now, set in a frown. "You are my wife and I command you not to write to them."

"Oh, how the lion he roar!" she laughed, determined upon disobedience.

Jules kept the neighbors away from his wife as much as he could. "*Grobian*' and coarse stable maids," he termed them. Actually he was afraid they would talk her against him as they had the blacksmith who came to open a shop on Jules's claim on the Flats, and the storekeeper from New York who was to put in a stock of groceries. Both went back. Besides, Henriette did not know about Rosalie, Estelle, or the debts to his father.

But when she saw no money coming in she determined to discover how others lived here. Apparently there was no market for cut flowers, canaries, goldfish, or fancy embroideries — the ways to pin money suggested by the women's magazines. At the neighbors' she heard about the debts and about Estelle, and she went home with darkness against Jules. But she had also heard about the Black Hills and that they furnished a good market for vegetables, butter, and poultry products through the store at Hay Springs. So she bought a cow, some chickens, and tried to get Jules up early to help with the chores and the garden. Even after he had eaten his breakfast he refused to go to the garden or field. "I got to rest after breakfast. I must think."

"You rest — after sleeping all the night. How does that come? And think, think. Why not do, do?"

Jules was up on his good foot. "Shut your mouth!" he roared. His hand shot out, and the woman slumped against the bench. Grabbing his gun, he limped out to saddle Old Jim and left for the sandhills.

But he didn't get any farther than Pine Creek. By evening he was back, sheepishly jolly, singing "Marguerite" while he dressed two grouse for supper. Smoking his pipe quietly, he watched them roast in the army kettle, now and then lifting the lid with a stick and filling the room with a steaming, wild fragrance. He pretended not to notice Henriette's swollen lip, the dark bruises on her temple, and the tear-wearied eyes.

The woman was intelligent, quick to recognize the potency of silence. With his wife's money Jules wanted to build, like the peasants he saw in France, a grainery, a horse stable, a chicken coop, and a pigpen, in a succession of lean-tos against the living quarters. Henriette waited until he was away on a hunt. Then she hired two men to build a story-and-a-half house, and laid out a yard with outbuildings. Emile abetted her.

"My family already working against me," Jules complained bitterly among the neighbors, but as soon as the roof was on he moved his guns, his drugs, and his new stamp collection to the new home on his wife's place. Without a regret he left his dugout on Mirage Flats forever.

Because Henriette did not intend to become a burden-bearing woman she bought a wagon of her own, and a team. Seeing others ford the Niobrara apparently anywhere and any time, she drove into the soft sands after the flood waters of a cloudburst and let the team stop to drink in midstream. The wagon settled to the hubs in quicksand.

"Oh, the fool!" Jules bellowed.

Hoping for a shift in the channel and yet afraid the

wagon might be swept away, he tied a two-hundred-foot rope to an axle and to a cottonwood shading the river bank. The next day the wagon was still there but the rope was gone, and Freese, living on the old camp site at the foot of Indian Hill, across the river, had a new picket rope for his milk cow.

For a week Jules met everyone in the yard, asking no one to the house. Finally Mrs. John from beyond the Rutter place made a special trip down. But she wore a red wrapper visible half a mile, and all she saw of Henriette was her gray skirt tail vanishing into the buffalo-berry brush where the fat woman could n't follow.

After that there was considerable headshaking. Even Sheriff Riggs, one of the old-time cattle trailers, stuck his saddle horse in the quicksand only the fall before and got his pants' pockets full of water pulling the animal out. It might happen to anybody. Besides, the wagon was Henriette's.

George Minten, living at the top of the bluff where Jules first crossed the river, three years before, told of seeing the early settler's wife pulling his socks off after he waded the river. Later others saw her about the place as usual, generally alone. Too often alone, the women said. It would be too bad if she was in for it already.

Before the wagon was entirely out of sight in the quicksand Elmer Sturgeon was caught by a storm below Henriette's place. He loped into her yard just as the rolling sausage of dust from the Flats swept down the bluffs and crossed the river above the ford.

Henriette was chasing a hen and picking up the chicks in her apron. The young man helped her, snatching them up as he ran and stuffing them into his shirt. Then the two stood at the door together, watching the greenish clouds boil overhead, the lightning split them in vivid red veins that left a lingering image on the eye.

Suddenly the wind stopped and through the breathless

silence a straight violet bolt fell, ripping a big cottonwood across the river from tip to five-foot bole, leaving half standing a ghastly scarred thing in the greenish afterlight. Thunder rocked the ground. A few drops of rain splattered like hot metal in the dust; then the sun broke through.

"The storms here, they are so savage, and yet nothing," Henriette said slowly, letting her tense arms relax.

The young man, who had seen her the day she married Jules, looked down upon the lining face.

"Yes," he said, tapping the toe of his boot with the forked end of his quirt. "Something like Old Jules."

The woman drew back as though he had fetched the leather across her face. Then she laughed with almost normal heartiness. When the man was on his horse, ready to go, she held out her calloused hand.

"*Merci.* You have helped me — with the chickens."

After that things went better in the home on the Running Water. Jules put on a little weight, wore cleaner shirts, and no longer rode around with his knees out. He stayed home more, spending long evening hours over his new stamp collection, his guns, and his reloading tools.

This was different from living with the illiterate Estelle. Sometimes he even talked of Rosalie. At first Henriette went out into the night, but after a while she kept right on mending. Towards winter Rosalie sent her a knitted cap, such as the sportswomen wintering in the Alps wore, tomato red and white, very pretty, and becoming to Henriette's dark eyes and straight brows. Jules had not written, but it was good Rosalie knew. Henriette kept the gift wrapped in tissue paper and wore a long brown fascinator about her ears instead.

Gradually the neighbors came back. They talked land and crops and shot target at Indian Hill, high over the Freese house, just as though he did not live there. Sometimes they stayed into the night and then Henriette brought out a loaf of bread, a platter of cold game, and a pot of coffee or a jug of new wine, still sweet.   Silent, she was always there, in the dark corner near the stove.

Gradually Jules went to the neighbors' again, to the Van Dorns' or the Mintens' or farther, as others dropped away and then rejoined the groups a few months later: Jed Brown, Nicolet and Aubert, even Tissot, getting blacker every day, with a girl wife at home who could not go much now.

"They stay home until you 're in for it and then they 're gone," Nell Sears, married and going through the experience, said with a deep laugh.   Not that she stayed home. She 'd dance when she was that way with her tenth.   But Henriette was still wearing a belt and getting steadily leaner.

Despite the disappointments, the migration into the Panhandle country was heavier every spring.   A new railroad, the Burlington, was pushing westward through the sandhills to Alliance and on to Crawford near Fort Robinson, stringing potential shipping points, white names on dark red boards, across the south sandhills.   For every settler that left, two more rushed in to fight the Russian thistles from his breaking or to push into the cattleman region.   Jules added to his Swiss settlement on Pine Creek and on the south Flats, interspersing his countrymen with any other determined farmers he could get.   "You stay until we get run out and you 'll be here to see the last of the cattlemen," he told any who seemed to be a little dubious or afraid.

To everyone's surprise the small cattlemen moved their fences without any particular protest.   Perhaps they had been bluffing all along.   Perhaps their eyes were on the greater opportunities deeper in the hills, along the new railroad, away from the locator and the rifles he was selling at cost.

When Sparks, United States land commissioner, suspended the issuing of patents until complete investigation of every proof, Jules's kitchen was filled with uneasy settlers. Did that mean they would not get their patents for years?

"Hell, no. Sparks hopes to keep the land out of the hands of speculators and the cattleman by preventing fraudulent proofs."

"*Ja*, but I got to have my patent now, so I can borrow money to pay for my horses or they take them away. Then how I farm?" Big Andrew demanded.

Jules refilled his pipe. "You'll get it. I'll write to Washington to-day."

Big Andrew kept his horses, but within a year Sparks was ordered to issue patents immediately upon proof of legal residence as established by two witnesses. He believed that the action was against the settlers' best interests and resigned.

"The cattleman with his lying cowboys can run fraudulent proofs through now like wild steers through a chute," Jules mourned.

The twenty-second of September brought three days of rain, to spoil the winter range, any down hay, and the cow chips. The Rushville *Standard* anticipated a hard winter and offered a year's subscription for every load of pitch-pine stovewood brought in. When Johnny Burrows showed Jules the item the early settler reminded him that a dozen eight-and-a-half-foot cane stalks and a squash weighing a hundred thirty-one pounds were on display in a bank window in Rushville.

"There's no limit to the stuff the country will grow under proper cultivation and the right seed. The land's valuable."

It was true good quarters of land near town sold for five and six dollars an acre, and there was talk of a pork-packing plant at Rushville, a cheese factory at Hay Springs, and grain elevators at every town. Six wagonloads of native lumber went down to the Niobrara for a flour mill.

Generally, however, it was conceded that times were hard in 1887, and the mugwumps, the socialists, and the anarchists were gathering strength. The Chicago bombings assumed local importance when a bottle bomb was found in the office of the Gordon *Herald*.

"Maybe it is only the newspaper joke," Big Andrew suggested.

During the fall Jules had received several letters from Neuchâtel. His father wrote that although his health had not been the best, he had been very busy with his clientele, his garden, and the agricultural exposition he sponsored. They were all glad that their Jules was at last suitably married and hoped he would do his best to make the Henriette happy in that isolated region which seemed not without promise. But knowing nothing about a daughter-in-law except her first name was too little. If they could not have a photograph, then at least a letter with her autograph.

"They are nice, this father and mother," Henriette said.

They hoped that Jules would care for his cattle and that Paul and Emile would not be alone in their shacks during the winter. Elvina seemed very well established in her teaching in Toronto, Canada, but the work was heavy. Henri was very zealous in his studies, more so than his brothers.

"They always like him better than me," Jules complained.

"They seem to me very fond of you," Henriette comforted.

William, next to Jules in age, was completely demoralized. He should be in America. There he could well make his way, for he is a worker. Ferdinand, Nana, send thanks for the stamps Jules enclosed.

Down on the Platte, Paul was doing well. He urged Jules to come immediately, for there, too, the land was settling fast. He was borrowing five hundred dollars from home. "Batching bores me," he wrote, "but I have not yet thought of getting married. . . . I do not need a rifle, here; the range cattle were all driven out this fall. They at home write that William is going from bad to worse. Suzanne is obliged to leave him. How I grieve for her who is such a good woman. If she were on this side of the sea she would be happier."

"Paul was always a ladies' man, washing his face and hands to get cakes from the hired girls," Jules said sarcastically. Then he wrote his brother to come to the Running Water for the New Year.

November and December were a chain of clear blue days, with a thin powdering of frost on the grass along the river in the mornings. Cattlemen from Dakota said this was more like the old days, when stock rustled all winter and came through strong and in good meat. The roads were open and the towns doing a booming business. Then, after a week of spring weather in January, snow began to fall quietly at daylight. By three in the afternoon the wind was blowing forty miles an hour, sifting fine snow into the tightest soddy, settling a white film over the floors and beds, hissing on the hot stove lids and sucking the fire from the rusty pipes.

By ten o'clock the thermometer was down to thirty-three below zero. Cattle, even horses, their eyes snow-caked, drifted before the wind to pile up and freeze in gullies and in fence corners. No one familiar with the West ventured out without a rope tied about his waist and securely anchored to the door. The settlers hunched over their stoves, their faces dark. There were few words.

Jules, always put in a good humor by vagaries of earth and sky, stuck his head out of the door and jerked it back. "Forty below by morning," he predicted. "I guess I hole up like a bear."

Henriette, a woolen shawl about her shoulders, her feet on a box, off the cold floor, made no answer. The house ivy she had kept with her ever since she left Switzerland was black, frozen behind the stove.

The third morning, when the storm was over, the wind down and the sun white and cold upon the iron-hard drifts, there was a crunching at the door, followed by a powerful thumping. It was Ned Dickerson, in a huge buffalo coat, his beard, eyebrows, and lashes frosted white. He slapped his hands and stomped his feet while Jules put on all warm clothing and looked to his supply of tobacco and matches. Last he slipped the morphine bottle and his doctor shears into his pocket. Dickerson's wife had chosen a bad time to be delivered.

Henriette watched the men move awkwardly over the drifts together, Jules limping badly. That poor woman, with no one to help her but these rough men.

She tried to read, to sew, but always she was back at the hole scratched in the frost of the window. Suddenly she ran out and tore armloads of sticks from the buried wood-pile, dumped them on the kitchen floor, and chopped and sawed until she had a big pile of stove lengths in the corner. Then she shoveled the snow from the chicken-coop door, found all but three of her hens dead. These she brought in to warm and feed behind the stove. She separated the cow from her calf so there would be cream for the coffee in the morning. Finally she went to look at Jules's coyote traps in a side-hill cow trail. Last week there was a big eagle there, fighting the Old Country bear trap. To-day there was an eight-foot drift over the path.

And always she shaded her eyes toward the bluff where the men had disappeared that morning. At last, tired and cold, she forced herself to sit quietly at the open oven door and wait.

Towards evening Jules limped slowly into the yard, his bad foot sore from three miles of crusted snow. Henriette set out his supper and met him at the door. "The woman?" she cried.

"Heah? Oho, she's all right. But my foot hurt. Pull the stuff off." Henriette dug at the crusting of snow and ice and cut the wire holding the gunny-sack wrapping Dickerson put about the tender foot.

"The woman was bad. I have to pack her in snow. Could n't leave until she stop bleeding."

"What was then wrong?"

"Baby backward," Jules said, scraping out his cob pipe.

"Oh, but that is serious, is it not? — Even for a doctor? What 'd you do?"

He tested the draw on his pipe. "Turn him."

"The poor woman!"

"Heah? Oh, hell, that 's nature. Woman have to have children to keep healthy."

Henriette hurried out of doors to shake the snow from the gunny-sack wrappings and did not return to the house until her hands were whitening with cold. Jules looked up when she came in. "Where you been?" he demanded. "I want the table cleaned so I can work on my stamps." Silently Henriette went about her task.

Two weeks later, when the trains began to run again, Old Jules pushed his saddle horse through to Rushville. The papers reported two hundred and thirty-five dead in the storm that swept from Canada to the Gulf — fourteen dead in Nebraska, a woman and two children on South Mirage. The Hay Springs paper admitted a slight chilliness of thirty-eight degrees below zero, but nothing comparable to Rushville, where a leg froze off a cast-iron heater and the thermometer dropped to the lowest point ever recorded in Siberia, one degree above Gordon.

"Well, we ought to have a hot spell now, with the journalistic pyrotechnics that quip will start up and down the railroad," Elmer Sturgeon laughed, but with no heartiness.

Many of the settlers lost their cattle, even milk cows, and some their horses and pigs. Two men and a woman were sent to the insane asylum on the first passenger East. Down at the edge of the hills a mother of three hung herself. North of Hay Springs a man killed his brother with an axe, sneaking up behind him and splitting his skull almost to the neck. There was much lawing. Contest sharks, swooping like buzzards about those with a few dollars left, had to be reminded of Akins and his checkered suit.

Using shot sacks filled with sand to drown the beaver, Jules caught half a dozen during the short winter season. The finest was a large, smooth, golden fur fit for the Queen Victoria he had seen as she came through his mail car on the way to Milan. This skin he packed for Dr. Reed, sealing the package with red blobs of wax.

A few weeks later he got a letter and a package from Louisiana. The doctor's five years in Nebraska were over, but when the wind blew there came a tightening about his heart, a longing for the Panhandle. He hoped that his former patient was completely recovered and, like the man on his seal, was planting the soil with trees that would grow and spread to feed and shade his people. The package of tobacco was just a little treat. Buried in it Jules found a five-dollar bill. He looked at the crisp paper a long time, took his gun and limped away to the bluffs, and did not come back until dark. Finally he spent the money, but he never answered the letter. That he put between the pages of his stamp collection with all those from Rosalie.

Henriette could still cry a little when she found their start in cattle, eight head, piled in a draw. Jules dismissed them high-handedly. He could make more than they were worth in one trip into the hills. As soon as the snow cleared a little, he and Young Boston, living east of Freese, went on a hunt. They poisoned several gray wolves and a dozen coyotes, caught mink, skunks, rats, and even a badger, out early, with spring just behind, but not enough to pay for the cattle lost. They brought home two antelope and might have shot more, but the hills were still full of drifts and their little team, thin from rustling, gave out. The dead carcasses all over the hills made wolf hunting slow business.

While Jules was gone a letter came from Washington,

telling Henriette she was appointed postmistress. Although he had suggested her application and circulated the petition, he took her appointment as a personal insult and protested to the Postmaster General. Had n't he started the mail service on Mirage Flats, worked four years to build up the country? Was n't he the only man in the community trained to handle mail? And now the government, denying him, gave the office to another, and to a woman.

He read the letter to Henriette, wooden on her box in the corner. Then he blotted it with ashes from the stove hearth, never noticing that she made no comment.

After that he wrote out a big order for ammunition and guns on time, and hauled out the pigeonholed shelves he had made for his dugout. Once more he was to assume his rightful position as the hub of his community.

Spring brought letters from Neuchâtel. The money Henriette had scraped together to pay Jules's debts to his father was received. William was on the way to America. His wife had died and there was a daughter, whom his mother would rear. The father was better; not so given to dizzy spells. But perhaps they would ask Elvina to come home, now that so many of the others were wandering.

A short time after a letter came from Elvina. She must return to the homeland, but first she would see her brothers and her dear friend Henriette. Paul had written such fine things of Jules's wife. No, she could not return to Neuchâtel without seeing some Indians and something of the magnificent venture of these young Swiss, her brothers. Jules planned greatly upon her coming, looking about among his friends for one to keep her in America, a good husband, a steady man with get-up.

Jules fattened and grew pleasanter during the summer. He was appointed notary public and won his lawsuit against Lamoureau — receiving seven dollars damage for his garden and the crops eaten up three years before. Lamoureau sold his cows, his implements, and his team to pay the cost and moved to Rushville.

"That's what comes of working against me," Jules boasted.

The Panhandle always took an active interest in politics, particularly in Presidential election years. Sheridan County had a vigorous group of young Democrats. They arranged a rally with a brass band, a barbecue, and provided spell-binders: one local orator and an import. The big day came. The torch-light parade ploughed through the jammed street. The local orator's words fell loud and lifeless as wet sand before the set, sunburnt faces of his audience. Then the imported man arose, a mere stripling, an unknown young lawyer from Lincoln. He opened his generous mouth and the noisy audience before him quieted. Words flowed over them in a flood swift and clear as the Niobrara. Jules pushed his cap back. The older heads began to nod approval to one another. The speaker established the issues, swung into the tariff and ended on free silver, and when he sat down the crowd was still as a lull in a dry-land thunderstorm. Then in a frenzy of applause the audience arose, climbed to the benches, and swept forward upon the prophet come to them. Never would these men see another such day as when the Panhandle first heard the young Bryan.

Jules watched the Lincoln attorney leave the building with the local bigwigs of his party, clean as a young tree beside the paunchy local politicians. A wonderful speech, yet Jules knew that nothing he said was remarkable, new, or particularly sound. It was the way he said these things, as a fine young crusader, armed with a voice that swayed the emotions of the crusted skeptic. What could n't a man with true vision do with such a gift!

It was four in the morning when he loped into his

yard, but Henriette must up and hear it all before he could sleep.

The winter and spring passed much as others before. The summer of 1888 was a good one. Half a dozen of the farmers Jules located raised more than three thousand bushels of corn apiece. Wheat went twenty-five and twenty-eight bushels to the acre on the Flats and brought eighty-five cents. The good crops and the lumber war between two companies at Rushville encouraged the settlers to build on borrowed money. Believing that lumber would never be so cheap again, they flung up large barns, larger houses of twelve and fourteen rooms — unheatable shells, anticipating family growth for twenty years.

The Catholic community about Jules's old place was caught in the craze. He gave them five acres of land and they built a white board church on it, the belled steeple overlooking the heat dance and the mirages of the Flats. Big Andrew and the Hollanders considered this a generous gesture. To Jules it was just the simplest way to keep Father McNamara of Alliance, an admirer of the Cæsars and a stamp collector, coming to the community.

The fall was a beautiful scarf of warm, hazy days that trailed leisurely over the Panhandle. Along the Niobrara the silvery-gray strips of buffalo-berry bushes flaunted clumps of blood-red creeper. Back from the river large, solitary cottonwoods, grown symmetrical and assured as men aloof from the crowd, rustled golden leaves in the light wind, and along the bluffs tall ash stood like slim, golden maidens against the darker brush.

A good fall for prairie fires, old-timers said, and particularly with so many new settlers, people who did not realize what a moment's carelessness in this land of long grass and high wind can mean. In October a fire started from a cigarette stub near the Niobrara and swept through the entire sandhills to the Platte, cleaning out the winter range and the hay flats in the lake country about the head of Pine Creek.

Blackleg, too, made its first serious appearance. Hundreds of fat calves and yearlings went lame, swelled up, and died. Too rapid gains in weight, some said, and starved their stock. Others changed pasture, with more success. Jules believed the disease spread through wounds, probably through dogs running loose over the country and chewing at the blackleg carcasses and then nipping live animals. He wrote to his father and to Washington, and in the meantime he shot every stray dog he saw and added to his growing unpopularity with neighbors whose packs of half-starved hounds scoured the community for food — particularly with Freese across the river.

The warm weather lasted until mid-December without a drop to zero in the Panhandle. There were literaries in the schoolhouses, husking bees, a feather-stripping party or two, and socials, sings, masquerades, and dances. The Cravaths, running a small ranch at the headwaters of Pine Creek, were known far for their week-ends. Their invitations were always inserted in the news columns of the *Standard:* —

Party and dance at Cravath's, December 2. Dinner from one to seven. Beds and breakfast for all. Everybody come.

Seventy, eighty people usually went, some of them forty miles in wagons and horseback. The next day the men slept between soogans in the haymow, the women all over the house. The young dandies of the Flats, Elmer Sturgeon, Scribner, even Johnny Burrows, went; strangers came too, perhaps ragged, with starvation appetites. Sometimes they had to be thawed out at the big-bellied sheet-iron heaters that burned cow chips well and twisted hay passably. Someone usually sang "The Little Old Sod Shanty on the

Claim," or played negro melodies and reels on a fiddle. And once a tattered, tired little man took the instrument and caressed its strings and made such music as the Panhandle never heard before. Liszt, Brahms, Strauss, Bach — snatches no one recognized. On and on he played, on a nail keg at first, then unconsciously he stood, his head up, his eyes down the long ceiling. The crowd pushed forward, even the boot heels still. Jules was well up in front, his cap back, his long hand on his beard.

And then the man stopped and in pathetic confusion sat down, the fiddle like a child across his knee.

"Ah, but it was beautiful," Mrs. Cravath told him.

The man blushed. *"Es geht nicht gut.* I cannot make my fingers go right. It is then the piano I play, *ja."*

While the others danced to a young Polander's accordion, boots stomping, girls laughing, Jules talked to the little pianist. All the rest of the evening their heads bent together over their pipes. Ach, *die Heimat.* When midnight supper came Jules pushed forward and brought the man a heaped plate. It was not his habit to wait on anyone — only a recognized superior.

In the morning the little man held the old settler's hand gratefully and then slipped out into the frosty sunlight and was gone. No one knew where he lived and no one there ever saw him again. Yes, the Cravaths had fine weekends.

Perhaps because the year had been good and the roads open to travel late, most of Jules's cronies were getting married. Even Big Andrew came to tell of a widow woman who would have him. Ah, this, too, was like the free land and his friend Jules — unbelievable.

It seemed like a fever. Up on the breaks of Pepper Creek a man ran away with his neighbor's wife, taking his five children and her six. And not far from Rushville a sky pilot disappeared with his host's wagon, team, and wife.

"I worked one whole summer down in the hills to get them horses," the deserted man complained.

Cattle rustling, too, increased. The sandhills, now full of stock, were ideal for brand artistry, butchering, and stock smuggling. Small herds swelled. Many ambitious cows reared twins. One steer near the headwaters of Pine Creek was credited with mothering seventeen calves one summer. In the meantime not even a picketed milk cow unbranded was safe. But usually such rustling was penny ante for any but the smallest outfits.

Whole herds disappeared into the hills, their tracks lost after a few hours in the wind-shifted sand, and were probably shipped from the south road. General suspicion pointed to cowboys of the Hunter ranch on the Niobrara, but the officials did no investigating. A report from Chadron said that the Sheridan County sheriff had been up and captured the leaders of a gang of thieves estimated to have stolen a thousand head of cattle. He received five hundred dollars reward from the stockmen, and some said the Pinkerton Detective Agency offered him five thousand dollars a year, but that his people could not afford to lose him.

"Lose him? Just wait and see what they do to him election time. You remember how slick Riggs got beat just because he got drunk now and then and talked too much around town," someone remarked.

"Sheriffs are windbags," Jules generalized. "Anyway, what's our man doing rounding up rustlers in Dawes County? How about them right under his nose?"

"Like a moustache, it is too close to see," Hans laughed.

In April 1889, Gordon voted for prohibition with such a hilarious last evening that many who doubted the wisdom of driving away the drinking trade were convinced that keeping it was a dubious asset. There were two shootings, a knifing, and a preacher in the cooler of the next town. Jules brought Henriette a bottle of peach brandy he won at a raffle. She put it away against possible illness in the community. Jules liked that, and with a gesture of satisfaction he filled his pipe and lit it with a twig from the fire. The women and the preachers would drive the good citizens out of the country, he teased Henriette. But she gave him no answer.

The next month Rushville went dry, temporarily, through a local feud that held up the licenses.

"Smooth as an old mare's mouth for business in Hay Springs," was the general conclusion. But even that town had its troubles. A committee of angry citizens called on a group of lawyers dealing in contests and protests against land proofs. It might be cheaper, the *Standard* pointed out, to buy a rope than to pay contest fees, and it might not be healthy to push the spirited homesteaders of the new country too far.

"Well, Rushville's had experience. They ought to know," Sturgeon recalled.

Jules made no answer. The lawyers took no chances. They boarded the next train west.

Improved methods of farming, better seed, and more rain brought good crops, made Christmas a good one. Down on the Niobrara there were music and songs, a long letter from Elvina, packages of presents from Neuchâtel. Jules read the letter to a houseful of guests: Emile, William, Paul, the Auberts, the Nicolets and their baby, Louis Pochon and his two sisters, and the Eugenie who had a place the other side of Freese and spent much of her time with Henriette. She was not pretty. Her generous mouth and the broad cheekbones prevented that, but she spread a wholesome sense of well-being about her and her wit disconcerted even Jules.

The only American in the company was Johnny Burrows, who had not forgotten Elvina, the petite, vivacious little Swiss girl who stopped to see her brothers on her way to

Neuchâtel.   He listened to the letter as carefully as if he understood every word of it.

Elvina acknowledged a letter from Jules and one from Madame Aubert.   "In them we had a moment of living in the midst of you.   I was able to see all of you in the kitchen, telling stories, speaking of the Old Country.   It was warming to us all."

And later, from the doorway, Jules and Henriette watched them go, Johnny Burrows westward, and the rest towards the frozen river, William with a lantern riding in the lead, the wagons behind.   The light silhouetted the trees, the heads, the mittened hands waving good-bye.   Gay voices shouted a reminder of New Year on Pine Creek and the dark bluffs echoed them.   A dog barked at the Freese place as the wheels crunched over the sand-covered ice of the crossing. A sound of singing came back as the wagons followed William out of the river valley.

Jules put his hand on Henriette's shoulder.   She reached up and touched his fingers.

"It has been a good Christmas," she said.

Yes, despite the fact that there was no greeting from Rosalie, it was a good Christmas.

VII

THE NIOBRARA FEUD

THE boomers, those who rush in upon the crack of the frontier rifle like magpies flocking from kill to kill, were leaving the Panhandle. They packed their bundles into their covered wagons, tied the milk cow to the endgate, her pot-bellied calf to her tail, whistled the dogs together, and drove on into the sunset. Hardship, even cold and hunger, they could endure for a while, but not the monotony of the walking plough.

Just when most of the habitual movers were gone another boom ran green as the promise of spring over the hills and the hard-land tables. A third railroad was coming, the Pacific Short line, westward from O'Neill, between the new Burlington and the Northwestern, tapping the hay country, the sandhills, and Mirage Flats. Eight hundred miles of grading was to be let immediately. Once more the settlers pounded the trails westward, some who had gone on reversed their dust. The new railroad would bring work and ready cash, markets for produce, lift land values sky high.

Jules took the excitement calmly. "The country's bound to grow," he had said from the start. The various booms and their dying echoes agitated him little. A community can't be planted like a potato patch, all in a day; a wilderness can't be tamed in a year. It took the drilled Roman legions generations to roll back the European frontiers.

"You can never get anybody to stick to a thing long enough to finish it. If it don't go like hell all the time

they quit. Then you got to start all over again, with new
men. Only a few got the intelligence to see more than a
day ahead, to keep their sights raised from mountain sheep
when there's only pack rats around. Here, along the
river, you see how it goes. The ignorant spend all their
ammunition shooting at mud hens and hell-divers and shite-
pokes because they make a lot of noise and are tame. In
the meantime the geese go by. Then when they can't eat
the fishy stuff they shot, they cuss and say the hunting's no
good."

"Your tongue's swinging loose like them newfangled
windmill things some's putting up to do their pumping," a
land seeker from down on the Platte told him.

The railroad did n't come and the penniless movers that
never got a start helped pile up county pauper bills. The
Farmers' Alliance was gaining strength. Jules went to the
meetings now and then, to talk deep cultivation instead of
organization. And at Adaton, north of Rushville, a Populist started the *Farmers' Hope*, immediately nicknamed
Farmers' Soap by the Republicans. But that did not help
scatter the dark cloud of Populism rising relentlessly on the
political horizon.

Gradually the cattlemen realized that the settlers were
flocking to the watering places and the meadows like flies
to syrup. When whole herds of stock vanished from the
range, the hated settlers were blamed. The cattlemen from
the mountains of Wyoming to the corn lands of Nebraska
organized against rustlers, the term stretched to include
anyone not connected with a ranch pay roll.

"Rustling ain't a hoe man's job. Takes a good cow hand
to run two-three hundred head of wild stuff out of the
country," Jed Brown, an old cowboy himself, remarked.

It was rumored again that a gang of thieves was butchering and shipping beef in big lots from the south road. Five
sheriffs from the north Panhandle counties combed the hills.

They found a few buried hides with the Newman brand. No signs of the other stock reported missing.

Even the older cowmen laughed — out of the wrong corner of their mouths, Jed Brown said. Any rustler worth his rope and running iron knew enough to cut out the brands unless he left them deliberately as a blind. The settlers did n't laugh at all. They knew that if anyone was charged with the rustling it would n't be any of the Hunter or Newman outfits. Jules hunted the brush and the bluffs and twice he let a flock of quail flush and disappear before he lifted his gun. He had many thoughts. At night he moulded bullets, reloaded shells, and cleaned a rifle or two not used since the Civil War.

On Pine Ridge in 1890 the Messiah craze was spreading among the agency-starved Sioux. A holy man had risen far to the west, one who promised the old buffalo days again, with the white man swept from the earth as the chinook clears the snow from the red grass. John Maher, of Chadron, kept the New York papers full of stories of depredations and atrocities. Jules complained. "Eastern people don't know better. They may believe them." But the stories made good reading.

And down in the Niobrara a feud was started, a feud that was to keep Jules's community in turmoil for years, break officials, undermine banks, almost bankrupt the county, drive three people to the asylum, and arouse hatreds that would live long after the leaders were dead.

From Baltimore Dr. Walter Reed wrote that he was studying his beloved bacteriology at last. Jules read the letter while the fire licked the lead kettle. He did not re-call the doctor's prediction: "This country will develop, but not until the soil is soaked in misery and in blood."

Across the river from Henriette's place lived Henry Freese, a thin, soft-spoken, pious little man with a watery nose. And since the first curl of smoke rose from his chimney towards the top of Indian Hill, there had been trouble in the community. His dogs ran the neighbors' colts into the barbed wire until Jules found one of his yearlings with its breast laid open red to the bone. The next time he saw the dogs on his place he picked them off, one after the other, as one might knock over clay pigeons at a county fair, as simply as he dropped bullets into the sand spot on Indian Hill.

It was soon after that the long rope, tied to Henriette's wagon in the quicksand, vanished. And all that summer mysterious fires broke out and only constant vigilance saved the homes, the crops, and the range of the community.

The Rushville people, fearing the rapid settlement and unification of the Flats, the Niobrara, and Pine Creek, favored this Freese who passed as a religious man. He called frequently upon God, not more frequently or more familiarly than is customary in a frontier community, but he called upon Him in a voice full of piety. And like Elijah he saw fire descend from heaven and he predicted where it would strike.

"Religion crazy," Jules said, "a most dangerous form of insanity." But he still used Indian Hill as a target.

"It is perhaps better if you do your target shooting elsewhere — " Eugenie told him when she came back from Rushville. "M. Freese has been making the complaint."

"I shoot target where I please. I found the country open and free," Jules shouted, pounding the table. Henriette wiped up his spilled coffee in silence. Eugenie, not married to him, was not so easily silenced.

"It is not well, but I have warned you."

The next week the sheriff took Jules away. Because of the old settler's influence with the voters of Running Water precinct and the Swiss settlement on Pine Creek, the county judge decided upon a compromise of advice.

"You say you were n't shooting at Freese but at a sand spot on Indian Hill?"

"I got four witnesses to prove it."

"Let us say you have. Now whose land is this Indian Hill on?"

"On Freese's."

"Then have you the right to use it for a target range?"

"You damn right I have, Judge. I came into this country when nobody was living here and shot at that sand spot with the Indians."

"Would you be willing to let Freese use the hill behind your, or rather your wife's, house as a target?"

Jules scratched his beard. "No, I don't consider him competent to handle a gun." He laughed all the way home.

Various reports of the encounter reached the river, and somehow all of them conveyed the impression that the judge had been bested. At least others had not got off so well. When Freese had Jake Morse arrested for attacking his fourteen-year-old girl the community had been aroused. Murder they might overlook, but not this. When half a dozen silent men armed with Winchesters tied their horses in Jules's yard he went out to meet them. They talked a long time, sitting on their heels, drawing figures in the dust with sticks, not lifting their eyes.

For once Jules counseled caution. He was pleased that they came to him, but they had better wait a week. Jake Morse was a steady man and a good farmer with a little money in the bank. There was the Kapic case a couple of years ago. Only quick work by the sheriff saved Kapic from a lynching, but before the case came to trial it turned out to be plain blackmail — an attempt to get money from a settler who had a few dollars. The men nodded to each other. It was so.

"When I see need for a mob I'll lead you," Jules told them.

The settlers scattered to their homes. Before long Freese

offered to settle out of court.   Everyone knew by now that
Morse was innocent.   On the advice of the men who would
have hung him not long before, he gave Freese enough for
shoes for the family, and the case was dropped.

Next it had been Rudolph Mutsch, an inoffensive, meek
little German with a shack against a bluff down the river.
He was arrested for shooting one of the Freese cows —
breachy animals, into everybody's crops.   The cow died outside the Mutsch corn, bloated like a bladder, but the entire
Freese family went to Rushville to swear they saw little Rudolph shoot her.   Because Jules did n't trust the county officials he advised settlement out of court.   The next day the
Freese cows came home with heavy pokes on their necks, put
on by neighbors to prevent their fence crawling.   The God-
fearing owner apparently looked upon the planks as so
much lumber sent by heaven.   He used them on his hog
pen.

Now he was after Jules.

"Nobody 's safe with a man like that in the country,"
Jules told Hans and Emile as he poured hot lead into his
bullet mould.   Henriette said nothing, but her face was
haggard, her hair laced coarsely with gray.

"Somebody hear you talk like that mabby mak' you
trouble, mabby tak' post office away," Anton Smolka suggested as he spit out his tobacco and licked the flap of a
letter to his wife in Poland.

The next week the sheriff was out again.   Before the
judge at Rushville Freese claimed that Jules shot at him
across the line fence, trying to kill him for fifteen minutes.
The judge, who had shot target against the accused and
hunted quail with him, looked down upon the sniffling
plaintiff.   "You don't seriously expect me to believe that.
You 'll have to bring a better story than that.   Everybody
knows that this man is a crack shot."   But Jules was placed
under a peace bond.

The next morning he came back to the river in a cold, oathless rage. Henriette saw that his eyes were like smoky agates and fearfully approached him with the suggestion that he go on a hunt. Young Boston had left word he saw two deer up Pine Creek, in the Hippach range. It would be good to have fresh meat. She did not say that Freese was talking visions of fire again as he did before the Blackman barn burned down and before Lever lost all his range. Another fire would bring trouble. The deer were fine young bucks, Young Boston had said.

That night Henriette watched alone at the dark windows overlooking the yard. At the slightest noise she slipped out, a gaunt, angular ghost armed with a garden hoe. Across the river the Freese grain stacks reddened the night.

Once more Jules was arrested. This time for burning his neighbor's grain, uninsured but carrying a heavy mortgage. Some said eight hundred dollars, others fourteen hundred, on the three stacks of hailed grain. It looked as though the bank might get the money now, for Freese and his entire family swore they saw Old Jules riding around the stacks with a burning torch, firing one after another until they all burned high.

The old settler was violent but not uneasy. He had spent the night at the Hippach hay camp with half a dozen hay waddies. They all remembered the event clearly because he brought in a deer and deer were getting scarce. After supper they sat around a mosquito smudge and listened to Jules tell stories of the early days. The next morning he cooked deer liver for them and then started the fifteen miles home with a quarter of venison across the back of his saddle.

When the case came up the settlers looked uneasily over the cattleman representatives packing the front of the courtroom, strangers among them, strangers with Eastern clothes, Eastern money. Perhaps Old Jules was right. Perhaps the cattle outfits were using Freese to run the locator out of the country.

From the first it was clearly not a question of evidence. Would the settlers on the jury sell out to the ranchers? Jules watched them file out. Last went Dickerson, whose wife and baby he had saved the winter before. And with him was Manson, the man Jules had driven from his place. The old settler limped slowly away and had no words even for Big Andrew when he came.

In the end the jury disagreed.

But in the meantime Jules and Henriette signed a warranty deed for the place on Mirage Flats to Thomas for a thousand dollars. "My land," Jules grieved, "that cost me my good foot." But lawsuits are expensive. Freese borrowed too, also from Thomas, cashier of the bank holding the mortgage on the burnt wheat.

"No matter how it come out," Jules told Henriette, "they clean out the settlers."

Yes, it looked that way.

When several prominent Rushville and Gordon sports, including Jules's most active enemies, came to the river with jugs and guns, they stopped at the old settler's place. They sneaked up on a flock of Canada geese on a sand bar and emptied their expensive guns with no result except a sharp, metallic echo.

"I am a dangerous man. I shoot at people, destroy property, but when the Rushville gang wants game they shoot my decoys full of holes!" Jules laughed, his mouth full of roast goose.

Before winter set in Jules was in jail again, charged with attempting to do great bodily injury to one Freese. Down on the river and along Pine Creek, particularly among the men with whom Jules spent the night of the grain burning, there was a growing resentment. This thing had gone far enough. Repeated complaints at Rushville against

Freese as a pyromaniac brought no results. He was destroying the peace of an entire community and still nothing
could be done.

"Up at Rushville they think only ruffians could fail to
appreciate the good man Freese," Hans said.

When the first case against Jules, for alleged assault on
his neighbor, came to court, it was discharged and the costs
taxed to the plaintiff. The old settler rode home singing,
and those along the way knew that it was good with him;
perhaps there was to be justice here after all.

And then word came that the Indians were out.

Ever since the reduction of rations in 1887 there had
been trouble at Pine Ridge Agency. The Messiah craze,
spreading from the west, aggravated the situation, bringing
the Sioux an illusion of hope. Perhaps the white men
could be driven forever from the plains. Then once more
the Great Father would send the buffaloes forth from the
caves of the south, to spread as a moving black robe over
the grasslands northward.

Everywhere there was talk of another Indian war.
"They are not hurting anybody," Jules reasoned. But even
those closest to him recalled the annihilation of Custer and
advocated troops. The first squaw men and breeds that
slipped into Rushville and Gordon asking protection sent
the settlers into a panic. Not a week before three young
Sioux had been to the Niobrara looking for Jules, who was
in jail. Henriette barred the door and cried for them to
go away. A long time they sat on the hog-pen fence, waiting
for their friend. Finally they rode into the darkness and
all the night Henriette sat at the window, watching.

When Agent Royer whipped his lathered team into
Rushville, shouting that the Indians were on the warpath,
the town loafers fled into the saloons, expecting to hear
bloodcurdling whoops at their heels. An hour passed, two,
and still the plain to the north was bare. "Them there In-

dians you was telling about — they musta broke the other way," an old mule skinner told the agent. But Royer had wired for troops and would not return to the agency until they came.

Jules rode up to Rushville, seeking word of his friends. Not a fire smouldered in the camp ground across the tracks. Towards evening General Miles stopped the old settler and asked him to join his forces as scout.

"You mean hunt Indians?" Jules asked, so astonished he dropped the butt of his rifle to the ground.

"Yes, shoot Indians, if it comes to war. They need fire-arms, and their old guns repaired. You could get through and talk them into coming in to the agency. It's for your protection, remember, yours and your Niobrara country."

Jules took his pipe out of his mouth and looked this general of the United States Army up and down. With his thumbs hooked in his leather belt, he was very important and just a little condescending to the shabby, crippled foreigner.

"Hunh —" Jules grunted, putting his pipestem back into his beard. "I have lost no Indians. You lose any, you hunt for them." Turning, he pushed through the crowd that gathered. There was a weak laugh or two. Not much. Few felt as safe as the trapper from the Running Water.

Up on the Flats, against Jules's amused protests, the new-comers stopped their work, ran their teams together, turned the freezing earth on Tom Sears's place, the nearest approach to a hill they could find, and threw up a sod fortress. The only opening in the lower floor was a double plank door. The upper section jutted out with gun slits, planned accord-ing to an old cut of a blockhouse in the school histories. Here the timid came to sleep.

"A death trap like a sheep pen for a gray wolf if the Sioux really were after them," Jules snorted when he saw.

General Miles, remembering a little difficulty the United States Army had in getting the Cheyennes out of the sandhills once, sent his nephew down to Deer Creek where Jules had hunted with the Oglala. The young man put up at Modisetts' little sod ranch house occupied by the two spare Virginians and their mother. At night they barred the door and slept with guns beside them, but there was nothing more disturbing than the howling of coyotes before a storm.

The war news manufactured by the correspondents was so convincing that even the county sheriff believed in the danger and distributed rifles among the remoter settlers. Opportunely someone recalled the pile of bleaching bones once found on the Preston place on Pine Creek by the early settlers, with smaller bones — women and children. But Jules went about undisturbed.

By the fifteenth of November, 1890, the town of Rushville, the nearest railroad station to Pine Ridge, was swarming with war correspondents; even Theodore Roosevelt, writing for *Harper's*, was there. Buffalo soldiers, as the Indians called the curly-haired colored troops, swaggered through the little town. Impatient to shed blood and emboldened by the potent frontier whiskey, they declared a little war among themselves, whacking a few dark heads with revolvers and smashing a few mouths. After a week of this the citizens began to wonder if they did n't prefer the Indians, even ghost-dancing Indians. The Rushville *Standard* noted sadly that some of the high privates seemed less civilized than the Sioux. "If they are able to punish the redskins as they are red liquor there will not be an Indian left in two weeks." But the midwinter march of sixty miles to the wind-swept Pine Ridge cooled the buffalo soldiers.

December first the citizens of Rushville and vicinity called a meeting to which Jules was particularly invited. What had the Sioux done to justify troops on their reservation? But the business men saw that an Indian war meant freighting, a good market for local produce. A Rushville miller contracted 68,000 pounds of flour for the troops.

"Big government are always bulldozing somebody," Jules complained. A petition of protest was signed and sent to Washington. The Indians had withdrawn to the Bad Lands.

By the middle of December the excitement among the settlers had quieted down. Not an Indian had been seen, not a warwhoop heard, and the thermometer hovered about twenty below zero.

Then came the news of the shocking annihilation of Big Foot's band at Wounded Knee: men, women, and children mowed down by Hotchkiss guns while they and their sick chief were surrendering their pitifully inadequate arms and asking for the peace they had not broken.

Jules heard the news the same day at Rushville and rode up in the face of a coming storm. From a hill to the north he looked down over the desolate battlefield, upon the dark piles of men, women, and children sprawled among their goods. Dry snow trailed little ridges of white over them, making them look like strange-limbed animals left for the night and the wolves. Here, in ten minutes, an entire community was as the buffalo that bleached on the plains.

Although Jules shivered in the torn old army coat, he did not move for a long time, did not even know he was cold. When Old Jim snorted impatiently the man suddenly knew that he was very sick, sick as he had been at Valentine, six years before. Slowly he turned his horse with the storm.

That evening at Pine Ridge he heard of a wagonload of whiskey that came up from Rushville the day before the battle, and of the drunken soldiers. The next morning he started home. At the Rushville post office he wrote to Rosalie, the first letter in a long time. In it he poured out all the misery and confusion of what he had just seen. A deep pessimism held him. There was something loose in the world that hated joy and happiness as it hated brightness and color, reducing everything to drab agony and gray.

Back on the river Jules let rumor wash over him as he hunched over his bad foot beside the stove.   Pushed for his opinion, "A blot on the American flag," was all he would say.

"You damned foreigners is all the time running down the government.   If you don't like the way things is run here you kin go back where you come from," Dickerson answered him furiously.

"You talk like an ignorant fool!" Jules answered him in slow, cold words.

Dickerson waited for no more.   He went, and without paying for the gunstock Jules made for him early in the Indian scare.   Henriette scolded.   Why must he talk so to people?   Another enemy, and just when he needed friends. It was not good.

After the first few weeks the Panhandle treated the uprising as a joke, mostly on the Indians.   When a Chadron paper reported the finding of a petrified man near a stone fence not far from town, another editor commented: "Probably a hardened old sinner who laid down to wait for the Indian outbreak and fossilized waiting."

Jules and several of his neighbors bought Winchesters cheap from settlers who were getting over their fright. Jules polished his, blued the metal, smoked the sights, and bragged to Henriette of all he could do with it.   Although he made no mention of his thoughts, he posed before Henriette's dresser with the gun in the crook of his arm.   But his eyes could never be impersonal as those of the man he saw in the saloon in Valentine.

February came in warm, breaking the bitter cold of December and January.   Snow water ran in the rutted roads, filled the gullies, and scarcely skinned over with ice at night. The settlers hitched up and went to town.   They got news. The officers in charge of the soldiers at the battle of Wounded Knee stood court-martial.   But nothing seemed to come of it, and the dead were dumped frozen into long trenches and covered like so many blackleg cattle. The ghost dancers had surrendered, subdued, broken; their religious rites forbidden. But to the settlers the chief topic was the weather.

"Looks like we'll be sowing wheat in a week or so," an optimistic Easterner said.

Jules's freighter friend from Valentine, hauling for the government, twisted his fingers into his moustache. "Sowing wheat, like hell! You'll be sitting on the stove lids a-keeping your tobacco juice from freezing."

The next day was even warmer, but midafternoon a swift gray cloud bore down upon the hard-land region. The wind turned the soft mud to iron under the horses' feet. Powdery snow filled the air. A young woman living six miles out of Rushville started home to her year-old baby just before the storm. Four days later, when the sun shone warm again over the glistening, drifted plains, she was found curled up in a blanket in the slat-bottomed cart, a mile from home, frozen.

When the snow softened and the roads were passable the mail carrier brought Jules a letter from Rosalie, the first in three years. He had tried to compose a note to her in November, when he wrote holiday letters to his family and friends in the Old Country. He wanted to pour out all the distilled venom of his repeated arrests, the sense of persecution that was growing on him. Even Henriette, who had endured one thundering rage after another for almost four years, now sometimes gave the man as good as he sent, both in curses and in blows. "This is my place," she could always remind him.

But as he wrote he remembered that Rosalie had failed him, and he crumpled the sheets together and threw them into the wood box. Henriette found them there. "I do with this like you do with mine three years ago!" Between thumb and forefinger she carried the ball to the outhouse.

"I don't give a damn," Jules called after her. "Neither

one of you is worth a damn to me," and for the moment he was convinced of it.

But to-day he had a reply to the letter he wrote to Rosalie after the massacre of Big Foot's band.   She, too, was angry at the slaughter of the Indian women and children.   "It is inhuman, this America!" she wrote.   She inquired of his health, his family.   Had he any children?

But the next paragraph drove everything from his mind except the Rosalie he knew so long ago.   "I cannot explain to you my delight," she wrote, "in hearing from him for whom I shall always keep in my heart the best place.   *Ich liebe dich so sehr*.   One day, my dear Jules, you sent back my photograph, piercing my heart.   An unhappy day for both of us."

Twice she referred to her last letter, written all in German, in answer to his photograph and his request that she come to him immediately.   He had never answered.   What was she to think?

Jules had no oaths now.   He was drained dry as an old buffalo head and as lifeless.   His pipe lay cold on the floor, forgotten.

He had received no such letter.   If he had — ah, the whole miserable mess of quarrels, lawsuits, unhappiness — all would have been avoided.

Slowly he put the letter into his stamp collection and called to Henriette to saddle his horse.   No answer; her cart was gone.   He caught up his horse himself, rode away from the place, without direction, without attention.   Once, twice, Old Jim stopped at fences.   He got off, kicked the staples from the posts, led his horse over the wire and went on.   He met several riders, but gave no sign.

Hours later Old Jim stopped at a corral gate.   Jules looked up.   The squatty buildings of the Green place. Three of the grown sons, lanky six-footers, with long black hair hanging to their shoulders, gathered about him.   Old Jules must be sick or drunk or crazy.   Never had they known him to look upon anyone without acknowledgment in his eye.

"Oh, git away with you — you passel of fools! Run and fetch me the old man's pipe and 'baccy and that bottle with a nip in 't!" Ma Green ordered as she led the man to the low rambling sod house. While Jules took a drink of whiskey from the bottle, and smoked the pipe a big fellow held out to him, Ma fried a steak that just fitted her big skillet, with onions simmering around the edges.

And while Jules ate she told him how the other small cattlemen were trying to run her boys out of the country, accusing them of stealing cattle. Well, she was n't saying they did or did n't. How did the others get such a fast start, two yearlings for every cow and buying none?

"But the Old Man don't want no trouble. He 's talking of getting out," Ma Green kept repeating. "The trouble is, we ain't got no pull to Rushville, no friends where they counts."

At last Jules raised his head.

"Tell the Old Man to stay — and if they bother him — come to me."

The next morning Jules started back home primed for a scorching letter to the Post Office Department. It must have been Lamoureau, hired by the cattlemen to hold up his letters, or to missend them; working against him so he could n't get a good wife, so he 'd have to leave the county, and with him the settlers who looked to him for protection, for courage to stay. Particularly to keep him from bringing in more.

Even now he ignored the paragraph saying, "If you had remained in Zurich we would have been so very happy, or if you had come back as I asked so prettily and humbly in German."

The Freese grain-burning case was coming to trial again early in May. Jules's attorneys, Westover, who had moved to Lincoln, and Harrington of O'Neill, with practice defending vigilantes, warned him to prepare his case well and indicated how much money he must raise before the trial — two hundred fifty dollars. Where would he get that much? So he let everything go, did nothing except save the letter he got from Young Boston, the brother of Freese's wife, at David City, now, in business: —

DEAR FRIEND:

Mr. Freese and his wife have written letters here trying to bribe us witnesses now. If you wish to use these letters next spring you must not neglect it. I have written to Westover about the letters. Freese has written some letters down here that are terrible. I wish you could see them. You must not fail to have them given in as testimony. They will help you and I think clear you.

I hope you will make good use of them. When will district court set?

Very respectfully,
A. W. BOSTON

The little town was full as for a celebration the day of Jules's trial, but there was little hilarity. The gaunt, burned men gathered in little knots, not talking much. Here and there a half-drunken cowboy with his palm on his gun joked of the fool hoe men that ought to be run out of the country.

"Don't pay any attention," Elmer Sturgeon warned Jules. "You can't afford to lose your head to-day. You 've plenty friends if you just don't get excited."

Court was called and along the back of the room sat the river, the Flats, and the Pine Creek crowd, together, without talking. Freese looked at them once and then his eyes kept to the floor.

The jury found Old Jules not guilty.

"Well, I 'm glad you came out all right, Jule," Johnny Burrows told him.

"Come out all right? I had to mortgage my place, probably lose it, to defend myself."

"Yeh, I guess you and the bank did n't make much.   Nobody did, but the lawyers and hotelkeepers and the livery
stables."

But Jules sang most of the way home as he had when he
brought Henriette to the river the first time.   Without a
hat, her gray hair flying, she drove the team and hoped that
this time the peace would last.

The *Standard* seemed glad too.   The Niobrara feud had
cost the county two thousand dollars, but it was over at last.

One warm evening in middle June Jules tied Minten's
mail in a roll, and with his shotgun over his arm he left,
saying he might see a cottontail for breakfast in the brush
somewhere.   Henriette was sitting on the doorstep, her
lined, leathery face between her hands.

"Don't talk too late," she answered, not caring particularly.

When the yard and the well-kept garden beyond were
lost in the gray of night that crept like fog from the bluffs
and canyons Henriette straightened up.   One pale bar of
light from between two dark clouds in the west reached
towards the zenith.   Lightning flashed far away, a mere
wink of light on the eyeball.   Probably it would not rain.
It never rained, she said, speaking aloud, perhaps to the low
star burning steady as a lamp above the Freese house across
the river.   Frogs croaked and a low gurgle and smell of the
river came up to her on the night wind rustling the cottonwoods.

She stretched her stiff legs and went into the house, feeling about for matches.   With the lighted kerosene lamp in
her hand she started towards the table.   As she passed the
uncurtained window the bowl burst in her hand, crashing
the room into darkness.

A second Henriette was paralyzed.   Then, as a heavy shot
boomed up and down the river valley, she dropped to the
floor, into the stinking wetness of the kerosene, the broken

glass cutting her hand. But she did not notice. Clawing along the wall, she found the open door and ran between the clumps of buffalo berry that tore at her dress and her hair — towards Minten's, calling, "Jules, oh Jules!"

At the foot of the hill she met him. He had heard the shot from the Minten place. Together they went back to the yellow-windowed house at the top of the bluff. The group of men in the kitchen looked up at the hurrying steps, exclaiming when they saw Henriette's face, blood-streaked where she flung back her hair with her cut hand as she ran.

The calm, bulky Mrs. Minten washed Henriette's face while Jules dressed and bound up the bleeding palm. Then the men, five dark, silent figures in the night, armed with rifles and an unlit lantern, slipped down to the house at the edge of the river. They surrounded the place, but found nothing outside. By the lantern light they inspected the inside, the broken lamp, the oil spot, the blood. Across from the open window was a hole in the wall. Carefully Jules dug the bullet from the soft wood with his skinning knife. He looked at it, passed it around in the light of the lantern.

"I never see one like that before," George Minten said.

"I have." Jules scratched his beard and took another look at the base and the rifling. "The gun belongs to Jacob Schwartz."

The roadhouse Schwartzes. The men considered that a moment.

"We better look into it," Big Andrew said. The dark circle about the lantern nodded.

"Yah, to-morrow," Jules told them, and then they went away into the night.

Henriette sat at the dark window until dawn spread an ash-gray light over the yard. Jules slept, but not in bed. He carried a feather tick into a corner of the kitchen, hitting the table and chairs and swearing softly through the darkness.

The next forenoon he rode through the mist over the

Flats and along the river. He wanted only certain followers. Youths of sixteen and eighteen he turned away. "No
excitable fool kids," he told them, to their intense disappointment.

That afternoon twenty men rode in silence through a slow
whisper of rain to the Schwartz place at the edge of the
chophills, the range country. Old Jacob gave one look at
the ring about him in the yard and began to shake like a
chilled puppy. Jules turned his horse so the Winchester
across his saddle pointed at the quivering mouth of the gray
little man.

"We come to get your rifle," he said.

"But I have not got any," he pleaded, rubbing his bony
hands together.

"Oh, come off! Did n't I repair it for your boy this
spring?"

When the man still denied the possession Jules produced
the heavy bullet, like the mashed end of a finger, told him
where he found it, and demanded the gun again. The
frightened man looked around the dark faces, the cold eyes,
and began to cry into his moustache, admitting that his wife
had lent his rifle to Freese two days before.

"With ammunition?"

"*Ja,* with ten shells."

In a lope the men rode back to the Niobrara, before any
of the Schwartz boys could circle to the river and warn
Freese. Two of the crowd were sent ahead to get him away
from his house and the rifle. Then the rest rode out of the
canyon down upon the house. Jules stopped his horse on
a knoll, keeping his Winchester leveled upon Freese while
the rest got the old gun and five shells, all he had left.

One of the cartridges was fetched to Jules. He pulled
the bullet with his teeth, compared it with the one from his
wall. The base and the heft were identical. The men,
holding Freese by the arms, had stopped to watch. Now,
without a word from Jules, they set to work, packing the

family into a wagon. The man shook. The woman cried a little, quietly. That was all. The children flattened themselves against the sod wall of the house, as so many little antelope might hug the ground.

Once the little man tried to run away between two horses, into the brush. They brought him back with a rifle in his ribs. With a rope around his neck and over a branch of a cottonwood they swung him off his feet and then let him down. On his knees, now, with his prayers to the mob, he admitted getting ten shells, shooting over his own house to scare his family. Yes, and through Jules's window. He stopped. They swung him from the ground once more. "Yes, yes, so Mr. Jules would get the blame," he cried in a high, frightened voice. He would leave the country, never bother any of them again. Only let him go. Against the sod wall his family waited.

The men got on their horses and in a silent semicircle they watched the pitiful wagon, with its weeping woman and huddled children, draw away into the thickening rain. The squash of the wheels on wet river bottom and the crack of leather lines across the horses' flanks came back to the watchers.

Jules turned and splashed his horse through the river and into his yard. Henriette unsaddled, went in and gave her man his supper, and let him go to bed without questions. That night the community razed the Freese place, tearing it as buzzards would a rabbit. One man cut his hand on a broken pane, another was caught under a falling ridgepole. By morning the place was as one where a house had stood years ago. No block of sod was left upon another.

The next day the sheriff and three deputies came down and demanded Jules's gun, which they did not get. But there was no way to prevent the arrest of the entire mob. The creditors of Freese were once more hopeful. The mob arrested included, in addition to Jules and his brothers William and Emile, half a dozen other Swiss, a good sprinkling of Hollanders, Johnny Burrows and three other Iowans, Hans, Big Andrew, and Anton Smolka — the more prosperous settlers of the Flats, Running Water, and Pine Creek. The Rushville papers discussed the case. Old Jules had no right to run anybody out of the country, and when his rifle was demanded by the sheriff he should have given it up. On the other hand there was some color to his contention that he needed the gun for protection. Apparently his wife had a narrow escape. Besides, as the *Standard* pointed out, Charles Grayson, in no way connected with either faction and whose word none would doubt, said Freese came to him two nights before the mobbing claiming his wife and family were afraid Old Jules would kill them all. The next morning Grayson went down and found that Mrs. Freese had heard three or four shots after her husband left the house, but thought nothing of shooting in a community of hunters. What she wanted was peace.

Yes, it looked as though Henry Freese was either crazy, as his neighbors had insisted for two years, or that, for some reason, he was trying to influence the community and the Rushville officials against Jules, or perhaps both.

The morning of the preliminaries people milled through the little border town and flowed towards the building housing the court, breaking about its walls like the waters of a cloudburst about a settler's shack.

And when the doors opened, only a small part of them could get in. Court opened with thirty men armed with Winchesters standing around the back of the room. After a farcical half hour court was adjourned, the crowd dispersed, the doors locked. But eventually Jules was put under nine hundred dollars bond, which ten of his party signed immediately.

The balance of the mob were charged with assault and battery, pleaded guilty, paid fifteen dollars and costs each, and went home. In the meantime the grain-burning case, on which Jules had been tried twice, and found not guilty in

May, was revived.   Chances for a verdict against him looked good now.

"What sort of justice is this?" demanded Elmer Sturgeon, risking his neutrality in the Running Water feud.   Even Johnny Jones, connected with the bank holding the mortgages on the Freese property, admitted that reopening the grain case was paring the cheese pretty close to the rind.

Plainly the situation demanded open war with the officials at Rushville or a compromise until election.   War would bring bloodshed and the militia, for the governor was bound to uphold the local officers.   Jules's friends quietly felt out Freese, to buy him off, since money had always been his goal before.   But this time he was firm.

As before Jules refused to do anything about his defense or the raising of money for it, claiming he would take no voluntary part in such lawing.   Actually it was his characteristic apathy, his way of letting everything slide, neglecting everything except his meals, his postal service, his locating, and his experiments with fruit, grasses, and grains. He read more than ever — world news, bulletins on lucerne (alfalfa), hardy grains, prehistoric animals in America.   He talked these to his neighbors and to Henriette.   Several times he went up into the bluffs on the Koller and the John places where there were banks of volcanic ash and petrified snails, where fossil turtles were scattered down the washed slopes, and where a thigh bone fourteen inches across stuck from the soft rock.

At the fall term of court, Jules faced a strange judge, entirely unprepared, a suicidal procedure, his friends and his attorneys insisted.

The trial dragged on, with the customary crowd, the customary hedging, evasion, and perjury, the customary attempts to confuse the witnesses who could not understand English well.   The judge looked weary, bored, with distaste for his task sitting clearly at the corners of his lean mouth.   The spectators from the Flats and the Running Water began to move their feet uneasily.   Things looked bad for Jules, sitting with his fingers pressed along his nose, his rifle locked up in the sheriff's office.

When the evidence was in he asked permission to make a plea as he had always done before, and been refused. But this judge was a stranger. He looked down into the far-focused eyes of the early settler and nodded permission. The next second he was compelled to pound down the buzz of remonstrance and anticipation that swept the room like puffs of a coming storm over ripe wheat.

Jules rose to speak, his old hunting coat hanging in loose folds of buff duck about him. He opened his mouth and an eloquent flow of impassioned German, held back for two years, broke over the jury, the courtroom. From far back twitters arose, then laughs, boot stampings; even a juror or two grinned. John Maher, court reporter and newspaper correspondent, scribbled like mad.

In a minute the entire court was up, the gavel pounding before the defendant stopped. How was the court to know what was being said? He must speak English.

Jules scratched his beard. He was sorry, but he was only a poor foreigner, come to find a home in America, the land of the free. He could not express himself well in English. Was there any law forbidding his use of German?

He bowed like a pine tree and let the battle of the attorneys pass over him, waiting with a patience strange and unnatural in him. At last an interpreter was brought in and once more Jules started, slowly, clearly, the interpreter wrinkling his brow and struggling with his words. Gradually Jules gathered speed. Suddenly he switched into French and despite the pounding gavel, and two men jerking at his sleeves, he ended in a fine bit of oratory, a plea for the settler, for protection against the cattlemen and their outside money, a plea for the little fellow in a world of powerful, selfish privilege, of gross corruption and graft, while the reporter scribbled on and the interpreter pawed his hair and sweat.

Long before Jules was through, the courtroom was in such

an uproar of laughter, clapping, and cheers at the discom-
fiture of the officials that no one heard the end. His attorney had the good sense to ask for dismissal. The chuckling judge consented, and the doors were almost rushed
from their hinges as the crowd poured out and down the
street to celebrate.

The judge beckoned to Jules and spoke very sternly over
his clasped hands. "See that you keep out of trouble in
the future. You will never get to make another plea in
this court."

Then his eyes twinkled; he gripped the early settler's
hand. "Man, I never heard anything like it. Learn to
do that in English and the sky's your limit."

Jules was halfway home before he remembered that he
had left Henriette in town.

The women of the Running Water wiped the worry of
lawing from their faces and looked hopefully to their husbands. Not Henriette. Jules, aggressive in his justifica-
tion, fought the battles over and over. His neighbors could
walk away from him, but not his wife. She heard it late
into the night. And in the morning while her husband
snored she pounded the stove lids and banged the water
bucket until he awoke and cursed her from the bed. Finally
at ten one morning she emptied the wash basin upon his
head and then, her hair flying gray strings in the wind, drove
her cart away towards town. From the doorway, his ragged
underwear dripping, he called her foul names. Standing
up in her cart she hurled her challenge in his face, defying
the rifle in his hand.

"Is it then not my bed — this where you rot in laziness?"

But the damage case against the mob was unsettled. The
Freese property was undeniably destroyed and, although
there were no witnesses, the mob was considered guilty.
Anticipating this, Jules and Henriette deeded their land to

William's new wife, Lena, the sister of Louis Pochon. His followers did the same. Freese got a judgment of $1000 against the mob and $650 against Jules for the wheat.

"I don't believe that would stand in any real court — not after you was acquitted once," Elmer Sturgeon said, risking his neutrality again.

Jules pounded his pipe against his palm and refilled it.

"I don't intend to pay a damn cent. More than that — I got suits against Thomas that will have to be settled."

He was gone most of the month before election. Once he got clear up to Chadron and spent a pleasant evening talking to John Maher, who could never hear too much of the Switzerland, the birthplace of this Jules. Most of the time he talked politics about the fringes of his community where the Niobrara feud was only an interesting diversion. And January first brought in an entirely new courthouse ring.

In Neuchâtel Elvina talked only of America and this place that they call the Running Water, where the brothers found so much of high adventure. At last the father lifted his hand for silence.

"Next month we sail."

Elvina and her father had been in America a long time now, almost a year. Much of that time the peace-loving old Swiss spent with Paul on the Platte. He was confused by the silent animosity between Jules and his wife. But the turmoil of the Niobrara troubles was really too much for him, although his brothers, Paul and Louis, whom Jules had located along the river, and those strange young men, his own sons, seemed to endure it well enough. Even Elvina married into the feud when they first came; married the sober, hard-working Johnny Burrows.

Before the father returned to Neuchâtel he came to the Niobrara to bid them a kind good-bye. They had one last evening together in Henriette's kitchen-living room. The next morning his leave-taking was interrupted by a loud fighting in the pigpen.   Henriette ran out.   With her hoe she fought the old boar from the litter of pigs he was eating despite the sow's vicious slashes at his eyes and ears.

"You are a good wife, my daughter," the father told Henriette.   "You have your husband's interest at heart. The pig he is not to be censured, but locked up.   He cannot know that he does this thing because some day these young will take his place."

"I 'll fill him full of lead!" Jules threatened.

"Do not excite yourself.   Shut him up, by all means, and restrain the act.   The urge you cannot deny."

"Urge, hell!   Damn cussedness!"

The father shook his head, still disturbed by the undercurrent of conflict that always ran so close to the surface with him and this eldest, this son of whom he would so gladly have been proud.

On the way to Hay Springs they stopped at Elvina's poor little sod home on the Flats and then went on.   Weary and ill, the old Swiss hunched into himself on the board seat beside Jules and wondered at the courage of these children he had fathered — even the delicate Elvina giving up an easy and secure life for an American hut of blocks of earth. And Emile living in the ground, as an animal in its burrow.

While the father waited for his train a horsebacker dashed up to tell him that his daughter had just given birth to a girl child.

"It was quick — good to be so quick," he said.   "Not three hours since I saw her moving about her work."

But he did not go back.   He must return to Neuchâtel, and swiftly.   He took the train East and never saw any of these wanderers again.

By the first of March Thomas proffered a settlement that Jules could find commensurate with his victory.   The patented quarter of Freese's land was deeded to Henriette, sub-

ject to a mortgage for $575; he surrendered Jules's note
for $850 and canceled his mortgage for $1850. He satisfied the $650 judgment for the burnt wheat, settled with
Attorney Westover for the defense fees, and gave Jules a
relinquishment for the Freese homestead. In return the
man from the Running Water signed a mortgage for $675
and promised that he and his followers would resume
friendly relations with the banks in which Thomas was interested.

It was a typical pioneer settlement involving days of
abusive talk. When it was finally signed and witnessed by
Sol Pitcher and Green from the sandhills Henriette threw
down the pen and pounded her team homeward, leaving
Old Jules in Rushville afoot.

The Niobrara feud was over.

It was over, except that none of the mob, including Jules,
could own attachable property until the Freese judgment for
$1000 was outlawed; over except that the county was in
debt $5000 for its three years of lawing.

Several disastrous and mysterious fires in town soon convinced Rushville business men that they had a pyromaniac
on their hands. Henry Freese was pushed on once more,
the asylum this time. And down on the Running Water
Henriette threw Jules's guns and traps into the road and
went to Rushville for her divorce.

VIII

RAIN MAKERS AND A HUNT TO THE BIG HORNS

THE early nineties were so dry even the old-timers wondered if it would ever rain again in the Panhandle. They had learned not to expect too much moisture in June or July, but when the young August moon, horned as an antelope, settled into the black wool bed of the horizon, and the hay was down, there should be rain.

All summer the homesteaders cultivated deep, under the spur of hunger, cracking the clodding earth, trying to maintain the mulch Old Jules believed would hold the moisture. But there was none to hold. They watched the skies until their eyes were like old wounds, and still it did not rain. A man on Box Butte Creek fortunate enough to get a shower from a June thunderhead won first prize for winter wheat at the state fair.   But on the Flats the wheat never headed; oats sat white and curled as grass, the root soil baked and cracked.

About the time the clouds of blackbirds from the painted wood of the river darkened the fields in search of nubbins, the settlers began to leave. The Iowa colony went first, leaving only Elmer Sturgeon and Johnny Burrows. Several of them had shipped in carloads of goods and stock. They let their claims go to Eastern loan companies for the money they once needed for cattle, horses, implements, seed, wire, lumber. They drove out with nothing except a crow-bait team and wagon. Scarcely were they over the horizon before their homes were torn down and hauled away by those who needed the lumber to hang on a little longer.

First the stores, then the banks of the Panhandle, went bankrupt. Of the four banks in Rushville only one weathered these years.

"Now is the time to buy land cheap," Jules pointed out, but there was no money — and his father with five thousand dollars out at 2 per cent in the Old Country. Jules did not go to Mirage much any more. To him a hundred sixty acres of wild Susans was not a field of gold but a field going back to sod, a dead venture.

Rain makers arose. In eastern Nebraska a Pawnee Indian promised a shower for ten dollars, a soaking rain for twenty. Someone gave him a jug of whiskey and the hail pounded the grass into the ground. It was a good story, told not without envy.

At Goodland, Kansas, Melbourne and his assistants produced half an inch of rain within forty-eight hours for a thousand dollars. They were given the same offer at Sidney, south of the Platte. Jules, mounted on a sturdy pinto he got from the Indians for two eagles, rode down with several of the Flatters. From their horses they watched the three men carry a long black box into an old barn, well guarded. Three times a day baskets were taken in full of food and came out empty. Once, the second day, the sky clouded over and awe swept the watching crowd like wind in a young field of wheat. Thunder rumbled, a few heavy drops splattered like shot in the dust, the wind blew, and the sun was out with a double rainbow.

"I'll keep catching skunks for a living," Jules told his neighbors.

Rushville tried powder and the Flats, both the Lutherans and the Catholics, prayer. Some said that the church steeples split the clouds. Jules laughed — only empty houses with the dead smell of religion in them.

When the settlers got clear down in the mouth a walking sky pilot appeared and called a revival at Alkali Lake, on the Flats, not far from Hay Springs.

"Would n't you jest know them critters 'd have to come to pester us! Ain't we got troubles enough as 't is?" Ma Green told Jules as she stopped her team for a rest at the river. The boys were haying and the freighting had to be done, so she had climbed the heavy wagon.

"Guess I kin handle them eight broncs 's well as anybody!"

She was timing her loading at Hay Springs so she would make Alkali in time for the revival.

Two days later she stopped while her horses blew before they took the long climb out of the river valley. It had been a fine spectacle, with folks thick as flies around a puddle of syrup, and that sky pilot, with his red beard cut like Christ's in the Sunday-school pictures, preaching hell and damnation from the back of a grasshopper buggy, and women crying and men ripping their only shirts. Then they all moved into the lake and the preacher stuck them under like so many old rag dolls until the Flats smelled of stale water and dead salamanders. "It done me more good to see that dirty parson get wet to his middle. I 'll bet he ain't ever had a bath all the way up."

Mrs. Schmidt, with eight children at home and a husband laid out behind a saloon somewhere, sang all the way home from the revival. The next week they sent her to the insane asylum and scattered the children. The youngest Frahm girl took pneumonia and died, and a lone Bohemian from the Breaks hung himself. Henriette came away sad. Only Ma Green seemed to have enjoyed it.

Still there was no rain.

The Mirage Flatters talked irrigation day and night, held meetings. Jules sent for government bulletins showing corn man-high with a little water. But when Pine Creek settlers sold out and bought land on the Flats, hoping to reap the irrigation profits, Jules protested. "Better stick to what you got."

Mirage Flats had the choice of drilling for artesian water

or depending on the flow of the Niobrara, one to two hundred feet below the level of the hard-land table. If they got the water up at Dunlap, south of Chadron, it meant ditching through twelve miles of waste land and building long flumes across Pepper Creek and Sand Canyon before they could apply a drop of water to the parched land. That would take money, much money. Those most able to help finance the project set their bearded faces against it. It was taking too great a chance with their last few dollars. Surely the Lord would provide, some said piously.

That was too much for Big Andrew, who had never spoken ten consecutive words at a meeting and who always hunched over his heels along the back wall of the schoolhouse, his head against the blackboard. He rose awkwardly to his feet, opened his mouth, and talked steadily for twenty minutes.

This was no time for caution or waiting on the Lord, he cried to them. They had waited and prayed; they had been cautious, and what did it give? Look across the Flats, so level and fine a farming land as God ever made smooth with trowel — and not grass enough this year on all of it to keep a sheep's ribs from wearing the wool off his sides. It gives crops when it rains. He pointed out half a dozen there who raised two and three thousand bushels of corn alone in good years. Water was all they needed. For three years it had not come; maybe it would never come. Now it was not the time for caution, but for courage; not for prayer and waiting, but for work. If they sank their last dollar in irrigation and lost, was that worse than if they did not try? A year or two longer, — at the best, — with more of them hanging from the ridgepoles by ropes and more getting free rides to Norfolk to the crazy house. In the end it was all gone anyway.

"Money I have nothing. But a good team I have — and a strong back for the scraper and two hard hands for the spade. Take them!"

When Big Andrew was through he saw for the first time
that every face was turned back toward him. Gulping,
he pulled his head into the protection of his shoulders and
sat down upon his heels, his ears standing out stiff and red
in embarrassment while hobnails and burlap-wrapped feet
gave their approval.

Mirage Flats would have irrigation.

While the hard-land settlers talked of artesian well and
surface irrigation, those along the Niobrara and Pine Creek
got along somehow. The wet years would come, Jules
preached, pointing to the rain graphs of the state. Nebraska
rainfall came in cycles. There must be wet years just ahead.

Hans looked at him dully. He had taken to drinking
lately and the last shreds of the boy his Anna kissed good-
bye were going. "It will be dry all the time," he said.
He would plant no more.

When the Flats no longer had socials and dances, no
longer saw anything amusing in the drouth parodies of
church hymns, the Pine Creek settlers and the small cattlemen took them up, singing lustily: —

> I've reached the land of drouth and heat,
> Where nothing grows for man to eat,
> The wind that blows with burning heat,
> O'er all our land is hard to beat.

> O! Nebraska land, sweet Nebraska land!
> As on your burning soil I stand,
> I look away across the plains,
> And wonder why it never rains,
> Till Gabriel calls, with trumpet sound,
> And says the rain has gone around.

These things did not amuse Jules. Part of the time he
batched in a shack he had moved to the Freese place, but

most of his time he spent at the post office. Usually Henriette did not object, even cooked for him now and then. Perhaps she met him with a pail of water in the face. Several times she drove him from her door with the hoe. There was no accounting for what a balky woman would do.

Often Jules rode the grub line, as the settlers called dropping in on the neighbors around mealtime, usually with something for the kettle: young prairie chicken, a mess of fish, or a sack of summer squash or carrots. Often, too, he made trips to Pine Creek or up to Box Butte to William's place to smoke and fight the battle with Freese all over again.

Even his brothers were ready to settle down to the dusty monotony of the corn plough, the security of hay in the stack and cow chips ricked tight and high for winter.

"Manure stink bad if you stir, stir all the time," Big Andrew suggested mildly, yet listening with more patience than any of the others. He never forgot his gratitude for a good farm when the rains came, for a quiet and industrious wife.

But Jules pounded his pony homeward in anger. The whole country was against him. He would pull up, go on a long hunt to the Big Horns, probably never come back.

He loaded his young pinto with rifle, ammunition, frying pan, and a couple of wolf traps, filled his pockets with several ounce bottles of strychnine and a supply of matches and tobacco. He was just a little sad as he rode over the short, browned grass of the Flats to meet Parsley, a young deer hunter.

Parsley was loaded down with heavy clothing, a buffalo coat, cap, mittens, and high overshoes. Jules had on an old hunting coat and four pairs of pants, only one of them not through at the knees.

Together they headed into the Northwest. When evening came they stopped with settlers, sheepmen, or ranchers, offering fresh game and good talk for their supper and bed. Sometimes they were taken for road agents or horse thieves, sometimes for officers or vigilantes, but the West still offered an open door to the traveler. Suspicion usually turned to cordiality before the promise of the strychnine bottle.

"All you gotta do is split a snowbird, put a pinch a this white stuff inside and drop it round the pens?" a sheepherder in a smoky wagon asked, the words coming slow as a wheel in deep sand.

"Yes, and the next day you pick up the coyote and skin him."

With a grunt the man granted them permission to stay in his wagon overnight and opened his last can of peaches for them. Along about noon the next day they stopped in a creek bottom and steamed the graybacks from their clothes.

They found the foothills of the Big Horns covered with light snow. In the thin timber they ran across a huge spoor, like the tracks of a squat man barefooted.

"Grizzly!" Jules whispered to his partner, and spurred his pinto ahead.

But Parsley hung back. They had passed lots of deer in the lowlands. Besides, he had a bad case of saddle-wolf. Maybe he 'd better not get too far from a ranch.

"Then go to hell!" Jules advised him, and followed the track alone, up through the light scrub timber. Here the huge claws tore up a mouse nest. There the animal lumbered through the thickets, leaving a low round tunnel behind. Finally the tracks led up a rocky gorge towards a sun-warmed cliff where the soft-footed pinto could not follow. Afoot, the man climbed the farther side and with his cap off he crawled to the edge.

Below him the bear lay curled up, sleeping in a crevice, his fur gleaming silver-frosted in the sun. For the first time in his life Jules's trigger finger shook. Raising his rifle again, he fired. The thick neck flattened, a hind foot jerked once and then lay still. The rock face across the canyon hurled the echo back to him.

It was almost dark when the thick hide was off. Jules rolled it up and sent it down the steep slope, guiding it between trees and gray boulders. That night he slept warm rolled in the fur side of the skin. The next morning he snubbed the pinto close to a sturdy young pine and by much manœuvring, puffing, swearing, and grunting he finally got the rolled hide over the saddle and tied securely under the pony's quivering belly. But as soon as the pinto's head was free he smelled of his load, snorted, jerked the bridle reins from Jules's hand, and tore away through the timber. When the horse was almost out of sight down the canyon a quarter of a mile away Jules raised his rifle and sent a bullet after the flying heels.

Then he calmed to the emergency. West and north were the mountains, the unbroken blue-black granite wall jutting high above the timber line, the rugged rock faces cut by streams of snow like the glaciers of the Alps. South and east the foothills sloped away to lone buttes and gray sagebrush plains. Somewhere, sixty miles across there, was the last ranch they had seen, sixty miles to travel on his lame foot, most of it without a tree for shelter or wood and a storm due any time. Southeast, about ten miles away, black tree tops, pine or cedar, snaked across the plain, probably clinging to the bluffs of a long canyon; a stream surely, with a trapper, or a sheepman — maybe an Indian.

Fortunately Jules had taken his rifle from the scabbard, hoping for a chance at game. Using it as a walking stick, he set out for the trees.

That night Jules camped in the river canyon cut deep through cross-bedding of gray and black, with a brownish seepage that he suspected was oil. In the protected pocket of a bend he built a fire, and between that and the bluff, on a bed of pine branches and grass, he baked his sore foot, cursed his luck, and finally slept.

The soft pad of hoofs in the loose escarpment below the bluffs aroused him. He sat up, his rifle across his knees, listening. Not far, faintly touched by the red of the dying fire, stood a horsebacker. Jules rolled himself out of the direct light and stood up, his rifle ready.

"What you want?"

"Oh, a Frenchman," the man said low, and reined his horse into the light. Jules dropped his gun to his arm in amazement. It was the man he had seen in Valentine with the beautiful Winchester.

"Heard anyone ford the creek the last hour or so?"

Jules rubbed his hand over his eyes. "I guess I been asleep. I was played out. My pony run away up in the mountains," he felt driven to explain.

"You mean that you are afoot here?"

"Yah, I shot a grizzly and the hide scare my — " He stopped. Together the men listened. From below the bend came a stealthy, slow swish of water.

"Stay here," the man warned, and keeping his horse to the soft wash along the foot of the bluffs he vanished noiselessly in the pale light of a hazy moon.

An hour later Jules was still smoking his clumsy chokecherry pipe and toasting his foot over coals. Once he thought he heard a shot, and finally he fell asleep. Something wet hit his face. He sat up, stretched himself, stiff with cold, and piled more wood on the fire. There it was again — snow. Now he was in for it. Last winter two men from Nebraska got caught in a storm in the Big Horns and froze to death. Searching parties went out to look for them, but they were n't found until spring — what the wolves left.

Forgetting his aching ankle, Jules built up a huge fire, and in its light he piled up a pine shelter against the bluff and gathered a big heap of firewood from the scrubby trees crowding the edge of the bluff as though driven to the very brink by the wind. He looked at the blackish strata. Lignite, probably.   He 'd find out when day came, dig in a ways, where it was n't air-slacked.   Then he lay back down, but not to sleep.   He would not let the snow drift over him, at least not yet.

Before the ground was completely white, hoofs boldly clattered up the rocky incline.   It was the man, back, with a pair of heavy-looking saddle bags he did n't have before, and leading a saddled horse.

"There 's a blizzard coming — no place for a crippled man afoot.   You better come with me."

"Where you going?"

"To shelter while I can.   Jump on this horse, if you 're coming.   We had better be riding."

After some difficulty with the animal, unaccustomed to approach on the off side, Jules was secure, his left knee through the stirrup strap, his foot comfortable.   Together they struck up a draw the way the man originally came.   In the darkness Jules smelled of the stickiness on his hand from the saddle.   Blood.

Ten days later, when the storm was over, the early snow shrinking from the foothills, Jules started home, headed for the Davis ranch; thirty miles due south to a cottonwood grove, and six miles east.   He rode a shaggy sorrel with long silver mane and tail, a good, easy traveler.   Once he looked back, but he could not locate even the approximate spot of the log house of his host.   A strange man, Jules thought.   He had come to the pass with him that morning to point out the shortest route.

"Another storm is blowing up, but Old Fox here will carry you through to-day.   All we ask is that you never ride him up this way, hey, Foxie?"

Gently the man Jules had seen at Valentine stroked the eager nose of his horse.   "So long," he said.

Before noon snow like corn chaff sifted from the gray sky and blew along in little swirls on the older, darker snow.

Just when Jules began to wonder whether he had missed the cottonwoods he saw the smoky gray mass. At its edge something dark moved, ran in circles, fell, and was up again. Jules pulled his rifle from the scabbard and spurred the sorrel.

By the time he neared the trees the dark thing was down under a fighting pack of gray wolves. Jules emptied his rifle into them, reloaded for the three escaped to a knoll. Two more went down, a bullet throwing snow as the last wolf vanished into a draw.

Tying the snorting sorrel securely, Jules limped to his kill. Five bloody-chested wolves lay dead about a big Hereford bull, the flesh of his hind quarters torn from the bone, his entrails strung over the bloody snow, his forefeet still pawing. A bullet through the head stopped the rolling eyes and the moving hoofs. On the knoll a tawny bitch dragged herself snarling over the snow. Jules killed her too and piled them all into a gray, bloody stack. Then he headed Old Fox towards the Davis.

At the ranch he told about the wolves. The ranch boss lifted one end of his heavy, graying moustaches and spit fastidiously. But Jules was so convincing that he sent two men from their game of seven-up into the storm.

"An' by God, Frenchy, if you 're lyin' we 'll stick you under the ice in the hoss tank when we gets back," they warned him.

It was late when the men brought the wolves in. Davis came into the bunkhouse, spit into the horseshoe tobacco box of sand beside the red-hot stove, and squatted on his heels next to Jules's chair.

Towards bedtime the foreman came in, his black moustaches ice-tipped.

"What in hell 's that Fox sorrel doing in this corral?" he demanded.

Not a jaw moved while Jules tapped the contents from his newly filled pipe absent-mindedly. "I rode him in."

Chairs scraped back. One fell with a clatter. Davis rose from the floor and stretched languidly.

"Keep your seat, Frenchy, now you got it warm," he advised. "I don't give a damn where you got that horse ner how. I said you was welcome and by damn you are, so long as you kill a gray now and then."

With that he stalked through the men and slammed the door on his spurs.

"For I'm a young cowboy an' I know I done wrong — "

somebody hummed in a rumbling monotone.

The foreman threw down his buffalo coat and went to the cookhouse for his supper. At the card table a deft brown hand dealt. Jules blinked and refilled his pipe.

The man from the Running Water stayed at the Davis ranch for several weeks. He killed forty-four gray wolves and scattered enough poison to kill a hundred coyotes when the snow thawed off. Several times he went elk hunting, and once he and Bill Davis followed mountain sheep for two days, but never got a shot. On all of these trips Jules rode a ranch horse.

"You might get lead colic on that sorrel — nothing personal, you understand, only a case of mistaken identity," the rancher suggested.

Jules wiped the snow from his rifle. "What you got against the man with the Winchester — the owner of my horse?"

Davis straightened in his saddle and looked the lean, bearded cripple over in surprise.

"By damn, there ain't no figgering you out, Frenchy. Don't you know the habits of Gentleman Jim? Holds up the hold-ups, and if anybody ever gets the drop on him there'll be one man jack deader'n a doughnut, unless it'd happen to be some a them he's helped out of a hole."

"Robin Hood of the foothills," Jul s chuckled to himself.

The man jerked his horse to a stop. "By damn, you know his real name?"

"No," Jules said gravely, "but I know he likes Villon and kirschwasser."

The mystified ranch boss observed the custom of the West and asked no further.

One night when Jules and Davis were coming in from a hunt through moonlit folds of bluish gossamer hovering over the snow-patched plain, the settler was overwhelmed by a desire for his mail. He wanted to know what the Panhandle was doing. And by this time he could get married again.

The first nice day he started for the Niobrara, leaving his pelts behind. He pushed the sorrel to the limit, riding him the last hundred twenty miles with only an hour's stop for a glass of whiskey and a plate of beans — nothing for the horse. When he took the saddle off Old Fox in his own yard the horse went down flat and did n't lift his head for two days. Henriette carried corn and water for the horse, but he was never limber-kneed again.

"You ought to be skinned alive for treating an animal like that," a neighbor told him.

"I got no time to fool with horses," Jules said.

Henriette brought the mail, mostly duns — duns for interest on the mortgages, for guns, ammunition, traps, wolf poison, groceries. The letters from prospective settlers he answered, agreeing to meet them all at the railroad, help them to free land. The duns he used to light his pipe. He was n't even very angry when he found that Henriette had traded his gelding to an Oglala for a buckskin mare.

"She is good for the hunt, the Indian say."

"Probably leave the country the first time I shoot from the saddle," Jules predicted.

"I hope so, and throw you on your backside in cactus patch!" Henriette shouted to him over her shoulder.

But Daisy was a compact, dark little buckskin, with shaggy black mane and a tail that dragged the ground. And she was not afraid of a gun. With a little training she stopped dead-still at the lift of the barrel, stood unmoving until the report came, then charged upon the game. But she shied at every Russian thistle, and if Jules dozed in the saddle he sometimes awoke on the ground. But Daisy never left him, and once when he turned his bad foot under him and lay unconscious she rubbed her wet nose over his face until he sat up and painfully pulled himself into the saddle.

In two months everybody in the country knew Jules as far as the little dog lope of the buckskin could be seen. He hunted and trapped, and talked of his trip. Once more he looked forward to spring, with a sack of new wheat coming from Russia, and a new orchard. The Freese troubles were almost forgotten, except that the interest was due, and he could n't hear from his wolf hides in Wyoming.

He told no one about the night along the creek far up towards the Big Horns, and nothing of his ten days with the man he saw in the Valentine saloon. He told much, but never where he got the horse Old Fox.

Once more Jules's thoughts turned to a woman. There was Tante Jeanne, governess to the Hyde Park Roosevelts. She had always sent him Christmas greetings, even during the long years in America. Perhaps she knew of a country-woman for him, and already in America. He wrote her a friendly letter; spoke with his customary optimism of his prospects, and mentioned his need of an intelligent wife. Then he waited.

The next week Tante Jeanne replied — a long, reminiscent letter of family news. So Ami's Jules owned so much land now. She must see this region of wonder. Countrywomen she knew almost none in America. But there must be many in the homeland who would gladly come. And in the letter was a picture of her charge, the youthful Franklin Delano

Roosevelt, cousin of the Theodore whom Jules had seen hunting in the Bad Lands.

All around him the settlers were taking Jules's advice and marrying. Eugenie was the wife of Louis Pochon; Paul and William married Fanny and Lena Pochon, the sisters of Louis. Emile and half a dozen others got their wives direct from Switzerland. Hans, a dilapidated, drink-sodden Hans, had answered a matrimonial advertisement and got a mail-order wife. She was a few years older than he, and correspondingly grateful, and now, only six months later, he was once more clean and sober and laying fat on his ribs.

Ah, a good wife, that's what everybody needed.

Once more Jules thought of Rosalie as though the inter-vening years had not been, and wrote to her again. She answered in her usual loving tone, but still she would not come. He tore the letter across and threw it into the fire.

As an alternative there was still Emelia, the modiste friend of Madame Degaillez, who was to have come to America for William. Jules went to Pine Creek, came back with an introduction to Emelia from Fanny Degaillez. And once more he wrote of things as he imagined them to be.

Emelia answered promptly, her writing beautiful purple tracery on thick, creamy paper. She was much flattered by Monsieur's offer. Unfortunately she was not, like him, en-dowed with fortune. She had not even the money for her passage. But she understood perfectly how to maintain the place of a mistress in a fine and prosperous home and how to receive in good company. In order to make herself loved by her husband she would be all obedience. That would be her entire aim in life.

Jules read the letter and sang a snatch of the almost for-gotten "Marguerite." Emelia was twenty-four, not yet spoiled. She would raise a big, healthy family. He wrote her to go to Neuchâtel to meet his people and obtain the passage money. She hesitated, preferring that he pay her way, but still, apparently, believing in his affluence.   Finally Jules borrowed the money at Rushville and with it sent a letter promising the girl a glowing future.   "I have enough fortune to put you out of reach of want if you should lose me.   The lands I have keep five or six farmers busy and take my time just to oversee them.   The country here is magnificent, with the air of the mountains and the sunshine of Italy.   I have six ponies, good health, except that I limp a little.   You will have your own saddle horse and sewing machine.   And if you are obedient you will be adored. Whatever happens you will never want."   And as he wrote he believed.

In the final draft he omitted specific mention of the six ponies.   With an eye to the welfare of his community, he added a postscript: "If you have a girl friend who would like also to come bring her to America.   She can get married here at once."

Then Jules went to Rushville, borrowed more money, securing the loan with stamps from Henriette's post office. Despite the divorce she was his good friend.   With the money he put up a house on the Freese homestead, on the bench halfway up the hill near the main road leading to the Niobrara ford, where he looked over to Mirage Flats that first time, so long ago.

He built the best house he ever possessed — two rooms with an attic and a cellar.   He sent for a good maple bedroom set, with a fine big glass and good springs.   With his name in eight-inch letters on a board over the door, there was nothing to do but wait.

IX

EMELIA, CATTLEMEN, AND MURDER

ONCE more Jules, hunched down on the wagon seat, brought home a bride. He had tried to keep Emelia's coming a secret — with a fresh shave, a moustache trim, a haircut, and a new suit. Every loafer in town followed him to the depot to see what got off.

A pale, slender, rather pretty girl in a well-tailored blue suit with fashionably large sleeves hesitated on the car step until those behind pushed her down into the wind-burned, sun-frowning frontier crowd.

"Mlle. Parel?" a hopeful voice asked at her elbow.

"*Oui* — But who are you?" the girl asked in French, drawing her arm away.

"I am Jules," he said proudly, glad to have them all see this fine young lady.

At first the girl could only drop her veil over her confusion. Then at last she whispered, "No, no — you are not the Jules — "

But it was he, and finally she consented to follow him down the street towards the courthouse, dully, without realization, carrying her valise herself. Once she stopped and let the man go on, but he only went a few steps and returned for her. An old man. Gray under the greasy cap; limping despite all he could do — a slouchy, stooped, careless figure with burning eyes. Then she noticed the hands: long fine fingers, smooth, almost white. They showed no brutalization, not the hard lot of a peasant that his appearance suggested. Perhaps it was with him as he said. Perhaps he needed a wife to look after him, to show him how to make the most of the money his lands brought him.

Besides, what could she do?

They reached the Niobrara late in the evening. If there was any beauty in the sky or in the land, Emelia did not see it. She sat as far from her husband as the board across the wagon allowed, and kept dabbing her eyes with a lace handkerchief that smelled like Mayflowers.

Fording the Niobrara in the pitchy blackness frightened the girl, but she only pulled more closely within herself when the wagon lurched forward in the splash of water. At the house Jules tried to sing, to joke, but he lacked the self-assurance of his earlier ventures. After supper, which they ate from the frying pan because there were no dishes, he showed his wife his guns, his traps, his stamp collection, his notary-public seal. She looked at them all, her hand never leaving her lap, and when she could she stole glances about the bare room, the floor of rough foot-wide boards with big cracks between, the homemade table with no cloth, the two windows staring blankly out into the strange darkness, unrelieved by curtain or shade, the rusty stove with a brick for a fourth leg.

Once a horsebacker rode up, but Jules had been listening for visitors. He went out into the darkness, closing the door behind him, and sent the man away.

At midnight Emelia still sat before the stove. Jules was in bed, between greasy blankets. He had not waited until she got her beautiful hand-woven sheets from her trunk. Now she sat with them in her lap, not daring to ask the man to get up again.

Suddenly he appeared in the door between the two rooms, his legs thin and hairy below his blue shirt.

"Come to bed!"

Two weeks later Emelia was gone. Paul Wuthier, a young Swiss Jules located in Pine Creek, took her away to

Rushville. She must have sneaked out to plan it in the night, for Jules watched her carefully in the day.

"I don't stand for any damned running around!" he had warned her when she smiled down upon his acquaintances who stopped him on the way home.

So Emelia was gone, and all he had for the passage money was some fine dresses and a hat with many feathers on it that she left hanging in his closet.

This time Jules sat with his head in his hands, not moving for a long time. Somewhere the thunder of the beaver was heavy under the smoke of autumn, the whistle of the bull elk clear. But he had chosen to take root here, on the Running Water, and in return he was made this poor, miserable thing; crippled, and spurned by women.

At last he took his gun and went to the river.

Much usually of moment to Jules went unnoticed that summer and fall. The new ranches deep in the hills were infested with road agents and hide-outs. Shooting, knifing, and disappearances became common as sand lizards and wind. The Northwestern was held up, the mail sacks found slit and rifled in a blowout. The divorces of the community were offset by shotgun weddings. A neighbor on the south table hanged himself in his well curbing and dangled unnoticed for two days in plain sight of the road, so nearly did his head resemble a windlass swinging.

Up on Box Butte a woman was fined five dollars and cost for horsewhipping her neighbor over a prairie fire he set. "There is the woman to teach The Black's wife something!" William said, sucking his moustache in anticipation. But unfortunately Tissot's frightened little wife was no such Amazon.

Although sheriff sales increased, the Burlington offered half-price excursion rates to homeseekers; Mirage farmers were raising thousands of dollars in the East, among relatives, mostly for irrigation. The Niobrara and Pine Creek settlers used their friends and relatives to take up adjoining land. Some day the rain would come. If not, they would need range, much range.

Three crop failures were enough for the Bannels, living beyond the John place. They laid out a race track in the dead grass, built on a room apiece for the three girls, and made money enough for red plush furniture with fringe.

All these things were less than the wind on the bluffs of the Running Water to Jules now.

When he finally had to admit that Emelia was not coming back he cursed her luridly to her friend, Madame Degaillez. She showed him the black hole into the night that was the door, and he took it, swearing that they could starve and rot before he would enter it again. The next day he rode deep into the sandhills to trap, and when the snow filled the passes he went to Knox County.

His friends received him with joy, but were shocked by his changed appearance, his acid tongue, his violent speech. He seemed grizzled and worn for a man of thirty-five. Still, it was ten years, and in a wild country.

Between accounts of western Nebraska he inquired about his first wife, Estelle. She and her boy lived with her parents. Jules wrote her a note — asking to see her. She did not answer. The next day he left for St. Louis. There he arranged to buy furs for a large company, stopped in at the drug house that sold him the wolf poison, and looked around for a steady market for frozen ducks, grouse, and perhaps rabbits. He stopped at saloons and at clubs whose members were mostly foreign, preferably French, German, or Swiss, and talked land and western Nebraska. Many were coming in the spring with wives and families. Jules got off the train at Rushville alone and discouraged. In a saloon he heard that his wife worked at one of the hotels. So Emelia was still there — perhaps waiting. He wrote her a note: —

DEAR EMELIA:

I returned from my trip to-day. I saw many of my old friends and had a very good time without ever forgetting that you are yet my wife. If you now have more tender sentiments towards me I beg you to let me know it. I have almost forgotten the sorrows which you caused me. I plan to leave to-morrow morning for my place and if you permit it I would like to have a word with you. Only I do not care to come to your hotel. If you wish you can see me at the other hotel this evening.

After the signature he added a postscript: —

They tell me you said to Mrs. Porter at the hotel that you are now "in hope." If that is true I should like very much that you let me know it. In that case, what do you intend to do?

In fifteen minutes the boy who took his note to Emelia brought her answer. It was written across the back of his letter, in French of course, without salutation or signature, and the penmanship had more determination then the delicate tracery she wrote from the Old Country: —

My sentiments have not changed and I beg you not to write me any more. I do not want to know anything more about you. After the things you said about me at the home of Mons. Degaillez I do not understand how you can still have the effrontery to ask me to return to your home. I am not in the position that you believe and I do not know how I could have said anything of the kind to Mrs. Porter, she not knowing the French and I not English. It is just another of your lies.

Jules read it and threw it with disdain upon the table. "That's what you get when you try to help a woman!" But on the way home he passed a flock of prairie chickens, close to the road, without seeing them.

When he got home he found his mail on the table where someone, Henriette, probably, had left it, and in the pile was a letter from Rosalie. With uncertain hands he opened it. But it was only a holiday letter, written just before Christmas: —

MY FRIEND:

Although you have forbidden me to write you any more if I do not wish to come to you, I cannot help but address you several lines and I beg you not to hold a grudge against me that everything is changed like this. I hope that you are happy and I beg you to accept my sincere good wishes for the New Year, and to believe that I take a very lively interest in everything that concerns you. Keep this note as a little souvenir and know that I shall always keep for you my old affection.

Later he noticed that there were two letters from Estelle, in Knox County. He opened them, stared at the uncertain, slow lines, like those of a very old person, the spelling that of a child. She had not realized that he expected an immediate reply to his note. "My heart aked with grief to hear you were gon in anger. I seand a note to Mr. Nippel sadady morning but you wer gon. If you will seand me five dollars I will seand you Percys photograph with lots of kises from Percy I will close. . . ."

Jules laid the incoherent letter beside that from Rosalie. But comparisons were futile. Both had fooled him. Rosalie would not come, Estelle would, and on his conditions.

Every few days there was another letter from her, asking for money, asking that Jules remarry her at the depot. If not then, when? Instead of admitting he had no money and that he was married, he asked her how old she was and if she could still raise children. She answered with an attempt at coyness. Jules lit his pipe with that letter. Two weeks later another came, returning to her query and saying she enclosed a lock of Percy's hair.

Jules looked about the table, found a tuft of hay-colored hair tied with a poor bit of ribbon. "Oh, that stuff git in

my grub!" he grumbled, and dropped it into the stove.   A
momentary stench and it was gone.

The next letter promised that if he would send her the
money for a new dress, a coat for Percy, and other small
items, she would come to Hay Springs, but he must marry
her right way.   Jules, impatient, wrote her the truth.   He
was married.   Her answer was as vacillating as before.

With this letter came one in the beautiful drawn charac-
ters of Nippel, the architect.   He said Estelle had apparently decided to rejoin Jules immediately, on the sole condition that he remarry her when he got his divorce.   She
seemed sincere enough.   But between the lines it was evident that the deliberate, responsible man disapproved of the
woman, her indecision, her childishness, and almost as much
of what America had made of this Jules, his friend.

Without even a beard clip Jules brought Estelle and
Percy home from Hay Springs.   The boy was small, dark,
thin-faced, unruly, and because he heard someone at Hay
Springs call this man Old Jules he did the same — and got
a sound thrashing for it.

"I teach you to respect me!" Jules panted, shaking his
stinging hand.

The mother tried to intercede.   No, no.   Her boy had
never been whipped.   He was nervous.

"Nervous?   He is a son of a bitch!"

"Oh, Jules, how can you use such bad words before your
son!"

"My son!   He's no son of mine, the bastard!"

When Percy discovered that Jules expected him to work
he ran away to Elvina.   Johnny Burrows disapproved of
whipping children, but he had always worked and saw no
reason why the boy shouldn't help with the chores and the
baby.   When Percy was left to look after the place, he cut
the knot from the well rope, let it run through the windlass
and drop, bucket and all, into the 180-foot well.   Then he
put his hat beside the curbing and started for the river.

Thinking the boy had fallen into the well, Johnny and Elvina aroused the neighborhood, dragged the well, finding nothing except the bucket and the rope.

Perhaps a light whipping would n't hurt the young scamp, Johnny decided. But by this time Estelle was trying to order Jules around again. She went to Rushville with a cut lip, Henriette shaking her fist after this woman she had once pitied.

The next week the United States Marshal came for Jules. The post office was short three hundred dollars. Jules, one of the bondsmen, had access to the money and stamps. Against his protests he was taken to Omaha and put in jail.

A few days later Johnny Jones, in Omaha on business, came to see Jules. The two had remained friends since 1885, even though Jones was with the Thomas bank and had to side against Jules in the Freese troubles. For reasons that the old settler never analyzed, he did not quarrel with the outspoken Jones.

"Oh, by golly, I am glad to see you," Jules told him. "Get me out."

"I don't think I should, Jule. I made some inquiries before I came up and it 's not much over two weeks until your case comes up. If I bail you out you 'll just go home and have to come right back — spend a lot of money and not do yourself any good."

"I got to look after the government property Henriette 's got, the stamps and stamped envelopes."

Jones ran his fingers through his thick, curly hair, chuckling. "The post-office inspector 's looking after the stamps, Jule, including those you left with me for security on that last loan. He inquired about them around town and I told him you brought them to me — safekeeping. That leaves you just one of the bondsmen. They can't hold you."

"That the best you can do?" Jules asked, as though he did

not know that his friend had saved him from the charge of appropriating government stamps.

Jones understood this Jules. "That is the best for you," he said.

In the meantime Henriette mortgaged her land for three hundred dollars to send to Omaha.

When the case came up it lasted a matter of minutes.

"This man you brought all the way from Sheridan County — he is not the postmaster?" the federal judge asked the post-office inspector.

"He is not, Your Honor."

"Then why do you take him from his business and bring him down here on a charge of shortage in the office?"

After a few days of celebration that kept Jules uneasy for several weeks, he went home. Grayson had the post office.

"And don't forget — there are n't many women would mortgage their homes for their divorced husbands," Jones pointed out to Jules.

"Heah?" he grunted. But at last Henriette and Jules had achieved an understanding — now they were friends.

Perhaps for that reason Jules was uneasy about her. He believed she was going the way of so many women there during the dry years. Many considered Jules crazy too, unconfinably crazy.

Gradually Jules caught up with national events, saw anew the unrest of stringent money and unemployment. During the railroad strike of 1894, affecting twenty-three railroads in twenty-seven states, Cleveland ordered General Miles to keep the mails moving. There Jules was divided in his allegiance. The mails must never be held up. On the other hand he saw Miles once more the instrument of force that he had been at Pine Ridge, and at Wounded Knee.

The county Populists were planning carefully. Because of his following they appointed Jules to the central committee. The secretary of the State Historical Society wrote for a photograph of the early settler and an outline of his work. Jules liked that, but the fact that a horse worth a hundred dollars four years before brought only fifteen, and that the state had no money for coyote bounty, was more vitally important than recognition just now. Everywhere preëmptions, early mortgageable, were being foreclosed.

"Boston loan sharks will soon be all that 's left to fight the cattleman," Jules predicted in a gloomy moment.

Eastern capital was once more the enemy, and the foreclosed places were stripped of even the upper sections of well curbing and the cellar steps the instant the settlers were gone. The night after Mrs. Masters, near Box Butte, was to leave, six wagons drove up to her house. Two men climbed to the roof and tore at the shingles while the rest attacked the door and windows. At the first rip of wood there was a commotion and the woman came screaming to her door, a white ghost in her nightgown. Shouting apologies, the men whipped their teams over the nearest hill. Jules listened to the story and did not laugh.

Lamoureau, cleaned out by the damage suit over Jules's garden, came back to sell his place. Knowing that the house would be torn down the hour anyone discovered he did not intend to live in it, he tried to sell the lumber to Elmer Sturgeon, who was building extensive corrals and sheds. They dickered all night. Towards sunup Sturgeon went down to establish his ownership. But there was nothing left except the foundation stones from Jules's limestone quarry and several fresh wagon tracks trailing off across the nigger-wool sod.

Although there were no tracks to Jules's place since the rain, and his wagon had n't been moved, Lamoureau stopped. He found the old settler cooking a late breakfast.

"Know anything about my house?" he asked.

Jules scratched his beard. "Nothing except that it is not worth what you want for it."

"Want for it! Some sucker stole it in the night. You and Sturgeon was the only two fellows that knew I was n't coming back, and I was with Elmer all night."

"Well, I be damned," Jules laughed, and pushed another piece of pitch-pine two-by-four into the fire. "You won't find any of it on my place."

Lamoureau picked up a piece of the firewood. "That looks like some of it."

"Hell, no. I got that up near Rushville before the rain. The sheriff helped me load it up."

In the Panhandle men far outnumbered women, with the usual adjustments. Roadhouses came early. When the ranchers spread into the sandhills they needed halfway stations for the freighters. At first these were little more than pasturage. Then a place to feed and bed the men was added. Later comforts and luxuries were provided — roadhouses. The Schwartz place was a good day's travel for loaded wagons from Hay Springs or Rushville — at the edge of the soft-sand region that demanded rested teams and men.

It was said that hook-nosed Mollie Schwartz first saw the opportunity; that she drove her sons out to forage for lumber to make room for freighters. She had two daughters, tall, full-eyed girls, with ready laughter and kind hearts. But Nell and Rae did n't restrict themselves to freighters long, particularly not Rae, who was slender-waisted, with narrow hands, who danced well and rode wild horses with considerable assurance and grace in a pair of chaps borrowed from her admirers. After a couple of years others besides Jules were faced with divorce suits. The wife of a Rushville business man jerked away the plaid horse blanket from about a bundle he was smuggling to his buggy, uncovering a nice dress piece of wine silk. She felt the heavy material with expert fingers.

"Exquisite! For the enchanting Rae? But you forget one thing that goes with a new dress like that." Smiling, she went to the house and brought out something white. "Here," she said, holding up her husband's nightshirt for all the window watchers to see, "you will need this."

"Outfits like that ought to be run out of the country," the women grumbled.

"If it was n't for places like that, no decent woman would be safe anywhere," their menfolks told them.

Murder was common in the Panhandle, but during the early years of settlement it was usually open, in the heat of anger or alcohol.   Now the secret murder had come.   The first of these to cause much local excitement was the shooting of Harold Still, night operator of Hay Springs, killed through the depot window at two o'clock in the morning. Later it was recalled that he was to appear in court the next week in a cattle-stealing case against Carl Schwartz, the eldest and blackest of the roadhouse brothers, and that he seemed to dread the duty.   The sheriffs of Dawes and Sheridan counties organized a posse, but nothing came of it.   They never went into the south river country.

By the time the Schwartz case came up all the state's witnesses were gone or dead.   But the butcher accused of buying the stolen meat was convicted and sent to the penitentiary.   He swore to get Carl Schwartz.

"You can't do nothing," Jules said.   "With a dozen thieves behind them to swear to any lie, outfits like that can run the country.   Only way to stop them is with buckshot."

"But who will do it?" Hans wondered.

"If that outfit bothers me or my people I will not hesitate to get any of the criminal layout I want," Jules bragged. Yes, perhaps that was the only way, some said.   Rae Schwartz had made friends among the county officials.

The same spring Green's son-in-law, Johnny Musteldt, was found dead at the far end of his field.   He was slumped down between the plough handles, a bullet hole clear through him. The night after the funeral Harve Green rode into Jules's yard.

"You heard?"

"Yah, I heard."

A long time the stooped little man sat on the broken kitchen chair, his fingers running through his thin, sandy hair. "I bin looking for it. I was down here a couple times lately. You was n't to home."

"Women and post-office troubles," Jules said briefly, filling his pipe. "But every damn one of you is in danger now."

"Yah, things was getting pretty hot for that gang down the river so they put it off on us. That 's what I come for." The man pulled at his hair with his blunt red fingers, his flat face puffy with grief and bewilderment. "John was a good boy and my gal was right fond of him — so was we all. Mebby I should a left three-four years ago. But we bin doin' well and the old woman 's so cussed contrary. She still don't want to go. Says she won't be run out by no damn cow outfit."

"Hunh — Well, I guess I go down with you — to hunt." Jules was already digging through the pile of tools on his workbench under the east window for the bullet mould. While the lead heated he cleaned and oiled Green's old rifle. The next day they shot target at a sand spot across the river to adjust the sight. At last Jules blew the gases from his rifle, smoked the sights. Then they rode away into the hills.

Ten days later Jules was back. He had been to the Spade ranch, owned by Bartlett Richards, the man who almost ran over him in Chadron while he was still on crutches. The old settler rode a horse carrying Green's brand plain for all the ranch hands to see. He stopped at the Spade to shoot a little target, raising unfailing sand spurts in a spot the size of a horse blanket across the broad valley. The

rough men saw and dropped away before him, and the foreman sent word to the cookhouse that Old Jules was to be
fed; he ordered Green's horse grained and watered.

Jules rode his own horse, Daisy, back to the river, smooth
with oats and the currycomb. Her back was easier, with a
hole cut in the blanket over the old saddle gall. Jules's
clothes were scrubbed clean and mended, his hair cut by Ma
Green's skillful shears.

Next Dave Tate, openly accused of the Musfeldt murder,
was arrested in Dakota.

"Well, they got him, now will they do anything with
him?" the settlers and some of the newspapers wanted to
know. Tate was on the pay roll of the Spade. There was
a buzz of talk. It was said that Jarvis Richards had looked
after the Spade ranch while his brother Bartlett was in England with a new bride. Perhaps because Jarvis was a mild-
mannered, religious man, rustlers worked the stock strong.
When the owner came back his face purpled. Steal his
stock the minute his back was turned! He would find the
rustlers, and when he did there would be hell a-popping.
When things got hot cowboys from the Newman and Hunter
outfits offered evidence against Musfeldt. Next day he was
found shot through the forehead and neck, a rifle bullet fired
from a horse.

A few days after Jules's trip to the Green place, William
and Emile rode down to the Niobrara alone. The three
brothers sat about the kitchen in the round-shouldered
hunches characteristic of the family, from Jules, the tallest,
straightest, and dirtiest, to Emile, short, and always knotted
up over his crossed knees as if he were perpetually blowing
his flute and stamping his foot in time. But to-night there
was no music.

"I understand they were getting close to a certain outfit — " Emile, always cautious, never mentioned names.

The noise of Jules's clogging pipe was loud in the room.

"You mean that outfit down the river —   Hell, yes, they

got out of it the last time by the buried hides with their brand on them."

William sucked his breath with a whistle under his clean, clipped red moustache, as he always did when amused. "I hear Richards is harder to fool than our sheriff. It was getting, as we say here, warm."

"The Greens bin having trouble for years — " Emile spoke as though making a secret accusation.

"Oh, hell, yes," Jules admitted. "The big fellows bin trying to run them out."

William was not making his amused sucking noise now. "You bettaire keep out of it — now that you are out of your own troubles."

Jules chuckled. "Everybody knows I am not a cattle thief."

"To be sure, but it is not much better to be a dead defender of the — ah, of the frightened than to be a dead thief — no?"

Jules scratched the tender spot under his chin. So that was why his brothers had come. They had heard of his trip to the hills with Green. He said nothing, but laughed into William's eyes as he used to when they shared some secret escapade as boys. They were good friends, these two.

"Some day the trouble will come down Pine Creek — " Emile mused, still concerned with his own thoughts.

"I hear some of the Swiss are getting a fast start in cattle too — cows with twins — " Jules admitted regretfully.

"Yes, it is a reflection on us." William spoke with the first heat he had shown. "And it will make us trouble."

The three launched into a discussion of the future, and they made it seem bright — if they could keep clear of the cattle troubles. "I won't let no arrogant rancher run me out," Jules said.

"No, but could you not do something besides locating settlers?" Emile asked.

"The land is free!"

William looked towards Emile under his bushy brows. Together they held their peace. They knew Jules. Opposition would only drive him deeper into the coming struggles. An exciting elder brother, this, but a difficult one.

Dave Tate was acquitted for lack of evidence. There were headshakings.

"You can't convict a man on what everybody knows," the judge explained privately in the back room of his favorite saloon. "You have to have proof."

Perhaps it was as well. A serious probing would have disrupted the county. "Make the Niobrara feud look like one of them ice-cream socials gettin' so popular with the parson's hen yards."

The drouth exceeded all probability. Corn did not sprout. On the hard-land fringe the buffalo grass was started and browned before the first of May. Even lighter soil south of the river produced nothing. The sandhills greened only in strips where the water-logged sand cropped out. The lake beds whitened and cracked in rhythmical patterns. Grouse were scarce and dark-fleshed. Rabbits grew thin and wild and coyotes emboldened. Covered wagons like gaunt-ribbed, gray animals moved eastward, the occupants often becoming public charges along the way. Carloads of supplies, particularly clothing, were gathered in the eastern counties and distributed over the country west of Broken Row. One car reached Rushville. Jules was in town and went down, limping along behind the rest.

By the time he got there everything except a handful of candles was gone.

"I rather burn skunk oil and a rag wick," he chuckled. The nice woman in charge looked from the dirty toes of his crippled foot sticking out of his overshoe to the top of his greasy cap.

"All worthless stuff," he told her, and limped away, leaving shocked silence behind him.

But the hard times were not an unadulterated calamity to the Panhandle. The shiftless, and those who live from the prosperity of their fellows, drifted to greener fields early. Only the strong and the courageous, the ingenious and the stubborn, remained. Common need knit them closer. It was no longer the Americans, the Hollanders, the Germans, the Slavs, the Swiss. The Catholic Church lifted its steeple over a depopulated Mirage Flats, but over one that would know little of religious or racial antagonism for a long time to come. None was hated for his prosperity.

Jules, with confidence firm against the unprecedented deviation from the rain graph, kept up his agitation for mail service, for bridges across the Running Water, for passable roads to the railroad; kept up his search for crops that would withstand drouth and ripen before a frost.

He planted a small orchard about his house — only a hundred plums and a hundred apples, all his credit would stand. Two plum trees he set to lean hard against the east wall, as in his childhood home in Neuchâtel. He drew water for the young trees until the well in the yard went dry. He sent samples of the dark berries, delicious and heavily sweet, that grew on the north slope of his rock quarry to Lincoln. Professor Bruner wrote that they were Juneberries, rare in Nebraska. They would thrive under cultivation if sufficient roots could be grubbed from the rock. Jules already had a row north of his house bowing under white tufts of bloom in the spring, purpled with fruit in July, red and gold and russet clumps in the fall; shade for his pet antelope all the summer.

The county put in a bridge west of Jules's house, at the foot of the bluff from which he first looked towards Mirage Flats in 1884, where willows hung over the stream and trailed their fingers in the water. If the south river country and Pine Creek ever raised anything again the road to market was open.

Fall brought wind that swept away the brittle grass and bared the knolls. The Panhandle was spotted with the black path of prairie fires. Old-timers advised ploughed guards, with a burned strip between. A rancher near Alliance, on the Burlington, let his guard fire get away. The wind freshened, swept the flames through Sheridan, into Cherry County, then southeast, burning range, hay, cattle, and homes, even two men, overtaken by a sudden shift in the gale.

There was almost no snow that winter and the cattlemen wondered if the grass could ever start again. Not Jules. He unfolded his rain graphs once more and pointed to the high years. Rain was as inevitable as comets, meteor showers, eclipses, moon changes.

"But when?"

Jules shrugged his shoulders. That he did not know, and so his neighbors went away to advertise their pathetic handfuls of household goods and the breaking ploughs with rusty shares that once shone like silver platters.

Jules took up his fight for mail service with the local committeemen, the Congressman from his district, the fourth assistant Postmaster General, and the President. He accumulated many polite letters. Then one day Grayson, the postmaster, aired his own disgust with the whole petty business. There was no money in a post office where nobody lived. The inspector had been there, found him seven dollars short, and acted as though he were trying to defraud the government of the Northwest Territory.

"It was a most humiliating scene — soon 's I get the money I 'm throwing it out."

Jules pulled out seven dollars, dumped the whole equipment and undelivered mail into a gunny sack, and printed a sign for the office door: MAIL AT OLD JULES. With the pack evenly divided across his saddle he started home, spurring

his Daisy mare into her short lope with his good foot.   He
would pull out the old board stored in the attic, with black
grease from a wagon wheel he would renew the sign: POST
OFFICE.   When the six months required for his divorce
from Emelia were up he would try again.   In the meantime some of the settlers from St. Louis were on the way, including a young German Swiss and his sister.   Jules planned
that they would stay with him during the six months allowed for the establishment of residences on the claims they
were to take up.

When the new postmaster got home there was a light in
his kitchen.   One of the young Beguins from lower Pine
Creek was frying cottontails, the white meat turning golden
brown under his watchful eye and filling the whole smoky
room with a delicious smell.   Jug Byers, a former Hunter
cowboy who had taken up land and rigged up a riding at-
tachment for his breaking plough, sat on the floor, his spurs
sticking into the soft wood.   He was pounding coffee in
the corner of a flour sack with a hammer and making a hollow boom rise from the cellar beneath.   On the old couch
under the south window three of Jules's countrymen sang
while Emile hunched over his flute on an old box, keeping
time with a muddy shoe.

And after the cottontails, with baking-powder biscuit fried
in the gravy and a glass of raisin wine around, — the best
Jules could do, for the drouth ruined the wild fruit, —
Emile told of the beaver dam he found up Pine Creek.
Jules dug up two shot sacks to be filled with sand to drown
the *castor*, oiled and smoked his traps while the others sang,
with a strong French flavor: —

> *Im Wald und auf der Heide',*
> *Da such' ich meine Freude,*
> *Ich bin ein Jägersmann,*
> *Ja, ich bin ein Jägersmann.*

Young, all of them, and for such as these hard times pass.

X

MARY, AND A LAND–STEAL PLOT

ONCE more Jules pounded the calloused backs of his ponies towards the Running Water, a strange woman beside him on the wagon. But this time she was not his wife, and so he wore two leather shoes and hid his limp as much as possible. Nor was there a pipestem under his moustache, neatly clipped to-day.

Mary had the fair skin of the German Swiss, with blue eyes and soft, curly brown hair under her brown rosetted hat. She was small, her head reaching just a little above Jules's shoulder, but she was the eldest daughter of a family whose vitality had receded to its women, and to her Jules's masculine boasting was as the wind on the dry buffalo grass. As he talked grandly of the country she considered the inauspicious beginning of her venture in western Nebraska. She had had a premonition the day she left St. Louis that it was not best to go. And then her brother Jacob did not meet her at St. Joseph. Even her trunk was carried past Hay Springs.

"Probably your brother just got on the wrong train; one before you," Jules reasoned. "He is likely out on my place now."

"Ach, but could he find it?"

"Everybody in the country knows me."

That seemed true enough. Business men and rough, sunburned farmers in patched and torn clothing were constantly hailing Jules, asking him about crops and the prospects for the summer while they looked curiously at the woman with him. Would there be any rain this year?

"Hell, yes, lots of rain," Jules told them. And then before they could begin their plaint of hard times he shouted "Git, git!" to his ponies, and with a squeak of ungreased wheels they were off again.

Mary's practical eye appraised the homes on the Flats, soddies, dugouts, unpainted frame houses, often with dead sunflowers choking the yards. To her Jules's weathering house with its two blank windows and a door towards the road was not so much of a shock. But Jacob was not there; no one was there.

"Have you then brought me out here alone?" she demanded.

"I 'm no wild man. I won't hurt you," he laughed. "Besides, it will be only a few minutes until somebody comes."

One look inside the house firmed Mary's long chin. "Have you no water and no soap in this country?"

Without waiting for an answer she rolled up the velvet-trimmed cuffs of her brown traveling dress and scoured pots, pans, knives, and forks with wood ashes spilling from the hearth of the cookstove. She piled the catalogues and newspapers into an old box and prepared to sweep the litter from the door.

"Don't throw me anything valuable away!" Jules warned from his chair. "You had better then keep what you want from the floor," she answered as she sprinkled water to lay the dust. Jules escaped into the yard and brought his young antelope to the door. The animal nozzled Mary's palm and tried to follow her into the house.

"No, not inside," she shooed, but she stopped to watch the beautiful animal trot away.

After supper Jules interrupted the cleaning again. The entire west was a sheet of rose, with the Minten house and barn two dark blocks against the sky. A path of red gold rippled on the river. It recalled a childhood rhyme to

Mary. Something about "Fire, O! The Rhine is burning!" with a final quenching by a hundred thousand croak-
ing frogs.

"That is a fine sight," Jules pointed out, hoping to please.

But the pain for Switzerland and all it once meant to her
closed the woman's throat.

Three horsebackers clattered over the plank bridge, but
Jules met them in the yard with their mail. When he came
back into the neat, orderly kitchen the two talked of Mary's
predicament. There was no telling what delayed her
brother. "A woman maybe?" Jules asked. Mary did not
know. She had given him the money to come to America
six or seven years before and he had not yet repaid her.
He was frankly without the initiative she thought any self-
respecting person should show.

But she, a town woman, could n't make a living here on
a claim alone, and with scarcely enough money to pay for a
shack and a team. And work for pay there was probably
none. Of course she could have her position in St. Louis
again. "Both Dr. and Frau Geiger told me I was a fool,"
she moaned, into a sensible handkerchief.

"Marry me and you always have a good home," Jules suggested a bit timidly.

Mary looked at him, her blue eyes perplexed, uncertain
whether this was a Frenchman's idea of romance or a joke.

"But I know nothing of you. You may then be a divorced man or a drunkard."

"Do I look like a whiskey soak?"

No, there was nothing of the drunkard about those sharp
eyes, the smooth, fine-textured skin.

Sifting the chaff from Jules's accounts of himself and his
country as well as she could, Mary decided that if she married him she would have a house to live in, a garden, trees,
brush with wild fruit, a team for the heavy work, a big roan
milk cow with a deep udder coming fresh, and the river.

It was not her Rhine, but at least it was not the sullen Arkansas she saw in flood water, with bloated cattle and poor homes moving slowly towards the ocean. The Niobrara was clear-bottomed, pretty, peaceful. There would probably be little money; perhaps the advertisement Jules showed her, asking for cattle to range during the summer on his school section, might bring in a little.

By the yellow kerosene light she watched the man across the newspaper-covered table. He seemed old to her twenty-eight years, graying, nearing forty. His restless hands annoyed her, and the foot he moved a great deal. But if his eyes were fanatically piercing when he spoke of his enemies, those who worked against him, more often they twinkled as he related stories of his hunts and of the early days, authenticated by his well-worn guns and the attic full of antlers. And sometimes his eyes were pleading as those of an unhappy dog, almost brown, and lost, hungry.

Unfortunately Mary did n't like dogs.

Jules showed her his notary-public seal, his certificate of justice of the peace, the pigeonholes of his post office set up in the corner over his workbench at the east window, and a gunstock he was making, pointing out the locks mortised into the walnut without a tissue paper's thickness of space anywhere, the wood rubbed with animal oil until the grain stood out as though worn by years of affectionate hands.

At bedtime Mary cleaned the old papers, catalogues, and dirty socks from the ragged couch in the kitchen-living room. "That lounge 's full of bugs," Jules warned her from the bedroom door.

"Bedbugs?" Mary stepped back in horror.

"Yah, lousy with them. Nobody can sleep there," Jules answered, rubbing his shaven chin to hide his smile. Mary looked at him squarely, as no woman had before.

"I have not said we would marry."

Spreading clean newspapers over the greasy tapestry upholstery, she lay down on the couch and covered herself with her coat.

The next morning Mary saw Henriette standing barefoot in the road, staring at the house through her stringing hair. "Old woman living down the river," Jules dismissed her.

After breakfast they planted radishes and lettuce, watered the seed bed, and then went to Hot Springs, across the Dakota line, to get married. Mary did n't understand that, when money was so scarce. But it had a romantic tang, and the sheer red rock, the evergreen timber, the cascades of Fall River, cress-grown and sparkling as moving glass, pleased her.

Brought up in the tradition of a lifetime of subordination to man, she gave Jules her savings, a hundred dollars. Three days later, with her trunk in the wagon, they were back on the Niobrara.

There was a letter from Jacob. The sheriff made him marry a woman the day he was to meet his sister at St. Joe.

"Ach, disgrace me like that! What will people say?" Mary complained, showing Jules the letter.

"Oh, hell — some woman trying to get his money."

"But he could not have much."

The next day Minten stopped by to tell Jules the Rushville bankers had been down and wanted to see him. Urgent business.

"I know what they want. I don't go," he said cunningly, laughing, and giving his wife no explanation.

In a few days the men came again, with a quart of whiskey. They gave Jules a big drink and demanded that he and his wife sign a mortgage on the place for a back debt of two hundred fifty dollars.

"We can never get that much money," Mary wailed.

Johnny Jones, who was with the men, comforted her. "Old Jules makes quite a bit. He catches every skunk in the country and he can skin them with the best," laughing inordinately.

"Now where will we live?" she asked as soon as the men were gone.

"Heah? — What 's the matter with this place?"

"But we signed papers for it. It will go," she said dramatically.

"Go, hell! I bin signing that kind of paper ever since I bin in the country. There 's more than one way to skin a skunk."

The next morning, while Mary was watering the garden, a loud cursing and a puff of smoke came from the open door together. She dropped the pail from her head and ran in. The stovepipe, never wired in place, had fallen down, scattering smoke and soot over everything.

"Oh, the lazy bitch!" Jules fumed.

Under her husband's raging Mary put the pipe up and fastened it in place. "Ach, now," she kept saying. "Ach, now, thunder in the morning brings more storming before the night."

"Heah? — Old woman's stories," Jules scoffed, holding his head. "Damn that whiskey."

After breakfast he dug out his pipe. By noon he had changed his leather shoe for the soft rubber one he always wore on his crippled foot.

"First it is the smoking you did not tell me, and now it is lameness also!"

Jules forced a laugh. "I can make a living better crippled than lots of men with two good feet."

"It is the lie I can't stand."

"I did n't lie. I did n't say anything."

Mary set her mouth in a thin line and did not answer.

Jules saw. "Oh, hell," he growled, and with his gun he started for the brush, but he came back almost immediately. Any minute a neighbor might come, talk his wife against him.

That day Mary worked until her arms were tired enough to break, her blue eyes thick with tears. If she had only kept back a little of her savings. Such a fool, to give him all.

Jules read his newspapers in the open doorway. When anyone came into the yard he met him with the mail. When Mary moved to the well to wash the blankets for the second time Jules carried a box out and talked while the antelope nibbled at sprouting weeds along the fence.

"You always sit around, not even pulling me a bucket of water. Have you then nothing to do?"

"Heah? — You can't drive me. Henriette tried that — " His face went flat; the pipe fell from his mouth.

Mary stopped; the blanket she was wringing uncoiled like a thick snake from about her arm and dropped back into the water. "Who is Henriette?" she demanded.

"Oh, hell — " It was bound to come out anyway. Yes, he admitted, he had been married. Was divorced from the woman down the river. Later would be soon enough to admit the others.

"And you heard me say I would never marry a drunkard or a divorced man!"

"Well, I don't get drunk."

"What can I believe now?" the woman cried. Her arms still dripping, she ran down into the brush along the foot-hills. If she had only kept her money. Now most of it was gone for the roan cow and her calf born last night, ammunition bills, the trip to Hot Springs.

For an hour Mary cried, moaning like a child. She had not cried like that when her parents sent away the black-haired, gay young musician who came to ask for her. He went, got heartily drunk, and everyone at home said, "See what a fine husband he would make!" Angered, she pointed out that her father was slowly dying of alcoholic cancer of the bladder. Before they recovered from the shock of her disrespect, she had taken her savings and gone to America.

But now there was no escape. She had nothing; Jacob only a shotgun wife. She could n't admit to Dr. Geiger what a fool she had been, letting a strange old man get her last penny.

And even so it might be too late.

At the thought she clutched her apron. If she stayed longer it would surely be too late. Swift as the antelope she ran towards the house, paying no attention to the plum thorns and the rose briars tearing at her skirts.

But there was company. She had just time to wipe her eyes on her torn apron before William and his wife and Eugenie turned into the yard. The women ignored Mary's red eyes and in mixed French, English, and bad German told her how nice the house looked, with the floor scrubbed almost to splinters, the windows shining, the stove black, the tools neatly piled on the workbench. And Jules most comically clean.

"Your man is like a storm — pfuff! — and then it is gone. You bettaire get mad too — call him bad name, worse name than he call you. Then he go off on big hunt and come back singing," Eugenie advised Mary. William teased her laughingly. "Jules looks better already. See that he is not the only one to get fat."

Mary flushed at their broad laughter. After chocolate Lena invited them to spend Sunday on Box Butte Creek, then, with a resounding French smack on each cheek for Mary, the women climbed to the board across the middle of the wagon behind William and drove out of the yard and up the hill.

Jules, not knowing that anything was wrong at all, called Mary and limped beside her to the garden. The radishes and lettuce they had sowed were up in neat rows. There was a mess of asparagus ready to be cut. Then he took her along the bluffs and showed her how he shot cottontails. From there they went to the Juneberry patch, the bloom-fragrant brush spilling like snow down the slope. On the way back they found a hillside golden yellow with spikes of blossoms. "Wild peas," Jules said. "Poison."

But the flowers were n't dangerous, and with a large bouquet Mary felt better. The cottontail Jules shot and the asparagus would make a good supper.

And as they came over the gravel-topped hill east of the house the late sun glinted the windows of the Minten place on the far bluff to gold. Two horsebackers, black pencils against the west, moved down the section line towards the house that was already home to Mary, home because she made it so by hard work.

Jules stopped, leaned on his rifle, and sang a little in his awkward German: —

> . . . *Ich geb' für dich so gerne,*
> *All mein Leben, all mein Gut.*

When the sun was gone, the river in powdery shadow, and the fireflies streaking the dark, they went down the hill together. But the hour of violent tears in the currant patch was still there, in a dark, hidden place in the woman's memory, to be added to the other resentments, the dirt, the bedbugs, and the many, many things to come.

The next time Mary felt that she could not stay it was too late to go.

To Jules's letter announcing his marriage Rosalie sent her congratulations. This time she hoped that her friend had found a place of rest for his turbulent heart. She too was married — last week, to M. Droz, a superior officer in the mail service. Perhaps Jules remembered him. "He is so very kind and now it seemed clear that other things could never be." She did not wish to face a lonely old age. Perhaps everything was better so. She preferred the smaller, the more familiar things, while her Jules saw only the far, the large, the exalted canvas. "Good luck and contentment to you both."

"Well, so Rosalie is married." Jules could not realize
it even when he made the words. Somehow she should
always be there, waiting, with her fine hands and dark, intelligent eyes. A long time he sat deep within himself, his
thin wrists crossed over his knee. Rosalie, the little Rosalie . . .

Late in the evening when he roused himself he noticed
that Mary was not there, that she had not been there since
he showed her the letter. No supper.

A week later another letter came. Rosalie and Droz were
in New York. They were coming west, perhaps even to
Rushville. They would see this land that stole so many of
one's friends.

Jules went to town the next day and with what remained
of Mary's money bought lumber for a lean-to of two rooms
on the north. "We will need the space when your people
come to America," he explained.

But Mary knew why it was built and was slyly elated
when a regretful note came from Omaha. "It could not
be," Rosalie said. That was all. Jules threw the white
card on the table, got on Old Daisy, and went for a hunt.
But he was back by night.

And across the road were three tipis, White Eye and his
people. They had tried to make friends with the new
woman, the Curly Hair. Now Straight Eye must make her
see that their hearts were good toward her. They brought
her a pair of beaded moccasins, beautifully soft. Mary put
them away with her old country linens in her round-topped
trunk. Jules talked late to his friends, of hunts and battles and the buffalo days.

The two rooms built for Rosalie and Droz were convenient. Jules's workbench was moved into the east part
and set up, his vise and his forge with the anvil beside it,
in good light. In an old cabinet bought at a sale for twenty-
five cents they put away the little drug store, as the neigh-

bors called it: menthol, phenol, alum, carbolated vaseline, Paris green, rosin, glycerine, tincture of iron, potato dip, and other community essentials.   In the poison drawer were small vials of iodine, morphine, blue vitriol, balsam copaiba, bichloride of mercury, alcohol, and strychnine — drugs which Mary's money and thrift made possible.   Mary was glad to get these things off the shelf in the living room, where they reminded her of Dr. Geiger.   The back door to the lean-to was a convenient avenue of escape when she must run to the brush.

Late one evening in August a man loped into Jules's yard. Mary got up from her seat on the dark doorstep and lit the lamp, blinking over it at the gray-faced, unshaven man.

"Where 's Jules?" he asked.

"I think he will be home soon.   He is by Mintens' over on the hill."

The man's head waggled loosely in acknowledgment, like that of a limp rag doll being shaken.   He went out, but from the dark bedroom window Mary could see him, a black, motionless figure waiting beside his horse.   It was hours before Jules came home, but when he limped into the yard the man was still there.   They talked, the man in low, hoarse tones, Jules louder.

"I bin looking for it," Mary heard him say.

The men came into the house.

"I have nothing but reloaded shells — not as true as the factory ammunition for long range."

The man mumbled an answer and spread a red handkerchief upon the table; carefully he laid a handful of long brass shells into the centre, twisting the corners together, mumbled again, and was gone.

"What was it?" Mary asked anxiously, her eyes dark as she came out of the bedroom.

"Been some shooting down on the Hill range.   Fackler, a man working for Dan Hill, was shot by a settler, Buckminister. Fackler claims he filed on a hay flat Buckminister held for four-five years. When Fackler went there to cut hay, he got shot."

"Was this man the — was that Buckminister?"

"No, this fellow filed on a hay claim down there too and is getting ready for his turn to be run out."

Clasping her hands helplessly, Mary retreated into the dark bedroom.

The next day Jules's place was full of gaunt, sunburned settlers from the fringe of the cattle range. He cleaned an old revolver or two, repaired several rifles, and cast bullets and reloaded shells. He discussed the homestead laws and thumbed through the Nebraska statutes.

"If any son of a bitch comes on your place and tries to run you off, shoot, and shoot to kill," he advised them all.

Yes, and go to the pen for life, maybe stretch hemp, they remarked gloomily.

"A man has a right to defend his place against all invaders."

"Right? What right a settler got? Don't the bums the ranchers hires to kill you — like the bastard that shot Musfeldt — go scot-free?"

Jules scratched his chin. "Yah, the cattleman got the money and money runs the rotted officials, but they can't free a dead cattleman tool."

"Ach, it will give trouble, with such talk," Mary objected. But they ignored her. She was new and could not know how it was.

The Rushville *Standard* carried an item about the Buckminister shooting, reminding its readers that the valuable hay flats of the hills had long been a bone of contention between ranchers and settlers. Two or three had been killed the last year and cattlemen blamed. Now the settlers seemed to have inaugurated a little war themselves.

"Settlers, hell!" Jules told his neighbors. "Fackler is a tool of Hill, who wants the Buckminister flat. All the government corners down there been tampered with by the cattleman. Nobody can be sure where his land lays."

"Well, how's it coming out?" a settler from down that way wondered.

"I guess Fackler is not dead, so it is not yet murder, and if I remember right I saw the corner of the section east of Buckminister's place when I was hunting deer in '84. It all depends on whose land the shooting was done."

And once more the courts started their slow and wondrous process. Jules was pessimistic. "There'll be no end until the settlers learn to stick together or the government takes a hand."

Soon it was known that Jules's new wife was neat and quick as a blue-wing teal and gay when she could be. The neighbor women invited her to their homes, asked her to join their *Kaffeeklatsche*. But Jules rose in anger when she would go, and so she faced him with tear-swollen eyes across the table for a meal or two.

But usually things went well enough this one more summer of no rain. Through the confidence fostered by good food and a clean body Jules went into politics. The votes of those he helped to homes would make a substantial block in themselves. He wrote a letter to the *Standard* calling the attention of the Populists to the number of foreign voters in the country. It was only an act of justice to back one foreigner for county official. Before sealing the letter he read it to Mary.

"Yah, I guess it is all right, but it sounds like begging."

"Heah? — Begging? — Women don't understand politics," he told her, licking the flap and sealing it with red wax with injured emphasis.

"Jules's wife sure cleaned him up. She must be a rustler," the neighbors were remarking.

"Yeh, doing a lot of work for nothin', hoein' them spuds like she does. Elbow grease is good, but it ain't rain."

But even if Mary had known what they said she could not have stopped.

Her hands blistered, calloused, and then grew horny; her back ached, but if she worked hard enough and long enough, she could sleep.

When Jules came home from his rounds of the county political meetings Mary cut his hair, fought to make him change his shirts and wash his hands. While he slept she cleaned and patched his clothes. From a gray walking skirt she made him a pair of pants and a cap, consoling herself with the thought that it was too heavy here anyway, would only collect devil's darning needles and beggar-lice. From two aprons of the same light percale she made a shirt. So, looking better than any time since he left Neuchâtel, Jules sold the antelope and filed for the nomination of clerk of the district court on the Populist ticket, and while he rode about electioneering Mary picked the few scattered chokecherries along the river and spread them on papers in the attic. She dried a little sweet corn too, all she had, and wondered about the winter to come.

During the lone evenings she read in the Rushville papers that Buckminister was out on bail. "They won't do nothing with him," Jules predicted. There did n't seem to be much they could do, as the shooting was on his own place.

In the same paper Mary saw that Sousa's band played at the opera house at Rushville. So, one might see and hear something now and then, even here, if one were in better circumstances. She had heard Sousa last winter. A blond young baker had taken her to many concerts — gay times, sometimes they went dancing. And now she would probably never hear a band or an orchestra again.

But there was the comfort of the cold mist creeping down the Niobrara in her isolation. None of her friends need ever know. Jules was difficult, but he was intelligent. He ridiculed all that she held right and sweet, but he was always interesting, and even the road running past the house was more entertaining than a street. Horsebackers, cowboys in chaps, broad hats, spurs, leather cuffs, slouched over the horn as they passed towards the bridge. The Schwartz girls, in chaps too, and white shirtwaists, galloped by with their admirers. Long wagons, trace chains rattling going west, came back creaking up the rise, the horses straining through the sand to the bench where the house stood, to pant and rest there, and then to lean into the collars once more at the crack of the long whips swung by men toiling along beside the logier animals. Dusty men slid from shying ponies or left their teams to rest while they drew water from Jules's cool well, tipping the bucket to their dry lips and spitting out the first mouthful, then drinking deeply, their eyes looking over the rim at Mary curiously, friendly, sometimes bold.

"You Old Jules's new wife?" or, "How you like this wild country?" — queries she answered in hesitant English. Many waited for Jules, ate her biscuits, her lamb's-quarter pie or grouse soup with homemade noodles, good, but of little variety because there was no sugar and little lard.

"Mary puts out good grub," Jules bragged, and while half-pleased she could not forget that one does not boast of the food of his own table.

Mary looked with some disfavor upon the few women who passed or stopped, gaunt, generally, and sunburned, in unattractive wrappers, often in unbecoming, garish colors.

To the farewell dance at the Mintens', driven out by drouth and mortgages, she wore a soft cream-colored dress, sprigged with tiny blue flowers, the blue shirred front in the basque exactly the color of her eyes, a woven silver brooch at her neck. The women hung back from her, but the men, particularly Arnold Peters, soon discovered that she danced well. Arnold, exactly Mary's age, took her to his wife, relegated to the wall with one baby asleep in her lap and another under her wrapper. Other men crowded about

Mary for dances, and the eyes of the bench warmers who could not dance followed her enviously.

During the evening Hans hesitantly came to tell Mary that Jules had taken his gun and gone home in a temper. She flung her curly head and said it made no difference to her. But as soon as she could she slipped away.

She found Jules sitting in the kitchen, his rifle across his knee. When he saw her in the doorway he arose and cursed her until he was dry as a bleached bone.

With tears marking indelible lines down her cheeks Mary put the blue-sprigged dress away. She never went to another dance.

The road past the house brought other things too: big herds of dusty cattle headed into the hills darkening the lane west, spreading down the rocky ridge, running in a brown sheet at the smell of water. Sometimes the sheet was a slow-moving blanket of gray-white: sheep, eating everything as they came. Then Steve Staskiewicz, the Polander living in the grove across the river, ran out shouting Polish curses, his little collie hanging back from the big sheep dogs, letting the gray blanket spread under his barbed-wire fence into his bit of meadow, sometimes even into his shirt-tail patch of pop corn and cabbage.

When Mary called "Sheep!" Jules always limped out and stood at his fence with his rifle across his arm, his cap back from the piercing gray of his eyes, and when the men saw him they called their dogs and drove the sheep quickly up the hill and away, their rifles used to push the laggards on.

Despite the drouth there were some who made money. Three ranchers who came in years after Jules, and as penniless, shipped out a trainload of cattle together. "I'm a business man, a builder of the community," Jules defended himself against the unvoiced accusation. Next thing his post office was discontinued. A citizen of his locality had reported to Washington that the office was too close to another and that he had once been arrested for violation of the postal laws.

"Was n't I freed from every charge?" Jules demanded of anyone who would listen. "The goddamn cattleman tools — steal me my post office that I worked to start, cripple me my business, prevent me from getting homes for honest settlers."

He wrote to Washington, to the post-office inspector, to the Congressman from his district, to anyone who might listen to his complaint. He received polite replies with promises of investigation.

Then he was defeated at the Populist convention.

"Offices are lazy man's jobs," Mary tried to console him.

"You want me, an educated man, to work like a hired tramp!" he roared, and threw her against the wall. He wrote letters to the local papers charging that he had been slandered, pictured a criminal, accused of shooting a hog on the way to Hay Springs, when what he really shot was a hawk. Was he to be held responsible for a Dutchman's pronunciation? He had been defeated by vote-trading and slander and would go before the people by petition.

He read the last paragraph to Mary, compelling her to listen.

"By voting for me you will help to some extent to repair the damages done me by malicious criminal prosecution of which I have been the object for years and which have deprived me of land and living."

"Ach, you ought not to put such things in the paper. It sounds like those cranks who think somebody should give them a living," Mary complained, but to herself. She was trying very hard to live in peace.

In September Jules took Mary to Rushville for the first time. He left her in a store and limped away to talk politics. She spent the entire day waiting for him there, without dinner, without a cent of money to buy anything to eat.

Once or twice she walked to the door and looked up and down the street, patting her folded arms impatiently. "Nu-un, why don't he come?"

From the dark corner at the back of the store, where she had retreated in humiliation, she saw Mrs. John and her daughters, Mrs. Koller and Mrs. Arnold Peters, come in to try on hats. They laughed and talked among themselves, and with other neighbors who stopped in. Even the head-clothed Mrs. Staskiewicz from across the river bought sugar and coffee and had the money to pay. And still Jules did not come.

"Oh, hell, I forgot about you. I can't remember one wife. I've had so many," Jules laughed when Mary reminded him on the way home how badly he had treated her. One more resentment to be stored in her heart against him.

Towards election time a couple of the leading Democrats of Rushville called on Jules and offered him the entire Democratic vote if he would support their candidate for county sheriff. Jules pondered this suspicious offer for an hour or so and then ordered Mary to saddle Daisy and rode away to Rushville.

The next issue of the *Standard* carried the story of a threatening wholesale land steal. Referring to the offer of support made to Jules, the item showed the reason. The Musser outfit, controlling a local bank, had bought up two hundred quarters of land at tax sales. To obtain titles the land must be put through regular foreclosure proceedings and sold for not less than two thirds of the appraised value. The appraisement was under the control of the county sheriff, or anyone who controlled the sheriff.

"Well, I be straw-feathered!" was the exclamation in varying vernacular when the paper came out. It was a neat scheme, this that Jules and the *Standard* uncovered. The land was now valued at about $400 a quarter and could not be sold under $266. Allowing $50 for foreclosure expenses, the owner would get $216, less costs, but if the land could be appraised at, say, $75 a quarter, it could be sold for $50, leaving enough to cover the costs and nothing for the settler who proved up on it or paid the government $200 a quarter — saving the Musser gang at least $40,000. And all for the small matter of electing the right sheriff to make the appraisement.

"What did you say to them, Jules?" he was asked everywhere.

He had told them what they could do with their proposition, laughing until he choked.

Now the preëlection exposures were on in full array. The rival Rushville paper ran three items that Jules read to Mary and discussed quite calmly with her. The first was about the Musfeldt murder: —

Who struck down this young man and left a widow and a fatherless child? What efforts have been made to ferret out the crime or punish the criminal? None!! Can life be taken with impunity and the murderer released from all responsibility? Let us have an Answer!!

The second was about the murder of Still, the telegraph operator at Hay Springs: —

Where is the assassin? Who has ever heard of the sheriff attempting to bring the foul murderer to justice? Has human life ceased to be sacred? Answer echoes, why?

The other was about a man found dead down along the Burlington tracks just a few weeks before. Jules said he heard it was over a woman.

"They must say that."

"Heah? — Well, the papers says that 'on account of his political engagements' the sheriff has been unable to take the necessary time to investigate the matter."

"Anyhow they think something ought to be done." Mary took a bit of comfort in that.

"Yah, but this paper is backing the Musser candidate for sheriff, trying to help that gang beat the settlers out of $40,000. The editor is against settler-killing cattlemen but not the settler-cheating kind. Fence-straddling like that will make the son of a bitch good and long-legged!" And Jules laughed at his joke until he lost his pipe.

The Minten sale was a big event, and a surrender. The owner of the largest house and barn, with a limestone cave larger and finer than the homes of many families, was leaving the country.

By ten o'clock the yard at the crest of the bluff towards the Flats was black with teams and saddle horses. Many close settlers plodded with dusty shoes across the weed-grown fields. Jules and Mary went over together and separated, one to the men about the barn, the other to the house, where a roomful of women talked, the mothers in the back stuffing limp nipples into their crying babies' mouths like birds feeding their young. Some went to the kitchen to help prepare the lunch — a meat sandwich, two doughnuts, and an apple, in a paper sack with the neck twisted. On the stove a wash boiler with a dark bobbing sack of ground coffee steamed and sent its pungent odor out into the yard to awaken hunger, in some cases to irritate a hunger that seldom slept any more.

Mary helped, glad to be busy. She knew no one in the big room except the Peters women, and they looked side-wise at her tailored dress with its shirred bosom of change-able blue and brown taffeta, at her neat waistline. Perhaps they held Jules's eccentricities against her, perhaps her popularity at the dance was not forgiven. They did not include her in their talk and Mrs. Minten was glad to have her help in the kitchen, and when the lunch was ready help take it out into the yard, where the sacks were thrown among the men, the wreaths of tin cups on strings broken and filled with steaming coffee.

Then came the selling, by a loud-voiced auctioneer from Rushville. The stock, the implements, the household goods, were going for almost nothing. A team that had cost three hundred dollars two years before sold for twenty dollars; a good milch cow for seven, and so on until they had to take Mary Minten into the house and calm her with camphor.

Big Charley Grossenbach was the sale joke. "So close he makes the bark of a tree look like a tent hung over a post," the community wags said. To-day he bid guardedly upon almost everything to confuse the practical jokers until he got the barrel of dishes he wanted — and found he had mostly excelsior and broken bottles. The Peters', managing the sale, gave him ha-has instead of his money back. Somehow they overlooked Jules's bid on the sewing machine, a woman's necessity since he had known Emelia. Mary need no longer push a needle through the thick cloth of his pants.

Hans, Elmer Sturgeon, and Big Andrew stood about and bought a little. Aubert and Nicolet were there with their families. Tissot too, without his wife, and Mary overheard stories of his brutality.

"That's the fellow who dropped me in the well."

So? Mary told Jules something of what she had heard — that The Black left his wife to draw water for all his stock when her baby was only three days old, and could not keep out of her bed even one week.

"A coarse fellow. I saw him drop toads into my well to hear them plotch."

"Ach, what kind of men are these then?" Mary asked herself. The two did not talk much on the way down the hill towards home, and what was said was subdued, as though they were returning from the funeral of a friend.

West Mirage managed to get up a grand opening of the irrigation ditch at Pepper Creek, with four hundred people and still no water. Everyone hoping for it, however, went,

and the local sports curried up the trotters and with picnic
hampers took their girls to spend the day on the bare prairie
fifteen miles west of the county line, far from arable land.
Westover did n't get there, but other candidates grasped the
opportunity to predict a golden future, with water for the
crops, and the Republicans or the Democrats or the Populists,
as the speaker chanced to hope, established in office.

As election drew near the whispering campaigners con-
centrated on the candidates for district judge. Kinkaid
was not fit to hold office; he was a bachelor. Barrow was
married six years and had no children. Westover was
married six years and had eight.

"Don't everybody know about Mrs. Westover's little
trick of surprising her man with twins?"

"Anyway, they bin married fifteen years. What's this
business of children and marriage got to do with making a
good district judge?"

But it was all to divert the attention of the voters from
the race for sheriff. When the Democrats' deal with the
Populists was exposed, they bargained with the Republicans,
who took what votes they were given and then swung to
the Pops almost in a body on the sheriff, the one office the
banker Democrats wanted.

Jules went the way of the petition candidate. He received, as the Democratic paper put it, not an office, but a
skinned nose. Daisy shied on a bridge and threw him off.
Perhaps the old settler had overlooked his best bet anyway,
the editor suggested. Perhaps the voters would have been
more interested in his varied experiences with women than
his reform ideas.

"When you run with black sheep you get tar on your wool
too," Mary pointed out to the disgruntled Jules. "I hope
you can see you have to work if you want to live." She was
secure in the knowledge that he would hesitate to kick or
strike her too hard now.

But there were other problems. All fall, when Mary

worried over the future, Jules promised he would be making a good salary after the first of January as clerk of the district court.

"What must become of us — we will lose our home — and not even potatoes enough for the winter," Mary sobbed, crying easily these days.

It was true they had raised nothing. The nine bushels of potato seed yielded seven.

"Don't bother me!" Jules growled, without looking up from his stamps.

But when the bank tried to collect on the mortgage he laughed. "I don't owe you fellows anything. I can prove in court by my wife you got me drunk before I signed the papers."

They were glad to take a note for fifty dollars instead.

"I don't understand this way," Mary complained. "If you do not owe them, why did you sign the papers, and if you do why don't they make you pay?"

"I just skinned a skunk," he told her.

Although Cleveland came for his Secretary of Agriculture to Nebraska, and it looked very much as though the young Bryan Jules heard at Gordon years before might be President, times were desperately hard in the state.

With a borrowed shotgun, — Jules had sold his during the Freese troubles when money was so necessary, — he shot many prairie chickens, ducks, and several hundred quail. Packed frozen into barrels they sold on Eastern markets, paid for the absolute necessities, including a pair of heavy men's shoes for Mary.

"But they are for diggers of ditches!" she protested, thinking of the soft, fashionable slippers she was accustomed to.

"No, they are what you need here," Johnny Burrows told her kindly.

And as she plodded through the snow to look after

Jules's traps while he slept until noon, she knew what
John meant. Sometimes she saw the Polanders across the
river, the woman always three steps behind her man —
peasant fashion. So, too, was she — a peasant.

During the fall Jules's father died. He had come in
complaining of dizziness. In a few hours he was dead.
Jules seemed to remember only the natural antagonism
between them — that this father had refused to send him
more money — and nothing of the fine old Swiss that he
was, the father who had wanted so much to be proud of this
eldest, to be loved by him as he was by his people in
Neuchâtel.

Mary's father died too, leaving her mother and the sister,
Susette, alone in Schaffhausen on the Rhine. They should
come to America, Jules said. Mary wrote to them how it
was here. They prepared to sail in April.

The mild, dry winter seemed long and cold to Mary, who
had spent the last few years in Arkansas and St. Louis.
She carried home a huge pile of wood, mostly on her head,
and built up hot fires and then sat before them knitting new
heels and toes to Jules's socks, or making blue-sprigged
baby clothes from the dress she wore to the dance at the
Minten barn.

Often Jules and his friends sat about the kitchen as she
worked; sometimes they sang, now and then in German.
Then she joined them and was happier. But usually they
laughed and talked in French, looking at her, maybe, saying things she could not understand — perhaps that she
was only German or getting very big. Often she slipped
away into the unheated bedroom and stayed there until she
was wooden with cold. But Jules's friends were glad
enough to eat her well-cooked meals, to throw ashes over
her neat floor. By this time Mary had given up trying
to get Jules to spit into a can or a box of sand. When he

OLD JULES

Photograph by Dwight Kirsch

"THE SILVER RIBBON OF THE NIOBRARA"

JULES AMI SANDOZ, 1886

had I been permitted
to fully exercise my
judgement, I should have
amputated at the ankle-
joint, but your son
would not consent.
The wound is nearly healed,
+ I anticipate that he
will yet have a use-
ful foot. You may rest
assured that he shall
have my best attention.

I have the honor
to remain very respectfully
+ sincerely yours,
Walter Reed,
Captain + Asst. Surgeon
U.S.A. Army.

FACSIMILE, LAST PAGE OF LETTER FROM DR. WALTER
REED TO FATHER OF JULES, FEBRUARY 12, 1885

THE OLD BARRACKS, FORT ROBINSON

A DUGOUT AND HOMESTEADERS

MARY, FOURTH WIFE OF OLD JULES, 1895

THE SOUTH ORCHARDS

THE NORTH ORCHARDS AND VINEYARD

IN MIDDLE LIFE 1905

THE GREAT HERD

───NEBRASKA───
STATE HORTICULTURAL SOCIETY
18TH HORTICULTURAL DISTRICT
COUNTIES OF SHERIDAN, BOX BUTTE, DAWES AND SIOUX

SANDOZ
EXPERIMENT STATION
JULES A. SANDOZ, DIRECTOR
ALSO NOTARY PUBLIC, SURVEYOR AND JUSTICE OF THE PEACE

Life Member State Horticultural Society.
Honorable Member National Geographic Society.
National Forestry Association.
National Rifle Association, and American Philatelic Association.

Hay Springs Nebraska, *1/28* 190*8*

Francis Bannerman *New York*

Dear Sir Enclosed check for $ 371.35
and please ship me by freight to Hay Springs
Nebraska the following goods:

10 Mauser Rifles 7 m m. @ $10.	100.00
1 M. Cartridges 7 m for above	18.—
1 m Cartridges 7 m Dum Dum for same	18.—
1 M. 45/70 - 405. Copper Cartridges	14.—
1 Set of new Reloading tools for 45 Rifle and 45 Colt.	3.85
1 M 45/80 - 500. Long Range crtges	18.—
1 m 45 Colt. Goot made Crtges	8.—
3 Pairs #05 army Shoes a 1.50	4.50
2 Pairs #6 " " a 1.75	3.50
2 Pairs #7 " " a 1.85	3.70
2 Pairs #8 " " " 2.00	4.—
2 Pairs # 9 " " " 2.—	4.—
2 Pairs #4. army Winter shoes a $1.00	2.—

FACSIMILE OF OLD JULES' ORDER FOR
GUNS AND MERCHANDISE

AFTER A HUNT

IN THE ORCHARD

AMONG HIS ZINNIAS

A WORD WITH FRIENDS

FRITZ (RIGHT) AND A FRIEND

JULE AND JIM (ON HORSE)

"ENDLESS MONOTONY, CAUGHT AND HELD FOREVER IN SAND"

left the house she wiped up the great nauseating splotches and a deep, dark anger against him grew within her.

But at last a thaw came. Thin rivulets of snow water trickled for an hour or so and were soaked up by the hungry, warming earth. A greenish-brown mist hung about the cottonwoods across the river. Gray April wept her dripping days away in mist that beaded every bush and tree, but there was no rain, not enough moisture to start the grass. Mary knew that they might raise nothing at all this year, have nothing to eat, but somehow she could n't stir out of her heaviness even for that. Soon her mother and sister would be with her, her own people, with news from the Old Country.

XI

RAIN

For three April days the wind drove Russian thistles like sheep across the fields, piling them in fence corners or flinging them over the bluffs into the brush below. Dust and sand hazed the sun, blinded the eyes and stung the face. It sifted into the houses, leaving a disconcerting gray furriness over Mary's blue and white tablecloth. Then it began to rain. At the first drops Jules came limping out of the young orchard carrying his cap to show Mary the dark splatters gathering upon the cloth.

That night, alone for once, they sat at the well-polished stove and watched the water stream down the windowpanes. Mary was knitting a little jacket of fine white yarn from Rosalie. Jules smoked over the black cat stretched purring across his knees and talked hopefully of the prospects for the summer that was coming early. This year it would rain plenty.

Mary answered nothing, only smiled a little. "That is way to keep woman still," Anton Smolka told Jules last week when he brought news of his fourteenth child.

Yes, this year, Jules predicted, there would be plenty of rain. But there were few left to profit. Grass grew in the trails. Long strips of ploughing lay mauve in dead weeds, empty cellar holes and sod walls gaped into the sky all over the hard-land region.

Some day the land would all be settled again if the sheepmen could be kept out. But south of Gordon and farther up on Mirage they were coming in with Winchester-armed herders. Their dogs — large, defiant brutes — chewed at blackleg carcasses and nipped the settlers' gentle calves and yearlings. They drove the horses into the barbed-wire fences, laying open the strong breasts, cutting their legs so they had to be shot. The sheep spread under the wire fences, tufting the barbs with wool, eating the grass out of the ground, leaving the prairie open to weeds and the wind.

The cattlemen saw the menace in the new invasion first and fortified themselves against it by expansion and aggression, squeezing the settler buffer between them and the sheep.

"More hard-working farmers is the remedy for both," Jules said tersely, and wrote more letters to Eastern papers, to Europe.

Although Valentine preserved its border flavor into the twentieth century, Gordon, Rushville, and Hay Springs were settling down under the hard time, becoming drab, dusty Western stock and farming towns. But Chadron remained the obstreperous youth of the north Panhandle. When the first boom days were gone, the rough, broken region, naturally fitted for hideaways, became noted as the headquarters of rustlers working from Valentine deep into Wyoming. Cattlemen complained it was impossible to get a jury to convict cattle thieves. Settlers accused the ranchers of using the rustling charge to clear the range.

Jules talked of these things to Mary until she began to doze. Finally she speared her steel needles through the ball of yarn. "Yes," she murmured, "looks like there might be trouble." Dropping the cat through the trap-door into the cellar, she went to bed with the splash of rain on the windows in her ears.

Jules sat up late writing to the colonization agent of the Northwestern Railroad. This year they would raise un-limited crops in western Nebraska. It was the year to get farmers into the country. It was to the railroad's interest to see the country settled, even on passes.

The wet weather brought Jug Byers, working at the Spade ranch, back to his claim on Pine Creek. He needed a new stock for his rifle. "Busted it square off running a gray wolf. Old Smoke stepped in a badger hole." While Jules blocked out a new one on a piece of dark, rough-milled walnut, they talked of the sandhills, rustlers, and the pressure used against smaller outfits.

"Yeh, I guess they do trump up a charge now and then or make a plant to get rid of fellers they don't like. But it don't always work." Jug bit off a chew of Battle Ax, and when it was juicing good he went on. "Yeh, I hear, just between you an' me, that they been tryin' to plant Old Man Green. The outfit's been spreading, fencing, stringing in a lot of young she stuff, and putting up a big jag of hay on them wet flats at the head of Pine Creek. Killin' Musfeldt seemed to make them stick tighter." He glanced to Mary, darning stockings under the lamp. "I hear you ain't been going down there so much."

"Heah?" Jules asked, his habitual query if his mind wandered or he wanted time.

"Oh, nothing, only you wasn't hunting round in the hills like you use to. I guess they gets the idea you was done. Anyway some of the ranchers gets together, half a dozen or so. Them Green boys is hard customers, so they picks a time when only the old folks is home. They plants a big calf that wouldn't wean in the Green corral an' leaves the cow outside the fence, mile or so away, to get anxious. Next morning, little before daylight, they expects to help her through the fence and find her, accidental like, bawlin' outside the Green corral. Well, the cow ain't there when they gets around to let her through, but thinkin' she's crawled the fence and is ahead a them, they rides over, Winchesters across the saddles. There ain't no cow at the Green corral, nor there ain't no calf, only a sorrel

horse, with lather dryin'. The Old Woman is up and sees
'em. The Old Man and the boys ain't home, she says,
but won't they light and set down to a bit a breakfast?
She gives 'em fresh deer liver, frying pansful while they eats
without talkin' much. But Old. Ma Green rattles on, all
about you bein' down that way the evening before and leaving the liver."

Mary looked up. Jules squirted oil on his whetstone
and ran a fine German chisel in little spirals over it. "I
ain't been down that way for a year."

Jug got up and spit a calculating shot through the front
draft of the cookstove, wiped his walrus moustaches, and
sat down again. "Yeah, well, as I was saying — plants don't
allus work."

The next day Jules saddled Old Daisy.

"You will not mix in those fights in the sandhills?"
Mary asked anxiously from the doorway.

"Oh, hell, no. I am just going down to hunt a little
and maybe shoot a little target around some of the ranches."
In less than a week he was back with the hind quarter of
an antelope sewed into canvas and in his hunting coat a jar of
purple sand-cherry jam for Mary. Ma Green sent it.

"I have bin to some of the ranches thàt want Green out
of the country, done a little target shooting," Jules said.
"By golly, but the fellows looked when I spurted sand five
shots out of five in a patch the size of a man as far as they
can see." Jules stopped to gulp a cup of coffee on top of
the half-ring of coffee cake he ate. "Old Daisy got all the
oats the old mare could hold."

Mary's people came and were barely settled in the lean-to
built for Rosalie when her time was upon her. She was not
of the broad, large-boned peasant stock that was peopling the
region to the west of them, and it went hard with her.
Perhaps Jules was made awkward and afraid by a softness
within him that he would not confess. At last, when a day

and a night went by and Mary was still in travail, Mrs. John, with her stiff, bearded lips and brutal, heavy hands, was brought. She left Mary more dead than alive, but relieved. And the next afternoon, when she awoke from the morphine Jules gave her to blot the pain and bring sleep, he was looking anxiously in upon her through the window and his arms were filled with plum blossoms.

Mary's second summer on the river was a good one — hard work, but joy too. With a baby she could never leave Jules, not so long as she could stay at all, so that was settled. And this year it rained. Not a lot, but they had a good garden and enough to eat. Susette, Mary's nineteen-year-old sister, was with them. Very small, without any particular prettiness except an elfin-like quality to her pointed face, her vivacity and her wit endeared her to the entire community, particularly to Mary, who had not seen her since she was a child of fourteen, and to the lonesome young bachelors who craved diversion and a wife. Tilted back on the wired-up kitchen chairs, they ate Mary's cooking, teased Susette, and laughed at Jules's pretended dreams of fat black wenches.

"You ought to shame yourself, telling such stories before a girl!" Mary objected angrily. But Jules only scratched the hair on his chest and laughed the louder.

Often Susette played checkers or nine-men's morris in the kitchen, or they all sang with strong young voices, led by Mary, who seemed always to know more and more songs of the homeland. Now and then a tear glistened in a wind-reddened eye as they sang of wandering lovers or sweethearts waiting and thought of those who did not wait or would not come to America. Jules always started the songs of faithlessness and the martial airs, singing one or two in French. Sometimes there was Emile's flute or perhaps Paul Wuthier, long ago forgiven the Emelia episode, with his accordion. Often Big Charley, the Bernese Oberlander, his

red-brown eyes teasing behind his thick glasses, yodeled for
them.   Then they frankly wept as they laughed and drank
of the sweet wine.   Ah, it was like the old homeland here
in Jules's kitchen.

Perhaps they danced a little on the scrubbed, rough
boards.   Sometimes Mary joined in, until her face flushed
and Jules glowered from his chair at the stove.   She was
a good dancer and no amount of work could make her feet
lag.   Was n't that why Conrad, the musician on the Rhine,
had first noticed her, so long ago?   And when it grew late
the talk turned to the Old Country, and the young Americans
sat wondering that such softness could be uncovered in
Jules, such a depth of wistfulness lie in them all.

> 30 miles to water
> 20 miles to wood,
> 10 miles to hell
> And I gone there for good

— carved on the door of a deserted shack on the dry-land
table near Chadron in the nineties.

Even Jules had to admit that the Panhandle was going
over to the cattlemen through drouth depopulation.   While
he preached dry farming the dwellers of the sandy soil
turned to cattle and the Mirage Flatters dug ditches and
hauled lumber for the two long flumes which must be
finished before a drop of water could be applied to the
land.

The irrigation project required a great deal of boosting,
and, as Jules pointed out, "several extra grizzlies thrown
in," to keep the work going without capital.   The boosters
whipped themselves into a good frenzy of enthusiasm.
Many hours were spent at the barns and about the pigpens
discussing the optimistic future, while squealing pigs pushed
sharp noses through the cracks.

A few of the conservatives kept their feet solidly on the
ground, but everyone was young with large dreams.   The

original twenty-odd-mile ditch lengthened to thirty-five miles. Next the *Standard* told of a 250-mile project that would reach from Dunlap near Chadron to Mirage Flats, across to Rushville, through the sandhills to the Snake River, whose bed was to be used for forty-five miles, by canal to a reservoir southwest of Valentine, and then down the divide of the Elkhorn towards O'Neill. Two hundred fifty miles for $1,500,000.

"Take the Amazon River to soak up the sand of a ditch like that," Jules tried to tell them. Eastern papers looked upon the gigantic plans as a serious suggestion and envisioned raids on the federal treasury. An Omaha writer predicted there would be enough water in the sandhills lakes to make the contemptible term "sandhills" lose its force; make the region "smile with harvest bountiful and varied, even when a pitiless sky and sun have done their worst."

Hard upon the optimistic predictions the rain ceased again; more banks closed their doors. Even Hans and Big Andrew were leaving, Big Andrew who had so eloquently offered his strong hands to bring the water, his shoulders rounder than ever now from the scraper. He would not come to Jules for good-bye. But Hans came; dully he talked a little, as though speaking of a stranger, one in whom he had bare interest. Jules brought out a pitcher of raisin wine, a loaf of bread, and a platter of cold grouse, but Hans shook his head. Only once he seemed alive — his face swift-purpled under the flush of steady whiskey. "Ach, this country — how I hate her! She has taken everything from us — from me, my joy, my youth, my music, *ja*, even" — his voice dropped to a whisper " — even my Anna."

Yes, so it seemed. Jules puffed at his pipe and scarcely noticed his friend as he slipped out and rode away without the good-bye he came to say. And now the deserted houses were left standing, their windows empty, yes, even Jules admitted that there must be much rain and soon. It came; washed away part of the dam at Dunlap. It soaked the deserted fields, and the sunflowers grew shoulder high once more. For Henriette, taken to the asylum at Norfolk, and for many others, it came too late.

Mary had three anæmic, undernourished children very close together, without a doctor. She lost her teeth; her clear skin became leathery from field work; her eyes paled and sun-squinted; her hands knotted, the veins of her arms like slack clothesline. There was little of the city woman about her now, little for the Peters women to envy. She still combed her hair the first thing in the morning, wetting it back, and it still blew out in unruly curls. She still used clean linen tablecloths for Sunday and company, and had a fringed spread on her bed every day.

In order that their names might not die from the Running Water, Jules named the first two children for their parents. The third and ever the favored he called James, Jim. To Mary's curious inquiry he gave some reply, forgotten immediately. Then, with his gun across his knees, he sat long on Indian Hill, Freese Hill, as he called it now, and watched a flock of powdery-blue mountain jays circle about the patch of sweet corn below. He wondered about the man who had found him afoot in the Big Horn country. And if he would be pleased that this fine new son would also be Jim.

Mary had little milk even for her beloved first-born son, and so the little Jule was taken from his father's bed and became his grandmother's charge and favorite. But there was no such escape for the mother from her first girl child. When the little Marie was three months old and ill with summer complaint, her cries awakened Jules. Towering dark and bearded in the lamplight, he whipped the child until she lay blue and trembling as a terrorized small animal. When Mary dared she snatched the baby from him and carried her into the night and did not return until the bright day.

But the night's work was never to be undone. Always the little Marie hid away within herself. She never cried out in the terror of her dreams or walked the house in her sleep as did the little Jule, but from the time she could walk she hid away, retreating into fancy. With Jule it was little better. Even behind the protecting skirts of Mary and the grandmother he could not escape the father's hand entirely.

The little James was more fortunate from birth. He was spared the sex animosity that is the inevitable heritage of the first-born son and daughter. There was more rain, more mother's milk, and his pretty girl face won him praise that the other two saw and envied darkly.

Jules still rested after breakfast. A half hour of furious hoeing still drove him to rest and read. Usually when Mary complained Jules grinned like a very clever fellow. Three or four times a year they took a whole day off and went to see Elvina or William or spent Sunday on Pine Creek, leaving the children with Mary's mother. The quiet, man-subordinated little woman effaced herself as well as possible, and she was not unhappy in this strange America with this strangest of all men, this son-in-law. She knitted and mended and kept an eye on the children, which pleased Mary. She kept an eye out, too, for omens, which amused Jules. When she found a snake in the little Marie's lap one day, both asleep under a tree, she was horrified. At her frightened shooing the tiny reptile slid hurriedly into the grass. With the child in her arms she ran to the house. No good could come of this.

"Ach, why did you let her go to sleep in the garden?" Mary scolded, examining the little hands for purple pricks.

"Probably the snake smelled milk," Jules laughed, not disturbed.

But the grandmother still shook her head. There was

a warning for women in Genesis against snakes. This traffic
was a mark of the devil's.

"More of the religion stuff — old woman's stories," Jules
scoffed. "More sense to the Greek notion that snakes
bring wisdom and healing."

After the mother came to America, Mary's brother Jacob
brought his wife and two children up and rented the Mutsch
place down the river, through Jules. Fanny, Jake's wife,
was a mortification to his mother and Mary and Susette.
She chewed horseshoe tobacco and could drown a fly at three
yards, but could n't seem to spit off the front of her loose
red wrapper. She was a good cook in an easy-going,
slovenly sort of way, and a hair in the fried potatoes was
just a hair. But she had her allurements, and after Jake
caught one bachelor or another with her every time he came
home unexpectedly he took her back to St. Joe.

A few weeks later Mary got a letter from a friend in
Arkansas, saying that Fanny and the children had come
down there with a crippled old man who seemed to have a
little money. Where was Jake? Perhaps they had killed
him?

"Ach, my son, my eldest!" the mother moaned.

"Be still. You 'll see he 's not dead," Mary predicted,
and wrote to his old St. Joseph address. After a few weeks
she got a letter, addressed in Jacob's vacillating scrawl.
Mary closed her lips as she looked at it again. She liked
good handwritings; her own was beautifully uniform and
restrained. As she had expected, Jake was all right. Nothing had happened to him except that Fanny got a divorce
and swore in court that the children did n't belong to him.

"But she made him marry her because of the first one!"
Mary objected.

Jules looked up from his plans for a larger orchard.
"That 's the way with a woman. Swear to any lie to get her
own way."

"You always make me eat out the cold soup for everybody!"

"Heah?"

"I said you blame me ror everything!"

"Oh, hell, don't bother me. Can't you see I 'm busy?"

But Jules was easier to live with now. He had a post
office again, his fourth.

When he convinced Mary's mother that she too should
possess a piece of this land so easily obtained in America
and so certain to be valuable some day, she wrote to the Old
Country for the few hundred dollars she had invested there.
All the free land near by was gone, but she could buy the
relinquishment to the Timmerman place, north of Jules's
school section, one of the finest quarters in the country —
level, with just enough sand to prevent excessive baking, and
not so far that she could n't go there a few nights a month
to establish a residence.

But Timmerman was impatient, he would offer his place
elsewhere. Every mail day Mary rode Old Jim, stiff and
slow now, to the post office at the John Peters place, north
of the Catholic Church. Still the money did not come.

One day as Jules dropped into the Rushville post office
to talk politics, the postmaster showed him a letter.

"I wonder if this don't belong to one of your Swiss on
Pine Creek?"

Jules looked at it. The delayed money, held up almost
a month and returned as unknown and uncalled for.

"Trying to keep me from getting the place for *Grossmutter!*"

Two weeks later Jules had a post office again.

The holidays brought letters. From Mary's cousins in
Schaffhausen, complaining of the hard times; from Jules's
mother and from Henri, and from Paul on the Platte, and
from Rosalie, who sent a present for her godchild, the

little Marie. She wrote in French, usually, with German paragraphs interspersed. The French Jules translated literally.

Dully now, with her hand on the wheel of the sewing machine, Mary waited for the end of the Rosalie anecdotes he told and retold every year: their walks in the greening woods of spring, their skating, all the promises of their partings.

Mary looked up at the old ebony Swiss clock. After eleven; the kerosene in the lamp burning low, and the children needing the moccasins she was making. The pieces of old overall stitched together, round and round, for the soles lay before her. Mary wondered at the perversity of her children, always out in the snow. She would gladly stay indoors if she could, but there was wood to be carried, traps to look after, the three cows to be fed.

"Droz," Jules read from Rosalie's letter, "is very jealous and I am having a great deal of sorrow because of this, although he has absolutely no cause. It is true I have told him I still think well of you and have not forgotten you. That perhaps is not a misfortune."

At last Jules put the Christmas letter away and went to bed. Mary rolled up the moccasins wearily. She dared not run the machine while he slept. So she darned socks; mended his pants, stiff with muskrat blood; considered washing them, but decided they would not dry by morning. There was no telling when Jules would get up, six or eleven. After the children's stockings were washed and hung behind the stove to dry, she got Jule up and took him out and stopped to cover James in the little bed with Marie. Then she stretched herself softly beside her husband and lay unmoving until gray morning.

By now Mary hoped for nothing more than that her children might have enough to eat and some day have shoes between their feet and the iron-hard ground of winter.

Others already had these things through cattle. Almost everyone in the community was taking herds on various share schemes, signing long-time mortgages for preposterous sums.

"That Boston outfit must have a lot of money to throw away. Looks like risky business to me," Jules said. But with characteristic enthusiasm he went in to the full extent of his credit himself, signing a mortgage for $4165, three times what the cattle were worth, to be paid from the increase, interest at 12 per cent.

Before long it was clear that the purchasers were doubly cheated. The cattle turned out to be culls, Southern stock and smooth-mouthed old cows. Even with the best of care they shivered and bawled and died while the native roan cow and her shorthorn heifers held in good flesh.

During summer Jules ignored Mary's ultimatum, "Now we have to put up hay," mainly because it was an ultimatum. The ranchers used to let their cattle rustle. Well, his stock could rustle too. So while the grass was under snow Mary eked out the bit of corn fodder with turnips and beets and rutabagas. Long before spring most of their herd was represented by a pile of warble-punctured hides that Gottlieb Sutter, a young Swiss wintering with them, helped her skin. Mary could not understand these share schemes. She saw only the load of debt weigh heavier.

"You never saw me lose nothing yet for debts," Jules reminded her, looking up from his new book on fossils and formations in the Bad Lands.

"No, but you can't always crawl out."

Jules's attitude was not unique. Sturgeon, Byers, Jed Brown, William, Emile, Koller and Peters, Pochon, the Beguins, and Nicolet and Tissot and all the others who bought from the cattle companies were losing heavily. They shrugged their shoulders. Eastern money. The East had lived off the West long enough. Should they worry now that the East was losing a little when it had planned to squeeze the last penny from the Western farmer?

In the spring the receivers of the bankrupt cattle companies gathered up what was left and departed.

"Did they get your cattle, Jules?" Louis Pochon asked.

"*Ja*, I 'm back to three head."

"Three head? But have you no more than before you start? Did you not keep the calves at least for your troubles? With all the canyons you have to hide them in you should have the good start now."

"I don't do business that way," Jules said shortly.

Although he never told Mary so, it was because she was such a hard worker, made all the other women he knew seem lazy, impractical, and irresponsible, that Jules turned his settling activities toward Germans and German Swiss. Here and there the sheep-grayed regions and the cattleman fences were pushing in upon what had once been settled land. He went to the land office, made a note of all unpatented land, and galloped Old Daisy optimistically homeward. He would build a new settlement, — not bachelors, men with families, — good, hard-working German stock.

He got passes for destitute families over the Northwestern, from Wisconsin, Missouri, Ohio, even New York, sheltered them with his own growing brood until they got on their feet, sometimes for six months — until the last bit of lard, almost the last potato, was gone. He sheltered them, but Mary did the work.

"Oh, shoot!" the Americanized young Susette scolded when a new group, father, mother, and four children, with bundles of feather ticks and checked tablecloths, arrived. "No wonder you never have the money for a new dress and the children go barefoot. But I guess it can't be helped. 'Marry when bees o'er May blooms flit, strangers around your board will sit.'"

"Susette is beginning to think of marriage and a man," Jules interpreted her complaint. Her mother was pleased, too. People were beginning to say she dressed like a pea-cock since she went to Rushville and Gordon to work; that she was too high-toned for any of the honest young settlers.

But Mary would n't push her.

"Let her have a good time while she can," she defended, her arms folded over her apron that never hung flat any more. She was nursing James until he was three. Cheat-ing the stork, Nell Sears called it. Nell liked Mary. She had burned her backside, but she sat on the blister.

Times were better in the Panhandle, but not for Mary. Sometimes there was no flour, no sugar, no kerosene for months. Then Jules revived the skunk-oil lamp of his batching days and Mary ground wheat in the hand gristmill until the perspiration streamed from her veining temples. She fed her hens hot mash, hoping for an egg or two a day for Jules's breakfast. He always ate three, complaining at the rye coffee instead of chocolate. He never noticed what the rest had.

But it was true that one after another the young men who gathered in the kitchen when Susette first came were dropping away. Hans Casper was gone. Paul Wuthier of the accordion was married. He wanted one of the religious daughters of Jules's Uncle Louis, living three miles down the river. But the family decided that her health was too delicate for marriage. Then he wrote to a matrimonial-paper prospect awhile, showed a photograph of a hand-some, Junoesque woman to his acquaintances, his pale little eyes lighting up behind the thick glasses. He even seemed a little more than his five feet five as he talked of this stranger, Andrienne. He saved his money and finally went to New York City, promising them all a big wedding dance when he returned.

But ten days later he sneaked back to Pine Creek alone. Andrienne, to whom he had sent ardent letters and nice presents, including a very fine beaver skin and money for

a wedding outfit, was a man.   So he married the daughter
Uncle Louis would give him, and later the one he wanted
went to live with them and helped care for the children
as they came.   And under the influence of the two religious
sisters Paul Wuthier put away his accordion and his lusty
stories and learned to pray.

But Susette was no longer interested in any of the young
men at Jules's.   She came to the river every month or so
in the top buggy of a young American who never got out,
but waited in the road for her as she talked half an hour
with her mother and Mary and then, with a rustle of many
petticoats, was gone again.

"Ach, she is ashamed of us," Mary told her mother, and
a tear moved slowly down the long line of her sunken cheek.
People had not always been ashamed of her.

"Susie has been spoiled by working for Americans in
town.   No good for a farmer's wife," Jules said, just a little
disappointed.   He liked the quick-witted girl and her clever
tongue.

The Germans and the German Swiss did n't visit as
much as the French, but they made good settlers.   They
carried lanterns until late at night, complained of the wind,
the cold, and the drouth, and prospered well enough.
At times they cursed Jules for bringing them into the
country, for helping them to stay when they should have
accepted defeat.   But most of the time they were too busy to
think of him at all.

They organized a church, with Jules's post office as the
logical meeting place for all.   Once a month a pastor from
near Rushville came down and preached for whatever they
could afford to give: a few worn dimes, a quarter or two;
butter, chickens, pork, if anyone butchered; or a few
bushels of corn for the buggy team.

During the first service Jules stretched out on the clean
spread in the bedroom to read, his knees crossed, his lame

foot high in the air. Crowded into the kitchen-living room were thirty grown people, their faces raw with wind and soap, the men in black suits well darned and brushed, the women in black woolens buttoned tight over swelling bosoms. One or two turned their backs to quiet fretting babies. The older children sat on the floor under the eyes of their parents. They all sang vigorously — "*Ein feste Burg*," "*Schäfers Sonntagslied*," other songs they could remember.

But during the sermon the serious young minister became confused several times, stammered, reddened, wiped his glasses, and then hurried on. After the benediction they talked the business of the church while Mary made hot chocolate. Mrs. Wittig pulled her unaccustomed corset down and bent to whisper to her that "maybe we should have an older man."

Mary looked up from the cups and saucers she was arranging on the table. Suddenly she laughed — until the tears ran and she had to pretend it was about one of the Wittig children. Wiping her eyes on her white lawn apron, she looked again. There, from where the young minister had stood, she could see Jules's crossed legs and the rubber shoe of his bad foot reflected in the mirror of her dresser, a dirty tuft of excelsior sticking out through the rubber sole.

"The looking-glass — I will turn it next time," she whispered to Pastor Haeckel as she helped him to a napkin and a cup of chocolate. He looked gratefully over his glasses, very boyish and blond.

Mary awakened Jules and he came out to visit and drink chocolate and eat of the little cakes. Every once in a while Mary laughed. Perhaps it was the service, the first she had attended in Nebraska. Perhaps it was only the foot in the mirror.

With the country full of sheep the coyote spread. From a scavenger and small hunter he became a killer. Emboldened by his success, he slipped into barnyards, attacking flocks of chickens and turkeys, leaving dead birds strewn behind him. Mary lost eight turkeys one morning — all she had. Many calves, even colts, were killed. The settlers and the cattlemen were ready to join even with sheepmen for the wolf hunt announced in the *Standard*.

At nine o'clock in the morning a relay of shots started the horsebackers off on a fifteen-mile front, from Box Butte, where William lived, to the Keplinger bridge, ten miles below Jules, and to Pine Creek. Yelling, whistling, running any coyote that tried to break through the line, they headed across the hard-land table to the Jackson place, near Hay Springs, where a big V had been built, the long arms made of hog wire and chicken fencing, with lath corncribbing where it narrowed to a wire trap in the point.

While the men galloped over the prairie the women unpacked baskets of food in the big barn mow for the dinner.

"Time they was running up a few coyotes," Mrs. Putney said as she uncovered a roaster full of browned chickens. "Henry lost twenty-five sheep last week, just killed and let lay, in broad daylight."

Settlers' wives exchanged looks. "Tsk, tsk," they said.

"We been having hunts for ten years and all they does is make the critters harder to catch. Never gets none," Mary Dorman, an old settler, commented as she measured out the ground coffee. "Dogs or poison, that fixes the sneaking devils that gets my turkeys."

"But where's the fun in that?" asked the girls from the Dutch community about the Catholic Church, just coming now, when most of the work was done.

By one o'clock black specks were running over the Flats like bugs. Shouts, commands, a cloud of dust. Horses tramping on each other's heels. A few shots. That was all.

Four jack rabbits, one badger, and three coyotes, for two hundred hunters.

"Got sight of a couple more, but they musta snuk out a the lines. Not many a the Pine Creek bunch showed up," Dorman said.

Now came the dinner, dished up on long boards over barrels in the mow. Windy fellows talked about the long-ago hunts, when there were real wolves, too smart for a mob. One told of the day he and eighteen others started after a gray in deep snow down east of Green's ranch, in the sandhills. They got the wolf near Hemingford, after traveling over fifty miles. The gray just laid down and let Old Jules and that buckskin of his ride up to him. Not another hunter in sight.

"Yah, and remember how he roared because somebody stole the skin and scalp and he never got the twenty-five dollars they offered for the wolf down in the hills?"

So they talked as they dug into the stacks of cold pies, drank coffee. With settlers, sheepmen, and cattlemen at one table it was safer to talk of the past.

After dinner cigars were passed by the local candidate for the legislature; an invitation to a hunt at Rushville the next week was read, and the fun was over.

The same day, the *Standard* reported, five coyotes were seen in a bunch at high noon near town. "Probably looking for the hunt," Jules told Mary. "You can't get game in a crowd."

Others beside Jules began to realize that the sheepmen were a menace. When the first herds came through in the '90s the range was open, grass plentiful. No one but Jules paid much attention to the undulating blanket of gray that spread slowly over the ground and left it bare. But the sheep-grazed regions grew up in weeds, the lighter-soiled spots blew into holes. Four-strand fences were as nothing against the herds. Settlers began to hurry them on with a show of rifles.

From the first sheep it had been war with the cattlemen. About Chadron and between Gordon and the Niobrara they got a foothold, but not without conflicts, lawsuits, destruction of property, and finally murder. When a herder was shot near Chadron the cattle range was fired. A new sheep outfit within ten miles of Hay Spring was burnt out the first night, the flocks scattered. Near Gordon the small stockmen organized against Bartow, running six thousand sheep and controlling seventy sections of land. He sent attorneys to the meeting, offering mediation.

"Just until he gets a footing and a bunch of gun-toting Mexicans, then all hell can't freeze him loose," a cowman from Wyoming told them, with convincingness.

Near middle Pine Creek two small ranchers thick with the Schwartz outfit were putting in sheep. The first flock brought Emile and Pochon and one of the Beguins to Jules.

"What can we do?"

"They will eat us up — run us all out in a year or two!"

"More Germans without money enough to leave the country, located in the sheepman's pasture, will break up the sheep game," Jules told them. He sent out more letters, hauled more families in from the railroad for Mary to feed until they were settled.

The sons of Jacob Schwartz, the cringing little man who cried before Jules's mob, were long, sunken-cheeked, dark-moustached men, their hats pulled to their yellow-brown eyes. Silently they watched much freight pass through their yard into the hills, saw large herds of grass-fat steers come out of them. Roadhouse business was all right enough to amuse their sisters, but they were hustlers, and the mother kept them hustling. With the Pine Creek settlement at their doorstep, the south hard-land farmers at their side window and the upper Pine Creek ranchers at their back door, they bought up-to-date rifles, hauled posts, fenced every foot of free range, ran rival cattle out and stocked their own place overnight — in the night, their angry neighbors said.

Now the Schwartz outfit was going in for sheep. Old

Man Bailey brought three thousand head in from Wyoming, where the cattlemen were organizing. He looked for range, found it by going into partnership with Carl Schwartz.

"Won't take them girls long to get the whole slough!"

The old man hung about the roadhouse several months before he left the country broke.

"They got every cent I had," he told Jules while waiting for the mail carrier to take him to the railroad. He was going back to Wyoming to start as a herder again, but the nights got cold up there and he was too old to sleep with a Winchester. Tears leaked down the weathered grooves of the old man's face.

"Ach, those girls ought to shame themselves," Mary scolded as she wrapped up a coffee cake and a piece of boiled ham for him to lunch on.

Jules located half a dozen German settlers in the Schwartz range, on free land illegally enclosed in their fences, as he had several times reported to the Department of the Interior.

"Well, Jules, you know your business, but I would n't bother that outfit," Jimmy Dorman, one of Jules's friends from the Freese troubles, felt impelled to tell him.

"You working against me too now! Sticking in with the land thieves!" The man went away sad and hurt.

In the meantime Jules was using every means he knew for getting the sheep out of his locality. Packing his surveying outfit under the wagon seat, with his rifle between his knees, he pushed into the Schwartz range with settlers. Then one day he came back in high feather, with a bottle of whiskey for himself and his friends and a patent potato chipper for Mary.

"I located Weigel, that big Prussian who had to skip Germany because he slapped an officer, right under Carl Schwartz's nose," he bragged.

"Don't you think you ought to do something about Old Jules — locating people so close to that roadhouse? Something will happen to him," Mary was warned.

"What can I do?" she demanded, all the resentment of years' accumulation murking her eyes to stony gray.

Somebody ought to talk to Jules, it was thought. One woman in the insane asylum was enough.

But perhaps because Old Jacob Schwartz once saw the wordless command Jules could wield over a mob, and knew his reputation as an unfailing marksman, nothing happened to the locator. He came and went through the fences and no one tried to stop him, until every tillable acre was covered. Then he sat back to wait until the settlers moved in.

In the meantime the big house the Schwartz brothers were putting up looked more and more like a crazy quilt, with wings and dormer windows of old lumber and new, wide and narrow, painted and unpainted. Nobody paid much attention to that sort of thing until the Dreyer district, halfway to Rushville, lost two new schoolhouses as fast as they could be put up. The irate patrons, with guns across their saddles, tracked the heavy moving wagons to the Schwartz fence. There they stopped and, turning their horses, galloped out of sight. The next schoolhouse they put up was of sod.

One after another the German farmers moved in. "Watch your lumber and your stuff every minute or you lose it," Jules warned.

They bought or borrowed rifles and, with their families, squatted and began houses and strung wire. Usually two or all three of the dark brothers rode up to each newcomer the first day. Rifles in scabbards and revolvers sagging shell-filled belts, they talked big. But Jules was always somewhere near, spurring Old Daisy from one soddy to another. After that the fences would be cut a few times, the horses and the milk cows driven off, or perhaps a young stallion shot to spoil him for service. But the settlers stayed, and stock shooting was a double-action business.

"I look them in the eye like the recruits they give me in the Old Country. I look at them so and say, 'Git,

Schweinehund!' and they go like the devil and make a big dust," the Prussian told Jules.

Their range shrunken to half, the Schwartz outfit cut down on sheep, to Jules's elation.

But they got his post office.

"I told you to let them alone. Now they got something you wanted damned bad," Dorman reminded him.

Jules protested to Washington. He accused everyone, Emile, Mary, her mother, even Susette, of working against him. Mary avoided crossing him or bothering him for help in anything she could possibly do alone. But there were times when she must have his help, as when the roof leaked or the calves were to be castrated. It took weeks of diplomatic approach to get him to look after the two bull calves before they were too big for her to handle at all. And when she could n't hold the larger one from kicking, Jules, gray-white above his beard, threw his knife into the manure and loped to the back door. "I learn the goddamn balky woman to obey me when I say 'hold him.'" He tore a handful of four-foot wire stays from the bundle in the corner of the shop and was gone towards the corral, the frightened grandmother and the children huddled at the back window.

They heard the banging of the gate, Jules's bellow of curses. Then Mary ran through the door, past the children and straight to the poison drawer. It stuck, came free, the bottles flying over the floor. Her face furrowed in despair, blood dripping from her face and her hand where she had been struck with the wire whip, the woman snatched up a bottle, struggled with the cork, pulling at it with her teeth. The grandmother was upon her, begging, pleading, clutching at the red bottle with the crossbones.

Jules burst in. "*Wo*'s the goddamned woman? I learn her to obey me if I got to kill her!"

"You!" the grandmother cried, shaking her fist against him. "For you there is a place in hell!"

With the same movement of her arm she swung out, knocking the open bottle from the woman's mouth. It rolled over the floor, strewing the white crystals of strychnine in a wide fan. Then she led Mary out of the house and to the brush along the river.

Jules limped away, saddled up Old Daisy himself, and with his rifle in the scabbard headed for Pine Creek.

And hidden far under the bed the three children cowered like frightened little rabbits, afraid to cry.

XII

HAIL ON THE PANHANDLE

THE late January sun slashed the fog to long white ribbons that clung to the gray bluffs jutting over the snowy slopes and the dead trees and brush. A flock of grouse perched upon the highest tips of the ice-glazed cottonwoods complained in sad little cackles. It was cold the night before, cold enough so the Minten barn, too wide for the little bridge, could safely be moved over the ice of the Running Water to Arnold Peters's place up the river.

Mary dropped her load of wood and, hidden in a plum thicket, watched the barn go, the men and teams like ants in the snow, straining, pulling, as it swayed dizzily down the hill and lurched out upon the ice. Once over the river the building moved heavily south towards the Peters homestead and the new ten-room house.

Now it was gone, as the blue-sprigged dress she wore to the dance there was gone. In place of the dress she had a coarse black hair-line wool Jules bought after he struck her with the wire whip. Mary hated black, needed calico. She would n't pretend to like it. And the bull calf was still to be looked after.

With a whir of wings the grouse flew over her to the cornfields of the table. She shivered in Jules's old coat, thumped her freezing feet, lifted the wood to her head, and toiled through the snow towards home.

The country around Jules was resettling. Ernest, brother of Jules Aubert, lived on the Minten place and hauled milk to Hay Springs for a separator and creamery company. Nicolet and his family were on the Mutsch place which Jules had bought for Mary because she had no time to establish a residence on a homestead, like Henriette and Eugenie and the rest. So they mortgaged the old Freese place for two hundred fifty dollars and bought the quarter.

A Hollander with a placid wife who looked upon her rapidly increasing brood with the unconcern of a mud turtle for the eggs she lays in the sand rented Henriette's place. Pat Burke, a bachelor, lived a mile east. South of him was the Johansen family. All these had moved in during the preceding year or two.

Farther away, too, there were more farmers, and telephone lines and mail routes were penetrating into the fringe of the sandhills. Some of Jules's friends on Mirage Flats went into sheep.

"What you think of that?" he was asked.

"A man got a right to run giraffes on his own land, so long as he don't interfere with other people's rights," Jules replied. "It's running sheep on government land, destroying grass that don't belong to them, and making it impossible for a poor man to get a home I am fighting."

Nationally, these early years in the new century were optimistic times for Jules. He watched the vigorous young Roosevelt rise, was pleased at his close contacts with Pinchot and his pet policy, the conserving of the nation's natural resources. He wrote them letters of approval, got large boxes of pamphlets and books on forestry and tree planting, distributed them, talked them. But the conservation most important in his eyes was that of the public domain.

With such important things taking place and his mail heavy, he helped Mary less and less in the orchard or field. He made a ritual of his letters, always sorting them into four piles: the duns, to be ignored as long as possible; the letters that promised something pleasant; those of unknown quality, and the advertisements. One day he hesitated over a flowing address in purple ink and stopped his sorting long enough to open it. It was from Henri Surber, a postal clerk he knew in Zurich. He was in America, in St. Louis. He had seen the name of his old comrade in a newspaper, mentioned as a horticulturist of note in western Nebraska. Surely it was not the fastidious Jules he once knew in the Old Country?

"Mary!" Jules called, and read the letter to her.

"It is good German he writes — a nice letter," Mary said in approval.

"You damn right. Surber is a fine gentleman."

Late in June Mary was whitewashing the bedroom, her face and clothing splattered. She worked even faster than usual, for she must finish before they came, these friends of Jules's, — the Surbers, father, mother, and the eldest daughter, — to visit all summer.

When Mary sat down to nurse James, her two-year-old baby, she looked over his blond head about the place. She knew what a shock it would be — after Jules's big-talk letters — to people who had three hundred dollars a month to spend. She knew how such people lived — thick carpets, upholstered furniture, and a grand piano like a mirror for the Elsa, who was to be a great singer.

"Come, come, don't play. I have work to do!" she scolded, but good-naturedly, for this was her pretty baby, not like little Jule and Marie, scrawny, persistently under-nourished. She buttoned her waist, dropped the boy to the bare floor, and went back to work. She scrubbed up the white patches on the floor and was pleased that the kalso-mine on the walls was drying much less streaked and much whiter than she had hoped.

With homemade lye soap she scoured the chairs, tied to-gether with wire where Susette's fellows had tilted back once too often. She dragged the lounge out and pounded it clean of dust, recalling that once there were even bugs

in it. But that was long ago, when she first came to Nebraska. She looked at her bedroom, white as a hospital
room, with the maple set Jules bought for Emelia. At
least it had a good mirror.

Mary had cleaned Jules up as much as possible, cut his
hair, clipped his beard, beginning to gray a little, but even
so he was plainly a shock to his old friend. Surber blew
his cheeks out and *Donnerwettered*. Where then was the
dandy who must maintain the style of a gentleman's son in
Zurich? It was almost to laugh!

"Oh, hell! I got no time to fix up. I 'm a busy man,
building up the country."

"Yah-so — and must one then become so coarse as the
land?" Surber's droop-mouthed, motherly wife demanded,
quite pleased with the preposterousness of her idea.

"Git, git!" Jules shouted to the team, swinging the whip
with a good leather lash. The wagon bounced over the
rough, rutted road and gave the woman all she could do
to stay in the seat and hold to her hat, while Elsa dutifully
dug out the huge black chiffon veil and, sweeping it around
her mother's head, tied it securely at the nape of her short
neck.

Although these fine visitors made more work, the summer went very well. Surber stayed only a few days, but
he made several more short visits, diverting them all. He
was a handsome man, with a way of looking up under his
bushy brown eyebrows that drove even the owlish Marie
into giggles. To him Jules could show his letters from
Luther Burbank, asking about these plant experiments in
western Nebraska, this growing of fruit in the region of
little rain. Jules gave them into the hands of his friend
and went out for a mess of quail. The letters were as the
man in the saloon at Valentine to him, the long months
with Dr. Reed at Fort Robinson.

The two old friends sat up late at night, in the warm starlight, smoking, discussing the old days and then the new

here in America.   Never in the history of the nation had
there been so much lawlessness and crime.   If something
was n't done soon the country would be in the hands of
bandits and thugs.   They discussed the Philippines.   "An
open steal," Jules termed it hotly.   The light of Surber's
cigar moved in agreement.   Then there was the Boer War,
the death of Queen Victoria.

"I saw her once, on the way to Milan.   She came through
the mail car and asked questions about the service.   *Ja*, England has seen her greatest day."

Surber let his cigar go dead.   "Empire crazy," he said
at last.   "All empire crazy.   England, France, Germany,
Russia, America — all except *die Schweiz*.   And there is no
future there."

That was it.   No future, and here there was, but the
country was in the hands of cattlemen, grafters, expansion-
ists.   "Bigger country, but not better."

"No, nothing better."

"Nu-un, now, you two, will you talk all the night?"
Mrs. Surber scolded softly from the bedroom window.

Mary was always up hours before her guests came to
breakfast, hoeing in the garden or in the corn, catching up
the horses.   There were occasional visits to William or to
Pine Creek, and the hours after the big dinners she cooked
for the Sunday visitors who came: Elvina and her four timid
children; William and Lena, unencumbered; and Eugenie
and Louis Pochon and others from the Creek.   Emile seldom brought his family.   He had nothing but posts over
his old wagon running gears to travel on, and the small children were always rolling off into the dust and cactus.

Then, too, there were the nice clothes of the Surbers to
admire, and quiet talks of what there was to see in St. Louis.

Elsa was seventeen, a frank and wholesome child, with
long, blue-black hair in a thick braid, smooth brown skin,
and a figure as graceful and straight and clean as a young
cottonwood.   She teased Mary a little about her coquettishly

curly hair, and the woman blushed like a girl with all the delightful unworldliness of Elsa herself.

Mrs. Surber made a virtue of two things: her bald frankness, telling everyone the worst she thought; and her headaches, for which she carried headache powders pinned into the folds of her hat. But she was a discerning woman, with taste and a soft heart and optimism. She told Jules frankly what his faults were and he did n't flare up in his customary anger, but grinned and shocked her with smutty stories.

"Nu-un, Elsa, go for a walk! Listening to such things!"

One afternoon Jules came home with the mail, pounding Old Daisy with a willow club, spurring her every protesting jump. Mary saw and ran out. Jules was like a wild man, wild as she had never seen him before. At last he could make words.

"He is the greatest doctor that ever lived — overcome yellow fever, found the damn mosquito the cause, will save ten thousand lives every year!"

"Who — who you talk of?"

"Who?" Jules dropped his gesticulating hands in disgust. "Who? Dr. Reed, the man that doctored my foot."

So?

The Surbers were told and received the news with sufficient astonishment. They had seen it, this yellow fever, and told of many cures and preventives used by the ignorant. Against such things all are ignorant, they agreed, until a Dr. Reed comes along.

"My uncle went through the bad summer in Memphis by soaking his undershirt with kerosene twice a day. Kerosene killed the fever," Mary recalled.

"Kerosene kept the mosquitoes away," Jules suggested.

"Yah, that can be."

Late that night Jules wrote the doctor a long letter of congratulations. "We are working together," he told him.

"It is important that a man have both a good home and a sound body."

Susette came home oftener now, and once she stayed two whole weeks to visit with Elsa. The girls went for long horseback rides. Sometimes they walked through the shadows of evening to the Johansens, who had several daughters in their teens. Sometimes Victoria Staskiewicz, the pretty fourteen-year-old daughter of the Polish family across the river, went with them. For hours they sang about the Johansen organ. On Sunday afternoons they spent long hours in the hammocks Jules swung under the trees for them, reading, singing "Listen to the Mocking Bird" and other sentimental songs.

This summer there were unbelievable delights for Mary's children: pictures taken with the Surber camera under a black cloth; candy, occasionally; bananas quite a few times; even pineapple once, and an entire suit each for little Jule and James and a pair of shoes and a new dress for Marie. It was like the stories Elsa told them under the trees.

Once when Mary came up through the orchard with an apron full of mushrooms she overheard Jules and Henri Surber talking under a plum tree, scarcely big enough to shade them both. They were smoking. She could smell Jules's strong old cob pipe and Surber's cigar.

"I ask her every way I know, but she would not come," Jules said, his long fingers laced about his knees.

"So?" Henri seemed to consider that a while. "She was a good conversationalist in those long-ago days — and witty, but it is twenty years — she must be fifty, graying when I saw her last."

"To me she is always young," Jules mused.

"Then it was wise — " his friend answered him. "She could never do the things Mary does, bear you children — "

Jules sucked at his pipe. "Yah, but with her by my side I could have been known far, legislature, perhaps Congress — who can tell?"

"Still the egotist," Surber laughed indulgently.

Mary slipped quickly away and stopped to weed the onion bed while she considered what she had heard. To Jules Rosalie would always be young, but to Mary she was fifty, six years older than Jules.

The next time Jules wanted to send Rosalie a picture the Surbers took of the children Mary brought them without protest. Rosalie was pleased, but disturbed. "They are not like children here, particularly the little Marie, who seems so wistful. Is there then not even happiness for children in your America?"

Early in September the visitors went back to St. Louis, and it was all very dull. Even Mary cried a little, although her tears came slowly, now, as though they were the last drops seeping from a drying spring. In April they would be back, to live on their own place, five miles east, between Emile and the Schwartz ranch, with several of their friends from St. Louis around them.

"Emile will not like that. He is keeping some of the cattle he has in herd for the summer on that land," Mary remonstrated.

"It 's in the Schwartz range — He got no business mixing with that crooked outfit — working against me and the development of the country," Jules orated. "Government land is government land to me. I don't give a damn who is using it."

In November Louis Casper, one of Surber's friends, hired to look after his interests during the winter, found the lumber he had hauled out for a house burned to a pile of ashes. He whipped his team through the darkness to Old Jules's place and told his frightened, incoherent tale. If these people wanted one out of there, might they not shoot? He doubted whether he could become accustomed to being shot at.

"Git a rifle and shoot back!" Jules advised, but he went to

Pine Creek with Casper to take a look about. There was no prairie fire; it was too late for fall lightning. Plainly a piece of malicious destruction. They drove to Emile, the nearest neighbor. His three boys, in tatters and barefoot, despite the cold, scattered behind the low shacks while the two little girls looked from behind their mother's skirts. Emile, more slouched and a little defiant, said he knew nothing about the lumber burning. It was n't his business to look after every greenhorn's property.

"Working against me, my own brother!" Jules muttered on the way home. Casper was ready to leave the country.

"Looks to me like a boy's trick," Mary suggested. "I believe the Schwartzes would have hauled the lumber home and used it."

"These range disputes promise to become interesting," the *Standard* said, reporting the news of the incident. "Blood is in the eye of the settlers."

Emile never crossed Jules's doorway again.

This year there was to be a Christmas tree. The children had never seen one, scarcely heard of the Santa Claus of the American children. Soon after Thanksgiving Mary began to teach them new songs.

Late in December a box at least four feet each way came from St. Louis. It was n't opened until after the children were safely in bed. When the box first came Jules thrust his pipe firmly upon the stem and ordered the claw hammer.

"Ach, can't we ever have anything for the children as it should be!"

"Heah? — Oh, hell, yes. I don't give a damn." He returned to his paper, and all day the children played over the box, sneaking little fingers into the cracks.

The day before Christmas Jules and Mary went into the Koller canyons. Towards evening the mother came dragging a little pine. It was set up in the window and decorated with long strings of colored glass beads fragile as

September ice, big glass balls, angels with tinsel wings, stars, and red and green and white candles. And when it was lit Jule ran to his grandmother as he always did before the bewildering. Mary, Jules, and even little Marie drew close together with joy. The Surbers had sent it all.

Mrs. Arnold Peters and her mother, Mrs. Van Dorn, saw the tree from the road and came in. They sipped a little of the holiday wine with a piece of fruitcake, baked and hidden away long before Thanksgiving, when the hens still laid. They would hear the Christmas songs. But the children could n't sing. Jule rumbled, Marie squeaked. When everybody laughed they cried and retreated, Jule to the grandmother, Marie behind the stove.

The mother dragged her from her nook. "Ach, can't you ever do anything right?"

But Old Jules, standing around with his hands in his pockets, his pipe drawing well, was expansive. "Let her go," he said, and lifted the girl upon a chair so she might look into a round silver ball that made her face bulge like Mrs. Fluckiger's. Everybody else had to see and laugh too. Then the father broke some of the gilded walnuts in the vise for the boys, and later they all went into the night to see the women tucked into their quilts and listened to the noise of the cart over the bridge.

The next morning there were presents for all of them. Stone blocks for castles, bridges, and churches with towers for Jule; a nested set of picture-box blocks for James; a doll for Marie that reminded her of watching babies and diapers. But there were picture books too, and these she wore out in a little while. She asked everyone to read the stories to her until she knew them by heart and could read them to herself as she lay on her stomach on the floor.

"Ach, she is like Jules — her nose always in a book," the mother complained.

"That 's all she sees before her," Susette pointed out.

New Year's they took the Christmas tree down and put

the trimmings away. Mary was depressed. The first stranger to enter the house was a fat old woman, Mrs. Fluckiger, on the way to town. That meant a year of bad luck. If it had only been a young person, a young man.

After New Year Jules took up his regular winter activities, hunting a little, although there was no market for game since shipping it was forbidden by law, trapping a little, poisoning a few coyotes. The evenings he spent with his visitors, his stamp collection, reading nursery catalogues, or writing letters complaining about the mail service.

Mary looked better than she had for several winters, but she still worried about bills, always overdue, and storms that threatened their eight head of cattle, dependent upon sliced beets and turnips, with an ear of corn or two now and then, until the hills were bare of snow once more. She tried to talk to Susette, to tell her that the first year of married life was the hardest. After that people got accustomed to each other. She had heard talk that the young American in Rushville gambled.

"You know what that means," Mary told her.

"Yes, and if I marry a foreigner, *you* know what that means," the girl retorted, and Mary said no more.

During the fall and early spring Jules and Mary cleared a new orchard patch north of the house, sloping down over the Oglala camp site and the old Freese yard. With a few days' help from some of the more regular grub-line riders, free boarders, Mary wielded the axe, the spade, and the grub hoe against the bushes and trees. Her mother bound the brush into sheaves, piled the larger wood into ricks. Jules drilled holes under the stumps with a post-hole auger, planted charges of blasting powder, called the family together, and lighted the fuse. From behind a big tree they watched the stump fly into the air with an eruption of earth, a shaking of the ground underfoot, an echoing up and down the bluffs, and a smell of spent giant powder. When the weather was too cold for grubbing, Mary, using wedges, split the stumps, mostly ash, into heater chunks.

After the snow water was gone and the Niobrara growled surly within its banks, Jules planted his new orchard. Mary dug the holes, Jule and Marie carried little bundles of trees or ran to anthills for Indian beads. Jules consulted his plan, selected a tree, snipped the end of every rootlet with the pruning shears, and spread them as they had grown, pulverizing the soil about them, pressing it gently with his knuckles. Then he cut the stem back to encourage low growth as a protection against January sunburn, and limped on to the next hole.

Trees that winterkilled to the ground in the old orchard were grafted with hardy slips and staked with laths to prevent the fast-growing shoots from wind-breakage. And when the meadow larks sang on the posts and the swallows living in the shed built against the lean-to skimmed over the blooming plum trees, Jules limped about the rows carrying sprigs of blossoms, tying them here and there, marking the branches and protecting them against other fertilizations.

And among the blossoming trees fluttered thousands of orange butterflies, so tame the children could catch them and let them walk on their palms, their feet tickling.

"Prospects look good for a fruit crop," Jules told Mary.

During the last year the only surveyor besides Jules who would take a settler into a cattleman's range was prosecuted on various charges, planned, he insisted, to drive him from the county. Jules wrote to Roosevelt once more, saying: —

This part of Nebraska is all fenced by stockmen who keep settlers away by misrepresentation, threats, and violence, and it is high time that the gov't step in to stop this lawlessness and avert further bloodshed which is coming surely if the small settler is not protected. It is almost impossible for the honest settler to get located because sur-

veyors and locators are being driven out by continual criminal prosecution.   I, for instance, have been locating settlers since 1884 and
have been arrested four times on the pretense that I shot at somebody.   The only other surveyor in this county able to find the maliciously obliterated and tampered-with corners is also being prosecuted
on trumped-up charges.   Settlers who dare enter the land inside of
the illegal fences are driven out, their property destroyed, beaten to a
jelly or killed.   It is high time the government took a hand!

Jules did not have to go far for a fight on illegal fences.
Across the road from his house was a constant reminder.
Inside the slovenly two wire fence of Koller and Peters,
whom Jules located in the early days, were several quarters
of free land covered with filings as blatantly fraudulent as
any.

"My stock got as much right in there as anybody's," Jules
announced one morning, before he had his coffee.   "Bring
me the ponies home from the school section."

"Ach, we have grass enough for them.   You only make
us trouble!" Mary protested.

"Obey orders!" Jules shouted, and Mary got on Old Jim
and went to round up the bunch of wild ponies led by Old
Red, a wily silver-maned sorrel mare, an unclaimed outlaw
that had come to Jules's pasture seven or eight years before,
evidently untouched by rope or iron.   She and her followers usually gave five good horsemen a lively two hours before she finally consented to step coyly through the wide
gate into Jules's high board corral.

With patience and trickery developed by practice and
aided by much apron waving and shouting, Mary got them
home alone, losing her sunbonnet, her hairpins, but fetch-
ing the ponies.   Jules cut a wide gap through the Koller
and Peters fence and turned the horses in.   He had mineral
claims inside the fence and contests on two quarters that he
hoped to turn over to settlers.   He had a right there.
Damn bastards, shut him out!

Mary knew trouble was coming, just now when they were getting on their feet a little. That was the bad luck Mrs. Fluckiger brought, New Year's. She wondered what drove Jules to these things. Was it peace he could not endure or was there something in him that made him destroy as he built? She looked down upon Henriette's house. The Hollanders were gone. Henriette was back. At least this insanity seemed not incurable. Quickly she gathered up an apronful of cow chips for her baking and went home.

Koller and Peters had ridden behind Jules in the Freese troubles. They helped swing the little man into the cottonwood, got some of the lumber from his house. They knew Jules's vulnerable spot. A week later the Rushville *Standard* carried a head: "More Troubles over Range." Jules had been arrested for shooting at Koller and his younger brother while they dogged his horses from their pasture. Peters, professing friendliness and no connection with the affair, rode up to Jules while the others ran his horses through the fence. The old settler was at the top of the hill, his rifle across his arm, empty shells on the grass beside him.

"What you shooting at, Jule?" he asked.

"Scare them bastards driving my ponies through the wire with their dogs!" Jules snarled.

That, the *Standard* said, was what defeated him. He was fined fifty dollars and costs. Jules appealed and was released on bond.

"That damn outfit knows me well enough to know that if I had been shooting at them they would n't be alive to have me arrested. I ought to killed that damned soft-mouthed Arnold Peters when he rode up to me!"

"Why did n't you say you were shooting at rabbits?" Gottlieb Meier, a young Swiss from Surber's place, asked. He was there. He would have sworn so.

"And have them get you so twisted you give me away! Next time I have no witnesses," Jules promised himself.

The case would be tried again in the fall.

Up on Box Butte Creek William was having trouble with sheepmen; Emile was being friendly with the Schwartz outfit, catching fish for them, taking his flute there to play. Jules seldom mentioned Emile any more, although he still stopped at Eugenie's and at the Beguins' on the Creek.

A few weeks after Jules's arrest he galloped Old Daisy into the yard, kicking her at every jump until she laid her ears back and nipped his leg. "Oh, hell!" he roared. "Mary, Mary!"

He had news. Another cattleman-settler fight was on down the river — the Sweeneys, trying to run Hamm and his wife off their homestead. Three of them attacked Hamm in his breaking, knocked him down from behind, bit a hole in his wife's arm when she grabbed the gun aimed at her husband. But she hung on and Hamm got away to his shack, with bullets hitting the doorframe as he went through it to get his single-shot rifle. In his excitement he missed the Sweeneys and only killed one of their horses, but they ran, like coyotes, leaving the wagon behind.

"That's the kind of woman every settler needs," Jules told Mary, filling his pipe and breaking the match he tried to strike on his pants.

Even the cattleman-controlled papers objected to such brutal methods and admitted that the Sweeneys got off cheap with a fine of $225 and costs.

"Ought to hang such people," Mary cried, aroused at last.

"Well, now, maybe Hamm was on their land," someone suggested.

That angered Jules. "The cattlemen know where the corners were. If Hamm was on the Sweeney land, all they had to do was bring out the county surveyor. A man got to learn to defend himself. The fool should have killed the whole outfit!"

Around the ranches there was open disapproval of such

sloppy work, particularly involving a woman. It gave the range country a bad name. Yes, the settlers told each other — better to hire a professional killer, make a quick, clean job of it.

In the meantime the local papers advocated leasing the government land to the cattlemen, bewailing the impending order that the fences must come down. "The barbed-wire barriers are the only means of separating stock, keeping peace among the stockmen, protecting the interests of the little fellows."

"Peace, hell! Every year three-four compelled to leave the country, like they tried to run out the Greens — dragged into a blowout or buried in a corral," Jules snorted. "What the country needs is two thousand hustling families."

"Not two thousand, Jules," someone remarked in astonishment.

"Well, fifteen hundred, anyway."

In the government fight against illegal fencing of the public domain it became evident that the entire Nebraska delegation at Washington was with the cattlemen. The settlers were nervous as horses before a storm. Jules sold fifty rifles in two months, at cost. A petition against leasing the government land to cattlemen was circulated along the river and Pine Creek. "The Bill in Congress would only make an illegal act legal, and keep the settler out forever," was the protest.

Richards, of the Spade, the Nebraska cattle king, Modisett of Deer Creek, and half a dozen other sandhill ranchers went to Washington to lay the situation before Roosevelt.

They did n't have much to say when they came back, but it got out somehow that the President had been terse.

"Gentlemen, the fences will come down."

Nor did the plea that the fences were on deeded land have any bearing on the case. No government land was to be enclosed. Richards was ordered to remove his fences from sixty townships already resurveyed, with more to come.

"A section apiece for over two thousand families," Jules said.

The papers objected; even the commercial clubs of the larger cities of the state passed resolutions against the proposed removal of the fences.

It was no use. Roosevelt's wire cutters were on the way.

Jules's orchard was becoming quite an important feature in the settlement of the country, denying the cattleman contention that nothing would grow. By crossing selected wild plums with choice tame varieties, but not quite hardy, he developed a new plum that stood the winter, was free of insect pests, of delicate flavor, and tender-skinned. In addition he experimented with cherries and apples, and grew all kinds of small fruit between the trees to hold the sand and the snow. Every spring he gave away wagonloads of shrubbery, sucker plums, asparagus, horseradish, and pie-plant roots to anyone who would promise to care for them. And in these activities he caught once more something of the early vision he had upon the top of the hill as he looked across Mirage Flats in 1884.

In recognition of his services, Jules's place was designated an experiment station and he was made director of the eighth district, from Cherry County to the Wyoming line. A bushel of Russian macaroni wheat was on the way for trial. Fruits, flowers, and grains for tryouts were available in reasonable quantities, from Washington.

"Well, Mary, you married an important man," he boasted.

"Yes, but I still have to wear men's shoes and carry home the wood."

"Heah? — Oh, hell, can't you be pleasant one minute?"

It was true that the financial return was small. The orchard was young, experimental, and all comers were welcome to eat as much as they could hold. All summer gay dresses enlivened the long rows; boys ran in gangs search-

ing for riper cherries, blacker berries.   Jules limped through
the crowd, his pipe at a happy angle.

But Mary was proud of the orchard too.   This year she
would take her friends through the cleanly hoed rows white
with the snow of blossom time or redding with fruit.   Then
she might forget her leathery skin and her work-crippled
hands.   With her apron full of large, firm fruit for her
guests she could forget the debts, Jules's quarrels with the
government and the cattlemen, even the coming trial with
Koller and Peters.

Surber spent his early summer vacation with his family.
They visited many Sundays on the Niobrara.   Walking
through the trees, they talked of many things, of the fine
fruit crop hanging thick along the young branches, of the
Boer defeat and the disappearance of two republics from
the world map, of the cattleman activities in local politics,
working to fill the Republican convention with Kinkaid
timber, of the fence fights, and of Jules's arrest for shooting
at Koller.

"Why do you blacken your fine hands on such besotted
sheep?" Surber wondered.

The last day of June the sun rose with a peculiar whiteness, casting a bluish shadow behind every post and bush.
About six o'clock a gray cloud started directly overhead and
spread.   Two sharp, dry bolts of lightning sent the grandmother and the boys scurrying into the house.

"Ah, I don't like this *Donner* in the morning we have
here in America.   It brings only bad before the night," the
old woman complained.

"We can use rain for the corn," Mary said as she strained
the milk into pans.

Without answering the old woman went out again, to look
at the clearing sky, shaking her head.

About eleven the five-year-old Marie ran into the house,
jumping up and down in pale excitement.   She and the
boys had found a snake, a great big snake, right under the

east window. Jules took the shotgun out and blew away the small head poised over the thick coils. Then, picking the writhing thing up by the tail, he stretched his arm high — over six feet of the heavy, twisting mottled body, the largest bull snake he had ever seen.

"He could crush you like an egg," he told the children.

"Does he bite?" Jule asked.

"No, I don't think so."

The grandmother ran up to see. "I said it gives something bad to-day, and right under the window, with the children — Ach, don't do that!" she cried to Marie. "Ugly thing, you, stepping on the tail, still alive, and then laughing. Are you bewitched?"

The child drew away, still watching the twisting tail.

Because it was clouding up Mary did n't go to the field after dinner. By two o'clock the sky was covered and a great green sausage cloud rolled in over Mirage Flats.

"Still!" Jules commanded the children, who were noisily pushing dirt in upon the snake's grave. There was a faint rumble — such as the Indians had warned him against, like a thousand buffalo stampeding over far prairie, their sharp hoofs cutting the grass to powder.

"Oh, hell! — Mary! Hail coming — Oh, ruin me my corn and my trees."

Mary, coming through the garden gate, turned to follow Jules's pointing finger, her skirts still tucked high under her apron strings, the well-polished hoe over her shoulder.

"Ach!" She slammed the hoe on the fence. "So it goes! Work, work, and then the hail comes and takes it all. Marie, where is the baby?"

"*Wo ist Grossmutter?*" Jules fussed. "Why don't she come home when a storm 's coming?" Just then she came through the trees, the short, plump old woman bent double under the weight of both Jule and the baby pickaback.

Sending them into the lean-to, Mary nailed old sheets and blankets over the windows to the west, while Jules carried a fifty-pound can of blasting powder out of the house and covered it with a wooden washtub. Then they huddled in the lean-to as far from the chimney as possible, Jules rolled in a feather tick, Mary and her mother on the floor with the children. By now the lightning was an almost continuous blinding violet; the thunder rocked the house.

Then suddenly the hail was upon them, a deafening pounding against the shingles and the side of the house, bouncing high from the ground in white sheets. One window after another crashed inward, the force of the wind blowing the blankets and sheets into the room, driving the hail in spurts across the floor, until white streaks reached clear across it. Water ran in streams through the wide cracks between the boards.

The wind turned, and the south windows, unprotected, crashed inward together, the house rocking with the blast. Mary ran to the bedroom, pushed the bed into a far corner, rolled the tick and covers into a pile. Outside the trees about the house were momentarily visible through the gusts of hail, only naked sticks, stripped of all fruit and foliage.

She walked the floor, the hail cracking under her heavy shoes, her knotted fingers twisting her apron, still tucked up.

"Ach, *Gott*, what must we do now? Everything, everything gone."

The next two days the drifts of hail lay thick in the canyons under the summer sun hot on the naked fields and prairie. Even the mocking bird that lived in the brush pile east of the house was gone. The children found him washed against a post, the feathers stripped from his back, dead. Pete Staskiewicz helped them bury the bird, and stole a little of his mother's holy water for the cigar-box coffin.

Jules came in from the garden and sat hunched over on a box before the house. All the trees were stripped, barked on the west and south, gone. Where her garden had been Mary planted radishes and peas and turnips as though it were spring. The corn and wheat were pounded into the ground, the orchard gone, but still they must eat.

XIII

A POLISH WEDDING

THE fall-deepened waters of the Niobrara hurried away between the bluffs so like the stiff, gaunt knees of old women.
From his blind Jules watched a wedge of geese slip out of
the paling rose of the northwest, circle over him, honking
softly in their white-marked throats, lower and lower. A
shot rang out, the leader swooped down, swifter, turning
over and over, to hit the ground with a plop, the bewildered
honking flock following. Four more shots, more crashing
bodies, and then the stragglers, with low, frightened honks,
scattered swiftly through the shadows.

"Run!" Jules ordered, and from behind him the little
Jule and Marie charged through the underbrush into the
cold river, Jules limping along behind. A flopping in the
rushes, a dark body dragged along by the water, a whitish
breast gleaming on the bank: three geese, two young ones
and the old leader.

Warming their hands under the wide wings, the children
ran to Mary with the game, and while they changed into
dry stockings they talked of the hunt.

"I got another one that crawled off in the grass. The
Polander and his dog will find it in the morning if the
coyotes don't beat him to it," Jules said as he loaded his
pipe.

Despite all his other activities, Jules still did considerable
hunting and trapping, particularly when snow stopped his
locating. Bare-handed he scoured the bluffs, ready if any
game was flushed, even when his breath made icicles to hang

from his moustache and beard and the snow that worked
into his overshoe froze to his sock and had to be jerked loose
by Mary's strong arms.

Perhaps because of his limp he walked so much, asserting
his will over a handicap; perhaps because he could watch for
strange plants and fossils.   He selected bits of petrified bone
and sent them to the geology department at the state university with an invitation to Dr. Barbour to come to the
Running Water, as was compatible with the hospitality of
the frontier that still lived in Jules.   He still met everyone
who appeared at his door with the query, "Had your dinner?"
And Mary, always pretending to be put out by grub-line
riders, was perhaps already picking another duck, catching
a chicken, or pushing the plates a little closer together to
make room.

The most regular of these grub-line riders was Andy
Brown, a little "yellah boy" from Virginia who never stayed
more than two or three weeks at any job, although he could
make good money husking corn, eighty to a hundred bushels
a day, even in the short Panhandle stalk.   But fencing was
his specialty and he always carried the latest combination wire
cutters, wrench, tin-snips, screw driver, can opener, and nail
file, all in one, in the voluminous overalls that bagged about
his little body, even with two pairs of pants under them.
His pockets were always full of little tools he did n't really
steal, just "took" along as trading stock.

The first place Andy struck when he "come No'th" was
Tissot's.   Perhaps The Black One saw something furtive
in Andy, said to have knifed a white man in "Viginie" and
migrated in the night.   Anyway, Tissot took him in hand
like a Simon Legree.

"Yah, it could be so," Jules agreed.   "The Black is a
devil."

Andy stayed with him three years, in itself a suspicious
circumstance.

The first time Tissot and his wife went away for several

days, Andy came to Jules, slipping into the noisy kitchen almost unnoticed, his clothes in a flour sack outside the door. The next day he bought an old .40-.60 rifle and a box of reloaded shells. "I'll bore him full of daylight," he said several times, omitting the usual expletives of the frontier. But Mary could n't hide her dislike for his curly hair, his color, and after a week or so he moved on.

Neighbors said that Tissot had used Andy to slip the irrigation gates at night, stealing the precious water. While Jules was busy with sheepmen and ranchers, his orchard and lawsuits, the irrigators on the Flats had dug. Under the initiative and tact of Elmer Sturgeon, secretary, men once more hitched up and went to work. A hundred thousand feet of Pine Ridge lumber went into the Pepper Creek flume, and the stockholders finally saw actual water run over the pitchy planks, leaking scandalously, but sure to swell. Young men went to work on the ditch as they later went to Chicago and New York.

And when the flumes were done and the ditch had swallowed over a hundred thousand dollars, it irrigated a little over a hundred acres. The one-foot drop per mile the engineer planned somehow dwindled, the soil was porous, and the Niobrara had a way of shrinking to a bar-choked rivulet in dry weather. The people of the lower Flats put in years of labor and got nothing. Only a few late-comers like Jules Tissot, with money to take advantage of another's extremity, profited. Big Andrew and his kind were gone. All Elmer Sturgeon got was years of lawing.

Then the flume across Pepper Creek collapsed. Few who financed the project and dreamed the magnificent dream remained for the crash. But it was something to have dreamed.

The Koller shooting case was to come up again early in December. Mary worried, as was her nature, getting thinner and more lined. Jules ignored it with all the profi-

ciency gained during the Freese troubles. Two days before
they went to Rushville Mary came to the house and found
her husband sitting at the stove. Across his knee was a
newspaper, but he was n't reading, and large tears that did
not break rolled from his eyes and slipped swiftly into his
beard.

"Ach, now, Jules," Mary comforted. "It is then not to
cry, not for you to cry."

Jules did not move, did not speak. She looked at the
paper. There it was, a small paragraph. Dr. Walter
Reed, the man who had conquered yellow fever, was dead.
Dead.

So. It was too bad — a young man yet, a fine young
man.

At last Jules took his gun and went among the gray trees
of his orchard and did not return until dark. The paper
he put away in his stamp collection with the letters from
Rosalie.

In the fall term of court Jules was found guilty of shooting at Frank Koller and fined one hundred dollars. William came forward to pay it.

"Hell, no," Jules told him. "I 'll board it out. That
Rushville gang git no more of my money."

"My children with a jailbird father!" Mary moaned into
her handkerchief.

For a moment Arnold Peters looked sadly upon his
hands. Why were he and this woman, neighbors, the
same age, two who had once danced well together, fighting?

"What will we do now?" Mary wondered. The lawyer's fees were heavy. Jules would have picked up a little
gun repairing, made a little trapping. There would n't
even be game for the pot this winter. Without flour they
had been before, several times, but they always had a little
wheat to send to the mill or grind in the handmill. This
year there had been only hail.

"If they take your man away from his family, make them

feed you.   Go and get flour and coffee at the store and let
the county pay for it," Mary was advised.

But she shrank from that.

The lawing neighbors were scarcely home when the worst
December blizzard old-timers could recollect set in.   While
it was not as cold as some January storms, only twenty-four
below, the snow was deep, and when the sun came out the
drifts lay hard over the garden fences and only the tips of
the six-year-old cherry trees stuck out like black sticks set
in little bunches.   The snow would break them down, but
it did n't matter.   They were dying from hail bruising anyway.

Old Jim and Daisy had drifted away and Mary was certain they were dead in a snowbank somewhere.   Grouse sat
tranquilly on the silver-iced cottonwoods as she gathered
wood below.   They even ate with her chickens in the front
yard, and when she tried to shoot one the gun kicked her
backwards and the grouse went on eating.

She trapped a few rabbits, but the snow was so deep and the
cold so constant that no fur-bearing animals were out.   All
of Jules's traps and his wolf bait were under snow and ice.

This was not much like the last Christmas.   The children
could n't even have cookie men and women this year — no
sugar and no flour.   Mary had known it would be so when
Mrs. Fluckiger walked into the kitchen last New Year's,
the first one there.

Jules was having a comfortable time in jail.   Three meals
a day, with all the company he wanted, for there were many
glad to ask his advice about crops, his predictions in politics
and the cattleman situation.   They laughed at his violent
denunciations of the government from the inside of the jail.
Here was a fellow who could n't be hushed up.   Still his
optimism for the Panhandle was unshakable.

Somebody brought him a copy of the *Standard,* still wet
and pungent with an announcement of the arrest of two local

land agents who hired soldiers' widows [1] for cattleman filings. The fraud existed in the vivid imagination of Investigator Mosby, the paper said. The investigation would cost the government ten thousand dollars and reveal nothing irregular. Now Jules stood at the window of the jail, eager to be free, to use the unlocked door.

The next week Colonel Mosby was recalled through the intercession of Nebraska's Senator Dietrich.

"The Senator 's a cattleman tool," Jules told his one jail mate, a youth in for bastardy and proud of his achievement. "The whole Nebraska delegation 's sold out to the cattleman, trying to turn the country over to the ranchers, establishing the most dangerous monopoly known to man — a monopoly of the soil."

"Yeh, guess you 're right — your deal," the youth said, pushing the greasy cards to Jules.

Mary got one postcard from Jules and then she heard no more. When the time came for his release he did n't come home, although he could have caught a ride with any neighbor, even Arnold Peters. But the *Standard* brought news of Jules, saying he took the train to Lincoln to attend the State Horticultural Meeting. He had been sent round-trip transportation in recognition of his work building up western Nebraska. There were those who considered the situation very amusing — out of jail into honor.

"Ach, why don't he write us?" Mary wondered.

Three weeks later Jules came back, his beard shaved off, his moustache clipped. He was full of enthusiasm for a new orchard. He had ordered a thousand trees for April shipment.

"Tch, tch — for the hail to ruin. How will we pay for them?"

[1] The service period of a soldier was subtracted from his widow's required residence upon a homestead, hastening the possible sale date. Further, these filings were made without actual sight of the location and without intention of establishing a home, as the oath required.

"Oh, I'll sell enough to pay for mine."

"I know how that goes," Mary spoke bitterly as she stuffed a newspaper full of grouse feathers into the fire. "You'll sell a few, at cost."

But the man's good humor was not to be dampened. "How do you like to have Papa home?" he asked Jule, trying to pull him from behind the stove. The boy jerked away. "I bet you don't run away from the grouse Papa got for you. Shot him half a mile from town right in the middle of the road. Just about made the team run away with the mail carrier's grasshopper buggy," Jules laughed heartily.

"I bet Old Daisy would n't run away if you shoot between her ears!" Little Jule came nearer now that he was being ignored.

"Heah? No, but I had a hell of a time to teach her to stand. Wild Indian pony!"

Yes, it was good to be home.

But before a week was up Jules missed the attention and praise he got in Lincoln. He was an important man to whom appreciation and mail service were due. The children were sent to bed early, and all evening Jules pushed his stubby pen in strong strokes across the paper. The next day he went to Rushville and showed the letters, addressed to everybody from Roosevelt down. The *Standard* was amused. If Jules down on the Running Water did n't get mail service right away he was going to Canada — and to hell with the American flag. The Yankees disgraced it. He would spit on it. In the meantime he was hunched over a nursery catalogue, planning another orchard up the canyon where he and his followers once waited for Freese to be lured from his rifle. Now it would be planted to cherries and strawberries.

The fall before, Mary's mother scratched her forehead on a thorn in a plum thicket. The wound did n't heal up well and left a loose, wart-like growth that caught in her dresses

as she pulled them over her head.   Exasperated, and without saying anything to Jules about it, she burned the wart
with carbolic acid, leaving a scab that never quite dried.
Then swiftly it began to enlarge, with shooting pains down
her neck and cheek.   To Jules's appeal that she go with
him to Omaha to a hospital immediately she was flatly obdurate.

"Ach, I won't be butchered."

Susette was married now.   For years four or five of the
young Swiss about Pine Creek tried to outstay each other
whenever she came home for a visit.   They sang, talked,
quarreled, poured dippers of water to freeze in each other's
overshoes, turned saddle horses loose, and put cactus under
saddle blankets.   Big Charley thought of most of the tricks,
and usually was the last to say good-night to Susette.

"Now, if you are going to stay up most of the night with
those young fools, don't burn the last stick of dry firewood
for the morning," Mary scolded.

"Maybe Susie and I better sit up *all* night.   Then you
won't have to have dry wood to start a fire," Big Charley
laughed, his red-brown eyes impish through his thick glasses.

"Ho, no — you don't get to kiss her good-night this
time!" the ambitious, hard-working little Ernest Beguin
promised.

Little Marie, who hung about the outskirts of all excitement, slipped into the dark nook behind the kitchen stove.
There her mother found her the next morning, cold, cross
because she had dropped off to sleep and knew no more what
kissing was than the night before.   "You wouldn't find
out.   Susette is not kissing these fellows.   She saves herself
for that gambler American that don't write," the mother
said, over the child's head.

The sister made no reply.

A week later, after watching the mail for a month, Susette
went to make some new dresses and shirtwaists for Lena on
Box Butte.   Her sewing was a wonder, and with such style.
She made even the ungainly Lena quite fashionable.

"I guess I been a fool," she told Mary as Big Charley, working for William, came to get her. "Harrison does not want a foreign girl."

"Don't feel bad — " Mary tried to console her awkwardly. "It is better. We get over those things easily when we are young — " But the tears in her fading blue eyes were not reassuring.

The next thing the community knew Susette had married Bernese Charley and gone to live on Mirage Flats with his brother, whose wife died the year before. A week after the marriage the letter came. Harrison, the young American who, people said, gambled, had been in a hospital, very ill. But now he would soon be better. Then she must come to him. They would be married.

Charley rode down to the Niobrara alone. But he did n't joke now, or talk. He just sat looking at his clumsy, honest hands. And after a long time he told Mary.

"What can I do? Susette she cries almost a week now that she is married to me."

"Yes, I know, but be patient. She will make you a good wife."

He blinked rapidly behind his thick glasses. Slowly he put his hat on his head and went away.

Jules planted the thousand trees, almost all of them. They came late, were badly grown, and he dared not wait to sell many. Mary insisted upon a patch of corn up on the east table, so, after the usual growling, Jules suddenly decided he had fathered the thought and hired a man to plough and plant about twenty acres. Mary, heavy with child and doubled up with lumbago, hoped that somehow she could keep the weeds down and that this year the hail would not come. They must have pork, lard to fry the game Jules killed. Elise, Ferdinand's divorced wife, was with them, and there was no telling for how long.

It had been planned early that Nana would be a doctor;

failing that, at least a dentist. By the time he was twenty-five he was finally ready to begin his professional course. But when his mother went to Paris to see how he was getting on, they knew scarcely anything of him at the school. She found him at last, with a burlesque dancer, his allowance spent. With violent denunciations she packed him off to America, to his brother Paul.

On the way he met the large Bernese girl, Elise, and, with a small man's fancy for the Junoesque, made love to her. They were married at Paul's house. But Ferdinand had nothing of Paul's love of system or his business sense, and little of the vision and the intellectual energy of Jules. He had never earned a penny, had done nothing more than entertain his mother's maids and drink himself into good-natured stupidity. America did not transform him.

After their baby died Elise left him and came to the Running Water.

"Big and foolish," Jules termed her, and felt free to pinch her while he talked prospective husbands to her. Mary, back in the dark, watched them. These men, she thought wearily.

Jules took Elise to see several of his bachelor settlers. Mary sent the little Marie along to sit on a forkful of hay or an old blanket in the back of the wagon. From there the girl marveled at the wonder of the fence posts traveling past while Jules told Elise smutty stories and watched her open her enormous mouth as she laughed.

In June there was a big wedding at the Staskiewicz grove across the river. Twelve-year-old Pete told it first, he who helped Jule and Marie bury the mocking bird that the hail killed.

It was to be Ed Skudlas, the gay, red-lipped young Pole from Cleveland, who drove a fiery matched team of blacks to a yellow-wheeled buggy. Not to fifteen-year-old Victoria, whom he had taken to dances and to town during the winter and spring, but to her older sister Maggie, who had waited table in Rushville for six years and only came home for two weeks every summer — never more, even with her mother bedfast for months with consumption before she finally died. Mary and the children used to see Maggie in a light dress with a ruffled parasol, strolling down to the garden or the cabbage patch where Pete and Victoria worked. But she never stayed out long. The sun was so hard on her complexion. Her skin was delicate, she told Mary. Not like Victoria's. Mary nodded. She remembered what Ed said about the younger sister when he first saw her, in broken German and with eloquent hands: A pretty girl, that Victoria, with cheeks like fall apples in Poland and eyes like blue-gray lakes. But he must have changed his mind, because it was Maggie he was marrying.

The evening before the wedding Victoria ran over to borrow some extra cake pans. The bride's cake was to be fifteen stories high, and they would need an extra coffeepot, too. Mary brought out what she had, pretending not to notice that the girl's eyes were dull as rain clouds over a lake. But Ed was not there to see.

"You must be expecting many people," Mary said.

"Yes," she hesitated a little, turning the tins round and round in her hands. "Over a hundred."

"So!" Mary was surprised. With only three little rooms and the place not paid for.

"Yes, Maggie wants it so," Victoria said slowly.

"Don't she see how bad that makes it for you?"

The girl did not answer. She dropped her hurt eyes to Mary's arms, folded under her apron, turned suddenly, and ran out of the yard and down the road into the sunset haze. Mary watched her, shielding her face. She had only meant to comfort her, to tell her she was too young and pretty to marry yet anyway. There were plenty who would help a pretty girl like that forget the red-lipped Ed.

All the next day and night there were dancing and music

at the Staskiewiczes', an accordion and a fiddle. Marie
sneaked away from the dishes to sit on the flat-topped gate-
post and watch the teams go into the grove. At night the
children sat on the wagon seat and watched the moving black
figures on the dance platform, making the lanterns come and
go like big fireflies. Every now and then someone laughed
loud or shouted in Polish.

"Git to bed!" Jules ordered, big and black in the doorway
with the light behind him. "There will be more hurry-up
weddings after this," Mary was saying to Elise in the house.
Jules pounded the ashes from his pipe and laughed.

"You would n't throw ashes on the floor in my house,"
Elise told him.

"That 's why you got no place. Mary knows how to make
a man feel at home."

Three weeks later Jules came in late for supper. He set
his shotgun in the corner and pushed his hat back, laughing
until his nose was red and he choked.

"By golly — I just heard a good one. Ed got Victoria
in trouble!"

Mary poured his coffee. "Ach, come and eat and don't
talk so before the children."

"Heah? — Oh, the little devils 'll know it all before
long."

The mother did not answer. After a long time she said,
"It is so?"

Jules nodded a mouthful of food.

"Poor girl. Men are hogs."

But she did n't have much time to think of Victoria.
That week her own fourth child was born in a thunderstorm.
Jules called the boy Fritz Theodore — Fritz after a relative in the Louisiana branch of the family, a naval gunner
in the United States fleet, and Theodore for the man who
ordered the cattleman fences down.

"Guns will thunder over him some day," the grandmother

predicted, from the bright hill of a pain-free moment. In the morning the children were brought in to see their new brother. James tried to hit the red-faced little fellow who had taken his place. Jule and Marie stood awkwardly by. They knew that this was the reason for their mother's cries in the night, and yet their father seemed pleased. Afraid, they ran down into the trees.

Because Fritz was born ruptured he was not permitted to cry. At the end of the second month he had outgrown the difficulty, but he had developed such a violent temper that the family ate no meal in peace for two years. He grew strong, lustier than any of the others, and screamed to be taken the instant Mary or Marie entered the house.

"Keep that damned kid still!" Jules commanded. Marie shrunk from him and carried the child on her hip until the boy's head reached almost as high as hers, making a funny two-headed animal shadow in the sand.

Early in September, when Jules's special plums were ripe, the Surbers came for Sunday dinner and Mary's Swiss plum pie. After the children had eaten and the grandmother's tray was brought back from her room, Elsa and her younger sister washed the dishes while Mrs. Surber and Mary went into the bedroom. They took the baby from Marie's lap and sent her out. The women stopped their whispering long enough to motion her to go on.

Marie knew what they were doing, talking about Victoria and the baby she was going to have. She listened under the window a little. It was too bad, they said, and her mother sick and dying for two years.

"I hope you do not let Marie go fishing and flower hunting with the boy — Pete — any more. You know I never thought it wise — a Polander!"

"No, she hasn't time, with the baby so cross, but you know how Jules is. He talks everything out and she has long ears."

Marie picked up a stone with her toes and threw it hard against the house, and then ran into the trees. Across the river she could see Jule and James trailing the tall, stalking Pete, with a spade over his shoulder like a weapon of war. They were going crawfish digging. She started down the hillside.

"Marie!" the mother called sharply. "Come and mind the baby while I go with Mrs. Surber into the trees!"

On the shady side of the house, under a plum tree protected from the big hail of last year by the wall, and red with fruit, Jules and Henri talked the afternoon away. Things were getting worse in Switzerland. Factories were taking the trade from skilled workers. The wood carver, the lace worker, the clock maker, once honored, were gone.

"In a few years there won't be a man left to repair a clock like the one I got. Every piece brass and handmade, running nice since the seventeen-hundreds," Jules lamented.

"Yes, and it is all in the name of progress. A million clocks that run only six months, and men and women growing not tall and strong as those of our ancestors who thrust the Austrian from our valleys, but short and afraid instead. Already it is happening."

"Land — that is what they need," Jules said as he emptied his pipe into the sand. "Well, Richards is indicted for fraudulent filings. Roosevelt is determined, and if he is elected there will be a wave of settlers West like in '84 and '85."

"*Donnerwetter!* You think so? Maybe land will be worth something then."

Surber buried the butt of his cigar and sipped the glass of wine Mary set on the window sill for him. "But for many it will be hard," he said, setting his glass down and wiping his neat moustache, "learning this dry farming after they have used only the pen. It is healthy, if one does not fall from horses or hayracks." His sensitive lip twitched the moustache as he wiped it.   He had been laid up twice during his vacations this summer.

The grandmother's illness annoyed Jules because he saw it as the result of her stubbornness.   The smell of decaying flesh sickened Mary.   Once she suggested that Susette might take her for a little while.   It could not be long now.

"You had her when she could work!"

There was no use reminding the sister that she had no place for her then, so Mary did what she could and Jules was generally patient enough if the old woman kept out of his sight.   The children were bewildered by the bandaged head that got larger and larger, until the grandmother could no longer push them up the hill in the wheelbarrow. When punishment threatened she had always taken little Jule away.   Now he knew no obedience.   He kicked and screamed and sulked and was beaten until Old Jules was out of breath and his hand stung.   Even Mary could see that this eldest son was excessively stubborn.

Marie, no one's pet, learned conformity early and developed a premature responsibility.   She was expected to look after the boys, keep James from building fires, Jule from breaking his father's delicate tools, both from fighting, and the baby from crying while the parents were in the field or repairing fences.

Towards winter the boys were moved to the attic where Marie slept, for by now no one could sleep in the room with the grandmother.   The old woman kept hidden as much as she could during the day, usually in the second lean-to, divided into a grainery and a stall for an occasional horse. When she did come to the front of the house she pushed the door open silently, almost as though a little wind were there.

Jules had difficulty now in getting morphine for her, and the pain demanded increasing doses.

Once when the tumbleweeds turned purple with frost

and the sun was warm again, Jule and Marie slipped up
to the door of the back lean-to.   The dark bowed figure was
there, on the customary box, but she could n't see them any
more.   Her hands were folded over her little black Testa-
ment and she was pleading low in German with the God
she used to speak of to the children when Jules was away.

"Please, *lieber Gott*," they heard her say in a half-whisper,
"what have I then done — that I must suffer so?   Please —
I wish so much to die."

The two stepped back and then, suddenly afraid, they
ran through the trees to their playhouse of fragrant tumbleweeds.   Even there they found no warmth.

Early in November, a year after the grandmother noticed
that the scab on her forehead was growing, she ran crying into
the kitchen.   A magpie had circled over her three times,
trailing his long feathers.   That meant death.   Three days
later she died.

Jules brought the coffin from Rushville.   Susette came
to the funeral in a stiff black taffeta blouse hooked up to her
ears, and with half a dozen ostrich tips bobbing from her hat.
Charley grinned sheepishly as usual.   Jake, back and living
on Pine Creek, was scarcely noticed.

Jules stayed with the two youngest children.   During
the short talk a man from Pine Creek made, Jule and Marie
shivered behind their mother's dress, the one she wore up
from St. Louis seven years before.   A woman handed each
of the daughters a red flower.   Mary dropped hers into the
open grave and burst into violent sobs.   Susette led her
away.

On the way home she quieted a little.   "To think that
I would n't have the money for a flower for my mother's
grave!"

At home Jules threw open the grandmother's room to the
November winds as soon as she was gone.   Sucking at his
pipe, he planned for another occupant.   Governor Mickey
had agreed to let him have a convict on parole.

XIV

THE KINKAIDER COMES

ONCE more that dream of every frontier, a boom, struck the Panhandle. Twenty years after the influx of settlers into the hard-land fringe north and west of the sandhills, another, and this time a swifter, more spectacular, wave surged over the free-land region and broke about Alliance, the land-office town.

The Kinkaid Act, allowing every *bona fide* settler six hundred forty acres of free land for a filing fee of fourteen dollars, went into effect June 28, 1904. Weeks earlier big shipments of cases, kegs, and barrels had arrived. Several new saloons were built in strategic spots in the little prairie town. Soft-spoken men, with knife-edged, peg-topped trousers and beautifully kept hands, appeared out of nowhere. A little weather-beaten church was suddenly overshadowed by the house next door, gay in a yellow coat of paint, a mechanical piano, a crystal chandelier, and painted glass lamps about which lolled women in lace blouses and waspish waists, chaperoned by Silver Nell, in wine-colored velvet and a dog collar of imitation pearls, winter or summer.

Two weeks before the opening, covered wagons, horsebackers, men afoot, toiled into Alliance, got information at the land office, and vanished eastward over the level prairie. Many turned back at the first soft yellow chophills, pockmarked by blowouts and warted with soapweeds. Others kept on, through this protective border, into the broad valley region, with high hills reaching towards the whitish sky.

Many came in hired livery rigs and generally went away again, for the drivers knew how to keep in the bewildering border of waste land all day. So stories spread through the East of a new Great American Desert, the sandhills of western Nebraska. The cattlemen should be paid to live in it.

Before the opening Jules spent weeks in the hills, only to find that every good flat was either covered or cut up by filings upon which no one lived. But after a lot of preliminary contesting he had over two dozen men ready to file. In Alliance they found board shacks thrown together and lined with rows of occupied beds and extra landseekers sleeping on the floor. Tents and covered wagons fringed the town. Pasture and hay were sky high. Jules stayed with Broome, his land attorney. His settlers shifted for themselves as they could.

In the evening Jules, his rifle across his arm, limped about among the newcomers and felt young again. It was like Valentine in the eighties, but different too — many more people and not so young, not nearly so young. Many of these were old — defeated old men. And about the hotels and the rude boarding houses were women with graying hair and fuzzy cheeks, women who spoke meticulous English and were horrified at the locator. They would never trust themselves alone with such a man. They wondered at his acquaintance with the wives of prominent people: bankers, newspapermen, attorneys, land officials. "The standards here — well, really!" a high-bosomed old soldier's widow remarked through her lace handkerchief as Jules limped through the packed lobby of a hotel, his rifle still across his arm.

The day of the opening long queues of homeseekers waited for hours, only to find that even the sad choice of land that was free had been filed earlier in the day. There was talk of cattleman agents who made up baskets full of filing papers beforehand and ran them through the first thing.

One woman was said to have filed on forty sections, under forty names, at five dollars a shot. The land was covered by filings that would never turn into farms. Yes, the Kinkaid Act was a cattleman law, as it was intended to be.

Nevertheless Jules was busy. His buckskin team, colts of Old Daisy, threaded in and out between the hills. In six months all unoccupied filings would be subject to contest. For twenty-five dollars Jules showed the land, ascertained the numbers, took the settler to Alliance to the land office, helped him make his filings, and later, when he was ready to fence, surveyed the homestead completely. If the homeseeker found nothing to please him, there was no charge. Otherwise Jules pocketed a twenty-five-dollar fee.

"That way you run around, skinning your team all over the sandhills, and for nothing half the time," Mary protested.

Jules's neighbors argued with him, too. What prevented a settler from getting the numbers of the land and then going to Alliance alone to file, giving the locator nothing for his work?

"That would be crooked," Jules pointed out.

"Funny how he reads his own honesty and his own cussedness into everything and everybody!" Nell Sears, married twice and now back and living with her brother Charley, commented to Mary.

And every few days some land agent or attorney from, say, Chicago suggested that Jules charge fifty or a hundred dollars and give him a fourth or half of the fee for steering the prospects to him. Jules stuck his cob pipe between his bearded lips and threw the letters into the wood box.

"I am not in this business for the money. I'm trying to build up the country."

After the grandmother died, Jules announced that he was getting a convict on parole from Governor Mickey.

"What kind?" Mary looked up dubiously from the children's plates.

"A Bohemian, forty years old."

"I mean — what's he locked up for?"

Jules had planned to avoid the question, but faced with it now he filled his mouth with potatoes and spoke through them. "Sent up for thirteen years. Trumped-up charge of criminal intercourse with a little girl three years old."

Mary wiped the baby's chin. "I do not like it."

Two weeks later a livery man from Rushville brought the convict Jim, a former packing-house worker speaking broken English. He was pale as tallow, couldn't draw a bucket of water, and had never touched a live horse or cow. He walked gingerly through the six inches of snow in his slip-on rubbers, shivering behind Jules, who took him to the edge of the hill and showed him the snow-bound orchard.

As soon as the two men were out of the house the Sunday crowd buzzed. "Old Jules is crazy, bringing a man like that into his home," Mary overheard Charley Sears say. She was putting up another bed in the lean-to for Marie and the baby, who slept with her because he disturbed Jules. Jim would have the attic to himself.

"Cold as the devil up there — freeze the poor Bohunk stiff," Jules objected.

"He has two good feather beds and I don't remember you ever complaining about the cold for the children up there."

"Oho."

At supper time Jim was still overhead, unpacking probably. They could hear him walk four steps this way and then four back, although the attic was made up of two rooms, each sixteen feet long. Four steps, always four.

The boys were sent up to call him. He came down the outside stairs into the house and stood, his hands behind the thin back, his head down.

"Pull up — what you waiting for?" Jules demanded impatiently.

The man looked about him without turning his head; only his brown eyes glinting in the light showed that there was movement at all.

"Here," Mary indicated the foot of the table.

Slowly the man came to the backless chair. Jules was already eating, seeing nothing, but the children eyed Jim over their spoons. When Mary had dished out for them all with little Fritz on her arm, she noticed in surprise that the man still stood.

"Sit down."

The heavy lines in Jim's face crumpled and broke as his reddish moustache spread into a reticent little smile, showing well-kept teeth.

"You mean it I should sit?"

"Of course."

"Thank you, lady." He slipped sidewise into the chair, without moving it, without a sound. He did n't seem to notice the quarrels of the children, or Jules's growls because his wife had overlooked his pointing finger.

"Don't go back upstairs until you want to go to bed," Mary advised. So Jim sat back in a corner, far from the lamp and the stove, his head between his hands. But she knew that his eyes followed her about.

The spring after Jim came to the river Jules put him to farming. The former meat-cutter had a lot to learn, but he worked, grew tanned, strong. He learned to laugh again, too, and sometimes he sang prison favorites, "Nearer, My God, to Thee," "Darling Nelly Gray," and "Till We Meet Again," during the evenings. Jules taught him to handle a repeating shotgun, to track the wily jack rabbit that made so cunning an end to his trail, to judge the speed of flying ducks. He made even a quail hunter of Jim.

The first Fourth of July Jim was on the river he took Jule, James, and Marie fishing in Spring Creek, in the school section. All the neighbors went to Palmer's grove,

down the river, passing Jules's house with bunting-trimmed
wagons and buggies, waving flags and shooting firecrackers.
And the children, would they not go? Jim asked. Ah, but
that was bad, and so he made a fishing holiday. They
caught a dishpan full of sunfish and had a fine time.

"Are n't you worried — those children with such a man?"
Mrs. Surber asked.

"Ach, no," Mary washed her hands preparatory to working her bread into buns and loaves. "He 's a nice man
with a family in Chicago and a little girl about Marie's age.
It was the strike made him go to Omaha, away from them.
Too bad — and he likes his schnapps much now his wife
got a divorce."

The golden ash clung to its leaves until they were
brown and wrinkled, the cottonwoods still yellow-green at
the time when Mary and the children usually raked up big
piles of dry leaves for the bottom bed ticks. She liked
cottonwood leaves better than straw or husks; they lumped
less and shook up easier and, with a loose quilt of wild duck
feathers over the top, lay well. But at last the ticks were
all stuffed high, the root crops carefully put away in the
cellar, and the ledge lined with cauliflower, cabbage, and
endive. And still the smoke of fall hung blue along the
bluffs.

Then, at three one morning, Jules awakened them all
with a loud hullabaloo to see the northern lights. From
east to west stretched a wall of reddish light, long tongues
of cold rose reaching towards the zenith, rising and falling
as though fanned by an Indian robe.

Winter was upon them.

All fall the farmers waited on freight cars to ship their
big crops. Now it was as Jones and Sturgeon and Jules
recalled, the land they saw in '84. Everyone was optimistic
and borrowing money on future good times, including Jules.
The Koller and Peters settlement gave him a lease at

twenty-five dollars a year as long as he wanted it on the quarter across the road; the adjoining quarter he bought for two hundred fifty dollars. In return he dismissed three contests, a protest against a proof, and his mineral claims against land in the ambitious neighbors' range.

"Your papa is a thief — he stole land from our papa," one of the Peters girls said to Marie on the bridge one day. But Jules's children were accustomed to such things. She giggled, turned, and ran up the road homeward, kicking sand back with her bare feet as she went, the nearest thing to nose-thumbing her mother permitted.

Christmas time Paul from the Platte and William, both just back from California, where they went to look around a little, came to the river for a visit. They brought their wives and Ferdinand. Emile, they apologized, had a cold. Mary understood. But the others came for Sunday dinner and stayed until late in the night. Fanny, Paul's wife, with one boy and a fine house, put on airs, bragged about her indigestion, and took soda and charcoal tablets. Her sister Lena, with no children, and still living in the old sod house full of fleas, was her own impulsive self, quick to anger and equally quick to laugh in unrestraint.

They drank a couple of bottles of wine they brought back with them, compared it sadly to that of the Old Country, and talked about the fruit possibilities of western Nebraska. Paul was starting an orchard. William had dammed Box Butte Creek, stocked the pond with government fish, and grew a fine garden.

And as the evening came on and the red firelight played over them they talked of the old days and the Old Country. Mary was the only one of them who did not speak French. But William, and particularly Paul, in contrast with the unchallenged leader Jules, gave her a phrase here and there in German and in English. They made her feel that her dinner was good and that her family was a nice one. She needed that, for she had heard that Paul's wife compared her to a rabbit in prolificacy. Jules only laughed. "Fanny would n't be sick all the time if she raised a big family."

"They seem healthy enough, our children, but they don't grow," Mary said when they spoke of the young ones. "And handsome they never will be."

"Every child is beautiful to his mother," Fanny said sweetly as she pushed her chair back to avoid the ashes from Jules's pipe.

William grinned a little, sucked in his breath, and looked into Mary's eyes.

"They will do well. They have a sensible mother," he said.

The new year promised to be an interesting one for Jules. The *Standard* reprinted a section of his discussion of tree culture before the State Horticultural Society. Gray wolves were dragging down strong fat steers and horses and eating them alive as they did the big bull in the cottonwood grove in Wyoming, where Jules shot seven. That was after one of his wives, — which one? — Emelia, left him. He heard she went from bad to worse, the way with women who won't work for a living. And here he had already this crop of little cotton-tops growing up about him from another.

The wolves were so bad that the Spade, Springlake, and Modisett ranches offered a hundred dollars for each gray killed in their region. Jules wanted to start as soon as he heard about the bounty, but the thermometer was down to twenty below zero.

"You can't go until it gets warmer," Mary pointed out. "You forget you 're not used to sleeping out like you were ten years ago, and not so young."

Yes, not so young. Then he rose to contradict her. "I feel as young as I ever did."

"You feel — but you are not."

The next two weeks of cold wave were severe. Range

riders nursed protruding, purpled ears and frozen feet. The schools were closed. And as in the early days close confinement brought out quarrels, aroused dormant conflicts. Four wives left their husbands when the sun came again. One could n't wait. She ran out into the storm and was lost for a day. Two men advertised: "I will not be responsible for any debts contracted by anyone except myself."

Jules spent the cold weather about the stove with his guns, his stamps, and his correspondence. He tried to get a pardon for Jim, who was a good honest fellow even though he could never learn to trap muskrats as well as little Jule. While he was writing to Lincoln, he complained about the new game laws. "Pay to hunt on my land, where I feed the game? Can't kill the grouse and the rabbits that eat the buds and bark off my trees! To hell with such laws. I found the country open and free and I don't recognize any restrictions imposed by a bunch of cheap politicians grafting on the taxpayer."

To emphasize his contempt Jules ordered a new lot of high-powered shells and another forty-foot fish net. But his interest soon changed. A letter from Washington informed him that hundreds of fraudulent filings were subject to cancellation whenever a *bona fide* settler applied for a filing. In a couple of months still another block would be opened. That meant another boom. Jules took his compass to town to have the needle remagnetized, put new red rags on his surveying pins, looped the chain neatly, and waited for the snow to go.

Twenty-two years brought many changes to the land of promise into which Jules drove so confidently in '84. By 1906 the Indians along the Niobrara, the big game, — elk, deer, even antelope, — were gone. The winters were still cold, but now there were railroads, good houses, fuel, warm clothing, better roads. The summers were still dry, and although Jules had moved out of the gumbo, as the southsiders called the Flats, the farmers on the table from Alliance to Gordon were doing what Jules said must be done: learning how to handle their soil, practising diversified farming, finding drouth-resisting crops. When corn failed, wheat often succeeded, and despite bugs and early freezes there were usually potatoes and Indians from Pine Ridge to pick them up behind the digger, in return for hard money every evening. The irrigation project was gone and with it its exponents. Where others lost everything, Jules Tissot sold his land and cattle for twenty thousand dollars.

"Did n't have a damned cent when I located him in '84, and all he ever did for me was drop me in a well," Jules told Ferdinand when he heard of the sale.

"He may come to see you before he leaves for the Old Country," Nana suggested, anxious to please. Paul, tired of having the younger brother drunk around the saloons, had sent him to Jules, who had even less patience with him. But Ferdinand stayed most of the winter, going to Pine Creek to his claim for his relapses. "No, a drunken man I won't have around the place," Mary said. Jules agreed. "A man ought to know when he has enough."

Other things were changing too. Most of the towns were alternately wet and dry, with the saloon element a strong factor in every election. But with or without saloons the towns, except Alliance, were the drab, quiet trading centres of a stock-farming region. Even the small stations in the sandhills went to sleep the instant the cowboys vanished over the hill. The blatant bad man was gone and the thieves and murderers pretended respectability, often most convincingly. Better roads cut down the necessity of halfway stations, and age did for the roadhouse girls what community censure failed to do.

Jules himself was changed, but much of it was only external — the crippled foot, gray hair, graying beard, a forward plumpness at the middle, and a fleshiness about the wings of his nose. Mary cooked food as he liked it, and in large quantities. When Mrs. Surber first saw him heap mashed potatoes in the centre of his plate, cover the plate with slabs of fried ham and two big dippers of unthickened gravy, — three thick slabs of bread stacked beside his plate, — she held up her hands in actual horror. When he repeated the portion in the same meal she was silenced.

"A man must eat if he is going to do a good day's work," he argued.

"Then you think you work?"

"I work my head. I 'm not a *Grobian* with a strong back and a weak mind."

"No, you leave the strong back to your wife. Nu-un, you will pay for such eating. It cannot go otherwise."

But at forty-seven Jules seemed annoyingly healthy even without the daily bath essential to a Surber. He was a little heavier, with pouches under his eyes, still the pessimist about anything anyone else was to do, satisfied the country was going to the dogs. He talked socialism to Ferdinand until late at night, but without the accustomed glass of wine, for Nana must not be encouraged. Evidently this Jules still hoped to build the community he planned, somewhere — Canada perhaps, or Mexico.

When Marie, learning to read a little, found Jules's name in the *Appeal to Reason*,[1] she took it in pride to her mother. Mary glanced at the item, an acknowledgment of a contribution of twenty-five dollars to the defense fund of the embattled Warren. So — throw money away — while she skimped and slaved, the children not in school because they

[1] The *Appeal to Reason*, 1895–1922, Socialist sheet, was moved to Girard, Kansas, in 1897, by Publisher Wayland, who set the vogue for muckraking. Under the pyrotechnics of Fred Warren, managing editor after 1901, the circulation ran into the millions. In 1905 he serialized Upton Sinclair's *The Jungle*.

had no shoes. She saw nothing in the ideal of a free press while she and the children were in need.

Jules could not very well strike her with the baby in her arms; besides, he was no longer certain that she would n't fight back. So he whipped Marie until he was breathless and left for a hunt on Pine Creek.

But age and Mary's resolution to make her man as comfortable as possible, with her determination to send as good as she got, were mellowing Jules. They got along well enough now — very well, the neighbors said, considering how William and Lena quarreled. When he sent the life-insurance agent flying to his buggy it was not entirely from a sense of persecution. Partly it was the imp and the devil in him that made him torment Mary by saying, "I don't intend to hire the Old Woman to kill me."

Although Mary sometimes said Jules told all he knew, he did n't talk about the man with the Winchester he had seen at Valentine and at the foot of the Big Horns until Marie was seven. They had been hunting, Marie following behind with her hands full of young grouse. As usual, Jules stopped on Freese Hill to rest his foot. With the sun glinting tardy rays along the blue barrel of the new repeating shotgun he held between his knees, he talked; looking away down upon the place where Freese once lived, now in young trees in neat rows, and over the dark block of Henriette's house to the shadowed bluffs beyond, he talked.

"He saved my life — when everybody else endangers it."

Marie liked the story, but dared not say so. Instead she stroked the head of a grouse, closed the soft blue eyelids. Here on this dark spot of gravel the Indians once built signal fires to be seen for miles along the twisting blue band of river and on the table from Box Butte to Hay Springs. Once Pete had shown her how to make wreaths of bluebells and yellow sweet peas here, but that was long ago too, before Victoria's trouble.

"Marie!" The mother's call came faintly up to them.

"Mama is calling — I better go," Marie stammered, grasping the scattered grouse by the necks.

"Heah? — Oho, yes, go. I be home after I rest."

Not until the sun was gone and the blued steel of his new gun was dark and cold to the touch did Jules limp down the hill and home.

A good wheat crop brought several new threshing crews into the community, and two of them crossed the river and pushed into the south region. Jules threshed two hundred bushels of wheat, assuring a bread supply — dark, because it was macaroni, but rich and nutlike. Pat Burke, living a mile east, raised a little too, the break in his bad luck. First the lightning had struck his haystack, then killed his team, and finally, during a morning storm, it struck his little house, ripping out all four corners, breaking the stove, tossing the lids about, and knocking Pat unconscious.

"He had it coming. He bin working against me ever since he lived there."

"Ach, you are crazy."

"Hold your mouth."

But Mary was in good spirits. "Now, you can tell me to hold my mouth, but that don't change things. You still talk like a crazy man. Pat Burke has too much trouble getting enough to drink to think about you."

It was true that as soon as the Koller and Peters troubles were over Jules and Pat quarreled over the fence, took up each other's stock for damage, lawed. Pat put up "no hunting" signs and, although there was no game on his bare little place, Jules immediately hunted there, with only the satisfaction of defying the little boards that said in black paint, NO HUNTING ALOUD. Next thing Jules would be arrested for shooting at Pat.

"But what can I do?" Mary asked.

Late one night in August someone pounded on the bedroom window, calling, "Hey, Jules, hey!"

Mary nudged her snoring husband, grabbed her dress, and, slipping it over her short gown, lit the lamp. Framed in the window was the befuddled, red face of Pat Burke.

"What you want?" Jules demanded, reaching for his rifle.

"Oh, nothing — just a match. Gotta match?"

Mary brought a full box from the kitchen. Pat tried to take one and spilled them all. But finally he got his pipe going and with elaborate thanks he stumbled away into the darkness.

"The drunken fool — wake me up at three o'clock!" Jules roared, and hung up his rifle. But before Mary got the light out Pat was back.

"Shay — " he asked thickly, "could I sleep here? It 's raining. M-my feet are wet."

"What 's the matter? Where 's your team?"

"Ghosts got them — ghosts under the b-bridge."

Jules got up, pulled on his pants, and with Mary carrying the lantern they went down through the soft starlight. One horse and most of the buggy were on the bridge, but two wheels hung over the four-foot railing and in the water below lay the other horse, tangled in harness and broken doubletrees.

They got the team out and Pat slept on the couch in the kitchen. In the morning while Mary was getting breakfast he sat up, rubbed his eyes, opened them cautiously, looking between his blunt fingers. She was still there.

"Where did you come from?"

"Maybe I do live here," Mary answered indulgently.

Pat buried his face in the pillow, moved his head until one eye could see, got up, walked all about the woman in blue calico. "An' it looks like you was intending to stay!"

After a breakfast of fried young grouse, biscuits, and hot chocolate, he was sober enough to go home.

"Why do you fight with the poor drunk?" Mary inquired of Jules. Surely his "no hunting" signs seemed unimportant enough to-day.

After threshing Pat took a load of wheat to town. On

the way home he gave an acquaintance a drink from a gallon jug of whiskey. The next man on the road found him on his knees, his throat across the front endgate of the double bed, his face black, his tongue out, dead. He had fallen off the high seat and was too drunk to get up.

The *Standard* was caustic. "We want such blood money to run our schools, so keep the saloon door open. It may catch another victim." It had already, at Rushville. Carl Fisher left town with a team and wagon, did not reach home. A neighbor searching the breaks of Rush Creek found the wagon upset at the foot of the bank, both horses dead, and Fisher crushed under the box. He left a wife and six children.

The Crawford *Bulletin,* taking the stand that anything happening in the Panhandle reflected on the entire section, carried a fiery editorial. "The county of Sheridan, in the state of Nebraska, lost two citizens last week through intoxication beyond human standard, and nothing is done, yet the marshal at Rushville chokes off free speech by the handcuff and bludgeon route, as he did when A. L. Schiermeyer, member of the state socialistic lecture bureau, attempted to say a few words to his fellow men."

Jules, usually an energetic exponent of free speech and leaning towards socialism, lost sight of these issues entirely when the saloons were attacked. "Just because a few fools don't know when they have enough they would prevent a decent man from having a glass of beer now and then."

"You think a man like Fisher, with a family on the county now, ought to be allowed to drink himself under the ground?" a neighbor asked.

Mary, down on her knees scrubbing up where Jules had greased his guns, looked up.

"Maybe some families would be better off if their men drank themselves into the grave."

But as usual Jules only heard what he wanted to hear, and that afternoon they all went buffalo-berrying. Jules ahead, with his shotgun for game, Mary carrying the pails, an old sheet, and the axe, the boys trailing along behind with the dishpan and broomsticks. Marie had to stay home with the baby.

Where the silvery buffalo-berry bushes were solid clumps of yellow or orange, the tiny, shot-like berries in round clusters all along the thorny stems, Mary held the bushes back while Jules chopped them off, to be threshed with broomsticks over the sheet.

Dishpans full of berries were taken to the river for preliminary washing, the worm-lightened fruit floated away, until all the pails were full. Then there was a day of jelly making in the big copper boiler and the wine press, until six- and eight-gallon stone jars were filled with the wine-red liquor to cool and set into firmest jelly for winter.

With the fall, animosity against the cattlemen flared higher. A man was murdered at the Spade ranch. Just a bum's quarrel, it was said at first. Then it was recalled that Dave Tate, who was still accused of murdering Musfeldt, had worked there, that Bartlett Richards was under indictment for land frauds, and that a relative of his was setting up a sheep ranch on the Spade range along the Niobrara, in a settled community, with thirty-five hundred sheep and two Mexican herders. Sheep would eat the grass roots out of the ground, cut up the sod, leave nothing but blowouts and wool-tufted fences, destroy the value of the surrounding land. There were more settler meetings. Richards, hearing of them, offered a reward for the murder of the man at the Spade and made overtures of compromise to the neighbors about the sheep ranch. Trying to make a good impression on the government now, the settlers said.

Jules's children were sent to bed or whipped to silence when he did n't want to be bothered. But when he talked of the sky, plants, and rocks, strange people and places over the world, of the coal age and the lumbering animals that lived then, they drew slyly near. Even the older ones, remembering his earlier violence, somehow lost their fear for the moment.

Jules taught them useful things: to pick the thick green worms from his trees and to trap the wily gopher. When a particularly clever one would n't be caught, Jules ordered the boys to bring the spade and help dig along the gopher's tunnel, leaving only a very thin crust over it, and a point of light at the end.

"Now fetch me my twelve-bore," he ordered. With the gun aimed upon the tunnel, Jules waited, and the boys behind him. Ten minutes, twelve, of absolute silence. Then suddenly the top of the tunnel boiled with fresh earth. The twelve-gauge roared and the boys ran through the black powder smoke to the hole splattered across the gopher's runway. Jule dug with his fingers, brought up a shattered mass that was gopher.

"Ach, your papa is so nervous he can't wait a minute on anybody, but he can sit still for hours hunting," Mary complained.

Often Jules took the two eldest, seven and eight, small, twin-like, to trail noiselessly behind him when he went on a hunt. Carefully they stepped through the rose-brush thickets, stooping to pull sand burrs and cactus from their feet. At his motion of command they ran ahead to scare up quail, dropping at the first whir of wings and watching where the birds fell. When the gun was silent they ran to retrieve the game, catching all the cripples, crushing the backs of the brittle skulls between their teeth as they had seen Jules do.

"Why, I never saw anything like it! Those children are better than any dog!" an Eastern hunter exclaimed.

"I learn my kids to obey instantly or I lick hell out of them," Jules chuckled. The man turned to look back at the two, slipping through the clearing, avoiding the dry rose-brush stems scattered about, each with two handfuls of quail held by the feet.   Jule was whispering about the man's high-laced boots.

"He don't have to get stickers, I bet."

Marie nodded, caught the stranger's eyes upon her, and fell back behind her brother.   The man did n't have a beard like Papa, but he was fat, and she was almost as much afraid of fat men as of beards.   For once she let her brother lead.

The Surbers built a house and barn.   Sundays they came to the Running Water, Mrs. Surber and the girls in the carriage with side lights, one of their young Swiss helpers driving, several riding alongside.   Sometimes Felix and Gus, sons of Jules's Uncle Paul living beyond the Koller and Peters homes, came down in goat-hair chaps with their horse-breaking friends.   They ran the bunch of ponies up from the school section.   When the plank gate of the high board corral finally clanked behind Old Red, the Surber girls and their friends climbed upon the fence and watched.

The wild horses pushed into a far corner about the wily-eyed old sorrel, noses aquiver, manes blowing.   At the flick of a clod they ran about the corral, crowding the wall.   The arm of the roper shot out, his heels tore up the dirt until he got a turn of the rope about the snubbing post.   Perhaps the horse leaped into the air as the noose shut off his wind.   Perhaps he just sat back stubbornly, wavering on his feet until he went down.   Perhaps another rope jerked a foot away and Felix was on his neck, his strong hand on the blood-flecked nostrils.

Finally the saddle was on the fighting horse, hunched up into a balloon, or with legs spraddled out, dun belly swaying to the ground.   When Gus was securely anchored in the saddle the horse was given his head and the sky opened over them.   With what skill the seventeen-year-old giant could muster he rode his horse, fanned him, scratched him, showing white teeth in his brown face for the approval of his audience. Perhaps a sunfisher left him in the dust, or a low-withered gray threw saddle and bridle 'clean, setting Gus ignominiously afoot.

Another horse, another rider.

Sometimes there were twisted ankles, hips, or a broken collar bone. Perhaps a cunning five-year-old, sensing the flying oval of rope was for him, bolted the high gate, crashing it down as he jumped, Old Red and the rest running at his heels, away over the hills, splashing the Niobrara high over them as they plunged through, stopping only when they reached the security of the school section north of Henriette's.

In the meantime Mrs. Surber and Mary walked through the garden pulling young carrots, picking a mess of peas or beans for the visitors to take home. Jules read or talked to Henri Surber or other visitors. He never went near the corral while horses were being handled. "I can't stand to see anybody get crippled," he said.

This spring Victoria and her pretty baby were leaving. Not so long ago even the Johansen girls, school-teachers, with an organ and a rose garden, stopped their side-lighted carriage for the little Polish girl on their way to dances and literaries. Now nobody came near her except Mrs. Van Dorn.

People began to talk again. Ed had been fooled. He had n't known how it was with Victoria, but the older sister had, and telling the frightened girl to keep her mouth shut, Maggie threatened Ed with the penitentiary. So he had been in the bushes with both. And here it was almost a year and his wife still flat as a board. But it was n't so fine for her. Mrs. Fluckiger told around that she saw the new bride with a black eye when it got out about Victoria. Her parasol with the ruffles and her fine, feathered hats were gone. Maybe Ed burned them that day he found out. Anyway, he rode down to see Victoria. Together they walked along the river over an hour, talking. Finally Ed kissed her, right out in the open, and then he rode away. Once when he was drunk he talked about it in Jules's kitchen. "I make that damn woman pitch hay till she have to burn her pants."

Pete never came over to take the boys fishing any more. His dog got poison somewhere and almost died. She dropped her pups and was n't much good for over a month afterward. Jules heard that they thought it was the strychnine of an old coyote bait he put out.

"If that damn dog got any of my poison he must have been on my place, and I have no use for stray dogs!"

One Sunday afternoon Marie sneaked away from the baby-tending to sit with her feet dangling over the river, looking down upon its dark green spring flow until the bridge began to fly upstream, carrying her far away. Suddenly Pete stood behind her. He did n't say anything, just stood there, looking at her, a long, tow-headed Polander. Finally he whistled to his dog and started his cows for home. Marie went slowly up the road, her game spoiled. The next day Steve Staskiewicz moved away to a sandy place in the Schwartz range, and young Ignatz from Posen settled his family in the grove across the Running Water. Jules saw that the young Pole was a fool for the accordion and for whiskey, but also that he needed work, and so he sent him to Modisett's hay camp and got him a job raking hay. Sometimes Ignatz and Pete, who drove the stacker team, rode down to the river on Sundays. Once or twice Victoria came too, pretty in her red waist and her tan divided skirt.

But the move into a new community did n't help the Polish girl. Before two years were gone she shocked the community again, this time by dying. She was taken by violent cramps, and before her father could make the sign of the cross over her she was dead. Everyone remembered now what a lovely, motherless little girl she had been.

Gardens were stripped of flowers, and the funeral procession to the church was the longest ever seen in the neighborhood.

Then it got out that the week before young Ignatz went to town to have his wife arrested for trying to poison him. He said she put green stuff in his coffee, the stuff he had for bugs on cabbages. But perhaps because she was the one to get sick the officials wouldn't do anything.

Several days after Victoria's funeral a stranger stopped at Jules's door and asked to see his record of strychnine sales. The large book showed that he sold an eighth of an ounce to Victoria Staskiewicz two weeks before, for gopher poisoning, price one dollar. Mary remembered that when the girl bought the poison on her way home from church with her baby and her father, Ignatz was with them, riding along beside the buggy. He admitted now that he knew about the poison. She told him "I got it" in English when she came back to the buggy. Yes, he had given her the dollar. He was working at Modisett's the day she died.

There was considerable trouble about it in the Catholic congregation. A suicide buried in consecrated ground!

"Ach, poor girl," Mary said sorrowfully.

Jules scraped the inside of his cob pipe with his pocket knife.

"When she was here for cherries last time she asked me if strychnine works on people like on dogs." He stopped, sucked the stem, and spit the nicotine into the fire.

"What did you say?"

"I told her all I know was wait on nature."

"Poor, poor girl," Mary murmured to herself. Then, louder: "But it's good with her now."

"Heah?" Jules asked.

"Nothing."

"Oho," Jules dismissed it as woman's grumbling. Already his mind was on other things. Deep down in the hills, farther than the little blue lake he saw from Deer Hill, was a large block of good land: deep, broad valleys, sheltered by high ridges of hills from the northwest wind. Here, away from corrupt politicians and pettifogging lawyers, a man could live. Good neighbors, good talk, and his family growing up strong to carry on his work.

XV

LAND FRAUDS

FOR the last two years the tempo of life in the ranch com-
munities of western Nebraska had accelerated. Government agents came investigating in shiny top buggies, sometimes with the mail carrier or afoot, secretly — pretending
to everyone, even to Jules, to be homeseekers. Often they
carried rolls of semi-transparent bluish maps, records of
the original survey. After supper they pored over these
with Jules, talking of ranges, corners, township lines, cor-
rection lines, old soldiers' widows, and fraudulent filings.
Over the shoulders of the less formidable the children
caught glimpses of these plats, ruled into squares through
which ran black, hairy caterpillars, indicating ridges of hills.
The men talked of obliterated and faked corners, of ploughshares and sickle bars buried to attract the compass needle,
of prairie-fire marks to be found in the genuine corner holes.
Jules delved into his deer-hunting days of the eighties
when the corners were still common, recalling where this
one or that lay. Then he brought out his compass, checked
and set the needle, counted the surveying pins, tied new colored rags to them, and talked of the early days.

The next morning they started into the hills, the government man usually holding the lines over the buckskins.
Jules never drove unless he had to. "Damn frisky team
run away with me," he would say, replenishing his cob pipe
with Big Bale. The truth was he wanted to be free to
watch the roadside for a grouse or a rabbit, his pump gun
between his knees, the barrel against his shoulder, brushing

his tangled beard. Now and then he pushed the old cap, muskrat or equally shapeless cloth, back from his eyes as he scanned the horizon. The .30-.30 rifle was always across the buggy bed at his feet.

These strange men came and went, men the children were forbidden to mention to their rare playmates. Always curious, Marie discovered that one of them wore a revolver under his arm and had a shiny button, like a star, that he kept hidden.

"Nosy brat!" he called her when she asked him why he did n't carry his gun like the cowboys that stopped to water the gaunt, dusty herds they trailed into the hills when the sheepmen fired the Wyoming range.

And now and then ranch owners called, ostensibly to look over the few Indian ponies Jules had for sale, or to buy a little fruit.

"We 'll see you 're taken care of, Jule," they promised, flipping the ends of packets of bills with suggestive carelessness.

But Jules was stubborn in his contention that he wanted to build up the country, even when approached more specifically at Omaha before the federal cases came to trial. No one need ever know, and he could provide his family with winter necessities, put a little in cattle himself. Jules spit at the rancher's feet and limped away.

In November the *World Herald* brought the news to the Panhandle. Two of the richest, most influential cattle barons of Nebraska, Bartlett Richards and his partner William Comstock, pleaded guilty of unlawful fencing of government land. Unlike John and Herman Krause, down near the Burlington, these men were not found guilty of intimidating settlers, the item said.

"No? — How about Green and the Musfeldt shooting — all the others that went down in the hay country and left damn quick or were never heard of again?" Jules demanded.

"Yeh, I know, but you can't compare them with that

Krause gang, still running settlers out just anyway, still shooting them down like dogs and getting off free."

"Damn lawless outfit," Jules admitted through his smoke.

Last June Richards and Comstock had been defiant, the *Herald* recalled, but the government set to work with such dispatch to survey their holdings, a region the size of Rhode Island, that by fall the cattle kings were glad to plead guilty. They were fined three hundred dollars and half the costs each, and remained in the custody of the United States marshal for six hours.

At the first sign of weakness the Panhandle papers flocked upon the cattlemen like blackbirds upon the raw backs of warbly cows. The *Standard* called the trial a farce such as could occur only under money-bought Republican officials. The cattlemen could afford to pay such fines more times than the government could survey their enclosures, and get richer doing it. If a small stockman had been found with an acre inside his fences, his hide would have been tacked on the corral. "Don't steal a quarter section of sandhills, but swallow an entire county."

More arrests followed, including the cashier of a Rush-ville bank and an official at the Pine Ridge agency — ac-cused of securing fraudulent homestead entries for the Mod-isetts, on Deer Creek.

"Looks like the government is compiling a social register of northwest Nebraska," Elmer Sturgeon told Jules.

"Yah, got about all the big bugs now," he agreed, pat-ting his growing waistline. He was expecting other cattle-man callers. They came, and he enjoyed his triumph and sent them away, and drove the buckskins into the hills as before. Soon the entire country would be open to settlers.

When winter shut him out of the hills and the orchard he remembered that a new post office had been given to George Peters, on the Flats towards Sturgeon's big new barn. A shiftless ground scratcher doing nothing but grow enough Russian thistles to seed the county, and now the government asked him, Jules, to go there for his mail. He shouted the children to bed, dipped his scratchy pen deep, and wrote to Washington.

Peters had a Kinkaid in the Koller canyons, a post office on the Flats. Legally each required his continuous residence.

He used his Running Water column in the *Standard* to strike back. "Skunk skinner," "dirty liar," he called the old settler.

"Ach, why can't Jules be satisfied with his cattleman fights?" Mary lamented. Things were bad enough for them. The county superintendent made Jules send the two older children to school. Because everything was generally done by townships, they belonged in Emile's district, with the schoolhouse five miles away, and so Jule and Marie trudged the two miles to the Peters school, unwanted outsiders. They were vulnerable enough, in their made-over clothes and their strangeness, to the innate cruelty of childhood. The community animosity towards Jules did n't help.

"Your papa 's crazy!" the Peters girls whispered for all but the teacher to hear. At recess Jule kicked his tormentors, threw clods and profanity with his father's aim and proficiency, and was punished. Marie stayed at her desk.

"You should run out and play. You 're so peaked-looking — " the serious young schoolma'am tried to tell her kindly.

"I got to study," Marie defended fiercely, squirming deeper into the protection of the double seat.

The teacher went away.

But the others caught Marie all right, and while two of the bigger girls held her hands from her ears the others read the Running Water column to her. Then they scattered, holding their noses. "You stink, stink, stink — like a skunk, skunk, skunk!"

"Are you sick?" Mary inquired crossly of Marie, hunched on a box behind the stove, the sleeping Fritz a heavy lump in her lap, the supper dishes not washed. "Don't bother her," Jules suggested from an expansive mood. But the table must be cleared for him, and the next day Marie did n't need to hear anything at school, nor the next. She was sick, was delirious, cried, "I got to go — they 'll all get ahead of me!" and turned the color of drying cottonwood leaves. Mary brewed camomile tea and elder blossoms, made rhubarb-root syrup, even steeped wild sage in a tomato can on the back of the stove until the brew was thick and black. Nothing helped.

A month later a Rumanian herding sheep up the river came for his mail. He looked down at the girl, a gaunt, yellow skeleton, that had no recognition for him, although he once bought her side combs and a postcard album.

"Ah, it is the yellow — what you call it — yellow jaundice. My little sister she die of it too." He did n't stay long, and late that evening he was back. From a pocket deep under his sheepskin coat he fetched a round box of white tablets. "From the doctor at Hay Springs," he said.

"Probably mercury," Jules objected. "Damn poisonous stuff." But Mary gave it to the girl, and in a few weeks she was able to sit up in a chair near the window.

"She does not get the right food," Mrs. Surber fussed, but the girl was getting better.

Jule did n't go to school while his sister was sick. He hated it. "He can learn more from me than from them ignorant American schoolma'ams," Jules bragged. So Mary sent the boys after Marie's books and said no more.

This winter the snow stayed on over the Panhandle for the first time in years. Bobsleds were pulled out from under the grainery or down from haymows and put together. The local dudes kept the few sleighs for rent at the livery barns busy. The bad snows made coyotes and wolves hungry — a good time for a hunt.

The old wagon was piled high with equipment and bed-

ding, a huge calico-covered feather tick roped down over
it, like a fat blue sausage, the morning Jules and the convict Jim set out for the sandhills on a gray-wolf hunt. Two
weeks later the unwashed men came back, half frozen but
jubilant. They had poisoned one of the largest grays ever
taken in Nebraska and Jules did n't hesitate to point out
that it was no mean feat, this poisoning a gray, as he generally eats only his own kill. Fortunately they found a
half-eaten rabbit on the animal's trail. A large dose of
strychnine did the rest.

The cattlemen had withdrawn the bounty offered some
months ago, but Jules made a circle of the ranches, showing
the wolf with a head big as a bear. Well, since it was the
old-timer the bounty would be paid. One hundred dollars.

At home Jules looked through a big stack of ammunition
and gun catalogues and filled out a long order blank. Mary
saw it over her knitting.

"It don't look like the children and I are going to get
much from the gray wolf."

"Heah? — What you expect? You did n't catch him —
and don't bother me. I 'm busy."

The national publicity given the cattleman trials in Omaha
and the large-scale cancellations of fraudulent filings attracted land seekers from everywhere. Times were hard
again, with employment scarce, and so once more the jobless
drifted West, in box cars, in wagons, afoot. Although there
were other locators now that it was a safer profession, Jules
was always busy and, except for his sudden storms of temper,
jovial and free from the bite of his persecution.

The mail carrier from Hay Springs reaped a considerable
passenger fee, and the livery stables added more teams to
their staff. And almost every evening at least one covered
wagon pulled up over the crest of the bluff west, swayed
drunkenly down the hill, and rumbled over the plank bridge.

The rise to Jules's house was sandy and the wagon creaked slowly upward, followed by perhaps two haltered colts and a lazy yellow cow, her calf tied to her tail.

With loud shoutings from the unshaven driver and nickerings from the hungry horses, the wagon pulled up on the level spot across the road from Jules's house. The boys usually lined up along the weathered house to see if there might not be children, and often there were, tumbling out the instant the wagon stopped, leaping, running, shouting in their release. Soon the man, tall, usually, and wiry, a pail on his arm, came to the house, looking up at Jules's big sign over the door with his name on it, and the antlers with a .30-.30 across them. Was the locator at home? Could they have some drinking water? Often Mary sent out a mess of pieplant or asparagus, radishes, peas, or whatever garden truck was in season. The women seemed grateful, but even so sometimes hitching ropes or spades and other loose articles were gone the next morning.

After supper, Jules, if he was at home, went out and sat on the wagon tongue and smoked and talked. The homeseekers had been to far places, Oklahoma, perhaps, and Oregon, and might be going to the Dakotas if they did not find what they wanted.

"Best land in the country here," Jules told them all. "The government's no good, but you're far enough from Washington so you can do well if you work."

If the baby was asleep, Marie might sneak away and listen too, or play hide and seek with the strange children until dark, skinning her shins on boxes, falling into gooseberry bushes, or hanging under a wire fence. And all too soon there was the call from the cupped hand: —

"Marie!" Never Jule or James, always Marie. Even strangers immediately put her in league with the elders, saw her the watchdog of the place.

"Funny little old woman — that child looking after the baby," a gentle, stooped little man said to the father.

"Heah? — Oho — Marie. She 's a little devil." Jules removed his pipe and spit into the sand, not unpleased.

And the next day the homeseekers would probably start up the hill, Jules with his nervous buckskins ahead, one of the settlers beside him to drive. Generally there was a new seriousness about the wagons. Jules never minimized the cattleman troubles. "And them kids ought to have shoes or boots. Country full of rattlers," he warned. "Little girl died last summer, bit by a rattler on the sand pile by the well. People want to be careful."

Every few weeks Clem Deaver, Burlington colonization agent, brought excursions to Lakeside or Ellsworth. Jules met these, and sometimes six or eight settled in a cluster, encouraged by numbers, for the road from the south stations to the good land was over eighteen to twenty miles of broken chophills, some of the worst land in the state, uninhabited, wild. Here a murderer could hide for months. A body could be cleaned, the bones bleached white, and nobody ever see it, until a bone picker came.

"The cattlemen are afraid of the government now," Jules told them.

"But I see you still carry a Winchester," a settler from west Kansas commented slyly. "I 'd a thought they 'd a shot you years ago."

"They were afraid of me."

But that was only a half truth. They were n't afraid soon enough. "Crazy foreigner," the Hunter ranch hands said in 1884, and laughed. "Crazy Old Jules," the Pine Creek ranchers called him a little less indulgently when he began to scatter Swiss up and down the creek; even then they were still certain that a dry spell would clear the range of them. It was n't worth the risk to mix with the old crack shot. No one knew what Jacob Schwartz and his long, gaunt sons thought. Apparently they were friendly enough before the Freese shooting, and after that, well, per- haps Jacob could not forget the silent men who came galloping out of the rain into his yard with Jules and his rifle at their head.

To be sure a bullet did whine past the locator's ear once as he loped along the hilltop in the Schwartz range, but his rifle was up immediately and there was nothing more than soapweeds and a horse running hard down the next valley. He never knew if it was merely a wild long-range bullet or a deliberate shot. He always rode the crests of the ridges, where his far-focused eyes saw what his friends, the Oglala, would see.

Now and then a settler left between suns or was hauled out of the hills like a log rolled in a tarp in the back of his wagon, his widow driving. But there was always a lawyer-proof plea of self-defense for the killer. Yet nothing like this had ever happened among Jules's settlers, and perhaps it never would. Still, every so often well-meaning meddlers warned Mary that sooner or later government vigilance would be lowered and the cattlemen would strike. But it would be a dangerous undertaking — attacking Jules. Besides, if anything happened to him just now it would go hard with the ranchers.

The first half of the summer was cloudy, wet. In July the heat came, but most of the crops were made — more land under cultivation in the Panhandle than ever before, with bigger crops. Sheridan County led the state in potatoes with approximately 5550 acres; Box Butte, second. Six years before everyone wanted to sell; there were no buyers. To-day no one was leaving. Here and there a farmer invested in an automobile. An impromptu race between a Gordonite's eighteen-horsepower Rambler and a sixteen-horsepower Premier ended in the latter's winning in a cloud of dust and stench, astonishing all the local experts — with two horsepower less!

In June Jules was called to Omaha again and notified that he would be wanted in the fall. The land indictments were piling up. The papers reported that one of the cattlemen coming to trial let his team run away and was killed, so badly torn and mangled that not even his wife was permitted to see the remains.

"Well," Jules looked up from the report. "That probably settles his case here, but Mexico or France may have a new citizen."

"I wish these land fights were over," Mary said, more to the pan of biscuits she was turning in the old oven that baked on only one side than to her husband.

"Heah? — Oh, hell, with a few more runaways and such tricks, the land will soon be in the hands of the settlers."

It seemed that way. Western Nebraska had become a land of glamour. Young men from everywhere came in search of danger now, and romance. Andrew Schulz, a saloonkeeper's son from Canton, Ohio, brought out three young men adventure bent. They spent most of their extra money for six-shooters and the Canton version of cowboy hats, large-brimmed, small-crowned, a pinkish-fawn color, with punched leather bands.

So equipped, the young men came to the Niobrara on the stage and waited for Jules, fairly content so long as their whiskey lasted. They spent most of the days upon the hill-tops watching the three or four homes they could see, and sang songs or looked for birds' nests along the river. But later they began to miss the Indians they had been led to expect, while the jack rabbits, only visible targets for their revolvers, proved devilish hard to hit. If Mary and the Polander's wife across the river were fair samples of the women out here, they must be a gaunt, unattractive, calicoed lot with too many children and too many tasks, too much suffering in their faces. The only girls they saw, Elsa Surber and a friend of hers from St. Louis, were not impressed. The girls here wanted a young man who spoke English well, danced well, had a nice top buggy and a spirited team. Girls were scarce and could be choicy.

"Oh, is that so?" drawled the handsome and spoiled Andrew as he adjusted his tie.

Sunday Jim took them hunting in the school section. They walked until they were tired and then sat around in a circle on the dry prairie to smoke and to rest and to wonder why they could not get game as Jim could.

They were scarcely back at the house when Jules came home. He talked to them about the land, the country. Suddenly little Jule and James came tearing through the trees, shouting that there was a prairie fire in the school section.

Everyone ran to see. Huge billows of yellow smoke boiled up in the north and trailed over Mirage Flats.

"The damned greenhorns!" Jules roared. "Burn me out of the country! Don't you know they hang fellows for that here?" Andrew started to laugh, but ended in a gasp. Jules was punching the .30-.30 against his stomach.

"Git to that fire!" he ordered.

Mary ran out with an armful of empty gunny sacks, dropped them before the men, and was gone, her blue dress a streak through the orchard towards the river. With a sack apiece the four followed, but not even the leggy Andrew caught up with her in the two-mile run. To them it was an unpleasant turn of events. To Mary it meant the range feeding the cattle they had in summer herd — the money for their winter clothing.

Two hours later they slunk back. The smoke signal had drawn over a hundred men and boys, mostly in Sunday clothes, with a sprinkling of women, all fighting for their crops and homes. When the fire was out the tired fighters dropped to rest, but not the four newcomers. Before the angry eyes gleaming white in the sooty faces and the mutterings against the "damn greenhorns," they could not rest. One could not say what these barbarians might do.

Jules called Jim all the names that came handy. The fool, not to know better than to smoke on the dry range.

The bed in the attic creaked early under the convict's weight. The four from Canton spent the evening brushing the soot from the pinkish-fawn hats.

The next day Andrew, who had the money, went back. The rest remained — two young Germans with fingers undefiled by shovel handle or ploughs but nimble on the zither, and a Rumanian who had found training for the priesthood a little monotonous.

When Jules calmed he found them jobs. Elmer Sturgeon took the Germans, and a sheepman up the Niobrara who kept his flocks well herded on his own property took the Rumanian. When they had the money they filed on land, sold their revolvers, and bought new, more fitting hats. Adventure, for them, was dead.

Jules's letters were always put away for him: fifty to a hundred strange handwritings — land seekers, probably — a week. One of these he ripped open carelessly, glanced over.

"Oh, hell!" he said, and limped out to the asparagus patch that Mary was salting. "A letter from Estelle's Percy, calling me 'Dear Dad' — and the ignorant American can't even write so one can read it."

Mary looked up. "What does he want?"

"He wants me to locate him, and get him started."

"Oh, so."

"Yah, he says he and his mother got seven hundred dollars coming from the government — Indian money."

"Then it's true that she went to an Indian."

"Hell, yes. They told me in Knox County I wasn't over the hill before she was moving in with a big buck."

But the letter, illiterate as it was, interested Marie. Percy said he played ball, baseball. He was a grown man. It would be nice to have a big brother like that. She stole a look at the address and wrote to him. But luck was against her. Percy had moved, and when the returned

letter fell into Jules's hands he took the buggy whip to her.
"He 's no son of mine, the bastard!"

The Surbers were established in the country now, with
their house done and several hired hands for the work, nice,
ineffectual young Swiss who knew nothing about farming.
The second daughter, Marie, taught school, and the father
still held his position in St. Louis. They had a new carriage with side lights, nicer even than the Johansens', and
went visiting, to town, and to dances in a crowd, with an
escort of horsebackers — something like a feudal family and
its retinue. Jennie and Felix, son and daughter of Uncle
Paul, spent much of their time with the Surbers.

Often they trailed down the hill to the Niobrara for
Sunday dinner with Mary or went up to Box Butte to
William to visit with Esther, the daughter of his first wife,
just over from Neuchâtel. Sometimes they stayed at home
and spent long, pleasant evenings about Elsa's piano. In
such an atmosphere romances sprout strong. Mrs. Surber,
still boasting of her frankness, nipped most of them early,
and then that young man's saddle horse or buggy was re-
placed by others. The girls did little to encourage serious
attention. They would have careers.

"A man gets his walking papers early there," a once-
ambitious youth from Hay Springs told Jules ruefully on
his way home.

Certain ones, however, seemed to be permanent members
of the train. Gottlieb Meier, working there, was long
conspicuous. The scrubbed, blond young Swiss had bad
teeth, already gold-filled, which made him less handsome
but not less interesting. To him Elsa seemed a bit more
kind.

When they came to the river it was Gottlieb with Elsa who
followed Jules to the reddest cherries, Gottlieb who made
whistles for Elsa and the little Marie early in the spring,
or pushed the swing in the big cottonwood until Elsa's feet

flew high into the air. It was Gottlieb who brought Elsa down into the garden behind Marie's bare heels for a glimpse of the mother quail and her eighteen young, striped as little brown skunks, but so sweet.

And when Elsa sang it was Gottlieb who never moved and whose knuckles showed white through his skin.

He came to the river often, whistling down the road out of the purpling east. But one evening he came quiet as a stranger and had no words for the boys in the yard. Jules was gone, and after supper, when the older children played in the dusk, he began to talk, his elbows on the table, his head between them. He loved Elsa. Mary nodded from her mending. It was so.

But he had forgotten himself and told the girl, and now Mrs. Surber resented not being approached formally in the old manner. But this was America! Anyway, now that she knew she sent him away for a week. What could that mean? They would telegraph the father, turn the girl against him. She had kissed him once at the well in the moonlight. Kissed him once.

"Yes, she is an obedient girl," Mary's voice penetrated his memories. "I think they had hoped she would make something of her voice."

The young man shook his head. "I know that well," he said gloomily. "And I have *ja* no money."

Mary let him talk until late, was not too kind when he cried, until at last he calmed and went to the attic to bed. The next morning he went to his own claim, crawled miserably into his dugout.

In a few days Elsa's father came up from St. Louis. But apparently the girl won him over. He went back and Gottlieb came to tell Mary it was all right.

"Better marry her right away," Jules counseled.

"Among cultured people it is not done so," Mrs. Surber told him.

There the matter stood.

But somehow Gottlieb was changed now. He no longer wanted to go with the others, did not want to go anywhere at all. "Nu-un, this is a girl's sweetest time. You cannot spoil it so," Mrs. Surber reasoned kindly enough. But when others saw the lovable qualities in Elsa that attracted him, he sulked. At dances he insisted upon the old manner, which he had scorned in his proposal. Elsa was to send all who would dance with her to him.

"Not really?" she dimpled at him. Gottlieb melted, but only temporarily. He thought too that there was no longer any need of her voice practice. She should be learning to do the more useful things — making soap from cracklings after butcherings, learn the correct planting time for peas and turnips. She should not waste time putting on gloves to replenish the fire with cow chips. White hands are a vanity in a farmer's wife. Henri Surber heard of these things and looked at Elsa's picture under his eyebrows and wrote her kind, chatty notes.

"You don't need to get so bossy, you 're not her husband yet," Hannah, the youngest, and a tomboy despite her careful training, told Gottlieb.

Then one windy day, as Elsa was pouring out the dishwater, Gottlieb came around the corner of the house and caught the most of it in his wind-reddened face. He was furious.

"Too lazy to look where you throw the dirty stuff!" he snarled. When he calmed a little he tried to apologize, but Elsa was steel. In the afternoon she rode alone to the river to say good-bye to Mary.

"Maybe it is good that you can go," Mary comforted. "In a few months away it may all be over. I would not like to see you be like the rest of us — here."

"Why must people kill the thing they love in you — if you let them?" the girl cried, covering her face with a lace handkerchief.

"Yes, he loves you," Mary had to admit.

"That makes it no easier." Elsa wiped her eyes, ran a chamois over her nose, kissed Mary's unaccustomed cheek, and rode bravely up the hill, a tall figure on a horse.

Mary turned and ran into the brush.

The next day Elsa went on an extended visit to an aunt in Cleveland, who had always predicted a future for this favorite niece on the concert stage.

By the end of a year Gottlieb and Elsa were writing again, but still she did not return.

"When is the Surber girl coming back?" Jules asked, between bites into a wedge of pumpkin pie.

"I know that not," Gottlieb answered, pushing a bit of potato around in his plate. "Maybe never."

"Oh, hell — you don't know how to get them. Look how that Ed do it."

The young man's hand shook. He flushed under the taunt.

"I had plenty chances — I could have done it. Now I could say to the old man 'Keep her, if you want.' And he would have begged me."

Mary set the coffeepot down hard. "Now it is enough!" she said to them. "Such talk I will not have about Elsa at my table!"

Gottlieb blinked at her as one coming out of a long darkness, a deep foul depth. He pushed his chair back and went quickly out of the door.

"Hey — why he don't finish his dinner? What's the matter with the fool?"

Mary looked with pity upon this man, her husband. "Eat," she told the children.

After dinner she washed the dishes alone, sending Marie into the bedroom to play with Fritz. Gottlieb came back and picked up his cap to leave, but it seemed he could not go. He stood there, running his finger about under the ear flap.

"Ach, surely," he said in German, too miserable to trust

his English. "*You* know I did not mean it, what I said. Elsa — she is all — all, the sunlight and the heavens, the summer night to me. Jules — he — "

"I know. Jules he must put his acid and his dirt into everything!" Mary hung up the dish towel without looking at the young man. "Perhaps she will return — soon."

"I know I never see her again."

"Ach, foolishness," Mary scoffed vigorously. But she wondered.

XVI

THE KILLER

WHEN the ordinary run of homeseekers — the covered-wagon people, the movers, and the broken-down Chicago lawyers, the Boston teachers, and the young adventurers — were located, the land hunger struck the Mirage Flats and the rest of the earlier Panhandle dwellers.

"Why did n't you fill out your section when you had the pick of the country?" Jules inquired, forgetting that he had just filed on the additional three quarters the law allowed him. He had not told Mary yet. The truth was he had no desire to leave the Running Water, but the sandhills drew him, still drew him as they had the day on the top of Deer Hill with the Sioux, as they had that first time on the Snake.

Jules located steadily, but he made little money. Usually the settler had only a part of the twenty-five-dollar fee, often none of it. He got his home on tick, on pump as the sandhiller called it. On credit. Most of them paid eventually, perhaps in rye or corn grown from seed also on pump from the locator.

"Ach, you let those tramps take your shirt — if anybody would want it!" Mary scolded, generally after she had added a gallon of sauerkraut or a half bushel of potatoes to the settler's provender.

"It did n't cost us anything," she defended, to no one in particular.

But Jules bought guns, shells, stamps for his collection, traps and fine tools, as though he got all the money he

earned.   The bills piled up.   Then one day he saw a large
herd of dusty white-faces plod through the hills towards
Ellsworth, pointed by the Spade cow hands, towards the
plank corrals and the long strings of silent box cars waiting.
And he remembered that Mary had complained more than
usually about the duns he ignored, the sight drafts returned.

"I made up my mind to borrow some money and go into
cattle," he told her when he got home.

"And the debts — the two hundred fifty coming due on
the Koller place?"

"Oh, I got good credit.   I 'll borrow enough to pay them
all."

Mary looked up from the catfish she was cleaning.   "All
right, but this time you have to get feed for them.   I won't
watch them starve and do nothing but skin after each
storm."

They went to town and borrowed seventeen hundred
dollars and paid two hundred and twenty of it to W. W.
Wood as commission on the Eastern money.   After the note
and the bills were paid there was little to put into cattle.
Jules bought six cows and five yearlings from John Sears
for $320, and later, in January, twenty-eight calves and
four yearlings for $432.

When Henriette first came back from the asylum she was
normal enough, went visiting, raised a little garden, milked
her Jersey cow, kept a dozen chickens, and drove to town
once a week in her two-wheeled cart.

But there was too much about the place that was un-
escapable.   Under isolation it settled like river mist over
her, damp, choking, distorting tree, bush, and rock.   Sometimes she jumped up from her chair in Mary's kitchen and
ran through the brush and the river, raising her skirts high.
Sometimes she stopped the children and told them strange
stories of visitors from far away, and about news she got
from China through her well.   She showed Jules the mail

box she nailed to a cottonwood along a cow trail. She never had a light any more because someone with a rifle was across the river, watching, watching.

Jules laughed loud and limped home to tell Mary. "Crazy as a shitepoke."

"You ought to shame yourself!" she told him, and took her anger into the garden, where she picked a syrup pail of Juneberries, lovely purple fruits in small bunches that stained the teeth but were sweet and smooth to the tongue. When she came in she felt better.

Gradually Henriette imagined the neighbors came to bother her, to do her dirt. After that the boys of the Flats went down to tease her on Sunday afternoons, to make her scream at them and swing her eighteen-inch butcher knife over her head, laughing when they scattered like frightened young quail into the brush.

She would n't have her bull calves looked after, although several neighbors offered to help Jules do the work. Finally some of the Peters' caught the breachy two-year-old Jersey that was running loose in the stock they were trying to breed up and did the belated business themselves. The animal went home, stood around for a few days, and died. Henriette was worse after that — from eating the meat, it was said.

Sometimes the Koller boys sneaked to the top of the hill behind her house and with a slingshot fired gravel down against her well. At the first pebble she was always out and with a club or a hoe handle she beat the curbing until the bluffs up and down the river echoed. It was good fun.

Soon the woman stopped using the well, carrying her water from the river. Next she thought the house was bewitched too, and so she moved into the cave dug in the hillside for a cellar. There she lived, humped over a fire of green wood, and when anyone passed she peered out, her short hair hanging in gray mats over her smoke-reddened eyes. And twenty years before she was the neat, comely,

cultured girl friend of Elvina that Jules brought from Rushville to the three-day rain in the leaky shack up the river.

Mary always spoke to the woman with kindness, although she was afraid of her knife and her tendency to set
little fires in the grass. As long as Henriette would take
them she gave her vegetables. But finally she cut up Jules's
melons, throwing them against each other, shouting strange
words, beating the vines with her hoe, shaking her fist against
the bluffs closing in about her. Towards winter she set a
dishpan of smouldering leaves and cow manure into the
house where she had lived with Old Jules for six years.
And when the smoke rolled upward from the windows
she pounded the ground with her hoe until there was only
a red pile of ashes.

That evening John Peters and a couple of his neighbors
sneaked up behind the woman, slipped a sack over her head,
tied her hands, and took her to Rushville. They drove
her cattle away and her horses, all except a crippled, flea-
bitten old mare.

"Want to get what little she got left," Jules complained
when he came back from the hills. He went to Rushville
to protest putting Henriette's property into the hands of the
Peters outfit. When he tried to reason with her she threw
the water from her wash bowl through the bars into his face.

The *Standard* reported his interest in Henriette's case as
news, saying that the woman brought up before the insanity
board "was sort of looked after by her former husband, who
lived on the other side of the river, surrounded by another wife and several children." Mary crumpled the paper
in her knotted hands and stuffed it into the fire.

A few nights later John Peters pushed Jules's door open
as a friend, without knocking. The kitchen was filled with
the family and several young men, — including Ernest
Markwalder, a black-haired young school-teacher the Surbers brought up from St. Louis, — still about the supper
table.

All talk stopped as the big Hollander closed the door with his shoulder, stuck his fingers under the lapels of his coat, and stretched his six feet of heavy body to the fullest.

"So — I hear you 're looking after wife number three again, or is it number six?"

"Heah?" Jules demanded, up and limping towards his gun corner.

"I mean — you keep your snoot out of my business or you 'll get it busted."

Jules pulled his cap back from his eyes, let it drop behind him to the floor with a soft thud. "You damned dead beat — Git off my place!"

John grinned into the roomful of antagonistic faces. "Oh, I 'll go, but there ain't no hurry."

Before this defiance Jules grabbed his rifle. The big Dutchman jerked it from his hand and stood shaking it in his face, laughing, rocking back on his heels in his mirth.

That moment Jules's face went gray-white, deadly. He jerked a revolver from its holster on a nail. As a snake poised to strike he cocked the heavy hammer, his aim slow and cold as steel, cold as the eyes above it. At last the sights met and before them John Peters crumpled. Flinging an arm about his head and crying open-mouthed, he jerked at the door and plunged into the darkness, the rifle still in his hand.

There was only the black hole of the open door and the noise of a horse running hard.

Mary was the first to recover.

"Now," she said in awe. "That time he nearly got it!"

"Why did n't you shoot him?" the young teacher, a stranger and the first to dare, addressed Jules. "He had no right to take the gun from you, in your own house."

But Jules was slumped into his chair, hunched forward, the heavy revolver across his knees, his beard like fine twisted wire in white wax. Like shadows the children slipped away to bed.

The next morning they found the rifle against the gate-post and deep horse tracks towards the bridge.   This time there was no arrest for drawing a gun on a man.   Nor was there much said about it, even at school.   A few days later Mary saw John Peters at the section line.   He took off his hat and spoke with much friendliness.   "Jule had n't ought to get mad like that — might hurt somebody," he suggested.

Mary laughed as she told it at the stove that night.   He had tried to help her across the river with her load of wood, until the ice cracked every way under him and he took long steps towards the shore.   "Run he can, when it 's necessary."

The same week the *Standard* reprinted an item from the Alliance paper saying that Jules had been up on land-office business.   "He is the patriarch of pioneers in the North-west country, and in his quaint language can tell much of experience and knowledge that would interest anyone."

Jules liked that.   But he was still not expansive.   He had been very near to murder, and it left him strangely weary and old.

The Hollanders about the Catholic Church were raising big families — eight, ten girls apiece.   The Peters school was getting crowded.   Perhaps because the four nonresident pupils were children of the community cranks, John Taylor and Old Jules, Arnold Peters, the director, came to school and told them to take their pencils and tablets and go home.

The two Irish children, older, and with school-teacher sisters, were defiant.   Jule grinned.   Now he could hunt and trap all day.   But Marie shrank down into her seat and could not believe it.   No school.   Never any school. Grow up like John Sears, who made funny motions with his mouth so people would think he could read.   But there was nothing to do except gather up their belongings into her apron and go home.   Jule swung the dinner pail be-side her.

After a while John Peters rumbled along the section line

in his lumber wagon and offered them a ride to the corner. Marie hung back, remembering the gun episode in their kitchen — but Jule was in the wagon. She got in too, in the back, her feet swinging, her arms about their school things, crying quietly.

At the corner John stopped to let them out. He swung Jule down by the arm and started to do the same thing to Marie. "What have we here?" he barked in a teasing way, and pulled her arm from across the reddened eyes.

"Why, Jule, your sister 's crying. What 's the matter?" Marie turned her back and blew her nose, and with a new grip on her apron started away.

John Peters, the father of eight girls, whistled a little through his teeth. "Want to come to school so bad?"

"Yes."

"Hmm — we 'll see," he said in his thick Dutch tongue.

Jules, who had opposed sending the children to school, was now aroused. The Peters outfit was trying to run him out of the country. He wrote to Rushville and to the state superintendent. Mary listened as little as possible and wondered what was to become of her children. She was so tired. She had n't recovered from her confinement last spring as she should have. Five now — and what was there before them?

Two weeks later John Peters sent one of his girls to tell Mary that the children might come back to school. "If anybody asks, say Jules fixed it with the board." Monday morning Marie beat the teacher there and built up such a roaring fire she almost burned down the schoolhouse. Everything was as before, except that the Taylors never came again. Jules talked big of his victory. "I would n't brag," was all Mary said.

Sometimes it seemed that Jules's purpose in life was to quarrel with everyone he knew, with the possible exceptions of Elmer Sturgeon, Johnny Jones, and his own brother

William.   With Johnny Burrows it was over horses he had
in herd.   With Big Charley, living three miles northeast on
Susette's homestead, it was over fencing.   With Charley
Sears, on the Pat Burke place, things had gone better, perhaps because he was willing to overlook a little for an occasional drink.   Then perhaps knowing Jules since the early
days made a difference.   He brought Mary's groceries from
town, offered to let them hook a telephone to his fence line.
It was a convenience and seemed to help overcome some of
the community animosity towards Jules and his family.
It was diverting, too.   Sometimes Susette's Charley yodeled
for them.   Sometimes George Peters, central of the Mirage
Flats high line, gave the general ring and played his new
phonograph for everybody, switching in the fence line too.
Jules could talk to his friends on Pine Creek in French.
Mary exchanged recipes with Susette.   But when anything
really exciting happened, the fence line was generally out
of order, a post down, the line wet, or wires twisted or
broken by one of Charley Sears's plank-poked cows crawling into his corn.

No one had ever been able to work with Jules long.
The settlers who carried his surveying chain often considered throwing it into the sand and walking to the railroad
without land.   Few went hunting with him more than once,
although they got game enough.   Only the choice of putting up with Jules's temper or going back to the penitentiary
kept the none too even-tempered Jim on the river.   Then,
too, there was often beer, and usually a glass of wine in the
middle of the afternoon, but no whiskey.   The warden's
explicit instructions were no whiskey.

But somehow Jim got a couple of drinks at Hay Springs
one Saturday and, immediately losing all restraint, he pur-
sued the fleeing girls and women in satyric glee.

"Oh, the fool!" Jules roared when he heard about it.
"That 's no way to get anything."

He climbed the attic steps to the miserable, crying man who had sneaked home to bed. "For drinking and acting like a fool you go back to the pen."

"Oh, no, no," he cried, like a crazy man. "Maybe they cut me — treat me like a dog!"

"Oh, hell, they can't do that."

"Yes, yes, I have heard — Honest to God, I'll never touch a drop again, honest to God!"

Jules rubbed the bare spot under his chin. "Well, I try you once more. Go to sleep and go cultivating corn in the morning!"

But Mary was uneasy after that, and there was talk in the community about a petition to the governor to lock the convict up. Not long afterward Jim spent a Sunday fishing on Pine Creek with Mary's brother Jake. Evidently he stopped somewhere on the way home. The next morning he answered Mary's call with complaints about a headache and did n't come to breakfast.

Because the cattle in herd were breaking out of the school section, Mary left the younger children with Marie, eight now, and big enough to look after them and the house. Once the mother stopped and looked back to the gray, weathered house. Before she got more than a mile away she became so uneasy she dropped the fence tools and ran back.

She found Jim holding the window up and pushing his head in, trying to coax Marie to open the door. When he saw the mother he righted his clothes and staggered back up the stairs.

"Let me in, let me in!" Mary cried, pounding on the door. Afraid of a trick, the girl pulled the spike she had wedged into the crack to hold the door. She opened just enough to see, her finger on the trigger of the .22 repeater.

"Ach, the dishes not begun," the mother scolded in her relief, all she could say even now to this daughter.

Next week they sent Jim to William. Lena was having

trouble with her hip, walking with a cane, and they needed a good hired man. Jim was all right now, where there were no children.

Once more Jules was called to Omaha. The Modisetts got off cheap. Their dispatch in removing the fences, their diplomacy and tact, their good treatment of the few settlers who stopped in the soapweed-grown chophills the old settler saw in '84 with the Indians, helped free them.

Jules heard at Rushville that if they had been in a tight place they intended to prove him, the government's star witness, crazy by one of his own letters of complaint about the mail service.

"Is it crazy to want mail service when I worked years to get it established? Probably afraid I might say something about the offer they made me a month or two ago."

Anyway, the thousand dollars it cost them meant a lot to the two lean bachelors. They wore old stocking legs to protect their shirts about the ranch and in the bank at Rushville. Penny squeezers, they were called, but their word was sure as winter in the Panhandle.

Next came a charge of favoritism. Mere tools, land agents from Rushville and Gordon, were fined for subornation in addition to the sentences for fraudulent land activities. Moves for new trials were overruled, and the fine of a thousand dollars each plus three months in the Douglas county jail stood. Yes, the Modisetts did get off easy.

And while Jules was in Omaha a cablegram came from Henri in Neuchâtel. The mother was dead.

At home Jules limped restlessly about the kitchen with the slip of paper in his fingers, still long and lean and fine — his mother's fingers, everyone said. He had once been her favorite, this eldest, and she had never seen him since that scene twenty-five years ago, when he slammed the door forever behind him and left for America. If he could have foreseen . . . But he was young then, so sound and strong, so certain of himself and of Rosalie.

At last he went to bed and lay a long time, his beard outside the covers — turning, and pulling his beard out again. Finally he slept and dreamed of his home on the lake. He was a small boy again, and his mother, with a guest for chocolate, tried to show off his knowledge. But he could remember nothing, and in a rage she flung him from the room.

He awoke, pulled the feather tick from Mary and over his heavy shoulders. Once more he slept and dreamed, this time of his boat, with his mother in it, and Elvina too, it seemed. The wind rose and splashed them and the sail fell over him, over his body and his head and his face. He fought with his hands, striking out.

"Ach, what is then the matter?" Mary asked. "Give me some of the feathers."

Jules awoke, sat up, blustered a little, and fell silent. The house was black and still, with a strange, new emptiness.

His mother was dead.

After New Year's the *Standard* asked for a report on Jules's experiment station. He sat down, thundered because the inkwell was dry, the letterheads gone, his pen scratching. The children ran like rabbits before a prairie fire into the lean-to and settled down around the heater. Papa was on the warpath.

Jules's report was published verbatim, two thirds of a column. Mary had to listen to it again ". . . Cherries: Dyehouse, Terry, Early Richmond, Wragg, doing well. All the sweets winterkill. . . . Plums: Sandoz for sale by the Crete Nurseries, grafted, or at the orchard on the Niobrara on their own roots, or five newer varieties, cross between the original and the DeSoto. . . . All Japanese and European plums winterkill. . . . Apples: Florence,

Martha, Hyslop, Whitney, Duchess, Longfield, Yellow Transparent. . . . Plant only yearling whips. . . . With four thousand trees this station looks like an oasis in the desert . . . a patch of California thrown by an earthquake into western Nebraska."

To all this Mary said "Yes."

Jules tapped the paper with his long fingers. "That 'll open their eyes," he predicted, and believed it.

Mary fished an old bone from the fire that Jules was burning to reduce to lime for the soil. She threw it sizzling into the snow, as she said something.

"You make so much noise I don't hear you. What you say?"

"Nothing, only 'Hide the new pinchers; here comes Andy for dinner!'"

"Oh, hell, I thought you said something." He put the paper away. Andy was not important.

The early cherry season was a happy time for them all, even Mary, whose fingers were permanently crooked from the hoe handle, her arms cramping at night.

Sundays there were as high as seventy-five people, many with picnic baskets to open under the trees. Most of them did n't come to buy, just to eat — young people from the Flats, the Kollers up the river, the Peters', a dozen girls with ruddy, Dutch cheeks and ripe lips. They brought their friends and ate cherries and paired off through the young orchard or went to sit in the shade.

"Don't break me my fine young trees," Jules admonished, limping proudly among these young people, dumb before him beyond a "Fine cherries you got, Jule!"

"It 's a bit of home to me, this orchard," a thin, gray woman with three children at her skirts and four more scattered through the orchard told Mary wistfully. "You know I lived in Ohio when I was a girl."

"Yah, I know how it is," Mary agreed, and picked a little

pail of dewberries, black and sweet, long as her thumb.
"For you," she said.

But the idyl could n't last. Early in July, Markwalder,
the school-teacher from Surbers', rode a lathered horse into
Jules's yard. His face was paper-white under the black
smudge of his beard. Mary ran to the door, her hands under her apron, her face anxious.

"What is the matter?"

"Emile 's been shot!"

Mary dropped her hands to her side. It had come.

"Emile! — How?"

"By Ralph Nieman, from the Schwartzes', shot before his
whole family. The hound rode up, shot him in the back,
and galloped away."

Weakly Mary dropped to the wood block in the yard.
So it had come as she had always known. Jules's brother,
who never located a settler, who was, in fact, friendly to the
small cattlemen, often went to the Schwartz place, shot before his wife and seven children.

And Jules was away locating, had been gone for three
days.

All evening the barbed-wire telephone line was busy.
The sheriff had been down; had the murderer. He did n't
have him; he had n't even gone out. Nieman shot himself. No, he had shot someone else. By the next noon the
situation clarified. The sheriff did n't come out of Rushville until morning. Community feeling ran high. If the
sheriff was afraid to act, there were others who were not.
The young school-teacher talked of mobbing the Schwartz
place, making them give up the criminal. If not, then
search the place, and willows of the upper ranch.

But without an able leader the plan dragged, collapsed.
They all waited for Jules. Ah, he would lead them. Old-
timers were prodded to speak of that other time he rode
into the Schwartz yard and made the old man shake like
a wet puppy. But Jules was still in the hills, in that land

of endless sun-colored hills where chops and blowouts follow each other like waves of a wind-whipped sea. Across
the road camped two groups of homeseekers, apparently not
understanding the situation, waiting for the locator.

A day passed. Emile was still alive with a bullet in his
lungs. Two days — three. Emile was dead. The settlers' wagons creaked back across the bridge. And still
there was no sign of Jules. The Woodmen offered a reward for the murderer, who, some said, was surely across the
border, north or south, by now. Or perhaps in the deeper
hills. Perhaps he would sneak up to a hilltop as hunters
once did for deer and antelope, bareheaded, looking from
behind a soapweed, only it would be a man he was stalking,
a crippled man below him, sighting his compass, his back
to the killer. Mary sent the children out, but they would
not play.

And then Jules came home.

With Baby Flora astride her hip, Marie ran out to tell
him. He knew. Above the dark beard his face, com-
monly so ruddy from wind and sun, was greenish yellow.
The child dropped behind her mother, afraid.

The funeral was that afternoon.

"You ought to go," Mary reasoned. "What will people say?"

But Jules did n't go. He lay on the couch under the
window, watching the neighbors drive past, his rifle within
reach above him. On their way back several of them
stopped, wondering, generally considering Jules's caution
wise. An associate of the murderer's, not debonair, handsome, as the killer, but stocky, red-faced, with whitish pig
eyes, stood at the outskirts of the crowd awhile and then
rode away. It was whispered that he was looking for the
locator, also that Emile was killed because he gossiped,
talked about a herd of horses stolen down in the hills. No,
it was cattle. Anyway, he knew too much. Marie listened
this far and then ran into the garden to hide under a low

tree to think. Was there anything about them that their father did n't know?

Jules just sat, reviewing the entire struggle against the cattlemen, from the first cowboy he saw on Mirage Flats — no, it was earlier than that. The men who pounded their teams back East because of the stories told at the Hunter ranch. Ah, it was a long fight, and now they killed his brother.

That evening while Mary was doing chores and Jules inspecting the orchard, using his rifle as a cane, Marie nailed down the windows with tenpenny nails. The house door had no lock. She drove a spike deeper into the old hole, and worked it out with pinchers, ready for noiseless reinsertion after everyone was asleep. With Jule she planned.

"I 'll rip his belly open with my toad sticker!" he promised, flourishing his open knife.

That evening Jules was doubly careful not to sit between the lamp and the unblinded window while he ate his supper. He found no relish in the accumulation of daily papers, no interest in the new *Geographic,* and contrary to all precedent he went to bed early. Every crunching step outside brought the eyes in the kitchen together. A belated pig grunted at the steps; the forgotten cat scratched against the door for her milk; even Keno, the pup, was gone.

When everyone was in bed and the house began to crackle, Marie sneaked out. But she could n't find the hole, and in her hurry the spike slipped from her stiff fingers to the floor with a tremendous clatter.

"Jules, Jules!" Mary whispered, shaking his thick shoulder.

To-night he was awake immediately, his rifle scraping as he took it from the wall above his head. Marie stood still. Bare feet limped toward her, a black hulk with a rifle moved out of the darkness.

"It 's only me! I had to go out!" she cried, through the silence of the listening house.

"Oh, the fool!   Got to scare me!"

In disgrace Marie went back to bed.   "And stay there or you get a damn good licking!"

"Did you fix the door?" Jule whispered.   "I wisht I 'd a gone," he said when he got no answer.

The next morning Keno, the dog, made his appearance. Mary hoed in the trees near the house.   Even the boys hung about instead of following the river.   Jules lay on the lounge staring at the ceiling.

After dinner, while the mother mixed up the bread, Marie searched the cherry trees for late fruits.   From the crotch of a tree she saw a horsebacker coming up through the young orchard.   There was no road there; only an occasional hunter from down the river came that way.   Hard upon the girl's shout announcing his coming, the horseman trotted into the yard.   It was the white-eyed man.

He swung from the saddle on the far side, his right hand free over his holster.   Just then Jules limped into the doorway, his rifle across his arm.

"How, Jule!"   The man used the old settler's Indian greeting in a surly growl.   There was no answer.   Under his shaggy brows Jules's eyes were sharp as gray gimlets, his palm caressing the grip of his rifle, his forefinger in the trigger guard.   Behind him Mary's blue dress showed and behind her the white faces of the boys.

"What you want?"   Jules asked the question always demanded of friend or foe.

"Oh, just riding through — "   The man's voice was insolent.   "This is the road to Pine Creek, ain't it?"

The two men's eyes held, riveted.

"Yah!" Jules spat at last.   "And take it — Get off the place, and get damn quick!"

Slowly the man turned his horse, mounting deliberately with his back to Jules.   He held the impatient animal still, looking down upon the locator in the doorway, his hand resting on the butt of his revolver.   Silence hung between them like a poised rattler. Almost imperceptibly Jules's finger tightened on the trigger, the knuckles of his hand whitening.

With a laugh, the man threw back his head, baring his teeth like a dog's. He jerked the reins and loped out of the yard, up the hill, and out of sight.

"They don't catch me unprotected," Jules commented, lowering his gun and going back into the house.

A few weeks later six short rings, the urgent general call, brought Jules to the telephone. He listened a minute. "Marie — come here. It is important and I can't understand the damn whispering."

The girl took the receiver. A faint voice was speaking from Rushville. An officer at Roswell, New Mexico, contrived to room with a man he suspected was Nieman, carrying a thousand-dollar reward up in Nebraska. To make certain he tried the antique dodge of uneasy conscience: rolling lumpy cigarettes that squashed in his hands, jumping up at every step on the creaky little hotel stairs. When the stranger finally asked what ailed him, he said that he had killed a man in a fight.

"Hell, that's nothing. I just killed one in cold blood and you don't see me losing sleep over it!"

"It sounds pretty thin, rounding up some tramp to get the thousand," was Jules's opinion, when Marie explained it to him as well as she could. But it was Nieman, leisurely riding towards Mexico, not expecting anything to come of the shooting. He was brought back and held for trial. His parents and a sister, well-to-do people from Kansas, — a banker's family, some said, — came up, hired the best attorneys their money could import and the best they could get in the Panhandle, someone who understood these people. The first two approached had refused.

Not since the Freese troubles in '91 had the streets of Rushville resounded to the heavy feet of a silent river and

Pine Creek crowd. But to-day they were mostly well-dressed, in buggies or cars, eating their meals at the better of the two hotels, even talking a little over their toothpicks. There was no milling around a little board shack long before the trial commenced, no talk of lynching, no firearms. To-day, because the streets were hot and dusty, everyone stayed in the shade until court time. Jules was the only man in town with a rifle.

The real battle was over the jury. With the county torn by cattleman-settler conflicts, the papers full of the cattleman trials for several years, with Jules and his activities always in the foreground, and the Schwartz outfit well advertised by their nefarious dealings, no man capable of an intelligent opinion was without one. No man who had been in the country for any length of time was without his prejudices. Slowly the jury was selected, mostly from riffraff, men Jules had never heard of, and of these he was suspicious.

"The Schwartz outfit got money and men who'll swear to any lie. Besides, they can buy up most of the jury."

But what could be done? Nothing, Jules believed, and limping out into the street he went home.

The defense tried to justify the killing. Emile had told of seeing Nieman and one of the Schwartz sisters bathing naked in Pine Creek. The gallant young man was only protecting a girl's reputation.

"Girl's reputation! Emile was giving the old roadhouse woman some free advertising she needs, with that wore-out kisser on her!" a partisan voice whispered loudly enough to reach all over the courtroom. Automatically Judge Westover's gavel pounded the noise down.

It was admitted that Nieman was wild, an unruly boy, a desperate youth. He had several knife scars, a bullet furrow or two. But his mother pleaded so eloquently for a new start for him, and her hair was white and waved and her cheeks beautiful, her dress of soft, blue stuff. On the other side sat the widowed Helen, the passion of her dark eyes imprisoned in a body heavy with repeated childbearing. Around her were seven sharp-featured, undernourished children. All of them were brown and wind-burned, their hands bony and calloused, their clothing old and patched, strange and frightened, the mother with no knowledge of English, no eloquence that the jury could know.

Perhaps the twelve men were busy considering the dark Schwartz brothers along the front row, directly under their eyes.

Not once was the real issue, the eternal conflict of the small man against the big, the settler against the cattleman, permitted to ruffle the surface of the trial. It was the old story of a hot-blooded young man whose loved one had been besmirched. It was just a coincidence that he worked for the Schwartz outfit, although no one had even seen him with rope or iron or hammer or fork in his hand. It was a coincidence that the vile-tongued foreigner he shot knew of certain irrelevant activities of his neighbors, that he was the father of seven children and the brother of Jules, that sworn enemy of all cattlemen and the Schwartz outfit in particular.

Nieman got off with manslaughter, because Emile lived three days.

"He died, did n't he? That 's murder," William and Jules insisted. But all Judge Westover could give him was ten years, which, when they talked it over calmly on the river, was really a victory. The first hired killer to be sent over the road. Generally they never were brought to trial.

There were people who looked for action from Jules to the last. Just what, none could say, but something. He had never failed his community. He fought drouth, cold, hunger, and loneliness for them. He brought them in as penniless homeseekers, many on passes, helped them to stay. When the Schwartz sheep threatened them he brought in German farmers, enough to cover the tillable land of the entire range, driving out the last ewe. He disposed of Freese and showed the Rushville bankers a trick about skunk skinning. He backed Green against the combined cattlemen about him, got three post offices against the government's verdict that he was unfit to have one. He it was who helped open the range and put the cattlemen and their agents under indictments, into the penitentiary. Jules would think of something.

But they forgot that Emile chose to side with the enemy against his brother. That he patronized the post office Jules believed Carl Schwartz stole from him. That when Jules came to him to find out about the burning of Surber's lumber, he drove him off. Emile, his brother believed, got what he bargained for.

"Just what I expected. I warned him when he first located there to keep away from that crooked outfit. He knew them and the dirty work they were doing. That's why they killed him. He knew how they tried to get me killed by loaning Freese a rifle and ammunition. This time they got a better shot to do the trick. In this country every man's life is his own lookout!"

"That bread basket Jules carries around these days is making him soft!" was the verdict of the community.

Perhaps it was as well, the calmer ones believed. War and wholesale bloodshed stalked very close to the Panhandle that year.

XVII

SNAKEBITE

WHEN the first fires of autumn ran yellow through the low places, Marie gripped the unaccustomed lines over the temperamental buckskins, while Jules swung the leather-lashed willow whip. With a jerk of the wagon they were off into the hills, the land of deep-grassed valleys, blue lakes: home to Jules; the habitation of gray wolves, cattlemen, and rattlesnakes to the girl.

All forenoon heat waves and low chophills undulated and blurred into a rhythmic pattern of mauve and tans before them. Not even a saddle horse stirred the ragweed dust of the trail. Game was scarce. They saw panting gray lizards, a rabbit or two, a grouse against the whitish sky far away, a rattlesnake slide into a prairie-dog hole. That was all.

At the gates Marie climbed over the wheel and strained at the stick or jumped on the wires to loosen them. Between fences Jules smoked and sang and talked of the first time he saw the country, of the deer and the antelope he shot in the buckbrush patching the last endings of the long, dry valleys, and of that happy time before his leg was broken. Then for a mile or two he was silent and there was only the whir of grasshoppers in the limp sunflowers along the trail, the creak of harness, and the grind of sand in the wheels. Finally he talked again — of the man and the Winchester.

"Now I got a better gun — more improved." He spit emphatically into the sand, but to-day even that masculine bolster of confidence failed him. "I got a fine rifle, but it don't make a show like his," he admitted.

Marie slapped the lines, not daring to answer.

They passed an occasional dugout against a hill, a little soddy or an old cattleman claim shack, dull gray and alone, tawny grass growing in the doorway and about the piece of pipe sticking up where Jules said there was no water, only a few feet of rusty iron driven into the ground. A fraud.

And often his long fingers pointed across the prairie and obediently Marie pulled the buckskins towards two dim, yellowish streaks or through a pass where there was no track at all in the rippled sand. They stopped at one of the Modisett mills, at the foot of Deer Hill. Marie slipped the bits from the horses' mouths and let them graze while they ate from the leather-hinged grub box and drank the clear cold water gushing night and day from the two-inch pipe into the low stock tanks. Then they went on. The hills grew higher; the valleys harder, resounding under the ponies' hoofs. Soddies were more frequent, with here and there a long strip of gray breaking, a few anæmic sunflowers pushing up between the sods.

Jules had kept his filing from Mary as long as he could, but it slipped out one evening when he was particularly pleased with his supper — quail, with potatoes fried into golden sticks, the last cauliflower of the winter creamed and specked with nutmeg, watercress salad, muffins, plum jam, coffee, and canned cherries with juice bright as deer's blood on fresh snow. By golly, it was fine. And it would be even finer on the new place.

Mary threw up her knotted hands and rolled her faded blue eyes back. Now, at last, he had gone crazy. The children drew away into the shadows, their voices buzzing softly. Got to live in the sandhills — where the gray wolves lived, and the cattlemen, the rattlesnakes.

But Jules recovered in a minute and went on planning his new community grandly as in 1884. During the summer

he helped circulate a petition for a school district, one of
the many cut from the cattle range, and called a preliminary meeting for the middle of September. "Let Marie
go with you this time, instead of the boys," Mary suggested.
They could stay overnight with Pete, Jules's cousin, married to Elise, Ferdinand's first wife. "Look good and see
how it is for fuel and a garden place," Mary instructed her.
"And don't get a headache from Papa's scolding." The
girl shook her head. He told her many fine stories when
the others were n't around.

By the time they got to the half-soddy, half-frame house
on Pete's Kinkaid it was filled with prairie-gaunted, sun-
bronzed Kinkaiders. Several slightly gray girl-women —
"Boston old maids," Jules dubbed them — sat primly on
improvised benches, squeezed in between women nursing
babies and men chewing tobacco. Few of the men carried
guns, although Pete had a rifle hung against the wall.
Someone told about a celebration given at the Spade ranch,
with everything free for the settlers, including ice cream.

"They shore steps around like an old Indian pony tangled
in bob wire since the government 's took a hand," a squint-
eyed boomer from Oklahoma said.

The meeting went well. Five months of school in a
work-donated soddy. Jules refused the directorship. Too
damn busy.

The next morning they drove to the new claim, bumping
over trackless bunch-grass knolls and finally rattling down
a steep hill into a high valley with a tiny yellow pine shack
leaning against the slope. "Your papa's new home," Jules
said grandly, as though it were the mansion of a cattle king.

The buckskins snorted and fidgeted about approaching.
"Hold the ponies; I 'll walk over. I just want to see
what the settlers stole from me now."

Before Marie had the nervous team quieted he came
running back, bobbing grotesquely in his limp, his mouth
to the back of his hand.

"Bit by a rattler under the house where I hide my hammer."

The words came in jerks between spittings of clear saliva. Groping frantically in his pocket, Jules pushed his knife into the girl's hands, jerked it away almost before she could open it, and slashed at the purplish swelling rising about two pinpricks. The dull blade sank into the flesh, puffy as dough, but it did not even cut the skin. With a groan he flung the knife from him and sucked fiercely.

Then his eyes turned habitually to his companions in danger — his weapons. He grasped the pump gun by the barrel. "Hold the team!" he commanded, slapping his palm down on the rim of the hind wheel, the muzzle against the swelling, holding the gun steady between his body and the wagon bed. A shot echoed from the hills. The buckskins plunged forward. The girl fell off the seat, but clung to the lines. Bracing her feet against the dashboard, she pulled and jerked until the ponies slowed to a short lope, to a trot. When she finally turned them, Jules was limping toward her, shaking great clots of black blood from the back of his hand.

Tying the lines about her waist, Marie ripped the blue shirt sleeve and made a handkerchief tourniquet just below the shoulder. Then, gray-faced, Jules lay down in the wagon bed.

"Drive for Pete's, and drive like hell!"

Too terrified to ask the direction, the girl swung the whip over the ponies, giving them their heads. They sprang out; her sunbonnet flew off; the board seat went next, and behind her the father bounced like a heavy bedroll as the wheels bumped over the bunch grass.

Foam from the ponies' mouths hit cold against the girl's cheek. With her feet wide apart she clung to the lines as they tore down a long hill and across a vacant valley. No house, no road, not even an animal. Another valley, and still nothing. Marie was sure she was lost.

Then the low house of Pete's swung around a hill towards
her and a man came running out to stop what he considered
just another of the buckskins' runaways.

With his wife he helped Jules into the house and ran to
the corral for a horse and was gone to John Strasburger's
homestead for whiskey. Marie stood inside the door and
looked at her father's swelling arm, the black-crusted wound
on the purple hand. He was still; his face like plaster, his
breath rasping. She twisted her hand into her apron and
remembered that John Strasburger was temperance. He
would n't have anything. Anyway, she had heard of a
sheepherder who died from snakebite while dead drunk.
This was September, the worst month.

By the time Pete came back with about an inch of brown
liquid in a tall bottle, Jules's arm was purple to the shoulder. He drank all the whiskey, choking, and sank back.
"It 's not enough," he mumbled, hopelessly. "Get me
home, Marie, I want to die on the Running Water."

Obediently she ran to the buckskins, but her legs were
like dead water. She did n't remember the road; the gates
were hard; the ponies would run away. Suddenly she
could n't stand it and, pushing her face between the spokes of
a wheel, she cried as she had never cried before. The buckskin mare looked back, pricking her ears sharp. Then she
went to sleep again in the harness.

In a moment Pete swung his buggy up to the door, called
to Marie to hold the restive horses while he brought Jules
out. Then he dropped her into the buggy bed at her
father's feet, they shot through the yard gate, and were
on their way home.

After four or five miles of sand the wild young team
slowed, their lathered sides heaving. Jules's face was sunken
into his beard, his eyes closed. Now and then he mumbled
— of the sheepmen, the cattlemen, all who had worked
against him. They ran through his head like dark waves
of cattle sweeping down the lane from the Flats to the

river. Then he seemed to sleep a little, talking as from
a dream of Neuchâtel and Zurich and Rosalie. And as he
dozed he swayed with the shaking buggy.

Marie reached her arm around his knees and held to the
seat to keep him from sliding forward. Once he looked
down on her.

"Swelling 's spreading into the lungs," he panted, thickly.
Pete whipped the jaded team into an unbelievably slow
run.

"If he kills his team getting me home tell Mama to pay
for them."

Marie pulled her skirt up to her face. "Your mama's
a good woman," he went on, the breath wheezing from his
beard. "You 'll get like her. Marry a farmer and help
build up the country."

The girl began to cry aloud. Pete touched her shoulder.

"Steady. We may need you to drive before this day
is gone."

Biting the gingham of her skirt, she calmed herself.
After all, they had faced bad times before, the time John
Peters almost got shot. Jules deep in the hills when Baby
Flora was born. The day when the killer stopped before
the door.

And still the wheels spun yellow sand. Jules did n't
answer any more. Pete stopped at two claim shacks, but
no one had anything. No whiskey, no potassium per-
manganate. Nothing. Frightened faces looked after them
as they hurried on; women clutched their children to their
flat chests.

They stopped a moment at Surbers' to say good-bye.
Henri was not there. It was too bad, his old friend . . .

Then at last they were in sight of the blue ribbon of the
Niobrara. Pete whipped up the thin-flanked, lathered
team and in a weary, flapping trot they stumbled into the
home yard.

"Ah, now, you let the horses run away!" Mary scolded

as she ran out. But when she understood she sent Marie
flying on cramped legs into the house for a cup of whiskey,
a big cup. Jules shot it into his mouth. Before they had
him in the house she was on her way to Charley Sears's, for
of course the fence-line telephone was out of order. She
could make the mile trip in less time than Pete's horses,
already down in the harness in the yard.

Dropping into a dogtrot previous emergencies had taught
her she could hold for the mile, she finally reached the man's
door, gasped out her need to the kindly bachelor, and was
sick over his doorstep while he called Hay Springs.

Long after dark she was awakened by the boys. They
were lined up beside her bed, poking her and whispering,
"The doctor's come — in a red automobile!"

A funny, short man came in, chased the boys out and
pushed her back. Old Jules would be all right, — cast-
iron constitution, — but he'd have been gone long before
this from the deadly September venom if he hadn't shot
it off.

In a week Jules, still pale, limped through the orchard
admiring his plum trees, but it was months before he could
use the two middle fingers of his left hand. Tendons heal
slowly.

Christmas Eve, 1908, the house was full of people. An
outcast from Austria played the "Marseillaise" aggressively
as he pulled his accordion over his thick knee and damned
Franz Josef vigorously. But after a big supper he mel-
lowed and played "Blue Danube" for those who danced,
his ear lovingly to his instrument, a reddish mist over his
pale blue eyes. Jules sat beside the stove and discussed the
year's progress with his cronies. A German Zeppelin with
fourteen passengers went three hundred miles at the rate of
thirty-four miles per hour.

"That is dangerous! It is good the air is not crowded."

Jules tapped his pipe against the stove. "It will be soon.

It's coming." He was in good spirits, stroking the three-colored cat that he sometimes fed from his plate when Mary was n't looking. He beamed under his heavy, bushy eyebrows upon the young people dancing until the floor shook. He expected a couple of young bachelors to find wives here to-night. They were crowded close enough in the sixteen-foot room.

Early in January Jules went to Omaha and Lincoln again. After a week he sent home a copy of the *State Journal* with a column-and-a-half write-up of the "Star Witness in Land Fraud Cases," with a full-length sketch of himself.

"Ach, why did n't he buy a new cap! That old muskrat thing!" Mary lamented. But it was a good drawing, his rifle across his arm, his loose overcoat hanging unbuttoned. The story interested Marie. It was garbled, even the snakebite incident, but it was fun.

Jules had planned to go to Louisiana to see his relatives, located there since the French occupation, perhaps on to Mexico to look for a new country. Probably never come back.

"Well, it's about time somebody else pulled your stinking sock off," Mary told him.

In two weeks he was home, with two slovenly, bleary-eyed Germans who stood uncomfortably at the door. "Papa picked up two more bums around the Lincoln saloons," Mary told the children. "Probably had to pay their way out, and now I have to feed them and wash for them all winter."

In answer to her remark that he was supposed to be in Mexico or Louisiana he said he spit blood, his lungs hurt him in the low, wet climate of Omaha.

"Ach, it is only your catarrh. But I 'm glad you did n't go. Only throwing money away."

"It's my money. I borrowed on what I 'm getting from home!"

The twenty-one hundred dollars inheritance money came. Mary thought the mortgage and the debts should be paid. Instead Jules bought a lot of stamps, threatening to order enough for a mattress, just to hear his wife scold. He bought a dozen new guns, including a .22 for the boys, and a barrel of candy and two gunny sacks of peanuts to sell to the young people of the community. And when they came he brought out scoopfuls and dumped them on the table. "Help yourself!" He ordered warm clothing for the entire family, even overshoes for the children, their first. No more chilblains and running sores. Finally he bought an Edison phonograph and three hundred records.

William, too, forgot his debts. He started a fine house with plate-glass windows for flowers, his hobby. He bought an automobile and let one of the Peters boys, working for him, run it. Elvina planned a two-and-a-half-story house of cement blocks. Emile's wife, Helen, died the year after the shooting, from grief it was said. William was the guardian of the orphans, but somehow the boys managed better than he. They were hustlers, going into cattle, and taking care of them. The sisters worked beside the brothers in the field, the corrals, and the meadows.

Ferdinand sent for the girl who looked after his mother the last few years before her death.

"Na, if she comes, knowing him as she ought to, she must be a fool," Mary told Susette.

Still, Nana was a sunny happy-go-lucky. He talked well and sang gay, off-color songs that he learned in Paris, twitching his forehead and his shoulder most eccentrically and comically — a little less amusing to those who knew the twitching went on all the time.

Although he was a good trapper, he never brought down the grouse like his oldest brother. "Schnapps don't help the aim," Jules said, with a fatherly fondness for this Nana. And knowing his brother's displeasure with alcohol-dulled wits, Ferdinand drank his whiskey in his dugout on Pine

Creek, the bottle beside his hay pallet — and waited for the rosy-cheeked Swiss girl.

Varied as the inheritance expenditures were, Jules had probably the most fun. There was the fine evening when they picked the records from the mail-order catalogue, the Kinkaider's Bible. At daylight they were still around the table.

"Throw dollars around to-day, scratch for pennies to-morrow," Mary could n't help saying. But Jules was in good humor. Among the French records he found several songs he learned when a boy. "They make me pay full interest for the five years anyhow," he answered her finally, having heard after all. "Do you want 'Stille Nacht' in a quartette or a solo?"

"Quartette, I like that best."

A couple of weeks later a neighbor brought the three big boxes and the crated horn. It was almost midnight; Jules was alone with his stamps.

"Everybody up!" he cried through the two bedrooms, pulling covers mightily, and thumping on the ceiling to waken Marie. "The talking machine has come!"

Mary built up a big fire with her morning wood. Marie buttoned her dress crooked and hurried down the outside steps. At the first screech of the inexpertly adjusted wax record the boys were out too, Fritz trailing behind, sleepy-eyed. Two teams going by late from visiting stopped in the yard. Everyone picked the records he wanted to hear. And Jules, like a god, wound the machine and adjusted the cylinders and stalked about, his pipe guttering, his hands in his pockets, happy.

It was a good time for all of them. Here, for once, differences in taste and temperament were countenanced — more, encouraged. Food they always ate alike, at least until the last two years, because there was no choice. Dress goods were ordered by the bolt, and Jules and the boys had

shirts, Mary and the girls dresses; even the feather ticks
had slips of the same calico.

To-night there were no superior remarks about woman's
ignorance because Mary preferred "Die Kapelle" sung by a
male quartette while Jules picked violin solos, the lighter
French composers, or "Listen to the Mocking Bird," with
something of the Slavs for his darker moods; stirring
marches when he planned more orchard or protested the
appointment of W. W. Wood, a ranch owner himself now,
as receiver of the land office. Jule and James liked "Rabbit Hash" sung with hearty negro laughter, and played
it as much as they wanted. Marie wore out the sextette
from *Lucia* that winter. And Fritz, convinced now that
crying got him nothing from his sister except the blackness
of the clothes closet, swung his short legs over the edge of
the chair and displayed his dimples at anything, the only
good disposition in that family.

All this music meant more company than ever. The
Surbers, of course, William and Lena and sometimes the
girl Esther. William had a player piano, but it was hard
on his knees, that everlasting pumping. "Noise, noise!"
Lena said, clapping her palms over her ears when she
talked about it.

The Germans from the Schwartz range came too, the
Swiss from Pine Creek, even Emile's children, walking all
the way to the river. The Kollers and Peters young people,
with fine homes, spent much time at Jules's. Jim, par-
doned the Fourth of July before and working for Elmer
Sturgeon, came every Sunday. He was moving to his own
land in the hills in the spring. Nell Sears, still with her
brother, stopped by for the mail. Then there were always
the grub-line riders, Andy, the two young Germans who
helped set fire to the school section, strangers, travelers, land
seekers — enough to fill the little rooms with humanity and
tobacco smoke.

All this company meant work for Mary, endless cooking

and baking. She used a sack of flour a week. Jules was
a little like William. He did not crave plate-glass windows towards the road, seldom traveled farther from home
than Omaha, but he too liked display. He liked to limp
through a houseful of guests enjoying his hospitality, to
sit at the head of a long table loaded with heaped-up platters.

"We got plenty to eat," he told Mary, and was invariably
answered by reference to the thinner times. It was her
nature and unchangeable.

When the father was home the phonograph was kept going, even during his naps, as though to make up for all the
miserable, musicless years. "I could throw the thing into
the yard!" Mary groaned as she panted in the black cavern
of a sick headache and tried to drown out "Die Wacht am
Rhein" under a goose-down pillow. But she did n't mean
that, although she missed the family song hours. The supper dishes were no longer washed to old Swiss songs or
to "My Old Kentucky Home," but more probably to a
facile piano solo, perhaps a fragment of a concerto that
stopped Marie's hand in the dishwater, or perhaps to
Ada Jones singing "If the Man in the Moon Were a
Coon."

In the spring Ferdinand's Marie came, a honey-sweet,
plump, milk-and-roses sort of girl in her early twenties.
The day after they were married Nana brought her to Jules's
place. He reeled a little and sang dirty songs in French.
Jules joined in the celebration.

"Ach, you ought not talk to her like that," Mary reasoned, but they only laughed. Nana's Marie blushed and
tried to ignore her husband's maudlin pawing, just a little
uncertain now whether it was so fine a thing to marry this
son of her former employer, even if he had inherited money.
Perhaps she was thinking about the damp, dark dugout
where they spent the wedding night. But there was to be
a house. He had promised her one.

After the rattlesnake bite Jules relinquished his first Kinkaid and filed on another, even deeper in the hills, not far from the little blue lake he saw from Deer Hill so long ago. The settlers were glad to see him take a new interest in them. Just the week before, the Kinkaid correspondent in the *Standard* asked what had become of Old Jules. "Always eccentric to a degree, you could depend on getting a proper survey and securing the valley land that he located you on."

The settlers, Kinkaiders, as they called themselves, needed his surveying but not his protection, apparently. The Spade ranch store presented every nester whose bill was paid up by New Year's with a ton of coal, and when spring came they gave a hundred box elder and a hundred cottonwood trees to anyone who came to the ranch for them.

"That's how they get the land now: sell the settlers high-priced stuff, get them in debt, and then take the claims," Jules tried to show them. But that was nothing illegal, only good business.

Jules hired twenty acres broken on his new Kinkaid and swung a spade over the smooth, flat sod, showing the young American how the corn was planted. Then he handed it over and went to smoke in the shade of his pine shack and to talk to the horsebackers coming through the pass.

When the Spade cattle ate up the corn, Richards sent Jules a check and a friendly letter. "They know they are on the wrong side of the fence now. Want to keep out of court," Jules said to Mary, frying potato pancakes.

Yes, it was different from the days when the rancher almost ran over the crippled foreigner in Chadron. Now he called him Mister and asked for information on tree planting for the home ranch.

Things were changing on the Flats, too. Where crowbaits and plough critters once turned the tough nigger-wool sod, now dappled Percherons and hairy-footed Clydesdales grew until Hay Springs was listed as the world's largest shipping point of fine draft horses. Johnny Burrows brought home his blue ribbons with the pride of a less godly man. They had silos now for forage, concrete storage cellars for potatoes if the price was low or cars scarce. They grew pure-bred cattle, supplying the range country with blocky black Galloway, or shorthorn, and Hereford bulls. Even the Hollanders did not mind the occasional drouth, with their cream separators and large families of milkers.

People began to read more, and soon as far away as Rushville it became known that Old Jules's girl was hungry for reading. "Takes after him." Even strangers sent her books, to be returned any time. If Jules was gone, Marie sneaked them to the attic until her straw tick was lumpy. At first they were girls' books, then paper-backed novels, and finally old volumes of Poe, Hawthorne, or perhaps Melville, and finally Hardy. Here, in Hardy, she found life as she saw it about her. So it was like that everywhere. Well, it was best to know.

Jules banned novel reading as fit only for hired girls and trash.

"And what does he think he is?" Nell Sears demanded when she heard his orders to return all books immediately. "Him with his backside out until he found a woman 'd keep him!"

The year Marie was in the eighth grade, John Peters's oldest girl taught the school.

"I don't send my children to no fifteen-year-old Hollander," Jules told his daughter flatly.

"She 's older than that."

"I don't give a damn. You don't go."

The boys showed white teeth in their browned faces when they heard. They could hunt, trap, and make sleds, perhaps even skates; who could tell?

Marie helped with the wood, looked after the house when her mother was gone, sewed, patched, and kept an eye on

Baby Flora, three, and not really much trouble in the winter any more. "You have to watch baby" was giving way to "Where 's Flora?" Soon the house would be free of babies forever.

But after a couple of weeks at home, Marie made a discovery. At first she refused to believe it, but finally she ran through the snow to the top of the hill where Pete had made the wreath for her once, where Jules told her about the man with the Winchester.

But she could n't stay there forever.

That evening Mary caught the girl's worried green eyes on her. "What 's the matter with you?" she demanded crossly, letting the dishrag drop between her hands.

Marie flushed but, driven to words, gulped. "I should think you 'd be tired having babies — I 'm tired watching them — "

The mother's wet hand shot out across the girl's mouth. "You talk so to me — your mother! Ach, such a hex I have brought up!"

Miserable, not understanding her mother's animosity, the girl took Flora up into the cold attic bed. And when the rest were in bed, Mary sat hunched over the stove for a long time, the light from the lamp beside Jules's stamp collection casting a big shadow of her halfway up the smoky wall. At last she spoke, and again, before Jules looked up.

"I want you to make out an order to Montgomery Ward for baby things."

"Heah? — I thought there was plenty time — not coming till May, you said."

"Yes, but I have to make them when I can now, with the children home all the time. That Marie 's getting so she notices too much for her age."

"Oh, hell, what 's the difference?" Jules was examining another specimen with a reading glass, then holding the stamp to the light for the watermark.

Mary rubbed her knotted hands over her tired knees. "I 'd give five years of my life if this had n't happened." She spoke between lips stiff as river ice that edged the dark, narrow current.

"Oh, that 's woman's business — raising kids."

Mary said no more. A long time the shadow on the wall did not move. There was so much to think about this winter.

Old-timers said that the winter of 1910 was the hardest since '84. 'Eighty-eight brought a worse storm, but this year the snow came the eleventh of October and stayed on. The few days of sunshine only thawed the surface enough to form thick, icy crusts that left reddish stains along the cow trails through the dirty drifts. Ranchers began feeding six weeks earlier than usual. By New Year's there were piles of hides at the railroad stations. Of the four thousand head of Texas-Mexican cattle the Spade imported, two thousand were already dead, despite all the care that could be given them. Several settlers worked steady, skinning with saddle horses, ripping the hides off at fifty cents a head.

All summer Mary had nagged Jules about hay. But Jules thought corn fodder would be enough.

"We have more cattle than last year," Mary reasoned.

"Don't bother me. Let them rustle."

She kept nagging, but she was unwilling to take the matter into her own hands, buy hay while it was cheap. Now, resentful of her condition and certain that Jules would withhold his hand, she cast her venomous predictions in his face every day. The cattle would all die. They would lose their home, be tramps on the road.

The children fled the house, the boys to the trap lines or to slide down hills on a sled they made for themselves, Marie to gather brush and wood. Mary could not get out much; her lumbago kept her doubled with pain.

"Dragging home wood on a crazy sled, when you have twenty, twenty-five horses running loose on the range!" Charley Sears scolded. "Why don't you hitch up the buckskins?"

"Just try to get the folks to let us do anything an easy way," Marie replied, half crying in her exasperation. With the rope over her shoulder as Mary had done for so many years, she dragged the wood through the snow.

At last hunger drove the cattle into the bluffs; weakness stuck them in the first drift. With shovel and rope Mary and the children dug them out, got them home somehow, usually to die of pneumonia. The pile of hides grew. And when the snow finally left, the young heifers began to calve. Because Jules did not believe in restriction of male freedom, the calves came too early, while the heifers were still weak. Even the cows had to have help. And Mary was heavy on her feet.

Every morning early Marie started out, carrying a rawhide strap with a loop in one end. She tried to cover the entire pasture, the tableland, the bluffs, and the timber along the Niobrara, two and a half sections, every day. She counted the cattle, looked for those apparently ready to freshen, hunted down the missing ones, helped them if she was not too late. Then, after washing her hands and the strap in the river, she went on. But even with the desultory aid of the boys, the pasture was too large. To cover it all on foot, look into every draw and gully and brush patch, meant walking fifteen to twenty miles a day. Every now and then a heifer or a cow she had n't found in time was stretched on the ground, bloated, dead.

"Have to run my legs off — when we have twenty-five horses doing nothing but eat!" she complained sullenly when she stopped at home for a lunch at two in the afternoon.

"Ha!" the mother cried, hot with envy of this daughter's slimness, her agility now. "Catch a pony and ride him if

you want. Takes five men to get them up and you know
how they throw Gus, saddle and all. You know too that
Papa won't have you run the risk of getting crippled."

"He's always gone. Anyway, he swears about so much
no matter what we do. Why not have Gus break us a saddle horse? He'd do it for five dollars — one calf, and
Papa would n't need to know until afterward. There have
to be about so many fights on this place anyway!"

"Shut your dirty mouth! Ach, to have such a thorn in
the side like you! Rather I go do it myself!" Mary
grabbed her sunbonnet and started towards the river, moving
heavily, her feet wide apart, like an over-weighted, sand-
filled duck.

Marie pushed back her untouched plate. She pulled the
strap from its nail and went out again, to come home at sun-
down, starved by the day's walking, to sit across from her
mother's silent, tear-scalded face.

Marie took her problem to her brothers, back from a
surveying trip with Jules. The next time he left them
home, the three put Uncle Jake's old saddle on the flea-
bitten mare that belonged to Henriette and took turns riding her. It was more trouble at first to get her to go in the
right direction than walking, and her lameness made it much
less comfortable, but they soon discovered that by enough
pounding the old mare could be kept in a short, protesting
lope that was n't bad when the swing was once mastered.

"Oh, hell, look at the damn kids. Marie, tell them to
git off that horse!" Jules called when he saw Jule ride the
old mare down to the river to water.

"Aw, it's all right. We been riding her for weeks,"
Marie said as casually as she could, without looking up from
her pan of potatoes. The phonograph, also by prearrange-
ment, was playing a violin solo.

Jules filled his pipe and watched the boy come back and
slide off in the yard, proud of his achievement. The father
went to the pieplant patch where Mary was pulling pink

stalks and pushing them into her apron. "Did you see that Jule — riding like a wild Indian on Henriette's mare?" he bragged.

That evening he told them how to use stirrups. They were only for the toes.

"Yes, but you fall off easy that way," Jule, who had experience, argued.

"Maybe, but you may fall off a hundred times without hurting yourself, but if you put your foot deep in and get caught just once you git dragged to death like that boy up on the Flats a couple of years ago."

The three children looked at each other. Toes it was.

Of course Jules raised a rumpus the next time he saw one of them start for the mail on the old mare, having forgotten his earlier knowledge. "Papa don't give me any rest all the time you are gone," Mary complained to whoever was taking the old mare out, but it beat walking the pasture.

Ferdinand's baby, a girl with a tiny rosebud mouth, was born late in April. They had spent much of the winter at Jules's, the pretty young woman of a few months ago sallow, her skin loose, her blue eyes tear-faded, her wrapper half-washed or frankly dirty unless Mary took it from her.

"Too lazy to keep herself clean," was Jules's verdict. Mary shook her head. She herself was n't half as disturbed by dirt as she had been. But Nana's Marie must have known he would n't be easy to love at his best, with the nervous twitching, the irresponsibility, the drinking. Ferdinand was intelligent and eccentric as the others, even as eccentric as Jules, but without the older man's violence, his sense of persecution, and particularly without his force and his ability to pursue an objective through years and a tangle of obstacles. Least of all was Ferdinand capable of following an objective without visibly nearing it, as Jules had all these years. Even now Jules was talking of Canada, of starting a settlement in British Columbia, where there would be good food, good wine, good talk, with strong women and sturdy children for the fork and the hoe.

Surber gave up his position in St. Louis, partly because of his failing health, partly because he had put so much money into his place that he could not afford to let it go. So he bought a pair of bib overalls that never quite hid his innate elegance, got the post office Carl Schwartz lost over Emile's shooting, and advertised egg preservative as a side line.

Elsa Surber was back too, and while her father could n't actually deny Gottlieb the right to come to the post office, he made it clear that as a guest he was no longer welcome. The young people met once or twice along Pine Creek, but they had little to say to each other. Elsa had done much with her voice. She sang in churches and at concerts for her friends in Rushville and Hay Springs. But these things did not pay, and it was evident that if they were to make a living here, they would need more land for cattle. So she filed on a piece of vacant range land a few miles from home. Surber's Marie located near Jules's Kinkaid in the hills. With only three years of residence required now, it would be easy. Land hunger was spreading, but as always those far away saw the opportunities first.

The Surbers still came to the river every other Sunday afternoon or evening, with a box of sandwiches or a cake now, to make things easier for Mary. They stayed up all night to see the earth pass through the tail of Halley's comet and talked about the things they had read. In the East some people stripped themselves naked and waited for the end of the world. Even Johnny Burrows got Elvina to put off building the house she planned because it would never be needed. However, he went right ahead with his stock barn.

At two o'clock they went out into the whitish half-light that permeated every corner, awed and strangely silent.

They thought they smelled ozone and listened to Jules's theory to explain it. But gradually the light died, and so they danced until the high tips of the cottonwoods along the river bottom caught the gold of the early sun.

Gottlieb was there. He could n't come with the Surbers, but Mary asked him anyway. He sat gloomily beside Elsa, holding her plate for her at midnight, trying to tuck a stray lock under her net. She tolerated it without moving, without even a change of expression, and the lover dropped his hands in embarrassment, as though he had made the gesture to a statue of stone.

Mary's sixth child was born in May, another girl, three and three now. Before the baby was ten days old the mother was in the garden, working as always, except that now and then she had to stop to lie between the rows because her knees were water. Early in July she fainted, for the first time in her life. She rested the next day and then resumed the hoeing in the cornfield. There must be corn for the hogs she was fattening for winter market.

When Jules came home he found his bed moved to the shed lean-to next to that of the boys. Marie was sleeping in her mother's room. He looked a little disgruntled, moved his guns over his new bed, cracked a few smutty jokes at the supper table. But Mary would not talk about it and thereby won her point. There would be no more children.

XVIII

THE HILLS

SPRING came to the range country with the swiftness of the swallows. In the morning snowdrifts lay deep along the wagon trails. In the evening the low valleys gleamed with lakes of rose and orange reflecting the delicate sky. In a few days translucent grasses pushed through the shallower reaches, misting the blue with green. Wild ducks darkened the open water and quacked and quarreled as they fed along the shores. In the swamps the hell-divers chattered and mud hens fought or led their early hatchings out for swims, a dozen wine-colored plush birdlings bobbing along behind the black hen mother.

But there was none of the fragrance of spring. Every puff of wind brought the stench of dead cattle piled in draws or fence corners by the long winter's storms. The secretary of the Homesteaders' Mutual Protective Association wrote a long letter to the state board of health, but by the time the officials got around to the complaint the stench was gone or lost to the consciousness. "Like the packing-house stink. The workers eat ice cream when you can cut the smell with a knife," Jim said. Even the maggots were dead, dried, and blown away, and bone pickers, Sandcherry Charley and his kind, were spotting the rich harvests a year or two of bleaching would bring.

The Kinkaiders were banding together, ostensibly to protect their crops against the ranchers' cattle, but actually to agitate the completion of the Pacific Short Line started westward from O'Neill toward the heart of the sandhills in the nineties. Although Jules was openly contemptuous of organizations, he was voted a member of the association by general request. They needed him and his reputation.

But despite all the talk, the demands and threats at the meetings, and the impressive scribbling of the secretary, protection against the cattlemen or even the coming of the hoped-for railroad was not as important to the settlers as the fact that the Spade was laying off all hands except the regular eight or nine punchers, the cook, and the choreman, until haying time.

"It looks like the beginning of the end," an expansionist Kinkaider told Jules, moving his tobacco out of its brown nest with satisfaction. But those who depended upon their pay checks to settle the grocery and coal bills at the ranch store scoffed — until ten thousand head of cattle were trailed down into the government reserves at Seneca to be summered at thirty-five cents a head. That meant less lease money, less work for the settlers. They failed to consider that their fences, their own growing herds, cut the range into inaccessible patches. The Kinkaid correspondent to the *Standard* looked about and asked, "What will the nester do for money without the Spade?"

"Go to work for himself," Jules suggested. "Nobody ever amounted to anything as a hired hand."

The convictions of land fraud against Richards and Comstock and their agents stood — one year each in the penitentiary and fines for the cattle barons, eight months each for the agents. Sooner or later they would have to serve their time.

Jules looked up from the paper at Mary. "Well, I got even with that outfit, like I did Freese and the sheepmen. Richards is n't going to run over any cripples for one year anyhow."

The gossips predicted that the Spade had about reached the end of its rope. When Mike Petersen, the foreman, heard the talk, he spit his dry ball of tobacco into the dust. Hell, the ranch would be here and making money when all the Kinkaiders were starved to death, ha, ha! Those among his hearers who still hoped to get back on the pay roll laughed in agreement. Christ, of course they'd starve!

Still more disconcerting was the news that the ranch no longer fed all who lined up along the oilcloth-covered tables in the cook-house. A sign, MEALS 50 CENTS IN ADVANCE, appeared over the door, and many a grub-line rider and his family turned away hungry.

In July Jules had lumber hauled to his new place, and put up a house. They would all move into the hills in the fall. Mary accepted the news without protest. She walked to the door and looked away over the river. It would be hard to leave here, where she had suffered so much. Behind her Jules was still talking, his words like rain on a dry stubble field. The time of residence was up. Somebody had to go live there now, for land was getting scarce. Beside, he had ordered a shipment of groceries hauled out. He would have a store, probably a post office.

In August Jules took Marie and Jim to live on his Kinkaid. Mary helped make an event of the leave-taking. She let Marie cut out two new dresses, a blue calico and a red one, and James got two pairs of new overalls. Both had stout shoes. No going barefoot as they did on the river — not with the rattlesnakes so thick. They even weighed each other: James forty-two pounds, Marie fifty-six, not much for thirteen.

For supper they had *Weinschnitte*. Mary dipped the slices of bread lightly in wild grape wine and into egg batter and fried them brown in butter. While still hot she sprinkled them with cinnamon and sugar and piled them high on a big platter.

After Marie was in bed Mary came to her, carrying the lamp high over her head.

"You're old enough to know right from wrong," she said awkwardly, and then she went away.

The next morning they started. When the crops on the Niobrara were harvested and the pigs sold, the beds and the phonograph and Jules's stamps would be loaded in the wagon and the Running Water left behind. Temporarily, until the Kinkaid was proved up, Jules said. But already he was circulating a petition for a post office at the new place.

Standing together, Marie and James watched their father swing his whip over the travel- and age-chastened buckskins and rattle down the valley out of sight. They looked at each other, just a little frightened, in a strange land twenty-five miles from home with a .22 rifle for protection.

Here they were, beside a squat board shack with holes for doors and windows. Nothing to keep snakes out. Their beds were on the dirt floor. There was no other house in sight, only towering ridges of hills to the north and the south, reaching low arms together to hold them in. No company but the burrow owl in the little dog town west of the dry water hole.

And in their ears ran Jules's last command: "Watch your fires or you 'll burn out the country. Ranchers don't plough the guards like they used to. Remember them kids that burnt to death in the swamp north and look out!"

They knew about fires. Jules's homestead was cut by the old line fence between the two big ranches of the sandhills, the Spade and the much smaller Springlake outfit. North of the pine shack the line fire guards, two strips of ploughing approximately eight or ten feet wide and sixteen feet apart, trailed over the knolls and dipped into the draws. They were weedy, neglected. South and east of Jules's breaking the knee-high bunch grass waved, reddening in the sun, dry.

The two children roamed the hills for game, for sand cherries, the heavy sprays of sweet, purple-black fruits, large as the thumb berry, dead ripe in the hot yellow sand. In the Osborn, north, above the old sod walls where the two boys who were burned to death in the last fire had lived,

chokecherries bent their bushes low over cackling young
grouse.   Along the hill wild plums swelled.

The swamp in the Osborn was drying, but a few ducks
stayed hopefully on.   These, with grouse and young rabbits,
kept the frying pan going and helped pass the time for the
two children.   They saw almost no one, and forgot about
fires.

Then one morning a vague, iridescent veil hung along the
horizon.   "It's far away," Marie consoled James, and herself.

The veil changed to piling billows of sulphurous yellow.
The southeast wind freshened.   Three heavy wagons filled
with men rattled off to the east, the Springlake hay crew
going to the fire.   Now and then a horsebacker galloped
over the hills.   One stopped at the shack.

"You kids better stay clost to the breaking.   Let the house
and the stuff burn.   Lay face down on the ploughing and
you'll be all right."

The wind blew harder, trailing pungent smoke in long,
blue-black sausages over their heads.   They tried to eat
dinner, but despite herself Marie kept talking about the two-
month fire old-timers still recalled.   Only a heavy snowstorm stopped that one.   James, his blue eyes round, rubbed
his hands over his curly blond hair and kept coming back
to the two boys who left their guard-protected soddy and
ran into the swamp while their father and mother were
fighting fire.   They were burnt in the tall rushes that looked
like green mist from the hill north.

By two o'clock the smoke streamed along in a gray blanket
only a few feet over the valley.   The hills on either side
were gone and the world was only the little shack, a plot of
tall-grassed earth and a corner of sod in the wind-driven
smoke.   The children moved about uneasily, looking over
their shoulders, restless as animals.   Suddenly they could
bear it no longer and together they ran to the knoll east to
see — farther, with only low dunes and chophills capped in

the moving sheet of gray-blue — and farther still, until the breaking was lost and they could hardly see each other through the stinging smoke.

A coyote tore past, not five feet away. Cattle bawled, their feet running below the moving blanket, shaking the earth. Then shouts and the dull roar of flames.

A gang plough with six horses burst upon them. A man was riding a lead horse; another, on the seat, hung to the levers as the sod rolled out in ribbons behind. Then came the backfirers, scattering flames along the windy side of the new guard. These little red fires burned back into the wind very slowly, spreading along the guard and widening it materially. Singed men swung sacks and old chaps legs upon any backfire that got too vigorous. All worked as the animals had run.

Suddenly a curtain of flame shot up from the earth on a grassy knoll, crackling, leaping through the sand grass. The children fled, as the cattle, as the coyote had fled.

On a bare knoll they stopped, panting, to look. The smoke was almost gone. The fire was down. Cautiously they stole back to listen to the exploits of the day. Men were plodding wearily along the new guard, beating out smouldering spots, stomping out burning cow chips and soap-weeds. Two groups closed in from the sides. They had tapered the fire and finally headed it, after contesting every step of the sixty miles between the Burlington tracks and here. The fighters, their faces smudged, their eyebrows singed, their lips swollen like drying liver, dropped flat to the ground, breathing gratefully of the clean air.

Two women drove up with a cream can of hot coffee. One of them, a music teacher, asked anxiously about the many settlers left homeless in the sixty-mile strip. It was fine that they had turned the fire from her little white house — "music box," the cowboys called it. She asked the children who they were. She knew Old Jules. She gave them cookies.

Down on the Running Water the smoke reddened the sun, and the smell of burning grass stung the nose and throat. "I hope Marie and James are all right," their mother said several times. Jules wandered restlessly through the trees. The next morning he started into the hills with a load of ash posts.

Once more Old Jules was coming to live in a new country, as new, in its way, as the Mirage Flats were in 1885 when he returned from Fort Robinson. Most of the good land was taken up. To some of the settlers the sandhills seemed a soft, undemanding country, ideal for loafing. But only until the ranches extended no more credit on pancake flour, an invasion of sand fleas came, or the winds of winter swept down upon them out of the Dakotas. To others the country was aloof, austere, forbidding; the wind sucking their courage as it sucked the green from the grass by mid-June. Some saw it as a great sea caught and held forever in a spell, and were afraid. And here and there were a few sensitive to the constantly changing tans and mauves of the strange, rhythmical hills that crowded away into the hazy horizon. They heard the undying wind rattle the seed pods of the yuccas against the sky, sing its thin flute song over the tall, sparse grasses of the slopes. They smelled the strange odors of marsh and mint rising from the wet valleys at dusk, saw spring run in sudden fire of yellow blossoms over the low knolls and give way to deep blue. Then that too was gone as though no flower had ever been, until August brought the long, graceful white phlox blossoms and the reddening bunch grass turned to russet waves under the stern caress of the chill fall winds.

These Kinkaiders came from the backwaters of the world's ends, driven by need. Often it was escape from some unendurable reality. Often it was land hunger. The victim of the latter found it easy to envy the stranger on the next section or to gloat secretly in his failure. The tramp, the fugitive, the ex-convict, the broken-down doctor or lawyer, the impoverished scion of a *Mayflower* family, the pack peddler, the refugee from a pogrom, the faintly tired music teacher, and the hull of a prostitute all rubbed elbows with the sturdy farmer and the visionary. Tragedies came swiftly.

George Booth, a young bachelor, settled uncomfortably near the Spade home flat. Along in July a hobo who helped him put up a little soddy the spring before came running to a neighbor's place. He said he had gone to Booth's to kill a little time. George seemed to be gone; a horse tied to the yard fence was down, stretched out, with deep pawed holes around the post. After carrying a bucket of water to the animal the tramp pushed open the soddy door — it caught, against the hanging body of the settler.

The coroner came out from town as fast as his team could travel, but it was July. Flies buzzed over the froth on the protruding tongue and the deep cut across the man's throat. They burned a little horseshoe tobacco on a stove lid and held an inquest. The soogans of Booth's bed were blood-soaked, with brown drippings in the sand below; a blood-crusted butcher knife was tramped into the dirt.

His neighbors went in, looked around, and hurried out for air. They gathered in little knots, talking low. The man's throat was cut. Could a man hang himself after soaking the soogans so with his throat's blood?

The verdict was suicide by hanging.

Three Kinkaiders got on their horses and rode over to Jules, running lines for the Strasburger brothers. They slouched in their saddles and told him their thoughts.

"Is that so? Looks like the hobo or somebody got a few dollars for putting Booth out of the way." Jules rubbed his fingers through his graying beard as he leaned on his rifle to think. Somehow he had hoped for peace. . . .

"Still an' all, the poor fellow was in a bad way," one of the settlers added. "Nothing to eat but two old pancakes without raisin' or syrup, an' not a smidgin of flour left. The place was full of letters too, from a girl out in California, somewhere, what did n't seem to want to marry him, just wanted him stuck on her."

"Fooling a good man — with love lies," Jules said bitterly.

Before the death of Booth had faded from the Kinkaiders' talk another story came to Jules's table. Two sandhillers clashed on the streets of Gordon. About a year before, Terran, working at the Spade, thrashed Briley, a settler too near to the home ranch, and destroyed his household goods. Briley, a widower with a little boy, moved to Gordon, but he would n't sell his relinquishment. Along in the fall he told his troubles to several neighbors up for winter supplies. Terran overheard and started trouble, but this time Briley had a gun. He shot three times, missing. The fourth time the hammer snapped dead and old-timers ran in to separate the men. Briley escaped into a store, where he was refused shells. The marshal came and started away with the settler without obtaining the gun, apparently empty. Terran followed along beside them, threatening Briley. Suddenly the settler reached under his arm and fired, hitting his tormentor in the stomach and spinal cord. An hour later Terran was dead.

Several versions of the story spread, depending upon the sympathies of the narrator. "More land fights," Jules termed these difficulties. "Richards always had a hard outfit hanging around his ranch," was a common complaint. "Yah, well, just let them try to run me out!" Jules answered, looking with pride towards the fan-shaped stack of guns behind the kitchen door — Old Jules's arsenal, his new neighbors called it. In addition, two guns always hung on spikes over the table, two in the store, and his usual .30-.30 and a pump gun were within reach over his bed.

Let them come.

James and Marie listened and went behind the house and whispered together.

"I wish Mama would come down," the boy said, scraping sand together with his shoe.

Jules's house building, not supervised by Henriette or conditioned by the hope of a young wife from Neuchâtel as his last homes had been, was a business of lean-tos that the Kinkaiders found highly amusing. It cost enough — took up an immense amount of lumber, but the centre building was only seven feet high to the eaves of the hip roof. The first lean-to was built around the entire north side and half of the west, making a thirty-two-by-twelve room with an additional ell of about ten feet, none of it over six and a half feet high, covered by an almost flat roof and lighted by only two small windows. Around that was another lean-to sunken a foot into the ground to maintain standing height, even darker than the first.

Mary was frankly disappointed.

"You promised me a nice house if I came down here," she reminded Jules almost every day.

"Oh, fiddlesticks!" Nell Sears, who had married Jim soon after he received his pardon, told Mary. "You ought to know Old Jules by now."

Mary held her resentful silence. That Nell Sears, married three times and locked up in jail with her husband at Hay Springs when they went to get married! They had a bottle of whiskey and Jim unbuttoned as usual and chased the chambermaid down the hall with Nell close behind, shouting good Irish curses. They spent the night in jail, both of them. But Nell was a hard-working woman. She helped Mary last summer, when she could hardly get around. Maybe she was right, after all.

The first storm proved that the small cookstove crammed with cow chips was entirely inadequate for the long room, particularly cold because of the flat roof. "What would n't I give for a load of ash stumps and the old heater!" Mary said many times that winter.

After New Year's the children, against Jules's protests, rigged up a buggy and started to school in the east district four miles away, a mile farther than their own school. But Jules had a feud nicely started with the people west. So, to keep peace and make things easier for their mother, Jule and Marie tucked James and Fritz into hay and blankets in the back and took turns driving when the weather dropped to zero.

"Well, we must be getting old, Mary," Jules said at the dinner table. "The kids are doing what they like."

It was true that they were both older. Jules's hair and beard were thinning, grizzled and straggly, and his forehead was heavily lined. But his hands were smooth and young. Mary looked old, much older than her forty-three years. Thin, work-worn, her face was long, her nose and her chin sharp, her hands knotted. But her hair was still touched with golden lights and curly. And there was no denying that the two were proud that their children went to school so.

Sometimes Jules and Johnny Jones, still dealing in farm necessities, shook their heads over the Kinkaiders. They were not the homeseekers of the eighties, young, optimistic, eager to battle wind and weather for their land. The Kinkaiders were mostly middle-aged, city-softened, dependent upon railroads and stores, too often set lone folk: bachelors, widowers, old maids, widows.

Jules preached marriage, wife importation if necessary. Here and there the isolation and perhaps the proximity of two soddies helped him. Generally the couple married, at least for a while. Sometimes they did n't trouble and blessed the community with diverting gossip.

But there were women like the retired high-school instructor and the music teacher from Boston, a little afraid of their neighbors and of the rough-appearing men in boots and high hats who loped past or stopped for a drink at their wells. These continued to live alone. Contrary to all predictions by the broad-hipped, obviously adequate women, even the music teacher stayed, grew ruddy of skin, liked the wind-ruffled grass about her door, the whistling curlew on the knoll, the yellow-breasted meadow lark singing his morning song on her plank pump, and the purples and dull yellows of the hills. The women who sniffed at her ideas welcomed her when there was sickness, or a new baby and a mother who needed coaxing to take up the weary burden once more.

Another kind of settler was the prosperous one who shipped in from Tulsa or Elmhill, or Cotter's Corner. Livery freighters planted dressers, an incubator, a cream separator, and rocking-chairs on the bare prairie and went away. With the awkward breaking plough the man turned smooth ribbons of gray earth in a low spot where the grass was densely rooted. With the help of the entire family a soddy was thrown up in two or three days. Plastered with gray mud from an alkali lake bed, it was cozy.

Different as these Kinkaiders were, they were united by two common bonds. They all wanted a railroad; still held meetings, consumed enormous amounts of chewing tobacco and time, and went home optimistic. The other was as most bonds are: a common need. Fuel. With no tree closer than the Niobrara River or the brush of the Snake, little money, and wretched roads over twenty to forty miles of sun-drenched or snow-glazed hills to the nearest railroad, wood and coal were out of the question. Cow chips were the solution. Most of the settlers had lost all the qualms that curse the fastidious long before they reached the hills. Bare-handed they took up the battle, braving rattlesnakes, which upon acquaintance failed to live up to their reputation for aggressiveness. City women encased their still-white hands in huge gloves and, with a repugnance no extremity could completely erase, endured the first few weeks somehow. The music teacher wore gloves to the last.

But the first winter brought the most squeamish to a proper appreciation of this cheap and practical solution of the heating problem. Mary forgot that she could not saw down a tree if the fuel ran short in midwinter, and after two months of only moderately cold weather, the family wore old coats in the kitchen and Caroline, the baby, was swathed like an Eskimo. The winter was unusually open and warm, as some wag has said everybody's first winter in a new country always is. The cattle that were there to pay off the $1700 mortgage coming due in the fall had survived fairly well on nothing except a bit of corn fodder and range. Now the faint green of spring was on the hills, and along the lakes the ducks were beginning to pair off. The last day of April brought a warm rain; it turned to snow by night.

"Three foot of snow by morning," Jules predicted, voicing a standing exaggeration joke of the hills, but one just a bit too near the truth. The next morning Mary tunneled out of the low door with the fire shovel and followed the yard fence to the windmill, invisible in the flying snow. The wind screeched and howled. Mary did n't return. Just when Marie decided that she took the wrong fence from the tank, the one leading off into the pasture, the mother came back white, snow-covered from head to foot, her eyelashes broad with ice.

"The cattle are gone!" she announced, exploding her bomb with characteristic abruptness. She had been to the shed and they had evidently drifted with the storm, to stumble into snow banks, to chill into pneumonia, to smother, to freeze. And there was the mortgage on the Niobrara place, on the cattle, even on the team, successors to the buckskins, mortgaged for the interest.

That May day was a gloomy one. Mary and the children foraged along the fence, tearing out alternate posts to chop up on the kitchen floor with the hatchet. No one was permitted outside the door without a rope tied about his waist. The lamp burned in the dark lean-to all day.

The next morning, long before daylight, the mother, without awakening Jules, called the two older children. The wind was dead, the stars were out; and the shed was empty of everything except Brownie and Blackie, the team, nickering for food. They were saddle-broke, and on them Jule and Marie were to track the cattle, dig out and save what they could. After gulping a hot breakfast they were bundled into what warm clothes the family afforded, an old fascinator wound about Marie's head. Climbing upon the old horses, they set out, equipped with a spade and a hammer.

Daylight stalked cold and gray over the knolls as the horsebackers crunched out upon the frozen snow. About two hundred yards away they found a cow up to her neck in a drift, her eyes already white — mad. Mary waved them on. She would tail that one up. From the top of a wind-cleaned knoll they looked across the valley, lightening into a pure sheet of white, with only a few dark spots, heads of buried cattle, moving or still, along the dim trail. Brownie smelled out the drifts that would support her, but if she or Blackie did break through to flounder there was nothing for it but to shovel a trench to a knoll or a harder drift. The first few critters the children found were range cattle, Herefords, evidently from a Springlake herd that drifted past and tolled Jules's cattle away.

By the time the horsebackers were half a mile from the house the sun was up, and with it came the wind. Little curls of snow began to run. Marie looked at Jule. In ten minutes they might be lost in a blizzard.

"We got to stick close together — The old mares'll see us through," the boy said, but his face was like a bleached gunny sack. The wind blew in puffs, dying down, rising, making a pale iridescence of the sun.

By now Mary had dug the cow out, a black hulk on the snow. Jules, a dark figure on the drift south of the house, his head higher than the smoking chimney, looked after the children. "Yu-hoo," he called, his hands cupped to his mouth.   But the two did not turn their heads.

Over the ridge of the south hills the trail was plainly visible between the white scarves behind the soapweeds, still blowing like chiffon at the ends.   Here and there a bit of hoof-balled snow showed where the cattle had passed.   Several range cows, thin and exhausted, lay flat, frozen.   One of Jules's calves was in a gully, only his starred forehead out, dead.

On the south slope the burning sun was already softening the crust, stopping the blowing that still filled the valley below with thin veils of white.   Perspiration started by the shoveling through the deep drifts of the slope chilled when they stopped to plan.   There must be a trail for whatever they saved.

The Strasburger homestead, belonging to a nephew of the man near Pete's place, was little more than two hummocks of white, blue smoke blowing from one.   At least three hours spent going a mile and a half.

In the next valley Jule found one of their cows up to her neck in the snow, her eyes wild.   They dug her out, changing off on the spade and keeping a sharp eye on her horns. The snow was softening, the children soaked to their hips. And when the cow was free and could stumble about on her frost-numbed legs, she rushed headlong at Jule and was stuck again.   In disgust they left her and plodded on, the snow too wet for the wind, too soft now to bear the small-hoofed mares.

The next cow was dead.   And still the two climbed on and off, digging and sweating, their feet clumpy and wooden with cold.   Noon came; Marie's face burned; her lips were blistering in the unshielding fascinator.   She thought about the smoked glasses at home in Mary's trunk.   Jule, protected by darker pigment and a huge cap, was hungry.

A neighbor who was digging out his saddle horse caught in a draw shouted to them.

"You kids better get for home!" He said more, but they let it go in snow echo. Cattle that stayed in the drifts much longer would be hopelessly chilled. So they pounded the tired, sore-kneed horses on; threw snow when the need arose, their shoulders and arms numb.

About four o'clock, in a choppy range, they found the cattle. First three head, then five, other small bunches. Crowded together by high drifts like a moose yard Jules had told them about. They bawled as the horsebackers plunged towards them.

At last, around six o'clock, the cattle were free. Only the two cows along the way and the dead calf were gone. The animals were gaunt; their skins jerked like palsied hands from cold, but they could walk, which was more than most of the range stock could do.

Slowly the cattle followed Marie, with a new little calf, still damp and curly, across her saddle, single-file, down the trail they had made. Jule, his legs kicking the tired mare along, brought up the rear. Darkness came gradually as the bawling string trailed into Jules's yard and up to the shed.

The children fell from the horses and were taken into the house with unaccustomed solicitude. Marie's head ached; they were starved; and the house was dark.

"Why don't you light the lamp?" the girl demanded crossly.

Mary made a funny noise in her throat. "A-ach, the lamp is lit. You are blind."

Before morning Jules was giving the girl small doses of morphine to quiet the pain in her head, the burning in her eyes. But the second day he dared not give more. A dozen times he limped in, his hands awkward in his pocket, to look down upon his daughter, twisting and turning in the pain, trying to hold back the tears that scalded like boiling water over the red eyeballs. He even renewed the cold pack a time or two, but he couldn't stand much, since the snakebite, and so he limped into his gun shop and filled the house with the noise and the tangy smell of the forge. When he had brazed the broken lock of Dick Weyant's gun, filed and polished the joining smooth, he stopped and scratched his beard over the first-aid book he got from Dr. Reed so long ago.

"She may go blind," he said gloomily to Mary. But it never occurred to him, to Mary, or to the girl to call a doctor.

A week later the pain was almost gone and the girl's face peeled in loose strips like gray tissue paper.

Old-timers who stopped in suggested all sorts of neglected precautions. A black veil, smoked glasses, soot smudged over the cheekbones. They talked of crippling cattle losses; whole herds scattered like Jules's had chilled and died. One rancher lost over two hundred head piled in one draw, smothered. Another lost five hundred head in one lake — wind-driven, their eyes caked with snow.

In a few weeks Marie worked about the place, rode the pasture almost as usual, and not until she aimed a gun did she discover that her left eye was blind. Still, the big snow assured Jules's new orchard a good start.

Most of the Kinkaiders suffered little from the late blizzard. Few had the money to stock their sections. But this was the year to farm, to set out trees. Jules argued as he did in the eighties, telling them that where sunflowers grew corn would grow also, that dark, well-rooted valley land only five to fifteen feet above ground water, with no intervening rock, will grow alfalfa; that the north slope covered with chokecherries and wild plum thickets would grow tame fruit.

The orchard on the Running Water was in bloom when the snow came, and the fruit was killed. Jules, Mary, and little Jule made several trips to the old place with a man and team to clean out the weeds. The second year the prospects were good. Jules ousted the renter, and the middle of

June, when the Dyehouse cherries began to turn waxy yellow, Marie and Jim packed their clothes in a goods box to go to the river.

"But you are not going to send that child with her brother to live down there alone!" Mrs. West asked in American astonishment at these foreigners.

"Oh, she is fifteen, old enough to know right from wrong," Mary answered, stuffing another raw potato into the food chopper. There would be potato pancakes as a special treat for the two who would be away until September.

Jules, who always heard everything not intended for his ears, looked up from his magazine.

"That Marie is a devil — like all the women. No good!" he said.

"Oh, you just talk to hear your face go," the woman told him through thin lips. "You don't believe a word of it. Where would you find children you can trust like you do yours? They are n't much to look at — Oh, they 're all right," she corrected, thinking of Mary, "only a little skinny, all except Flora, but there are n't many you can leave alone on the place for weeks and have anything left."

"I teach my kids to obey me!" Jules agreed, laying his magazine aside and limping out to get Mrs. West a mess of radishes and young onions.

Armed with a .22 repeater and a good supply of shells, Marie and James moved into the bare old house built for a woman they heard mentioned sometimes, evidently a no-good called Emelia. A whore, Jules called her, his eyes murky with anger. They knew what those were, of course. Gay, stylish women, like the Schwartz girls.

Because the renter let the snow flood of spring wash into the well, caving the old curbing, they drank river water, boiled at first, later in coffee. They were to hoe the orchard, but they kept putting it off. There was so much for two hoes. But they sold the fruit, collected the money, and turned it over to Jules every week or so — seventy-five or a hundred dollars every trip.

"Why don't you buy yourself a good dress out of the money?" Mrs. George Peters asked Marie. The girl looked at her in surprise. "Oh, I could n't. They would n't let me!"

One day little Jule, pale, tired, dragged his short legs wearily down the hillside to the house.

"Why, where did you come from?" Marie demanded, afraid.

"I ran away. Had a racket with the Old Man — walked the twenty-five miles to-day. God, but I 'm tired. Got something to eat?" He dropped to the doorstep, his thin wrists hanging between his knees.

They gave him what they had and let him go to sleep in James's bed. The next day the father came for him. The boy went back, but it was the first break, and it helped the more completely disciplined Marie. She had passed the county examination from the eighth grade in good standing, despite the little schooling. Now she sneaked to Rushville the first week in August, and in a pink cross-barred gingham dress took the teacher's examination in such subjects as arithmetic and civil government, and the theory of teaching. It seemed impossible that she could pass. All the other candidates were well-dressed young ladies and she was a child, but she must get away — peacefully if she could, because of her mother, but get away.

When Jules heard what she had done he was violent. "I want no goddamn lazy schoolma'ams in my family. Balky, no good for nothing!"

But after Marie got her certificate he bragged about it when she was n't around.

"That 's what comes of living with an educated man!"

And none denied it.

XIX

THE KINKAIDER GOES

WITH Richards, Comstock, and several other cattle kings finally in the penitentiary for land frauds, small outfits pushed up from the settler ranks like mushrooms about old stack butts after a warm rain.   But unlike the products of decaying hay, these toadstool ranchers were ready to fight for permanence.   Down near the Sowbelly two settlers were carrying guns over a line dispute, and in the Thunderpump Mrs. Beckler shot a cow every time she found the gate thrown back and her neighbor's cattle hogging her corn.

Spar Spargo, retired from farming by a lame back and a hard-working wife, reported the progress of all the land fights to the Saturday crowd waiting in the Spade store for the mail wagon.   Squeezed back into a dark corner, Jule and Marie waited too, and listened.

"Not bad, that Mrs. Beckler, for a Chicago widow woman," Spar was saying as he pulled a crisp moustache end.   "You ought to see her look down that .25-.20 of hers and tell them fellers trying to run her out to 'git the hell off the place!' — soft and gentle-like, like she was a-saying 'Amen, Lord!'   But they git!"

"The hell you say!" Old Birch, needing a cook and somebody to wash his shirt, leaned far off the counter and unloaded his tobacco juice into the sand box set convenient to the row of waiting heel squatters along the wall.   "The hell you say!"

Mike Petersen, permitted to sprawl over the counter because he was foreman, moved his thick legs apart and sat up. "Just a couple years," he boomed in his Scandinavian bass, "a couple of years and you nesters 'll all be gone. Even Old Jules and them gun-packing kids of his. No barking dogs and no squalling babies from Deer Creek to Valentine. No, by God, nothing but coyotes and the bulls fighting. Ha, ha."

The crowd snickered, especially those still hoping for credit during the winter at the store.

So it went, sometimes until long after dark, until a shouting and the clank of trace chains announced the heavy freight wagon. When most of the crowd was gone, some gayly, here and there an unshaven young man with slow, disappointed tread, the clerk beckoned to the dark corner. "Here 's Old Jules's junk."

Jule and Marie stuffed the mail into sacks, letters and small pieces in one, big catalogues and packages into another, tied them securely across their old saddles, and rode away into the darkness. At home Jules stalked in and out of the black yard, swearing. "Why don't the damn kids come! Liable to get crippled riding over the prairie pitch-dark, with wire fences and badger holes everywhere. Damn the rotten mail service!"

"Oh, they 'll come," Mary soothed, wearily, caught between husband and children.

"We had to wait for the mail, did n't we?" Jule defended sullenly as Marie set out their late supper in silence.

"Eat," the mother commanded.

So it went, three times a week.

Although the children never told Jules, he heard of the talk at the ranch store. "Trying to scare the settlers out, discourage them, like they did in 1884," he complained. But without the early violence. He was older now, and the upper button of his pants was seldom fastened any more.

"Somebody is coming; close the stable door," Mary would say.

"What 's the difference?" Jules always retorted. But

he prepared for any conflict with the cattlemen seriously enough. Once more he oiled his rifles, shot target at a sand spot against his own hill.

Despite the widely circulated petition and the many letters of protest to the governor, Ralph Nieman was out on parole before Emile's family was adjusted to orphanage. "Money kept him from paying the price of his crime in the first place. Money got him out of the penitentiary," Jules read from the *Standard*. Mary rolled out her crullers wafer-thin and dropped them into smoking fat in the army kettle. Jules filched several of the puffed, golden pillows. "But that Terran, who shot the Spade ranch tool, he'll stay in the pen until he rots."

Complaints were as wind on the bunch grass. Panhandle justice did n't look so good, Jed Brown admitted. Jules ordered forty Swiss army rifles carrying bullets thick as his thumb and sold them at cost to the settlers.

When he went to William on Box Butte for a visit he heard that Carl Schwartz was found dead down in Cherry Country, a load of buckshot in his back. The mother was gone too, and since then strange stories got around — how she had held them all together under her hand, to make money, much money. The weak, frightened Jacob died early, soon after the Freese troubles, but the mother goaded her long, close-mouthed sons on and on, and, being also sons of their father, they obeyed. She taunted them with the fear in their yellow-brown eyes. She played upon their ambition. It was even said that when one of the girls needed a doctor badly the old woman made her take patent-medicine blood purifier. Finally she had to go to Omaha anyway.

Now the mother was gone and Carl full of buckshot. Someone recalled the butcher sent over the road for buying stolen beef for which no thief was found, back in the nineties, the case in which the murdered Harold Still was to have been a witness. The butcher was out now and gone, and

no one knew where.   If his true eye aimed a load of buckshot for Carl Schwartz, there was no one to prove.

"Probably some of Old Jules's shells," someone suggested.   The old settler laughed.   He was too busy building up the country.

Anyway, the old woman was dead, and when Nell came
back from Omaha she would n't step inside the big house,
once like a crazy quilt of colors and now weathered to an
even gray to which the Panhandle reduces all things in the
end.   Then suddenly the big old place with its dormer
windows was gone.   Not burned down — gone, and in its
place were a dozen small buildings, some like claim shacks
with one door and one window, two with blank staring
rows of eyes, schoolhouses.   Several of these pushed together were the home of Nell and her younger brother
Frank.   In the newspaper-lined room Nell did the cooking, the washing; she cared for her turkeys herself, although she and the rest owned most of a Rushville bank.
The other brother and sister moved to the upper ranch and
seldom came to the old place.

More strange, even, was the change towards their neighbors.   They built good fences, helped keep the telephone
lines up, worked for better schools, for a county agent, and
came to Jules for fruit every summer.   There was little left
to remind Mary of the dashing girls she saw fifteen years
before, riding snorting horses in chaps belonging to their
admirers; nothing except the yellow-brown eyes that were
still restless, still seeking.   The once pretty Rae was pre-
maturely middle-aged, surreptitiously trying to help Emile's
orphans as much as they would let her.

The Spade and Springlake outfits still surrounded Jules,
their breachy cattle crawling and jumping his fences.
Mary and the children herded them away, but even so
Jules found occasion for complaint.

"Cow tracks all over my garden!   Ruin me the straw-
berry bed!"

He wrote to Comstock, got a polite answer. It would not happen again. And when the fall round-up came it was a big one, comparable, old-time cowmen said, to those of the seventies and eighties along the Platte, when representatives from the Dakotas met with the ranchers from Kansas.

The boys, out grouse hunting, saw the mess and bed wagons pull into camp at the Four Inch Mills, two miles south of Jules. Brand holders from Pine Creek to Brownlee and Valentine gathered. In the night the far lowing of standing herds was on the wind. When Caroline, the white-haired baby, was in bed, Marie slipped to the top of the south hill. A long time she sat there, the night warm about her shoulders. Far away was the faint song of night herders, tunes she knew, "Git Along, Little Dogies," "Lonesome Cowboy," and strange ones, plaintive, sad. Now and then a lost calf bawled, a milk-heavy cow flung her deep, long call over the hills, a dog owl hooted. From the dark road below came the sound of weary hoofs, the creak of heavy leather, a laugh. Cowboys, coming to Jules's for tobacco and candy. She hurried home, a little sad, without knowing why.

The next morning strings of bawling Herefords trotted through the passes into the big West Flat, south of Jules's Kinkaid. The strings thickened to tongues, to wide, flowing streams of dusty red and white; they met, whirled into a milling mass to fill the two-mile valley. Under the bawling and the rising clouds of dust, riders circled quietly about the higher ground, turning back any critter that broke from the herd. The range bosses gathered on a high knoll, their horses in a circle, manes blowing. The cutting began.

After an hour or two the eyes of the punchers gleamed white in dirty faces, their cow horses following lone animals through lightning twists and turns, nipping at the calves that would run between their feet. In pockets in the chophills solitary horsemen guarded the little cuts. Now and then a bawling cow broke towards the main herd, only to be turned back by a shaggy horse, sure-footed as a wolf in the shifting sand.

At the edge of a blowout, on a clean yellow spot above the turmoil, sat Old Jules, his shotgun between his knees, his pockets full of young grouse. He had seen many round-ups, but none so large as this. He cleaned his pipestem with grass, smoked. He would never see another, for this was the passing of the cattleman.

At last he rose stiffly, using his gun as a cane until his ankle limbered. Once he looked back over his shoulder towards the gray rags of dust blowing into the hills. Then, talking to himself and gesturing as boldly with his long left hand as he did in the dugout on Mirage Flats, he limped into his valley. Against the farther hill squatted the flat house, a weathered yellow. Beside it whirred the windmill overflowing the broad tank, and below it lay the green sweep of young alfalfa and the orchard along the slope, dotted with frost-yellowing young trees. In the yard were two strange teams, several horsebackers.

Jules spit into the grass and hurried homeward.

Christmas passed and New Year's, and still no letters, not even a note, from Rosalie. Mary remarked about it, not admitting that she was disappointed too.

"Yah," Jules said, drawing himself up and pushing his cap back with the old gesture. "That's how it goes. Old friends, they all turn against me."

Along in the spring he heard indirectly that Rosalie was dead, dead almost a year.

"And nobody write me," Jules said sadly. For a long time he sat at the reservoir of the cookstove, his fingers pressed against the ridges of his nose. At last he took his pump gun and went out, up the hill northeast.

"Papa's getting old," Mary told the children as she watched him limp along, using his gun as a cane.

On the hill overlooking the Osborn Jules stopped, and

with his hands around his knees he looked off across the brush below him, the wide mist of feathery swamp growth, the open water.

Rosalie, Rosalie was dead.

It did n't seem possible that one so young, with such soft hair at the nape of a white neck, could die.

And he had never seen her again. Sometimes, the last few years, he had talked of going to the Old Country. Now he would never go.

The afternoon passed. The wind died down before the sunset; the smell of new grass and warming water drifted up to him. Ducks quacked softly down there, and two grouse cackling a little, like friendly married folks talking, flew over him. Automatically he reached for his gun and then remembered that it was the nesting season.

Down the trail rattled a wagon, Old Tucker, probably, coming to plough the trees to-morrow. Two horsebackers rode over the chops towards him, directed by Mary. It was the Hiltons.

"Our contests are coming off the twenty-second, Jules. The Spade is putting up a fight, not losing that big meadow so near the home ranch if they can help it. We 're depending on you."

"You can depend on me. I never failed yet," Jules told them, and reached into his pocket for the old cob pipe. The creak of saddle leather died away, and the silence was a comforting arm, the hills like the bosom of a beloved mistress, the little winds her voice whispering.

He had forgotten that Rosalie was gone.

"Now — Jules, we ought to plant a big patch of corn next spring," Mary began in December. By May he believed it was his idea — to prove that cattleman tool, Petersen, a liar, saying nothing would grow in the hills. He hired three men to plough sixty acres, half for white corn, half yellow, ordered more Turkestan alfalfa through

the government, bought seventy shoats, and had lumber
hauled for a big barn.   He ran a plate up sixteen feet from
the ground, and from the twenty-foot gable sloped the
rafters gently towards the ground each way, sixty feet long.

"No stuff bigger than two-by-fours?" someone asked.
"Only a shell.   First wind will flatten it."

The wind came; the family ran out to brace the frame,
holding up the corners, spiking extra timbers here and
there.   Furiously, before another wind came, they worked,
Mary and the three older children holding boards, finding
the square where Jules dropped it into the sand, running
the level for him and the plumb line, nailing, sawing, and
enduring fits of temper as long as they could.   Then the
boys escaped to the hills or the swamp, Mary to the field
or to the hills to pile cow chips.   Usually Marie stayed,
accepting the abuse silently, without the spirit to rebel.

Before the barn was up a month the rubber roofing leaked,
just like the house.   But no matter.   It was shelter; kept
the cattle from drifting.

Jules gave a big dance and the river folk and the Pine
Creekers met the Kinkaiders.   The Surbers came, the two
younger girls, and the mother, with a shrunken escort.
Elsa was singing in Cleveland, never coming back.   Gottlieb Meier was married to Marcelle Humbert, a shy, red-
haired Swiss girl.   It was always said the Frenchy Jim,
her stepfather, had hoped his wife would die in time for
him to marry the daughter.   But Tante Mary was a
laster, and one evening Gottlieb waylaid Marcelle in the
cow pasture.   They rode to Alliance in the buggy bought
for Elsa and got married.   Unseemly, Mrs. Surber thought.

She thought other things too, and characteristically said
them.   These Kinkaiders, as they called themselves, were
they not an untalented lot?   And Mary's children!   Regular wild young Americans, like Indians.   The little Marie,
tall and thin as a horseweed, and so without grace in her
heavy men's shoes; Jule so uncontrolled.   Ach, who could

have thought it at all, from the high-collared dude in Zurich!

Big Andrew, graying, more humped than ever, sat in the dark kitchen and listened to her. He had gone away, come back, come back against his will, drawn by the land. He did not like Mrs. Surber.

"Jules is then only what he must be," Andrew defended. "One can go into a wild country and make it tame, but, like a coat and cap and mittens that he can never take off, he must always carry the look of the land as it was. He can drive the plough through the nigger-wool, make fields and roads go every way, build him a fine house and wear the stiff collar, and yet he will always look like the grass where the buffalo have eaten and smell of the new ground his feet have walked on."

"Nu-un, but you are a strange man!" Mrs. Surber said sharply, uncomfortably.

But evidently Big Andrew had voiced all there was in him to say. He was silent as he walked beside Jules through the orchard, listening to the old settler's undiminished optimism. Here was good soil, a new country, and perhaps there was still a piece of Kinkaid land for this old friend, somewhere. But Andrew shook his head. The next morning he drove west, out of the valley, and Jules never saw him again.

Twice a year Jules cleaned up — in January for the State Horticultural Meeting in Lincoln, in the fall for the teacher. The day she was to come he listened to Mary's "Go wash yourself" with a friendly ear. He even plastered his gray hair down with water and fastened a tie in a hard knot under his beard as a further concession to the new teacher, who always boarded with Mary for five dollars a month during the short term held in the bunk room in the barn or in a little box shack in the valley west.

Because they always got married, Jules met a strange young woman each year, showed her his stamp collection, his

letterhead, the orchard, and made her listen to his talk about
the rotten mail service much as he did Henriette once, and
Emelia and Mary. He invited all the lonesome old
bachelors and widowers to see the new girl, and was angry
when she remained behind the curtain that made a room for
her in the ell. "Damned high-toned women, can't see the
value of a good man with a place of his own and a cookstove and a bed."

"Must you always make everything vulgar, talking about
beds?" Marie cried, ashamed.

"Beds vulgar? Is it vulgar then to talk about the place
where you spend a third of your life, where you were made?"
he inquired, injured.

Jules raised two thousand bushels of corn, much of it
soft because of an early frost in the swampy Osborn. He
sent the family into the field, hired several neighbors, and
by Thanksgiving it was all in the new barn. After the big
dinner was over and most of the visitors gone except the
young folks, whom he barely tolerated, Jules limped in a
hurried lope across the yard and burst in at the door.

"Get to the barn — everybody. The corn's burning!"

Not burning exactly, but surely heating it was, so hot it
steamed. The old mares tied in a stall next to the corn-
crib wall jerked at their halters, their nostrils curling. Instead of dancing to the phonograph, the young people helped
scoop musty corn until morning. Every few days all winter,
until the hogs cleaned it up, Mary and the children moved
corn.

When Jules, who had been at various times a Republican,
a Populist, a Democrat, and a Socialist, was nominated for
county judge on the combined Democratic-Populist ticket,
the local correspondents enjoyed the occasion. "We hear
that Old Jules will be our county judge the coming year.
He has just finished a barn two stories high. The first floor

will be used as a courtroom and the upper floor as an arsenal for his firearms."

"Why must he always make us a joke?" Mary wondered.

Jules was pleased, but not sufficiently to send in the ten-dollar filing fee. He had been restless the last few months, restless and uneasy as an animal before a storm. The good land was gone. Bartlett Richards, who represented all the cattlemen to Jules, was dead, died several years before, with a month of his sentence left to serve. The old locator turned to his trees, but they were too peaceful. His first feud in the hills, with the other patrons of his school district, ended too easily — in their leaving the country without paying the groceries bills and the locating fees they still owed Jules.

Then suddenly he was in trouble again, this time with the Strasburger brothers, nephews of the man from whom Pete got the whiskey when Jules was snakebitten.

"Every so often — " Mary lamented.

It began over a fence-crawling cow, broken posts, a sow that dug in Jules's garden, and it crystallized over the telephone line. He tried to join his secondhand instrument and barb-wire fence line to a single strand strung along two-by-fours, spiked to the fence posts, and termed the Strasburger High Line because it was elevated. They wanted Jules to join, they said — even went so far as to have one of the meetings at his store. The old settler filled his pipe, pounded it against his chair, refilled it, and had little to say during the discussions, the motions, the voting. In the end he was obdurate. He would join; he would not put up a high line, buy a new telephone, or pay dues.

When they were gone he told Mary graphically, before the school-teacher, what they could do with their telephones, adding, "I don't want the sons of bitches on the place."

The next week he told them as graphically. But the ambitious brothers had taken over the leases of the Spade range around Jules and intended to ignore the old crank.

Unfortunately the main-traveled road, the only road in
Jules's valley, lay through his yard. The next time the
Iowans, two of them, rode that way Mary was rinsing
clothes before the door; Marie inside making starch. Jules
saw them come from the garden. Shaking with anger, he
limped to the house, grabbed his rifle, and pushed his head
out of the door as they stopped at the gate.

"Hello!" they called, their teeth gleaming pleasantly
white in their sun-reddened faces.

But there was no greeting in Old Jules. "I told you
bastards to keep off my place!"

They seemed inclined to argue. "This is a public
road — "

"Public road, hell — no section line here!" the old
settler cut them short. He jerked his rifle to his shoulder.
Before the steady barrel the two faces went flat, the men
without the volition to flee. Slowly Jules firmed against
the stock, his eyes like muddy ice. "I told you to keep off.
Now you git it!"

But as his finger jerked on the trigger Marie struck the
barrel upward. There was a report, an echo, and the sound
of horses running hard.

Automatically Jules ejected the steaming cartridge from
the chamber, drove another into place. Then he whirled
upon his daughter. For a long moment the two frozen
eyes looked down the blued barrel an inch from her chest.
Behind the man Mary let the suds run from her finger tips
over her apron. Up on the hill the sun shone warm and
bright on the yellowed bunch grass. The windmill rod
plumped pleasantly up and down, up and down.

Suddenly the man dropped the rifle across his arm,
pushed his cap back, and limped out of the house, across
the yard and up the yellow slope out of sight.

Mary got one bit of satisfaction from her uprooting on
the Running Water. "We won't have to keep all Papa's

little tools hid because Andy might pull in at the last minute for dinner."

But she underestimated the little yellow boy's ingenuity. He still traded, but instead of down, say from a pump gun to a set of husking pegs, he traded up, until he had a saddle with the cantle broken by a rolling broncho and a horse, iron gray, with rolling white eyes and stiff knees from bucking himself down on the frozen ground. So mounted, with a piece of soft leather for quirts and his fencing tool, he appeared at Jules's door in the sandhills.

"Aha," Mary greeted him, not so displeased after all. "You got homesick for us."

After that Andy came almost as he had on the river, for the holidays and eight or ten times between, until he committed the unpardonable sin in Jules's eyes. One might be without family connections, money, morals, or even education, and still be welcomed at Jules's door and table, but never careless with a gun.

Marie was running a comb through her short hair before the six-inch mirror at the wash bench. Behind her Andy examined a new walnut stock Jules had made for a neighbor. He admired it, clicked the hammer of the old pump gun softly once or twice. Suddenly there was a blast of air past the girl's head, an explosion in her ears, and the mirror crashed and splintered before her. She whirled. Andy's face was a blank yellow triangle through the film of spent smokeless powder.

Slowly, shaking like an old man, he hung the gun on the nails against the wall, gathered up his quirt leather and his extra coat, and stumbled out of the house.

The next instant Jules burst in at the back door. When he saw the inch hole the choked-bore gun blew clear through the double walls of the house he fumed.

"Oh, the fool! Now I'll have to run him off the place for good."

But Andy was already going, his horse wabbling grotesquely in an awkward lope up the trail towards the Running Water.

"Looks to me like you're getting a little familiar with guns," Jule teased his sister.

"If Grandmother was alive she would worry," Mary told her. "The next time there's a gun against you you'll get killed. Third time!"

Jules had nothing to say. He seldom spoke to the girl since the Strasburger troubles.

The boom enthusiasm of the Kinkaiders was short. So many were middle-aged, some old, dying. Claims were deserted or the relinquishments sold for a couple of hundred dollars. The *Standard*, having survived several waves and ebbs of population, showed no sympathy. "A shiftless, discontented class of people who would be dissatisfied anywhere on earth."

There was trouble with Elise, Cousin Pete's wife. Finally she was sent to Norfolk. "That family shore is tough on womenfolks," Dick Weyant commented. Mary heard that Pete kicked his wife until she almost bled to death. Now she was that way again and laying for him with the butcher knife. Not even Ferdinand had treated her like this, at his drunkest. To be sure, Pete never touched the vile stuff. No, indeed.

But Ferdinand's Marie wasn't happy either, it seemed. She tried to kill herself before the last baby. Three in less than four years.

"Seems to me all the women are a little crazy," Jules said slyly over his glass of wine, his mouth full of sausage and bread.

"They must be or they wouldn't put up with you men," Mary retorted acidly, scrubbing at the spots where Jules had just skinned half a dozen muskrats.

"Oh, hell — hunt me my pipe!"

When the fruit began to ripen in the river orchard Marie and James went down again to the Running Water. On one of his frequent trips Jules brought a clipping to read to the girl, an account of a man formerly from the Panhandle. He got lost in a blizzard while hunting in the Big Horns. They found him by watching the buzzards. He had built three fires, the last one not a hundred yards from his camp.

"It seems too bad to die so near — " Marie said, looking down at the gooseberries she was stemming.

"Heah? — Yes, well, he's gone — " Jules twisted the clipping and lit his pipe with it. He started to say something, took his gun instead, and went out to find a rabbit for breakfast.

The girl looked after him. That was the first time he had much to say to her since the day the Strasburgers came.

When Jules got home a settler from down in Cherry County was waiting for him. The government resurveying outfit was scattering new corners promiscuously over the hills and through the hay flats.

"Oh, the fools!" Jules exploded. "Don't they know that the original surveyors never entered all the discrepancies on the plats? They wanted their pay and no Washington official could understand how rough land can get in the sandhills."

"Yeh, well, we didn't have any good surveyors when we settled. Them locators down our way just made new corners. Now there's bad blood and trouble." The settler had lost his house, barn, and alfalfa, although he had what was clearly an original corner on his place.

"Kick to Washington," Jules suggested. He wrote, too. He might not have any influence with the Post Office Department, but the Secretary of the Interior, that was different.

"I like to let them know I'm still doing business, even if the free land is about gone," Jules told his family as he licked the flap of the envelope, dropped red wax on it, and pressed it with the man-and-tree seal.

"They must hire an extra girl just for your kicking," Mary answered him wearily as she washed the gray-green down of alfalfa dust from her face and arms.

Instantly Jules's good humor was gone. "Working against me! My whole family working against me!"

"Working for you, you mean," Marie snapped, and escaped to the barn, not strong enough for a hay sling, to take her mother's place mowing back the last cutting of alfalfa. She should have been out looking after the cattle, but the mother was easily overheated since Caroline came. Not Marie. She weighed only eighty pounds, but was resilient as broom wire. She plunged the fork into the heavy hay shutting out all air from the mow, and threw it behind her, an intoxication running through her arms. She had talked back to Old Jules and nothing had happened to her. The last time he whipped her with a chokecherry club, broke a bone in her hand, and then daubed it with iodine for months to reduce the hard white lump.

Some day she would be gone from flour-sack underwear, men's shoes; be teaching, have a winter coat, never come back.

Down in the low kitchen Jules was limping angrily up and down. "The damn bitch — I 'll teach her to respect me!"

"Always I have to eat the dirt between you and the children," Mary complained. She brought a pitcher of new currant wine, just beading. Jules poured a glass of the blood-red liquor, spilling it on the table. "I know you work them against me. I can see it," he told her, but the drink soothed him.

Two weeks after Jules's complaint the man in Cherry County had his home back.

And the next time Jules got together his important papers, his favorite rifle, and his stamp collection, and said he was leaving the damned outfit, going to South America, the three older children backed Mary in telling him to go. So he walked to the Strasburger place, the anger against his neighbor having cooled long ago, and asked to be taken to town. He was through with the rotten government, the country that he helped build up, the balky woman and the damned kids.

John Strasburger looked down the thin bridge of his nose, grinned a little, and said something about needing windmill repairs anyhow.

"Well, good luck down there, Jules. I got to be getting my trading done. Starting home around five this evening," he said, as he shook the old settler's hand in good-bye at the hotel.

"Heah? — Oho!"

When John went to the garage for his car that evening, Jules was sitting on a pile of old tires, waiting, a gunny sack of black walnuts at his feet. And on the way home he sang an old song he had almost forgotten, "Marguerite," and talked of his orchard and his grapes that would make wine for the whole community in a few years, all the wine they could drink. He shot five grouse at a gate in the chop-hills of the Modisett range and gave two of them to John.

By the time the supper table was cleared and a game of pinochle going, Jules was home, the sack of walnuts over his shoulder, his rifle in his hand, blinking in the dark doorway upon his family.

"Golly, you made a quick trip to South America," James said, still the favorite. Mary fried a thick slice of red ham, Marie set a place at the table and poured the coffee and set the coffeepot close. Everything was as usual.

Jules's immediate family kept unusually free from death or serious illness. There were accidents — James stepping into a kettle of boiling water, Jule cutting an artery in his leg on a broken water bottle in the field, Marie with a toe hanging by the skin when Jim, the convict, threw a spade at her bare foot. But nothing that did not heal with a good disinfecting, perhaps a stitch or two with a needle and linen thread, and plenty of clean bandages. Six children born and brought well toward maturity without a doctor. It was fine.

But others in the family were less fortunate. Paul's wife, never well, died leaving a week-old baby. He sold out, came to the Running Water, but not to the hills.

"So it goes," Jules said sadly as he dug his pipe deep into the red tin of tobacco. "My own brother leaving the country — without saying good-bye to me. And I got him to come."

Paul married again in Switzerland, began to raise boys, came back to America, to Oregon, the new land of promise.

William's wife was still crippled with rheumatism, but improving since she went to Rochester. Elise was better. The baby born at Norfolk died. She stayed there, working in the asylum kitchen, refusing to come back to Pete and more family. The children she had were scattered by now.

Then Jennie, Pete's sister, was killed while raking hay on her homestead, not over four miles from Jules. Her life had not been a happy one. Small, pretty, vivacious, fond of nice clothes, she went to Rushville to work — against her father's Old World commands that she stay at home and await a man to claim her. "Let her run!" Jules advised his uncle when he came for help to bring her back.

Perhaps because she was popular, there was envy and talk. When she went home to visit, Old Paul, with a show of the family's best violence, drove her out. She went, and then it was whispered that the man she loved was married, had a wife in Kansas City. True or not, Jennie gave him up and filed on a Kinkaid not far from Pete and Gus. She had style and was clever with a needle and found many school outfits and trousseaux to make. But girls about her were marrying, leaving her alone. Finally she came home from one of her sewing trips married to a Spanish-American War veteran with hair, eyes, and skin the color of dirty sand.

Jennie was n't pretty long now, but she never complained — even when Harry got angry at one of Jules's
barn dances, cursed her, and left her there. She smiled her
old, gay little twisted smile that used to make a dimple
where there was only a line now, and pretended that it was
only Harry's little joke. He always went home early. She
danced until morning, as laughing as ever, but by then she
looked very tired in her red mull dress with white ruching
like swansdown about the neck and arms.

And now the gallant young woman was dead. Harry
had used her harness and lengthened the tugs without telling her. In the morning she hitched the team to the hay
rake and started across the rough knolls, watching the hay
roll up before the teeth. On a sidling place the long tugs
let the tongue fall from the neck yoke. It plunged into
the ground, broke, pitching her forward, across the doubletrees. The team bolted, kicking the woman into the long
steel teeth that rolled and tossed her body, bruised her,
penetrated her flesh, — her arm, her eye, and her head, —
while her husband ran futilely behind shouting, "Whoa,
whoa!"

"Women got no business with horses!" Jules said over and
over.

"Jennie knew more about horses in a minute than you and
that man of hers will ever know!" Mrs. Tucker told him
hotly, her three hundred pounds of flesh quivering with
rage. "Any man with sense enough to come to the table
when he 's hungry ought to know enough to change back
any tugs he lets out or say something about it. Besides,
what 's a fine young woman like Jennie working in the
hay field for?"

Everybody felt sorry for Harry. He took it so hard;
could n't be left alone or he might harm himself. Frost
whitened the meadow where Jennie was killed; snow
banked over the torn rake; Harry still took it as hard as
ever, although he had the comfort of a sixteen-year-old

with soft lips and an easy-going mother. Finally he sold
Jennie's place and her fine saddle horse and left the country,
alone.

With half a dozen men for every woman at the sandhill dances, matrimonial papers began to circulate again.
Here and there a bachelor carried one about with him for
a few weeks, made a surreptitious trip to Rushville or Lakeside, and came back with a wife. Towards spring Elias
Worona, a big Bulgarian Jules located on one of the better
places in the Sinclair range, came to him. He bought an
old Vetterli for three dollars and a box of shells.

"Shoot some coyotes?" Jules inquired.

"*Na, Herr* Julius, another woman she come and noboddy
steal her these times from me," he said as he slipped a shell
the size of his finger into the chamber. Then, formally
shaking hands all around the kitchen of this great man who
had the power to give him six hundred forty acres of land
all his own, Elias departed.

Those behind laughed a little. But it was true he needed
a wife, had brought one out five years before; but to the
heart of the huge, yellow-skinned man there was something
obscene in this marrying a strange person at the railroad.
He arranged with a neighbor to board the woman while he
formally set about his wooing. But the simple factory
worker did n't understand, and married the red-bearded
Dick Weyant the first day she saw him. Perhaps she was
tired of waiting on Elias.

This time there would be no interference. *Na, Herr.*

In the meantime Dick's wife gave him a boy each year
and grew fat and lazy and complained about six people
living in a one-room soddy, until one night her American
husband got on his horse and rode away for good. Then
there were only five until the baby came.

But Elias and the second woman prospered. His neat
little place shone in white paint with green trim. He bought

his wife a top buggy and a gentle team and did not ask that she bear him children. *Na,* that he could not ask her until she offered it. And as he told Mary these things, his dark face glowed red on the wide cheekbones. "*Ja, Frau,* I am a lucky man."

And now, the summer of 1914, the world was suddenly at war.

"I saw it coming," Jules mourned, hunched over his crossed knees for hours. "High tariff, immigration shut out everywhere — Central Europe locked in, with no place to take her goods or her growing population, no place to get foodstuffs." At last he roused himself. "The big bugs in America have war in mind too — only a couple months ago our warships were shelling Vera Cruz. You can scare the ignorant American into anything. Look how Billy Sunday scares them with talk about hell, making them give him ten-twenty thousand dollars in every big town. The world is going backward."

Mary heard his explosions with relief. "Ach, I thought Papa was sick!" she confided to Marie. "He has n't been complaining much about his breast hurting lately, and he don't act natural. Now, when he starts talking religion I know he's all right. That and women — that's how I can tell."

"You're getting old," a neighbor told Jules after watching him for several hours, and seeing his fifty-five years.

"Maybe," he admitted. "I know I had enough fighting with the cattlemen, the sheepmen, dead-beat neighbors, the government, and four women — "

His eyes, faded to the yellow-gray of winter-washed grass, twinkled as he scratched his beard and looked over to Mary.

Marie and her mother exchanged glances. "See, I said he was all right," Mary laughed.

"Heah?"

"Nothing important."

"I hear you. You say I 'm all right. You damn right. All I need is a young German woman to warm me the bed in winter."

No, Jules was not sick.

Suddenly he remembered something. He dug in his pocket and brought out a handful of purple-black plums. Mary took a couple and washed them free of tobacco crumbs, tasted one, the rich red juice squirting over her lean chin.

"They are fine."

"Yah, and they did n't bloom until the leaves came out again after the late frost — ought to be ripe the first of August other years." He dropped his hand on Mary's rounded shoulder, stooping under the weight of hoe and fork. "The trees look fine, plums ripening on rows a quarter of a mile long. A couple of years and we 'll have one of the finest plum and cherry orchards in the state," Jules predicted. And now, at last, he said *we*.

Although Jules could n't get many to plant trees, most of the Kinkaiders still on their claims farmed a little. Rye and corn were reasonably successful. Crops brought better homes, more space, deep window seats with red geraniums and perhaps tinted walls to suit the fancy of the girls becoming educated through the Kinkaiders' Bibles. But the little white music boxes were still the same, with the ruffled curtains at the one window fading, for the hundred dollars annual rent from the ranchers spread over no luxuries.

But prosperity, unless too great, brings neighborliness. Where once each little shack curled pungent blue smoke from its stovepipe reaching crookedly into the sky, now wagons, buggies, saddle horses, and a few cars were grouped about certain homes on Sundays for big dinners. Three kinds of meat, perhaps, in big gray roasters or black kettles, beans, become a staple during the leaner years, corn, salads, choke- and sand-cherry jams and jellies, wild plum preserve, with cake, stacks of pie and cookies, until there was scarcely room for the plates.   Pure democracy excluded only the fat old widows who were afraid of horses and could not "hoof it," as the Kinkaiders expressed it.   People like the music teacher were always remembered by somebody who could just as well swing "round that way."

Jules's family seldom attended any of these, for he frowned on visiting.   The boys slipped away now and then, but not the others.   Every Sunday Mary cooked dinner for perhaps fifteen to thirty people.   Often all Sunday afternoon the uninvited came.   Young fellows slipped in from the corral to help Marie with the dishes when Jules took some crony out to the orchard.   They moved awkwardly about in crooked-heeled boots, snapped Flora's arm with the wet dish towel, and escaped to the corral when someone called, "Old Jules's coming!"   There they talked chaps and saddle gear and dogs.   They pulled Caroline's white pigtails, short as a pickaninny's.   She liked boys.   She was always trailing at their heels.

"Oh, let her," Jule suggested.   "She hears less dirt around us than around Dad."

So they let her.

XX

A NEW BOOM

TIME moved heavily over the tan-and-mauve swells like a plodding old woman with her shoes full of sand. Ranching gave way to stock farming, and war news was the only excitement. Bombs and machine guns and gas were strange weapons of death and far away. Besides, they made steers go up, and wheat and corn and hogs. On the Flats silos rose to stand against the sky, and long cribs with the gold of yellow dent corn showing between slats, and barns spreading like hovering hens. Down on the hard land around Sidney and Kimball, war prices for wheat brought the farmers their first taste of ready cash, while along the Platte sugar beets provided a living for the landless willing to work in wet, clumpy shoes or mud-caked toes, to bend their backs all day between the green rows.

No one starved despite the predictions of Mike Petersen, once foreman of the great Spade ranch, now boss of only a few sections. To be sure, there were bachelors, like old Amos, who still wore burlap and bailing wire for shoes, but not of necessity, as those of the dry nineties. Rising beef prices brought an offer for a good hay flat here and there. Kinkaiders who had never seen so much money before took their thousand dollars and went back home and wrote of the greenness and the trees and the rain. Here and there a music box stood empty, the ruffled curtains gone from the window, the owner glad, for the moment, that she need no longer live with herself alone. But the music teacher was loyal. With an old organ bought in Rushville she gave lessons. Her house would not be moved to a ranch for a tool shed.

Jules withstood the buyer when he came with a remarkably generous offer, even considering that the old settler was the key log in the jam.

"Ever'body left me in '95 and I got ten men to every one that pulled out. I can do it again. I have not been working to build up the country for thirty-five years to desert it now."

"Ach, only a little over thirty years," Mary corrected.

"It 's all the same!"

Then came the Bad Winter, unrivaled, old-timers said, by any ever seen in the hills. On election day the first white flakes began to fall, fell part of every day until Thanksgiving, until Christmas. Disappointed children were told that Santa Claus was snow-bound, but that Easter would be green and fine, and perhaps the Easter rabbit . . . By Easter there was desperation in many homes, even up on the Flats. The usual January thaw, with its frozen roads for coal hauling, did not come this year. Old hay burners were dug up and smoked the tinted walls, the oatmeal paper. Starving cattle bawled and then were still. No horse could plough far through the valleys. Illness, from long confinement, restricted diet, and the discouragement of mortgaged cattle dying, was in every home.

The first of May brought the sun and summer winds. Snow water filled the valleys and the cellars, drowning out the alfalfa. This was the buyer's opportune moment. The music teacher, weak from a severe cold, was one of the first to sell. Here and there the shrewder, the more courageous, sensed the promise in the latent hills and mortgaged their claims to buy out their neighbors. Sod walls gaped open to the sun, making good rubbing places for the cattle, lousy from lowered vitality. But Jules's family scarcely noticed the Kinkaiders go, so busy were they with the extra work of the orchards. To them, despite Jules's constant complaint of depopulation, it was not a general movement, an exodus — only the Wests, the Tuckers, and the Weyant family who went. They missed them; Marie missed the music teacher and the books she smuggled to her most of all. The woman cried a little the day she went away.

"But it 's four miles to the Zimmerleys' — and six to the next neighbors' — and I — " She choked a sob into a fine old lace handkerchief. "It 's no use. I 'm afraid of dying alone."

Quickly she put her arms about Marie's shoulders, kissed her unaccustomed cheek, and then climbed into the mail wagon.

Once more the sky pilots came, almost as they had in the desperate early nineties. One, an exceptional individual with a face as long and narrow as a horse's and a loose lower lip that was very red inside, stopped at Jules's for dinner. He had to listen to the old settler's talk on fruit growing, the government, the mail service, until the meal was ready.

"Does you occasionally permit returning a thanks at your table?" the man asked uneasily when the noisy family and two neighbors were gathered.

"Heah? — Oh, hell, yes, go ahead. Pass me the spuds."

This was just another story to add to those told about Jules and his four wives, his peculiar activities, his crab about the mail service, his aversion to baths, and his habit of bursting out upon strangers from the door of his low house, a rifle across his arm. Then there was the time when his wife, too, stuck her head out of the meat house with a long butcher knife in her bloody hands, a dozen big wolfhounds leaping before her at the smell of fresh meat, while two sunburned sons with rifles rode into the yard. The young Easterner did not stop to ask the way back to the railroad.

Only Arnold Peters seemed to recall the young woman in the blue-sprigged dress with a shirred front the color of her eyes. He told Marie about that once, and his neck reddened as from sunburn. Now even Mary liked to tell the story of the traveling man who lost his way and got to Jules's yard instead of Alliance one foggy night. The pack of hunting dogs awoke and fell upon him in the darkness; the door opened and Old Jules stood against the light with his rifle across his arm, and behind him was a room full of rough young men. No, the stranger said. He'd sleep in his car. But in the morning he found a warm woolen blanket over him and saw that half of the big dogs were red as spaniels and licked his hands. He answered the breakfast bell, stayed all day.

"How do you do it?" he asked of Jules. "Why, the roads around here are so sandy you can hardly get through at all."

But there were still shining fringed napkins for the geologists from Lincoln, the horticulturists from the East. Good food and good talk.

Early in July Old Jules went for a visit with William. Mirage Flats was booming. There was wild talk of ditching southward from the Missouri River with the machinery left from the Panama Canal, through Dakota to the Flats and the sandhills. It was like old times, only instead of the skunk-oil lamp there was the glare of William's carbide lights and Jules with the two top buttons of his pants comfortably open after Lena's big dinner.

Back in the hills the old settler wrote another complaint to the *Standard*, a hot letter, he told them all, as he sprinkled ashes on the wet ink, snapped it clean, and sealed it with the man and tree. But it was tame compared to those of twenty years ago, perhaps because he had a secondhand car now, one he believed endangered his life every minute, even with James driving.

He could not forget the wide deserted sections he saw at the fringe of the hard-land country, with gray strips of weeds, sometimes wind-pocked, the scars of old plough wounds, often with a few dying cottonwoods leaning sadly together where a house once stood and a gay mill spun in the wind.

The country needed more farmers; the lean young natives needed strong wives to help them settle down, strike deep roots into the soil despite wind and drouth and hail. He advertised his monthly dances much as Cravath did thirty years before, hired outside music, until cars came even from Gordon, Rushville, and Alliance, and there was no longer room to turn. But it did n't matter much for the bear dance.

The first time Mary saw Marie dance it she darted through the crowd, jerked her from the arms of a blushing neighbor boy. "Now! — Shame yourself!" she cried, her blue eyes white as a noonday horizon. "Disgrace me like that!"

The girl spent the rest of the night on her cot, staring dry-eyed at the ceiling.

When Jules heard about it he just laughed. "Dancing is for hired hands and stable maids. What difference how they do it?"

He usually stayed down in the store or kept the kitchen fire going, and talked to the Frenchmen from his colony south or with old-timers from Pine Creek or the river. Now and then he limped up to the barn to watch, coming down the middle of the floor through the ragging crowd, his old cap on, his hands in the pockets of his greasy hunting coat, his blackened pipe stringing strong blue smoke through the dusty room.

Sooner or later Mary saw him and the old coat. "That dirty rag!" she would complain, perhaps to John Sears's wife. It was a good joke on the Old Woman and Jules laughed until he choked.

If one of the dozen babies on the beds in the house awoke and cried, Jules came up with the interested infant held out awkwardly before him as though he had never fathered the three young giants talking horses and scratching matches among the stags at the door while the fiddler plunked his strings.

"By golly, somebody come and take the bugger," he would beg, out in the middle of the floor, tilting his going pipe away from the grasping hands and getting as much applause as Nellie Hyland, who had been on the stage, when she danced her jig after midnight supper. Unless some of his cronies were there, Jules went to bed and was up at daylight, before the dance ended, to invite the stragglers to breakfast. From the head of the long table he urged more food on them or cursed the fellow who tied his horse to one of the trees last night. "Break me the limbs, the bastard!"

If he caught one of the boys talking to his daughters at the well or over the corral wall, he was irritable, swearing about the place all day. Marie he simply ordered to the house, but Flora did not go as readily, and the day was coming when Caroline even returned his abuse. "Dirty mouth!" he called her. Sometimes he limped out with his gun, into the hills; sometimes he ordered the offending boys off the place.

After these dances little things were always missing — bridles from the hooks in the barn, loose tools, once even the broom from behind the kitchen door. Maybe it was old age, Mary thought. Anyway these people seemed unlike those of the river, surely not like William, the Surbers, Elmer Sturgeon; not even like Jug Byers, Charley Sears, and Peters or Andy — tasty seasoning for the pudding of existence. Here even those with schooling were dull, flat to the tongue. They saw wickedness in her glass of wine, were shocked at her mention of a bull or a calving cow. To Jules's pessimism of state and nation they answered solemnly that he must trust in God to see that right prevailed. "That's why there's so much injustice and graft and corruption. You Americans don't do nothing about the sand-burrs in the grass, and so they spread and take all the place!"

A broken-down Chicago lawyer eyed him sadly. "The state of your immortal soul is of vastly more importance — "

"Oh, hell!" Jules broke in wearily.

But it was not only the Americans who talked so to him now from their security, but the foreigners as well, the Strasburgers, the Hunzeckers, almost all of them except the Bulgar, Worona.

Land hunger, as undying as the wind over the Panhandle, increased during political and economic stress. But the free land was gone, and, because homeseekers seldom have money, Jules was driven to renters. "They never amount to anything. Won't improve the land because they don't intend to stay or afraid they 'll drive the rent up. Damn poor farmers."

"Yes, that is so," Mary agreed absently, standing back to admire her table full of black plums in hot quart jars.

Jules wrote more letters to the papers, bought the west end of his home flat at thirty dollars an acre, and the Tucker and the West places, from the old Spade. He built a small house and barn in the valley of the big round-up and rented it to a young family man. He hoped others would follow his lead in cheap rent.

"Why, you hardly make the taxes that way," Mary scolded. It did n't matter. Taxes were too high anyway. Some day they would be confiscatory, and the land would revert to the government, as it should anyway at death. Besides, he had seventy head of sleek cows now and the boys home part of the time. The hard times were over.

Soon after Marie began to teach, little Jule ran away to William. "Hitch up my horses!" the father roared, pulling his rifle from its nail. "I 'll have the bastard sent to the reform school!"

But Mary stood her ground for this eldest of her sons. "Yes — just go to town — and I 'll tell how you treat them and me!   You 'll see — "

"Hold your dirty mouth!"

But his muscular hand no longer shot out as it had so freely with Estelle and Henriette at first.   Long ago Mary had learned to strike back, and the last few years her children stood up to the father.   Before the desperate young eyes, the tight, bony fists, he fell away.   "Sons of bitches!" he called them.

At the first meal after his eldest son left, the father turned his pouching eyes towards the empty place along the wall and looked down into his plate.   There were no dirty stories that night.   The next meal Mary spread the places to fill the table, stopping once to blow her nose.   Always before she had crowded the plates.   Now it began to go the other way.

Jule went away an undersized, ill-tempered, sulky boy. Two years later he came back a young man, six feet tall, still slight, with amazingly slender wrists, but strong, courteous, and with a most engaging smile.   When his mother saw him she made a funny crying noise in her throat and blinked her faded eyes fast.   Jule lifted her from the ground, whirled her about him.

"Now, now, you!   Let me down!" Mary cried.

"Are you glad to see me?"

James came in from the field, and Fritz too, suddenly less the young giant.   The boys had little to say to each other, but Fritz sat on the reservoir of the range, his usual perch, and the dimples played in his cheeks as they did long ago when the phonograph came.   Flora, a pretty brown-eyed child with soft light hair and an ungraceful way of toeing out, hung at Jule's chair.   The white-haired, yellow-freckled, five-year-old Peggy — Caroline — hid behind Fritz and peeked around him.

If Jule had any qualms about the father's welcome, nothing was said about them as he sat at the long kitchen table, recounting his adventures up on Mirage Flats.

"How are you, Dada?" he said when Jules came in.

The father stopped in the doorway, pushed his cap up. "Oho — that your horse in the yard? Put him up and feed him. We got lots of alfalfa and corn now."

That was all.

Whenever anyone asked about young Jule's temper, he grinned. "I don't know; did I have one?" — his voice fine and deep. "I guess maybe I lost it when a feller gave me a good licking soon after I left here."

Mary, whose ninety pounds seemed suddenly nothing at all beside this six-footer, could hardly work for looking at him. Never before had anyone carried in water and coal, thrown her lightly over the yard fence, pushed her out of the barn. "The house for you."

Jule got along with his father now. "You know," he told Mary once, "I was surprised when I got up on the Flats. Even people who don't have much use for Dada think he's a big man — crazy maybe, but big."

And there it always remained for this eldest son.

War and the curtailment of German shipping brought a new industry to the sandhills — potash. And to the most unlikely place for a million-dollar development, to the wind-torn region south of the Greens, no longer needing Jules's protection, to a region pitted with lakes as stinking as old setting eggs, the gray water edged with alkali-bleached tufts of grass like worn-out scrub brushes.

Men let their cultivators stand in the corn rows, the polished shovels buried in the earth; left their mowers with the steel teeth in blowing timothy and purple-bloomed alfalfa. They squatted on their dusty heels, talking. They leaned over the hog pens in the evening sun, talking. Work was started at Jess Lake, four miles from the south road. A Chicago concern already controlled a thousand acres of the foulest, richest brine, quietly leased up before a foot of pipe

was shunted to the siding at Reno.   Five thousand dollars
went into a well and an evaporating tower before anyone
knew what was up.   A $50,000 plant was already on paper.
The report of the water analysis once more brought a stream
of Eastern money to the Panhandle.   It would carry away
the profits as before.

Someone went to Al Modisett.   Better keep the money
in the country.   But he pulled at his shrewd, lined chin.
Let the East take the risks.

Sunflowers grew through the cultivator wheels; dew
rusted the sickle bars.   Almost every Kinkaider with a mud
hole briny enough for water puppies (the sandhill sala-
mander) carried a bottle of the gray water with him and
thrust it hopefully on any stranger in leather puttees or
with a crease in his pants.

Big money was loose in the country.

"So it goes," Jules told his family gloomily.   "I pick out
a good place with fine grass and fresh water, and along comes
a war, shuts off German potash, and a lot of fools that don't
know any better than to file on stinking alkali lakes make
more money in a month than I can by working a lifetime."

"Ach, if our eyes were meant to see that far ahead we
would n't need our padded hinders to fall on," Mary tried
to comfort.

Then suddenly America was at war too.   Jules had refused to see it coming.   "Wilson promised to keep us out,"
he said to the last.   Now it was here, beside him in the
house, the orchard, even on his hunts in the hills.   He had
little to say.   Once more bereaved, he sat long beside the
stove, looking straight before him.

"Bankrupt the country for generations, paying pensions."

"It looks so," Mary agreed, considering the floor where
Jules had skinned muskrats.   It must wait until he went
out.   The wetness hurt his chest, and still he would not go
to a doctor.

Even before America went to war, two and a half million dollars in potash had been pumped from the south end of the county, and the rich lakes were barely tapped by the worms of corrugated piping strung over the hills to the evaporating plants. The sign, RENO P. O., on the roof of the one building that served as store and station for the stock corrals for years, was gone. In the sandy pocket a new town, Antioch, spread like a dark smudge from the tall flues rising over the big tar-paper hulks that were the evaporating plants, housing several vertical boilers each, with intricate coilings of pipe. "Look like the guts of a dinosaur," Jules told the family. Yes, the high chimneys, their long necks craned to look down the railroad tracks.

There was a rush to the south road to reap in the golden harvest of seven, ten, fifteen dollars a day. Long rows of tar-paper shacks were hammered together, each with a door, one window, and a piece of stovepipe sticking through the roof. Old Jules's boys stayed with their trapping. "No telling how soon the war will be over and German potash that can be dug out with a spade be back on the market," the father said.

In the spring Jules and Mary went to Rushville together. The orchard on the Running Water was not doing well. In the winter the neighbors' cattle got in and rubbed the frost-brittle trees. Many were dying. Help was scarce, with everybody going to war. Young Jule might be called any day.

The night before, they had sat quietly alone, the stove between them, Mary thinking of the smoky kitchen to which she came from St. Louis, the lusty young voices about the table, the singing, the talk of the Old Country. The evening sun on the river reminded her of her home on the Rhine, and at noon, sometimes, a blue kingfisher poised over the sandy stream, or a great gray heron rose from the slough grass into the morning sun. Jules smoked and thought of the bitter years, the lawing, the mob, and at last, a little sadly, of that first time he looked across the Running Water to Mirage Flats.

Yes, and now a barefoot Polish woman would walk the boards of the floor he laid for Emelia.

But in the sandhills there was a better orchard, and range, more hay land, cattle, and plenty to eat.

"Well, Mary, there goes the last of our early days together," Jules said. He spat on the polished floor of the courthouse office, felt reassured, and signed the deed for four thousand dollars, half cash, with a loud pen.

"You've come a long ways since the day you got that place from Freese," Johnny Jones told Jules when he saw them at the hotel. "A half-crazy fanatic, dirty, no credit, starving. And look at you now. Credit good anywhere; Eastern papers carrying page write-ups of what you are doing, with your picture."

"Yes, and look at the bread basket he's growing," Mary added.

"You are building out a little in front, Jules. Too much good cooking and comfort — and I hope you know who's responsible."

The old settler pushed back his cap in his habitual way. "I had to fight for it alone — for all I got."

Jones took one of Mary's hands, spread it over his thick, soft palm. "This shows whose work did it."

Quickly she pulled her red, knotted fingers away, up into her sleeves. "Come, Jules, we have to go," she fussed. On the way home she opened the gates, drove the team, listened to her husband. And underneath his talk she resolved that the next order she sent to Montgomery Ward would include a pair of brown gloves.

They crossed the river at Loosefelt Bridge, not far from the old Hunter ranch, and climbed the long, graded hill road. At the top Mary looked back. It was beautiful, but not comparable to the view from Indian Hill, with miles and miles of winding river, soft tuftings of trees tucked in against the steep sandstone bluffs. . . .

They would never hear the thunder of the ice going out on Niobrara again, never see the gold of autumn along the bluffs, the ash, slender yellow pencils, the cottonwoods rustling in chartreuse and orange, the creeper blood splashes on the silver of the buffalo berries. It was only a memory now, like her lover, he who made gay music on the Rhine.

"Some day every foot of the land in the whole country will be under scientific hands. The population of the world is growing. Wars no longer keep ahead of the doctors. In the future it means find new productive areas and better transportation and distribution, or millions will starve."

As Jules talked, the sand of the Modisett range followed the smooth old wagon tires and fell back into the tracks. Mary shook the lines over the gentle old horses. "Giddup, giddup," she scolded. Next time they would let one of the boys drive them to town in the car.

The Alliance paper reported the death of W. W. Wood, register of the land office, defeated candidate for county attorney in 1885. Akin, the other unsuccessful man, left the country in tar and feathers, while Westover, appointed by the gone and forgotten Newman and Hunter ranches, had been district judge for over twenty years, with many a man's destiny in his palm.

"Well, Wood caused me lots of trouble, ever since the eighties, but I lived to see him dumped in a hole!" Which wasn't literally true. Jules never went to funerals.

The next death, of Louis Pochon, Eugenie's husband, touched him more intimately. "One after another they go — I won't last long. My breast hurt me every day."

Surber was gone, too, sold out and moved to Missouri with Pete Staskiewicz, who once made wreaths for Marie. He was married to a mail-order woman now. She came for his father and preferred the son. He was twenty years

younger than she, but they needed a cook. Now Gottlieb
Meier bought the Staskiewicz place for his wife, and Pete
went into the chicken business near St. Louis with Henri
Surber.

"Leaving with that ignorant Polander!" Jules exclaimed,
not believing it at first. He had not seen his old friend for
years. The post office and Jules's outbursts had estranged
the gentlemanly friend of his youth. The Surbers came to
western Nebraska with high hearts, optimism, and a little
money — Henri spruce, with a good-humored mouth under
his neat moustache. He went away old, gaunt, brown, with
a little of the look of the land upon him, even as Big Andrew once said they all would be marked. He took away
bitter memories and animosity toward the friend of his youth.

"Such people are not fitted for pioneering," Jones said
as he saw them go. "No more than Old Jules himself —
but there's something in the old locator — maybe what the
old Sioux call a vision."

When Jules heard that Henri Surber had left the country
with hard words against him, he sat quietly in the kitchen
the rest of the day, his bad foot in everybody's way. But he
didn't move or swear when Mary insisted she must sweep.
He just lifted one foot after the other for the broom. Yes,
the people, the few people he loved, were going. Surber,
Dr. Reed, Rosalie. . . . Jules blew his nose into a blue
handkerchief. Suddenly he sat up.

"*Wo* 's my tobacco?"

They searched for it, all of them, found the red tin box
upset behind the counter in the store, the tobacco a stinking,
dusty pile. And when his pipe was going good, Jules
looked through the smoke to Mary, frying fish from the
lakes west, fish the Peters' left on their way home.

"People like that got no get-up."

"Who you mean?"

But Jules did not hear. He took his pump gun and went
to the orchard, where the grouse were eating the swelling
fruit buds.

XXI

WINTER

Heavily, as a woman approaching her time, Jules limped over the icy cinders of the depot to the mail truck that was to take him home. He did not have a post office, but twice a week the government brought the mail for his community to his store and filling station in a special locked sack, at a loss, which brought deep chuckles to the old settler and awoke the sharp thin wires of pain in his breast.

"Slow, slow," he commanded as the solid-tired truck bumped along the frozen ruts of the wet meadow. "I 'm a sick man. Every jerk hurt me."

The driver knew Old Jules. He slowed down a little and turned the talk to his orchard.

"I hear you been to Lincoln, to a horticulture meeting."

"Hell, yes," Jules said, and pulled a handful of ribbons, mostly blue, from his bulging pocket. "I bin collecting the last year. County and state fairs — and the last couple weeks. Over thirty, — " the sharp, yellowed eyes considered the unimpressed driver shrewdly, — "over *forty* prizes in one year."

"Hot ziggity!"

The old truck rattled along faster now, bumping over the corduroy bridges — pipe and cement contraptions used instead of gates at the few fences still cutting the range. It jolted to a stop at the mailboxes, usually rusty, battered, honey or Crisco cans nailed across the tops of posts like the shoulders of lone, beheaded figures, often with no house, not even a fence in sight. Perhaps a clump of dead weeds on a slope hid a rusty cookstove or an old cylinder hole with a piece of galvanized pipe still sticking up, remains of a once-optimistic venture. The long, gray streaks showed where corn and rye and perhaps alfalfa once grew, and, Jules told the driver, would grow again. For there was his orchard to show the skeptic what could be done by clean cultivation.

Besides, there were the others who stayed, whose mail boxes marked the hayed trails leading over the tan, snow-patched winter hills to the small stock farms, the land deeded, with no need of guns against homeseekers or wire-cutting troops. Fat cattle, busy windmills, wind slopping water from the broad tanks, old cornstalks, stack-yard-dotted meadows. Families that started twenty years ago in dug-outs, perhaps, to-day had large homes of ten or fourteen rooms, big family cars, and radios fed by wind-power electric plants. Sons and daughters left home for college or jobs in cities, driven by the same urge that sent their parents across the sea, over the plains in covered wagons or perhaps even afoot.

"Never satisfied — got to run, run," Jules complained of them, unreasonably. "And the old folks all playing the big bug, mostly on borrowed money. With South American competition bringing cattle down and the tariff running up everything they got to buy, half of the outfits will go broke, sell out for nothing, and then there 'll be a family on every section again."

The driver, who made considerable money freighting for Old Jules's store and got his dinners there, agreed as he flipped a cigarette into his mouth from a squashed package.

And at home Mary wondered how many bums Jules would pay railroad fare for, bums to be fed through the winter. If they were diseased like the last one, patches of matter and blood all over her sheets, she would n't stand for it. Peggy got rid of him. Put a section of bull-tongue cactus the size of a man's hand, with thorns half an inch long, in his mattress. He took the hint.

Jules had aged fast during the war and the years following. His hair was thin and white, his beard a dingy gray; he plumpened to two hundred pounds, although his hands and his knees were thin as ever. Mary had almost given up trying to make him wash. Once a week she tore the shirt from his back, stripped him of his underwear. That was the best she could do. She wasn't so careful herself any more.

The war days had stirred the old animosities against Jules. He was even less pleased with the government than usually, and his extravagant threats were taken up by the County Council of Defense. Al Modisett was a member. "Old Jules is crazy, but a lot of people listen to him. He ought to be locked up," he said, remembering certain incidents of the land-fraud trials.

But the county clerk, a woman, and for that reason despised as an officeholder by Jules, wouldn't hear to his molestation. The men laughed. "Funny how the old rascal gets women so far above him. You weren't planning on being number five — ?"

The tall, gray-haired county clerk brushed their irrelevancies aside as so much dust left on her desk by a Panhandle windstorm.

"Perhaps you never noticed his gentle hand on the twig of a half-grown pear," she told him pityingly. "You never saw him lean over his shotgun on the hill overlooking the Running Water and his orchard. His daughter took me up to him, resting there after a hunt. He pointed out what he saw in the country the day he came. There was something of the prophet in him, a prophet who remains to make his word deed. He is rooted in a reality that will stand when the war and its hysteria are gone, a sort of Moses working the soil of his Promised Land."

"Whew! Why don't you run for Congress? — But it's a good thing too that you never had to live under Old Jules's roof or join fences with him," one of the men told her.

Nothing more came of it but a few uneasy months for Mary.

With the end of the war the potash fortunes melted like snow before the bite of the chinook. Once more the Panhandle settled into monotony, relieved only by the growing consumption of bootleg whiskey. "Damn the women and the Methodist preachers," Jules swore hoarsely as he drank near-beer. Soon bootleggers brought him samples. He could n't stomach the yeasty stuff they called beer or the muddy wine they peddled. But the rising water level, probably due to cultivation and increased rainfall, ruined one cellar after another, and so Jules drank white mule while Mary reminded him that his mother had died half crazy from alcohol — drowning the memory of her wandering family, Ferdinand's Marie said. William was drinking more, too. And on the dark way home from Rushville Nana drove his team over a bluff into Pine Creek. As the wagon went over he fell off and sobered up enough to crawl into Jug Byers's outhouse. When Jug's old-maid sister went out in her nightgown she found him there, asleep.

"Oh, the fool!"

Yes, Nana had luck. Both his horses were killed. More luck than Carl Fisher up on Rush Creek, twenty years before.

Not that Jules got drunk even now. Mornings he complained of the pain. "Ach, why don't you go to a doctor?" Mary scolded.

"Doctor? I been doctoring the community myself for years!" he told her as he poured himself a cup from the colorless bottle he kept in his safe. Soon the pain was gone and he sat quiet, hunched over his knees. Once he escaped into hunts, to the hills, to the Big Horns. Now there was only this.

Gradually he left more and more of the management to
Mary and whichever of the boys was at home. Now and
then he noticed something he did n't like — haying going
up with a sweep and stacker, the boys dehorning and castrat-
ing calves. When he saw horse-drawn tools in his trees he
limped out with his rifle to reënforce his impotent hand.
But James took the gun away from him and marched the
sputtering old man to the house. When he ordered the
boys off the place they went, knowing that soon he would
send for them.

Mary worked as hard as ever, but she was fifty-nine.
She wanted peace.

During his better times Jules kept up his correspondence,
his reading, entertained everybody as always, from Andy,
who was back long before this, to millionaire duck hunters.
When mallards were flying, their wings singing in the
wind, he still dropped them without miss, but the wet of
the blind hurt him, chilled his chest. Nor was his talent
for growing things impaired. He supervised the planting
of a vineyard of a thousand cuttings, watched the grapes grow
heavy on the trellises, and learned to drink wine muddy and
badly made, but from his own grapes. He grew large beds
of iris and peonies and zinnias, cut armfuls of bloom for
everyone. When Mary told him that they sold four
thousand pounds of black cherries at eight cents a pound
directly off the young trees, he wanted to buy more cherry
land, plant another orchard. "The only place you can
grow them in Nebraska — free from blight here," he told
everyone. He had two new kinds of apples to show: Delicious and Liveland Raspberry, the first of these. With
more land he would plant a thousand of each. But by spring
it was forgotten.

The lean-tos leaked and everything moulded, even Mary's
homespun linens in her round-topped trunk. At last Jules
was ignored; the low, hut-like rooms were torn down and
rebuilt into an extension south of the store, high enough so

Fritz could come through the door erect. But neither the house nor the barn could be painted, and they weathered to a soft gray that blended into the hills, became a part of them.

South, in the potash country, there was drilling for oil. Like coquettes who could not believe that their days were past, the towns bloomed into an autumnal glow, but only until no more stock could be sold; then the wells were capped and winter hit the potash region for a long stay.

Sundays, when the ground was n't frozen, became ranch days, with a crop of Kinkaider cowboys to show off before the native daughters at the scratching matches. At Jules's or at Pete's place the corral was lined with young people watching the wild horses push into a far corner, away from the batwing-chapped boys in gaudy shirts, Fritz in an orange and purple one, as reckless as his coloring, Jule and James quieter.

Perhaps a sorrel gelding was snagged, wild and cunning as his ancestor, Old Red, the wild mare of the Running Water. Dust, the blind, the leather, and Al Beguin, the son of a Pine Creek Swiss who married the daughter of the blue-eyed Nicolet, climbed on. The corral gates flew back, the blind was jerked off, and the sky opened over Al, just as it used to open over Gus down on the river, with the Surber girls watching. Somehow there were always girls at the corral, dust and horses and girls.

The hazers caught the loose horse as Al picked himself up. "He 's a leetle young, but a good rider," an old-timer with a bunged-up hip told the line of heel squatters along the far wall of the corral.

Fritz tried the next one, slick-headed, a bad broomtail that sagged his smoky belly to the ground, made a few high jumps as he left the corral, swapped ends a time or two, his head between his knees, and then took off in a blind bucking run across the bare feed grounds straight for

the wire fence.   Unable to turn the knot-head, Jule, hazing
for his brother, pulled the rider from his horse just as Al's
rope crashed the broomtail to the ground, not a foot from
the wire fence.

"Saw daylight and plenty that time," a girl called as Jule
dropped his brother in the corral.

"Yeh, but I stayed with him till he went loco," Fritz
grinned, his teeth white.

James, shorter-legged than his brothers and with a way
of drawing bad horses, was thrown, his collarbone broken,
and became the hero of the day.   At last the girls slid
from the fence.

"See you all at our place next Sunday," Flora announced,
knowing that Old Jules would call them all damn fools to
risk crippling themselves for life that way.   But most of
them would n't mind too much.   So the cars scattered down
the trails and the horsebackers, including Jule and James
with their coyote hounds following them, shagged it over
the hills.   Another sandhill Sunday was gone.

Cars, better roads, and telephones did not entirely neutral-
ize the effects of the post-war letdown and the moody monotony of the hills.   The old conflicts broke through the
crust in lawsuits, fights, suicides, murders, and insanities.
One of the first to go to Norfolk was Fred Goshen, a young
Swiss who followed Esther, William's daughter by his first
wife, to Sheridan County.   Another steamer romance.
When she married her second cousin, Felix, the brother of
Pete and Jennie, Fred moved to the Surber train.   For
a while he even drove the side-lighted carriage.   Finally
he was relegated to a Kinkaid in Modisett's range, with no
neighbors.

Perhaps it was bad luck with women, perhaps living
alone.   Some thought the silver place he carried in his head
since an accident in military manœuvres in the Old Country
had slipped.   Anyway, he suddenly appeared on Pine Creek

as Christ — not a second Christ as the Denver Schlatter, now married to one of the sandhill widows and picking cow chips for winter.   So Fred Goshen had to go to Norfolk.

The slump in cattle prices and the sudden withdrawal of the government guarantee on wheat brought hard times to many in the Panhandle, while all about them prices boomed. Once more men walked the prairie at night, away from the roads and their glaring headlights.   One hung himself, another blew the bald spot from the crown of his head with a charge of buckshot in his mouth.

Mary was drawn into a murder trial as a witness, taken to Valentine for a week, where she saw her first moving picture and in it relived something of the old days in St. Louis. She wondered about the baker who took her to hear Sousa, and about Conrad, the musician on the Rhine.   Could it be that she had loved him so?   Now he seemed as shadowy as the people on the gray screen before her.   Perhaps it went like that to all of them: Susette, Elsa, Hans — yes, even to Jules.   She blew her nose vigorously, remembered she was not on the prairie, and sank deep into her seat.

Of the murder she knew nothing.   Soon after the Kinkaid Act Blaska had come to the Running Water.   She did n't like him because he kept the ends of his moustache bleached by constant chewing at them, and because his yellow-brown eyes reminded her of water-filled horse tracks in the barnyard.

He came every few months, usually with one of his boys, six or eight years old then, and four horses to eat corn for a week.   Jules ignored him easily enough, for Blaska talked little except to himself.   Even his boys would n't play.

Soon after the war he was caught shooting muskrats out of season, resisted arrest, and got a load of buckshot in the leg.   His wife left him, but through those strange, silent sons he coaxed her back.

One wintery March day, in the spring of 1927, when dry snow fell like dandruff from a gray sky, Blaska came to

Jules's with the younger boy, stayed several days, and went away. An hour later the sheriff from Cherry County brought a warrant for him.

"I could see there was something — " Mary said, and so unwillingly became a witness.

Yes, there was something wrong. The day before, the older Blaska boy had come to the Bixbys', the nearest neighbors, for help to bury his mother. Two of the men rode over, found the woman dead, stripped naked, in the open chicken yard.

In court Blaska insisted that his wife died of the flu. He had fresh meat in the house that he did n't want tainted and so he put her outside. He admitted that he had whipped her, as is every husband's right. She started to run away again and, handicapped by his crutch, he sent her sons to bring her back. They held her while he pounded her with a three-foot piece of wagon tug with a metal cockeye in the end. Was it his fault that she died?

He cried like a lonesome little dog when they took him away to the asylum, but the boys calmly watched him go and then started to the reformatory.

Mary came back in a windstorm from her first train ride since her wedding trip to Hot Springs. The family was glad to see her. Old Jules had been restless as an animal before a storm, limping about the place, commanding, swearing, complaining. "Why don't Mama come home?" he fretted the second day she was gone. At last he went out to shoot a mess of grouse for her, and then sat on a box watching the road.

While she plucked the birds in the meat house and put the feathers into a paper sack to be burned, Jules hunched over the *Standard* spread on his knee, reading to her, chuckling, hiding his pain. Alkali Lake, near Hay Springs, where the early sky pilots dipped their converts, was inhabited by a sea monster — with a head like an oil barrel, shiny black in the moonlight. Some thought it a survival of the coal

age. But Johnny Burrows and other fundamentalists of
the Flats knew better. The same devil that scattered the
fossil bones over the earth to confound those of little faith
could plant a sea monster among the sinners.

"Real estate must be moving slow on the Flats," Jules
laughed, and scratched the tender spot on the sagging dewlap
under his chin. When Andy came in he asked if he had seen
anything of the monster. The little grub-line rider took the
jew's-harp from between his leathery lips. "No, cain't say 's
I has, but I seen lots of the stuff them fellahs as sees 'im
drinks."

At the long table Jules ate grouse as heartily as he did
on Mirage Flats in '84. By golly, it was good to have some
of Mama's cooking again.

Jules bought his liquor from Pine Creek now, once a
community of congenial settlers who knew how to enjoy
life without breaking the law beyond picking up an occasional
unbranded calf. Now the region was torn by the suspicions,
jealousies, and hatreds of rival still operators and peddlers.
State booze hounds came out every few weeks. They
chopped up a still at Emile's place, where the eldest son
lived alone in the big, empty house. They took away
Ferdinand's kettle and worm. The son-in-law of Eugenie
and Louis Pochon was not disturbed. "If you got any
scabby cows in the lot, turn them out," the sheriff was said
to have telephoned him before the enforcement officers
came.

Next they went into the hills. They searched the Frank
Wildman place. The young Bohemian had worked for
Jules for several years. Perhaps because Flora grew up
even prettier than everyone expected, he endured the father's
abuse. But he must make money fast. Jules sent him
away, but bought his product. Hearing this, the officers
came and searched the old settler's house, barn, and orchard.
They found nothing except a fish net hanging openly along

the wall of the bunkhouse. They took it and fined Jules
a dollar a foot and costs. One hundred forty dollars for a
rotten old net fifteen years old.

"How can they do that — when they were looking for
Frank's still?" Elmer Sturgeon asked, even as he questioned
Panhandle justice in the nineties.

"The country has not changed since we run Freese out.
You got to fight for your rights — and I 'm getting old."

"Well, anyway, you have the money to keep yourself out
of jail. That 's what you have to have nowadays."

"Hell, yes." Jules shrugged his heavy shoulders much
as he did in the dugout on Mirage Flats. Government
officials were a lot of crooks. Fall, Sinclair, and that outfit indicted. A cabinet member implicated and dirty tracks
leading into the White House. But actually Jules was
more disturbed that wild ducks were dying by the thousands
around the south lakes. Too thick, got a strange disease,
old-timers from down that way told him. Then there was
always the pain in his chest, like a thin wire, cutting his
lungs at every breath.

He went from one doctor to another now, but they could
do little except speak vaguely of diabetes and arthritis, words
he did not understand, and give him diet sheets he would not
follow. In a thundering rage he limped out of the hospital
at Alliance, went home, drank all the grape wine he could
hold, and groaned and swore for two days and nights. It
was all Mary's fault, making him sleep alone. A man
needs a woman as he needs the earth, for relief. Now he
was gelded by disease.

Other times he insisted he was being poisoned. Somebody was killing him with a powerful, tasteless drug. And
as he made his venomous accusations his bloodshot eyes slid
in suspicion over the faces of them all. Mary moved her
cot into his room, kept a hot fire going all night, carried
everything to and from him. There were few minutes of
joy for the old settler. One of these was when he saw that
the Spade was advertised for sheriff sale.

"Well, the cattle king who run me down in Chadron when I was on crutches is gone — and his land selling under the hammer."

But even joy brought pain, and so he drank himself into numbness, where he could neither read nor sleep, just sit within his barrel-round body, a frightened old man in a huge, malevolent house.

Once more at Alliance the doctors cut off all alcohol, put him on a light diet. When he disturbed the other patients, the nurses held his wrist and gave him a shot in the arm. In two weeks he was roaring to go home. He stole his pants, climbed shakily into them, walked the half mile to a garage, and hired a man to take him into the hills. That evening he ate at the table and was better than for months. In a week he was helpless again.

But now he took everything anyone suggested, answered the patent-medicine advertisements until his room was like a pharmacy. Because he needed money he sold part of the land he bought from the Spade to Fritz. Now he had them all about him: James and his wife, a school-teacher from Gordon, in the valley where the big round-up was held; Jule, the only one who followed his father's advice and married a French girl, one from the colony towards Ellsworth, living a few miles west; and now Fritz coming home with his wife from down along the Burlington. It was good so, with the sons close about him, like young pines sprouting in the shadow of the old tree. Even the two girls in high school would teach near. Only Marie was gone, like a seed washed far by a flood, and that was not good.

With the money he got from the land he sold, Jules went to Rochester. But he was too impatient to endure the painstaking procedure of the clinic. At the end of the third day he left, got a bottle of spiked wine, and went to Chicago. While limping along the street, his huge overcoat fastened with a blanket pin where he ripped the button off in his impatience, someone stopped him, offered to take his picture for nothing if he would let one of them be used in a window display. He went, gave the man his address, and started home.

At Lincoln Marie cut her university classes and met him at the depot. She helped steady his huge body on the tottering, feeble legs, and listened to his wandering tirades. Bitter and violent he had always been, but not wandering.

"I 'm a sick man, Marie, a damn sick man," he told her when she put him on the train again. "I give you the money if you come home Christmas, my last Christmas."

When Jules was home a week the photographs came, a dozen, without a bill. Mary looked into one of the folders, laid it down, and slipped away to the frozen feed ground, where she wandered among the chewing cattle. After a while she came back, blew her nose loudly, and stuffed her handkerchief away.

"Damn fine-looking man you got," Jules told her, holding out one of the pictures. This time she was prepared for the eyes, by some trick swept free of their load of age and disease, the live, piercing, far-focused eyes of the man she saw thirty-two years before across the smoky kitchen on the Running Water.

Jules thanked the photographer on his letterhead with his long list of honorary memberships. He received an immediate and apologetic reply.

"See — I always tell you you ought to look decenter. The man took you for a bum."

Jules started to chuckle, shaking his loose belly, but the pain brought gray sweat to his face, and with his arm over Mary's shoulder he limped to his bed, the wine bottle on a chair beside him.

The girls came home from school for Christmas, the boys brought their wives, and once more the family was together, with Solomon, the Syrian peddler, Andy, Sandcherry Charley, and an old Austrian Jules picked up in Chicago. They talked of old times. Elvina had had another stroke, the third, and could n't talk. William was dead; Lena living in Hay Springs. Ferdinand was bootlegging again. Paul still lived in Oregon with his five sons. Henri, with a houseful of girls, had given up surgery and was a veterinarian in Neuchâtel. Henriette was out again, at Alliance, companion for an old woman in a wheel chair. At least she did not have to live alone with the past.

"Surber is broke, talking of coming back here and living with his girl who married an ignorant bronchobuster. All he knows is talk and blow and has not a cent," Jules told Marie.

"Ah, can he help it then that he was born when there were no schools? A few years earlier and your children would be the same," Mary defended.

"They could never be so ignorant," Jules insisted, dismissing the subject and turning to his illness. "You work in a drug house part of the time, you say. What you think I ought to take?" he asked Marie.

The mother lifted her hands in her old dramatic gesture. "Ach, it is a change before death! I never heard Papa ask for advice before, and from a woman."

"Well, the women of my family are the only ones that get any education."

"Not with your help or approval," Caroline cut in, her tongue as sharp as her hair was blonde.

"Oh, hell," the father groaned. "I ask Marie a decent question and I get a fight."

But there was nothing his daughter could say, except that it was probably best to do as the doctors ordered. "You have an iron constitution or you would have died at Fort Robinson or in the hills when you were snakebitten. And besides, you have luck — like that time in the Big Horns. If you keep to the diet you will probably get comfortable again."

"Get so I can hunt, eat, and drink like I did ten years ago?"

Marie looked down upon her fingers, long too, but a little broader, with the large joints of heavy work in childhood. "I 'm afraid you 'll always have to be careful — "

"Then what is there to live for?" he thundered, still the man who rose from his sleep and whipped a crying baby until he was breathless.

"Ach, Jules, don't fight with them and spoil Christmas for us all!"

"Let him eat and drink," James argued. They did. Marie had written to Rochester. It was only a matter of weeks, they believed. But she realized that the three days at the clinic were too short a time to find the man who still stood tall within the quaking house.

After a big glass of wine Jules's pouched and bloodshot eyes moved about the long table with the same pride he took in his young cherry orchard. "We got a fine, strong family, an improvement on the old folks — on Mary, anyhow," and his eyes twinkled for a second as they did the evening Mary first noticed his fine long hands and their way with chisel and sandpaper on walnut.

"There is nobody to carry on my work," he added, a little proudly, and yet regretfully, too. "If the Marie was a man she might — as a woman she is not worth a damn."

But as soon as the house was quiet the old call came again. "Oh, my lungs, my lungs! Quick, Mary, quick!"

And when he slept a little, noisily, a whistle in his breath, the mother sat before the fire with Marie, rubbing her work-crippled hands before the flame to take out the cramp of overwork that night brought to them. Where would it end with Papa? Alcohol, patent medicine, morphine when he could get it, doctors, hospitals, and more alcohol. It was costing them everything they had, all they worked so hard to accumulate. And as she talked the easy tears slipped down the long folds of her thin face. Now he wanted to sell more land, go to Mexico, where he might get morphine. Everything was mortgaged again. Even the stamp collec-

tion was gone. But what could she do? One would n't
let a dog suffer so.

Now his people could go insane, commit suicide, murder
and be murdered, even let themselves be driven from the
country, and Jules lay unnoticing in his dark well. At times
Mary got him into his wheel chair and brought him into
the warm kitchen. Other times he staggered out on his
dropsical legs, carrying his rifle. Demented by alcohol,
pain, and disease, he sought still an enemy. To quiet him
the gun must be kept hanging over his bed, so Fritz removed the powder from the shells, replacing it with sand.

Then one evening Jules called quietly. Mary ran to
him, lifted the water-puffed body, tugged and pulled at it
until she got him to the edge of the bed, his useless legs
hanging over the side.

"Mary — " he gasped weakly through the thin beard,
"Mary, we gone a long ways together. But now — I guess
it is good-bye."

"No, no, Jules, talk not so," she cried to him in German.
But his face was grayed, his beard lengthened as his jaw
relaxed. She laid him back. A long time he was like
that, his open eyes like milky marbles. Then slowly the
heavy lids closed. When they opened the eyes were clear
again.

The next day he looked through the papers and found
a small item announcing a prize for a short story awarded
to Marie. He tore the paper across, ordered pencil and
paper brought, wrote her one line in the old, firm, up-and-
down strokes: "You know I consider artists and writers the
maggots of society."

Then for several days he felt more like the old Jules.
He shot a hawk circling over the chickens in the alfalfa, he
even got to the orchard in the hired man's car. He tried
to read the articles in the Sunday feature sections of the

Omaha and Lincoln papers praising his work, calling him the "Burbank of the Sandhills." But the page cuts of himself and the trees tired him less.

Before long he was in the hospital again, at Rushville. His relatives came, strange, tall young people he did not recognize, until it seemed there must be over a hundred. Old friends stood at the foot of his bed. Ma Green, ninety, outliving her sons one after another, brought courage with her, even now. Westover and Wood were dead, but their daughters came. The sons of Freese, fine middle-aged men who never went to law and never talked of God, stood silently beside Jules's bed and thought, perhaps of the day a wagon left the Running Water, a circle of men with Winchesters watching in the rain.

Others came: the Schwartzes, the young Kollers and Peters', the woman from the County Council of Defense. Sometimes Jules talked as brilliantly, as exaggeratedly as ever, but any moment his mind might turn dark with the load of his body, a black night with no moon or star. And then even his enemies went quickly away.

One day the room was suddenly full of Indians. In the centre was White Eye, an old man between two graying sons. It was bad, this, to find Straight Eye in the medicine house with women in black robes to keep friends away. Jules was pleased, but soon the old Oglala led his people into the sunlight. "It is the land of the Gone-Before-Ones," he said, and the young Indians looked at him tolerantly.

When Jules could sit up, Elmer Sturgeon came to talk of old times, of the early days on Mirage Flats, forty-four years ago. Yes, there were two of them left, Sturgeon and Jones, only two, but forty-four years is a long time and two such as these are many.

Jones stopped in for a greeting every few days. Once he sat a long time, running blunt fingers through his fine white hair, still curly as a boy's. "Why did you have to spend your whole life fighting over stupid things like post offices, Jules?" he said at last. "You're good shot enough to know you have to aim high if you want to shoot far. Why, man, with your ability you could have gone to the legislature, the Senate. I've heard you make some pretty good speeches beside the old stove on the Running Water. You had ability and courage. You knew a trick or two, and where was the man among us who wouldn't have followed you through hell if you had only let him?"

"But the damned cattleman stole me my post office I worked so hard to establish. Everybody worked against me," Jules roared, his face flushed pale red with anger and weakness.

Jones brushed his hair back, put on his hat, and went away.

Early in November, 1928, Jules, seventy-one now, was rushed to the hospital at Alliance, and Mary sent a wire to Lincoln and then huddled beside the bed to wait. At daylight Marie looked out upon the first low sandhills, huge sprawled bodies under dun-colored blankets. So they must have looked from the east in 1884, a little grayer from the winter wash of snow, when Jules drove up the Niobrara. But then there were still deer, antelope, elk, wolves, Indians, and white men armed to turn back the westward invasion coming with the spring. Now ducks swam in melancholy file on the summer-shrunken ponds. Geese circled high to catch the swifter blasts of the north wind that moaned a little over the frost-reddened bunchgrass. The sunflowers, Jules's index to good soil, bowed their frost-blackened faces and rattled their fear of winter winds. And sometimes for ten, twenty miles through the choppy country along the south road there was no house, not even a horsebacker — only the endless monotony of a stormy sea, caught and held forever in sand.

The train stopped a moment at Ellsworth where the old

brick summer homes of Bartlett Richards and his partner Comstock waited empty-eyed, a door swinging open and shut. Past the shabby buildings a road led through the sandy pass north. At the fork stood a signboard: FORTY MILES TO OLD JULES.

At the potash towns the old plants loomed gaunt, fire-stripped, the boilers and pipings red-rusted, the large chimneys tumbled down to piles of brick. The tar-paper shacks were gone, the towns dead. And on all sides the hills pushed in.

With a loud shriek of the engine they were out upon the hard-land table, with large barns standing against the sky. Straight bare stretches of graveled road stretched across the prairie between telephone lines, reaching northward toward Mirage Flats and the Running Water, over deep, smooth black soil that raised corn tall as a man if the rain came. If not there would be other crops: flax, potatoes, cattle.

James and his wife and baby met Marie. Behind them was Mary, shrunken, tiny, her sleep-weighted eyes light as the windy sky. They took her to the hospital room where an old, old man lay, his face a thin gray shell of wax with a few straggling beard hairs like wire. His faded eyes opened. They slid over Marie without recognition and closed, but not quite. Behind the slits he watched that they did not leave him alone.

The sight shook the eldest daughter. From such a being, helpless, without personality, without fire, a man had grown as from a tiny cloud a storm spreads, to flash and thunder and roar and bring rain to the needy earth, in the end to disintegrate, to drift in a pale shred of nondescript cloud.

Two days later he seemed no worse. James and his wife had gone home to care for the stock.

"Beer, bring me beer!" the sick man moaned, his voice trailing into incoherent fussing, a constant stream fretting the thin ice of his sleep. Then he saw he was alone.

"Oh, the fools!" he complained. "Run away and leave me."

Marie, clipping rose stems in the bathroom, came forward with the flowers in her arms.

"Where they come from?" Jules demanded, his eyes alight as by a candle, far off, but gleaming, the horticulturist in him living stubbornly on.

"Lincoln."

"Oho — you are Marie."

"Yes."

"Sit where I can see you when I wake up," he said drowsily. He slept, just a little. "Ah, I have a thirst," he mumbled. The nurse brought a bowl of broth. He gulped the liquid in huge famished draughts. Nothing like the leisurely drinking from Sunday-night glasses of wild grape wine on the Running Water, plates of bread and meat on the table and a dozen sun-blackened settlers about it. There were songs then, too, and good talk, for they were young and there was much before them.

"Where 's Mama?" the sick man asked from his dozing. "I want Mama."

"She 's gone to the hotel to sleep a little. She can't be with you every minute — after four years, day and night — "

"I know — " he said, without opening his eyes. "She has to have sleep. A good woman, your mama." But in a moment he moved a little, pulling himself higher. "You ought to come home next summer. I 'm looking for a bigger cherry crop than ever before — and pears — and apples by the — by the truckload — " The voice died to a whisper as of dark waters under thawing snow. The long fingers moved a little from side to side. Purple points came out on the man's neck. Grayish shadows sat on his temples.

Then once more he raised his head, his face alive, his eyes far-focused, burning. He began to talk slowly, as though his lips were metal, stiffening. "The whole damn sandhills is deserted. The cattlemen are broke, the settlers about gone. I got to start all over — ship in a lot of good farmers in the spring, build up — build — build — "

His voice sank deep into the caverns of his chest. He fell back slowly, his head rolling a little, his fine long hands flattening on the sheet.

Outside the late fall wind swept over the hard-land country of the upper Running Water, tearing at the low sandy knolls that were the knees of the hills, shifting, but not changing, the unalterable sameness of the somnolent land spreading away toward the East.